SIX
VICTORIES

SIX VICTORIES

North Africa, Malta, and the Mediterranean Convoy War

★ *November 1941–March 1942* ★

VINCENT P. O'HARA

Naval Institute Press
Annapolis, Maryland

This book has been brought to publication with the generous assistance of Edward S. and Joyce I. Miller.

Naval Institute Press
291 Wood Road
Annapolis, MD 21402

Library of Congress Cataloging-in-Publication Data
Names: O'Hara, Vincent P., date, author.
Title: Six victories : North Africa, Malta, and the Mediterranean Convoy War, November 1941–March 1942 / Vincent P. O'Hara.
Description: Annapolis, Maryland : Naval Institute Press, [2019] | Includes bibliographical references and index.
Identifiers: LCCN 2019011248 (print) | LCCN 2019017475 (ebook) | ISBN 9781682474761 (epdf) | ISBN 9781682474761 (epub) | ISBN 9781682474600 (hardcover : alk. paper) | ISBN 9781682474761 (ebook)
Subjects: LCSH: World War, 1939–1945—Campaigns—Mediterranean Region. | Sirte, 2nd Battle of, 1942. | Naval convoys—Mediterranean Sea—History—20th century. | World War, 1939–1945—Naval operations.
Classification: LCC D763.M3 (ebook) | LCC D763.M3 O385 2019 (print) | DDC 940.54/5091822—dc23
LC record available at https://lccn.loc.gov/2019011248

♾ Print editions meet the requirements of ANSI/NISO z39.48-1992 (Permanence of Paper).
Printed in the United States of America.

27 26 25 24 23 22 21 20 19   9 8 7 6 5 4 3 2 1
First printing

Maps drawn by Vincent P. O'Hara.

CONTENTS

ILLUSTRATIONS

ACKNOWLEDGMENTS

I should like to thank the many people who have advanced this project with their generosity. I extend special mention to Enrico Cernuschi, who provided time, resources, and access to the vibrant community of Italian naval historians. Leonard Heinz, Michael Yaklich, Michael Whitby, John Burtt, and Richard Worth read the work and provided helpful comments and corrections. Commanders Marco Sciarretta and Claudio Rizza of the Ufficio Storico della Marina Militare secured material from Italian archives. Commander Erminio Bagnasco, the dean of Italian naval historians, gave his generous permission to use photographs from his many publications. John Roberts shared photographs from his collection. Jean Hood, Peter Cannon, and Simon Fowler copied material from the British National Archives at Kew Gardens. Joseph Caruana and Robert Dimech, prominent members of the Malta historical community, shared information. The Naval Institute Press has always supported my work, and Rick Russell, Tom Cutler, and my editor, Paul Merzlak, deserve special thanks. I am grateful for my family's support and I thank my daughter, Yunuen; my son, Vincent; and, especially, my beautiful wife, Maria.

Introduction

VICTORY HAS A HUNDRED FATHERS

La Victoria trova cento padre; a nessuno vuole riconoscere l'insuccesso.
(Victory has a hundred fathers; no one wants to acknowledge failure.)
CIANO DIARY, 9 SEPTEMBER 1942

On 23 March 1942—the fourth day of spring—a gale lashed the central Mediterranean. Two freighters, yawing through a heavy following swell, approached Malta, while a pair of Hurricanes patrolled overhead. Hundreds of islanders had gathered along the medieval ramparts guarding Grand Harbour. When the leading ship passed St. Elmo Light, the islanders cheered. The vessel was the first transport to reach the island in almost two months. "I felt a lump in my throat at our reception," a British officer wrote.[1] Yet, three days later both ships had been sunk and most of their cargo lost. The happy moment of their arrival had been a false promise, and almost three months would go by before another supply ship passed St. Elmo Light.

Why start in Malta? The Italian admiral and historian Giuseppe Fioravanzo wrote that two critical operational and logistical vectors intersected in the central Mediterranean—an Italian vector running from Italy to North Africa and a British one stretching from Gibraltar through Malta and on to Suez. "The war could have been won locally . . . if one of the two antagonists had, on their own, broken the line of the other," he wrote.[2] The chafing of these vectors generated much of the

1

conflict between the Axis and Western Allies from June 1940 through May 1943. The period from November 1941 through March 1942 is especially important. The intertwined struggle during these months to maintain Malta, and to supply the armies in Africa illustrates the importance of sea power. It shows how maritime dominance is secured, how it can impact land operations, how it is maintained, and what consequences its loss carries.

In October 1941 Great Britain had lofty expectations of winning a decisive victory in the Mediterranean; the Admiralty acted to intensify its attacks against Axis maritime traffic and assist a forthcoming North African offensive by basing Force K, comprising two small cruisers and two destroyers, at Malta. At first Force K proved wildly successful, and British warships won powerful victories in November and December 1941. By the middle of December, the Royal Navy had a chokehold on the Axis army in Africa. The British army had ended an eight-month siege of Tobruk and was advancing through Cyrenaica. Yet, over a span of just thirty-six hours the Italian navy won three critical victories that frustrated British ambitions and dramatically transformed the balance of power at sea. The period ended with the triumph of Axis sea power, confirmed in the late March 1942 Second Battle of Sirte; the failure of the MW.10 Convoy to Malta; and the suppression of Malta as an offensive base. Axis control of the operational-logistical intersection enabled the Panzerarmee Afrika's subsequent capture of Tobruk and its advance deep into Egypt.

This book's title, *Six Victories*, reflects how military success is often measured in terms of big events—and not without cause—yet its approach to this subject also reflects the cumulative impact of little deeds and the narrative will reflect this. It may seem full of detail, but detail is the essence of the matter. In these details such issues as doctrine, technology, training, and command are best illuminated. Only the details can show how communications and intelligence—along with logistics, infrastructure, and geography—influenced operations and impacted the application of sea power. In the details are found the lessons that apply today and into the future. These hundreds of details are the true fathers of victory.

The Importance of Time and Other Conventions

The Mediterranean war was fought over three time zones—Greenwich Mean Time, or GMT, labeled here as Zebra or Zone, included Great Britain and Morocco; Alpha, or Central European Time, was one hour ahead of GMT and included Spain, Italy, Germany, and North Africa between Algeria and Libya; and Beta Time, which was two hours ahead of GMT and included Egypt and the Middle East.

During the period covered in this work, late October 1941 through the end of March 1942, both sides kept summer time. Thus, clocks were advanced one hour from GMT, which was always solar and never adjusted for summer time. The Axis powers set their clocks to Alpha plus one hour for summer time, no matter what time zone their forces operated in. In shorthand this is expressed as Z+2. The British, on the other hand, generally, but not always, used local time as adjusted for summer time. As a result, forces in Malta followed Alpha plus one hour for summer time (Z+2) while forces in Egypt may have their clocks set at Beta plus one hour for summer time (Z+3). However, all messages containing information from Ultra, the allies' top-secret message-decoding process, were time-stamped with GMT, regardless of where or when the intercepted and deciphered information was generated.[3]

To avoid potential confusion, this book uses Central European Summer Time (Z+2) throughout. Because Ultra dispatches were always expressed in GMT, the reader simply can add two hours to any Ultra time stamp to reconcile with book times. Times are usually expressed in a code with the time in twenty-four-hour format given first; for example, 0010 is 12:10 a.m. and 1505 is 3:05 p.m. Next, if necessary, comes the zone where Z indicates GMT. If no time-zone code is given, book time is used. Finally, two digits indicate the date. So, "1015Z/19th" indicates 10:15 a.m. on the 19th day of the month, GMT; 2325/3rd is 11:25 p.m. on the 3rd in book time (Z+2). Generally, the month and year will be clear from the context but if not, they are spelled out.

In the terms "Axis" and "Allies," Axis powers means Italy and Germany, and "British" is shorthand for British Empire. Thus, when in chapter 1 the text states that British troops were sent to Greece, this shorter form is used in preference to the more precise description—that the force included Australian, New Zealand, and British troops. In similar fashion, Axis troops generally refers to a combination of Italian and German forces. Italian means Italian forces only and German indicates German forces only. The word "miles" always refers to nautical miles unless otherwise stated. The metric and imperial systems of measurement are used interchangeably, although the imperial system is preferred.

Chapter 1

Sea Power and the Mediterranean, 1940–41

To try to be safe everywhere is to be strong nowhere.
WINSTON CHURCHILL

From June 1940 to May 1943 the central and eastern Mediterranean and North Africa between Suez and Tripoli were the principal sustained battlegrounds for the air, land, and sea forces of the British Empire and the Kingdom of Italy. Germany entered the campaign in January 1941 and the Americans did not arrive in force until November 1942. The campaign was characterized by dramatic advances and sudden swings of fortune. With the Sahara Desert to its south, North Africa was like an island. "[It] produced nothing for the support of armies: every article required for life and war had to be carried there," one account observed.[1] These realities limited the size of the armies and made logistics the overriding concern. Relative supply states and long lines of communication caused the campaign's seesaw advances, retreats, and protracted duration. Because air transportation could satisfy just a small fraction of the materiel requirements, the combatants had to supply North Africa by sea. Accordingly, sea power was crucial to the conduct of the campaign and to its outcome.

In its broadest sense, sea power is the ability to transport personnel and material freely over the oceans and the ability to deny the enemy that use. Sea denial is the ability to limit the enemy's maritime traffic even if one's own sea traffic is limited. In 1940 the British and Italian admiralties

5

regarded the battle fleet as the principal instrument of sea power, and believed that defeating the enemy fleet was the best way to assert sea power. In 1937 Rear Admiral Oscar di Giamberardino, a well-regarded Italian naval theorist, wrote: "The objective of every offensive at sea can only be the enemy fleet . . . [and] the goal is always and only its destruction." Italy's war plans of 29 May 1940 expressed the intention to "commit the bulk of our naval forces [battleship squadrons] as soon as possible against the opponent, before its forces in the Mediterranean can be greatly reinforced and when the battle can happen closer to our bases than the enemy's."[2]

Indeed, both sides believed that a fleet action was key to exerting sea power. In the Royal Navy, as its official historian observed, "the tradition of seeking decision with the enemy by battle at sea" had long been a "fundamental precept in [the] maritime services." In his first action after Italy's declaration of war, Admiral Andrew Cunningham, commander in chief of the Royal Navy's Mediterranean Fleet, ordered the battle fleet to sweep the North African coast to test Italian reactions. His initial goal was to achieve "control of sea communications in the central and eastern Mediterranean." To accomplish that, he wrote, "the destruction of enemy naval forces [is a] necessary course of action."[3]

Appreciating this concept of sea power makes it clear why admiralties treasured their capital ships and regarded the use of battleships, cruisers, and even destroyers to defend or attack traffic as secondary assignments that only diverted such vessels from their primary missions. This concept of sea power determined the building programs of both nations and, consequently, prescribed the composition of the naval forces that faced each other in the Mediterranean; it defined their training and influenced their use. This was especially true of Italy's navy. The Regia Marina spent much of its limited naval budget on modern battleships and heavy cruisers; it trained its fleet destroyers to support the big ships in daytime actions. Its battle doctrine focused on long-range gunnery. When Italy declared war, it had a pair of excellent battleships about to enter service, but it did not have effective sonar or radar. Its secret special forces unit, Decima Flottiglia MAS, was equipped with unreliable prototypes. The navy had only five modern, purpose-built antisubmarine-warfare escort vessels. It did not have magnetic triggers for mines or torpedoes. It had no nighttime surface combat doctrine for warships larger than destroyers. Its doctrine for the defense of sea traffic did not envision the routine use of fleet units as convoy escorts. Its weapons and doctrine were important and useful, but in the particular kind of war in which Italy now found itself fighting, the weapons and doctrine that it did *not* have proved more relevant to the tasks at hand.[4]

The decision by both sides to fight an offensive war in North Africa— along with Britain's resolve to defend Malta—set the parameters of sea power in the Mediterranean. For the British, sea power was measured (in order of importance) by the ability to supply their army in North Africa from outside the theater; to maintain maritime traffic within the theater, particularly to frontline ports; and to supply Malta from both inside and outside the theater. For the Italians, sea power consisted of maintaining maritime communication along the Italian coast and between the main- land, Sicily, Sardinia, and Albania; supplying North Africa; and ensuring the movement of maritime traffic to the western Mediterranean (par- ticularly Spain) and in the Aegean and Black seas. For both sides, it also included the ability to interfere with enemy traffic and to conduct offensive operations—such as bombardments or amphibious landings—as required.

An underappreciated fact of the Mediterranean naval war is that each side had only limited power to interdict its enemy's most important mari- time routes. Between June 1940 and May 1943 the Allies did little to inter- fere with Italy's domestic traffic, which averaged more than thirty-five ships a day during this period, and there was hardly anything that the Axis forces could do to hinder Allied traffic arriving via the Red Sea—at least after April 1941, when the British captured Italy's naval base in Eritrea.[5] On the other hand, each side had periods of success in stopping enemy traffic traveling either from Italy to Libya or from Egypt or Gibraltar to Malta. Late 1941 to early 1942 was a transitional period when both sides waged the battle of sea control and denial in classic and innovative ways. After a brilliant start, British forces faltered, and the Axis powers emerged supreme in the central Mediterranean.

Some context is required to understand these changes fully. Major campaigns that last for months and involve hundreds of thousands of personnel, thousands of aircraft, and hundreds of ships are not fought in

British warships

BB: *Queen Elizabeth, Valiant, Barham*
1913/1940, 36,500t, 23.5kts, 8x15in/42, 20x4.5in/45, 32x40mm

CL: *Aurora, Penelope*
1937, 5,270t,32.3kts
6x6in/50 XXIII, 8x4in/45 QF, 6x21in TT

CL: *Ajax, Neptune*
1931, 6,985t, 32kts, 8x6in/50 MkXXIII,
4x4/45, 8x21in TT

CLA: *Bonaventure, Cleopatra, Dido
Euryalus, Hermione, Naiad*
1937, 5,600t, 32.3kts, 10x5.25in/50 QF,
8x40mm, 6x21in TT

CLA: *Carlisle*
1918/39, 4,290t, 29kts 8x4in Mk16, 4x2pdr

DE: *Avon Vale, Beaufort
Dulverton, Eridge, Farndale,
Heythrop, Hurworth, Southwold*
1941, 1,050t, 27kts, 6x4in/45, 4x2pdr

DD: *Maori, Sikh, Zulu*
1937, 1,959t, 36.25kts, 8x4.7in/45
QF MkXII, 4x2pdr, 4x21in TT

DD: *Griffin, Hasty, Havock,
Hero, Hotspur, Imperial*
1936, 1,370t, 36kts, 4x4.7in/45, 8x21in TT

DD: *Gurka, Legion, Lance, Lively*
1940, 1,920t, 36kts, 8x4in/QF
MkXVI, 4x2pdr, 8x21in TT

*Jackal, Jaguar, Jervis, Kandahar,
Kelvin, Kimberleym Kingston,
Kipling, Napier, Nestor, Nizam*
1939, 1,690t, 32kts, 6x4.7in/45 Mk XII
1x4in/QF MkV, 4x2pdr, 5x21in TT

DS: *Yarra,
Parramatta*
1935, 1,055t, 16.5kts,
3x4in/45, 1x3in/HA

DC: *Delphinium, Erica,
Gloxinia, Hyacinth,
Peony, Snapdragon*
1940, 1,170t, 16.5kts, 1x4in

Data includes: type, name, year of commision/reconstruction, tons standard displacement, speed, main battery, secondary battery, torpedo battery

Figure 1.1. **British Warships**

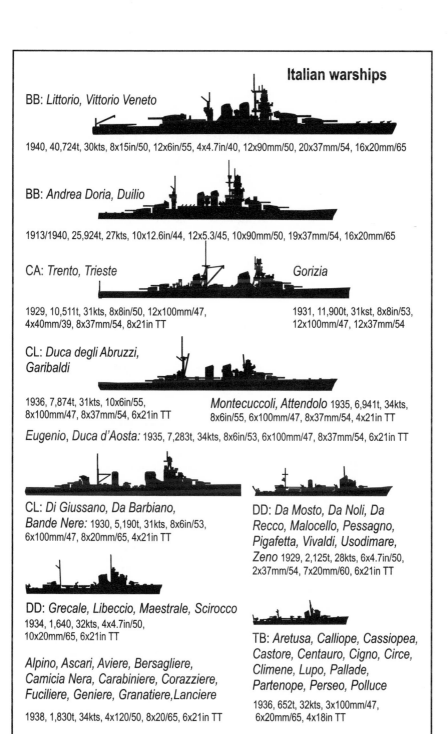

Italian warships

BB: *Littorio, Vittorio Veneto*

1940, 40,724t, 30kts, 8x15in/50, 12x6in/55, 4x4.7in/40, 12x90mm/50, 20x37mm/54, 16x20mm/65

BB: *Andrea Doria, Duilio*

1913/1940, 25,924t, 27kts, 10x12.6in/44, 12x5.3/45, 10x90mm/50, 19x37mm/54, 16x20mm/65

CA: *Trento, Trieste*　　　　　　　*Gorizia*

1929, 10,511t, 31kts, 8x8in/50, 12x100mm/47, 4x40mm/39, 8x37mm/54, 8x21in TT

1931, 11,900t, 31kst, 8x8in/53, 12x100mm/47, 12x37mm/54

CL: *Duca degli Abruzzi, Garibaldi*

1936, 7,874t, 31kts, 10x6in/55, 8x100mm/47, 8x37mm/54, 6x21in TT

Montecuccoli, Attendolo 1935, 6,941t, 34kts, 8x6in/55, 6x100mm/47, 8x37mm/54, 4x21in TT

Eugenio, Duca d'Aosta: 1935, 7,283t, 34kts, 8x6in/53, 6x100mm/47, 8x37mm/54, 6x21in TT

CL: *Di Giussano, Da Barbiano, Bande Nere:* 1930, 5,190t, 31kts, 8x6in/53, 6x100mm/47, 8x20mm/65, 4x21in TT

DD: *Da Mosto, Da Noli, Da Recco, Malocello, Pessagno, Pigafetta, Vivaldi, Usodimare, Zeno* 1929, 2,125t, 28kts, 6x4.7in/50, 2x37mm/54, 7x20mm/60, 6x21in TT

DD: *Grecale, Libeccio, Maestrale, Scirocco*
1934, 1,640, 32kts, 4x4.7in/50, 10x20mm/65, 6x21in TT

Alpino, Ascari, Aviere, Bersagliere, Camicia Nera, Carabiniere, Corazziere, Fuciliere, Geniere, Granatiere,Lanciere

1938, 1,830t, 34kts, 4x120/50, 8x20/65, 6x21in TT

TB: *Aretusa, Calliope, Cassiopea, Castore, Centauro, Cigno, Circe, Climene, Lupo, Pallade, Partenope, Perseo, Polluce*
1936, 652t, 32kts, 3x100mm/47, 6x20mm/65, 4x18in TT

Figure 1.2. **Italian Warships**

isolation. The Mediterranean was not a self-contained theater of war; it was only a corner in a global conflict.

The first item to examine is why the Mediterranean–North African campaign was fought at all. Given Italy's position as a peninsula in the central Mediterranean, its dependence upon maritime lines of communication to sustain its economy, and its demonstrated vulnerability to maritime blockade, the Italians naturally sought to control the central Mediterranean. Ideally, they also wanted to secure the British-held exits at the Strait of Gibraltar and the Suez Canal. Moreover, the Suez controlled the access to Italy's East African possessions, and in June 1940 the capture of the canal seemed an achievable objective. Accordingly, after the armistice between France and the Axis, a North African land campaign became a key component of Italian strategy.

At the same time, the Mediterranean had long been Great Britain's main transit corridor to the Middle East, India, Malaya, and Australia. When it became apparent that Italy was contemplating war, Britain terminated all trans-Mediterranean commercial traffic and withdrew all but a small fraction of its naval forces to Gibraltar and Egypt. Given this, it is natural to ask why Britain would fight in the Mediterranean at all if there were no maritime traffic to protect, especially when the British Isles were threatened by a possible German invasion. One answer is that Britain needed to defend the eastern Mediterranean to protect its supply of oil from the region. A second is that the British also decided to wage an offensive campaign in the central Mediterranean and to defend Malta despite the difficulty in supplying that island. The British War Cabinet made this decision in September 1940 as part of a strategy that identified the British Empire's vital interests and defined a road map for defeating Germany. This strategy persisted even after the Soviet Union, the United States, and Japan entered the war.

The British plan declared that the "foundation" of the Empire's strategy would be "the wearing down of Germany by ever-increasing force of economic pressure." A blockade was key, as it had been in World War I, from 1914 to 1918. So was oil. The document read: "Apart from ending the war by the defeat of Great Britain, Germany can only improve her oil position to any material extent by driving out our fleet from the eastern

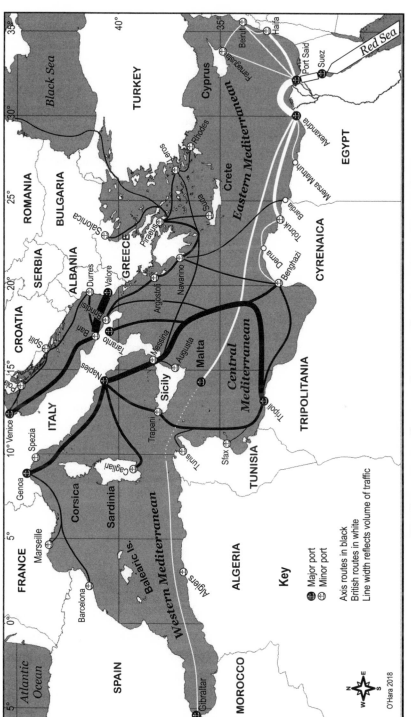

Map 1.1. **Mediterranean Convoy Routes, October 1941–March 1942**

Mediterranean, thus ensuring seaborne supplies from Roumania and Russia." Therefore, "the security of our position in the Middle East is of the utmost importance to our strategy, not only as a base from which to exercise and intensify economic pressure, but as a barrier to prevent our enemies from breaking the blockade." In short, London considered defense of the eastern Mediterranean and the Middle East to be a vital component of the only strategy that would offer a chance of winning the war. Moreover, the Mediterranean was also the only area where effective offensive action was possible. "Direct attack on Italy . . . may be the first important step we can take toward the downfall of Germany."[6]

In perspective, the Mediterranean–North African campaign was fought because it was there that the vital interests of Italy and Great Britain clashed. Still, Britain's top priorities continued to be home defense and the protection of seaborne trade, especially in the North Atlantic, and defending these vital interests sharply reduced the number of forces that otherwise would be available for the Mediterranean and Middle East. There was also the need to account for other threats to imperial hegemony, particularly in Singapore and Malaya, which up through May 1941 the British chiefs of staff (although not the prime minister) considered the most critical interest for the Empire after the home islands themselves.[7] German intervention in Africa in February 1941, followed by the Reich's invasion of Yugoslavia and Greece in April, upset the Mediterranean's balance of forces and threatened Britain's overall position. But the situation improved in June, when Germany invaded the Soviet Union. That attack transformed the war's strategic dynamics and gave the British Empire what it most needed—a powerful continental ally. The Soviets were a partner the British did not hesitate to embrace, despite mutual distrust and ideological differences.

Although in the short term the thrust of German forces into Russia exposed the Middle East to Axis invasion through Turkey and the Caucasus, London saw an opportunity to seize the initiative. In October 1941, after sixteen months of fighting, Britain had slightly improved its original position and was on the cusp of securing an important strategic success over Italy. An offensive that seized all of Africa would bring great reward, and Germany would be too busy in Russia to do much about it. To seize this opportunity, the British launched a campaign in Africa called Operation Crusader.

The Parallel War: June 1940 to January 1941

At the beginning of 1940 Italy deployed nine small infantry divisions in Tripolitania to watch the French, and sent five such units to Cyrenaica to face the British. Since Comando Supremo, the Italian high command, expected that the combined French and British Mediterranean fleets would blockade Libya, its War Plan of 8 April 1940 called for a defensive stance sustained by a six-month stockpile of supplies; the navy would not need to run convoys to Africa.[8]

The collapse of France in May 1940 invalidated everyone's plans. Italian Prime Minister Benito Mussolini declared war on 10 June, anticipating a quick victory and a seat at the peace table alongside German Chancellor Adolf Hitler. With the powerful French fleet and army no longer a factor, Africa suddenly seemed open to exploitation. Yet, Supermarina, the Italian naval high command, had only two battleships available, both refurbished World War I–era vessels, and lacked enthusiasm for the all-out naval offensive that Mussolini had proclaimed—at least until its new battleships were ready. As for attacking Malta, Supermarina concluded in an 18 June 1940 study that "It is not conceivable to attack from the sea with a landing of troops without an intense and protracted preventative aerial action of many days to produce the maximum devastation and exhaust the supply of antiaircraft ammunition."[9]

Italy attacked Malta by air on the war's first day. Ninety-four S.79 tri-motor bombers raided the island, dropping twenty-seven tons of bombs. But Italy lacked the aircraft, doctrine, and infrastructure required to maintain the type of sustained air campaign that the navy wanted. Moreover, the air force considered such a campaign pointless. Its raids were enough to keep the British Mediterranean Fleet from using the island as a base. With few forces on the island, Malta did not threaten traffic, and with peace anticipated before the end of the year, it would have been foolish to risk decimation of the Italian air force in a sterile bombing campaign. In June 1940 Malta was toothless, and the crystal balls in Rome did not foresee the island's future impact.

On 16 May, even before Italy declared war, the British Admiralty had suspended all merchant traffic in the Mediterranean. It had no choice, given Italy's large submarine fleet and the fact that traffic had to transit the Sicilian Strait within a few dozen miles of enemy air bases. The closure instantly added 20,000 miles and more than two months to the round trip between Suez and the Clyde. On 16 June 1940, when it was clear that France would seek an armistice, Dudley Pound, the first sea lord, wrote to Admiral Cunningham that he believed that "the Atlantic trade must be our first consideration," and ordered him to explore and prepare for the withdrawal of the fleet from the Eastern Mediterranean. In a narrow vote, however, the British Defence Committee, chaired by the new prime minister, Winston Churchill, decided to defend Malta. In addition to the obvious political reasons, "[Churchill] needed quick victories to maintain the nation's will to fight and its international credibility and sensed that they could be won in and around the [Mediterranean]." In Rome, meanwhile, the Italian government scrapped plans for a purely defensive posture in North Africa and decided instead to mount an offensive toward Suez. The capture of Mersa Matruh would bring Italian air forces within range of Alexandria and hopefully drive the British fleet from the Mediterranean. The eventual capture of Suez would open a supply route to Italian East Africa. The decisions on both sides gave the navies of Great Britain and Italy tasks that neither had anticipated before the war. The British needed to sustain Malta and the Italians needed to build up and support an offensive force in Libya.[10]

British strategy during this period presumed that Italy was the weak link in the Axis alliance. "The elimination of Italy and the consequent removal of the threat to our control of the Eastern Mediterranean would be a strategic success of the first importance," the British War Cabinet concluded. "Italy's power of resistance is much less than that of Germany and direct attack on Italy and her possessions in Africa may be the first important step we can take towards the downfall of Germany."[11] In other words, Britain undertook major offensive operations against Italy in the Mediterranean because it could not do so elsewhere.

In the war's first eight months the British and Italian navies fought two fleet actions and six smaller naval engagements. Britain attempted to control the central Mediterranean and reopen it to traffic with a knockout victory over the Italian fleet. This led to the action off Calabria in July 1940, which resulted in an inconclusive skirmish that saw both sides claiming victory. Whatever the claims, Italy's routine traffic in the central Mediterranean continued unabated, while British traffic from Gibraltar to Suez remained blocked, although the British did run heavily escorted convoys to Malta in September and October. A British carrier raid against the major Italian naval base at Taranto in November damaged three Italian battleships and permitted accelerated shipments to Malta, but its effects were relatively short-lived, and Italian battleships opposed the next Malta supply operation from Gibraltar two weeks later.

Malta had minor strategic value during the Parallel War period of June 1940 to January 1941. As a former head of the British naval historical branch wrote, "it has generally been claimed as having conferred 'command of the sea' upon the British. Such a claim is highly questionable at this remove of time . . . as [the Italians] were able to go about their more important occasions, supplying the Italian armies in Albania and Libya across the breath of the Mediterranean with near-daily sailing of convoys and single ships."[12]

The first convoy from Italy to Tripoli, carrying 937 men and 2,775 tons of supplies, arrived on 26 June 1940. There were also 73 return convoys involving 158 ships, of which only one was lost. In sum, during the Parallel

Table 1.1. **Italian Traffic to Africa, June 1940–January 1941**

Month	Convoys / Ships	Ships sunk	Tons sent	Arrived	Percent	Men sent	Arrived	Percent
Jun 1940	2/3	0	3,618	3,608	99.0	1,358	1,358	100.0
Jul	3/6	0	40,875	40,875	100.0	6,407	6,407	100.0
Aug	10/23	0	50,699	50,699	100.0	1,221	1,221	100.0
Sep	16/33	0	53,635	53,635	100.0	4,602	4,602	100.0
Oct	7/11	0	29,306	29,306	100.0	2,823	2,823	100.0
Nov	11/25	0	60,778	60,778	100.0	3,157	3,157	100.0
Dec	19/37	2	65,556	58,574	89.3	9,731	9,731	100.0
Jan 1941	18/35	1	50,505	49,084	97.2	12,491	12,214	97.8
Total	86/173	3	354,972	346,559	97.6	41,790	41,513	99.2

Source: USMM, Dati Statistici, 1:115–16, 126–27; USMM, Difesa del traffico, 7:436–38.
This table only includes sailings from Italy to Africa. It excludes sailings along the African coast or from Africa to Italy.

War period total Italian traffic to and from Africa (excluding coastal convoys) involved 331 commercial vessels, of which four vessels (1.2 percent) were lost. Traffic to Albania, Greece, and the Aegean Sea in this period totaled 1,480 commercial vessels of which 0.8 percent, in terms of gross registered tonnage, was lost.[13]

Italy's efforts to oppose supply operations to Malta were similarly ineffective. In the Parallel War period the British sent twenty-eight transports in eight convoys to Malta, but Italian forces damaged just one ship.

There were several reasons that British forces sank less than 1 percent of Axis shipping in the central Mediterranean, Adriatic, and Aegean seas during the Parallel War period. First, British rules of engagement were designed to limit unrestricted attacks to warships and escorted convoys; otherwise, stop-and-search rules applied. The Royal Navy maintained these rules until February 1941. Second, most Italian traffic to Tripoli favored the western route along the African shore, yet the British directed reconnaissance operations—and most submarine patrols from Malta—toward the shorter eastern route. It took British intelligence until mid-December before "the realization at last dawned upon the naval authorities at Malta and Alexandria that Italian shipping was being routed to the west."[14] Moreover, Allied submarines did poorly. For example, when the hostilities began, the three Allied boats that were deployed from Malta were lost on their first war patrol.

Table 1.2. **British Convoys to Malta, June 1940–January 1941**

Operation/ convoy	Date arrived	Transports	Loss	From	Tons Delivered
Hats/MF2	2 Sep 1940	3	1 Damaged	East	25,000
MF3	11 Oct 1940	4	0	East	30,000
MW3	10 Nov 1940	5	0	East	26,000
MW4	26 Nov 1940	4	0	East	30,000
Collar	26 Nov 1940	2	0	West	15,000
MW5A, 5B	20 Dec 1940	7	0	East	47,000
MW5.5	10 Jan 1941	2	0	East	20,200
Excess	11 Jan 1941	1	0	West	13,000

Source: Compiled from Cameron, *Red Duster,* Caruana, *Maritime Diary,* Playfair, I; Woodman, *Malta Convoys;* NSH, *Mediterranean,* I.

Although both sides could expect their convoys to arrive safely during the Parallel War period, British convoys were occasional and heavily protected, while Italian traffic was routine. London could not regularly reinforce the Middle East directly from Great Britain. Traffic to Egypt had to travel a circuitous route via the south Atlantic, the Cape of Good Hope, the Indian Ocean and the Red Sea—a voyage that was three times longer than the direct Mediterranean route and required three times the shipping to sustain the same level of traffic. At least the longer route was relatively secure, once the ships had gotten past Axis submarine patrols in the Atlantic. When the war began, Italy had air and naval forces based in Eritrea on the Red Sea, but these units were isolated and their efforts to interfere with the massive and strongly escorted British convoys moving up the Red Sea inflicted insignificant losses. The lack of fuel and ineffective doctrine greatly reduced the Italian threat, and in April 1941 the British eliminated the danger once and for all by capturing the port of Massawa, Italy's key naval base on the Red Sea.

Italy launched a half-hearted offensive in North Africa in September 1940. After a short advance into Egypt a large Italian army dug in, and in December a British corps counterattacked and eventually took 130,000 prisoners.[15] After conquering Cyrenaica the British seemed poised to drive Italy from North Africa. This threat provoked Germany to send in the 10th Fliegerkorps and two army divisions. German air strikes against Malta began in January 1941, and German troops disembarked in Tripoli on 15 February 1941, in the first of three large convoys to run between Naples and Tripoli that month.

In sum, neither side dominated the central Mediterranean during the Parallel War period. Despite all the naval and air activity, the Italians were able to meet their traffic requirements with little hindrance. The British were able to supply Malta, but had to abandon their most important prewar Mediterranean shipping route between Suez and Gibraltar.

The Period of German Intervention

Heavy air attacks against a British convoy to Malta and Greece, which departed Gibraltar on 6 January 1941 as part of Operation Excess, marked the end of the Parallel War period. None of the cargo ships involved was damaged, but German and Italian dive bombers hit the aircraft carrier *Illustrious* six times, German aircraft sank a cruiser, and an Italian mine crippled a British destroyer. Far worse from the British point of view, however, was the arrival of German troops in Africa, which came just as Britain was pulling divisions from Libya and sending them to Greece.

Between 4 March 1941 and 18 April some 20 convoys, totaling 173 merchant ships and three transport "lifts" of three cruisers each, departed Egyptian ports. In these convoys and "lifts" the Royal Navy delivered 58,364 men, 8,588 tons of arms and equipment, and much other materiel to Greece. German aircraft flying out of Sicily sank six ships from these convoys, while Italian aircraft dispatched one ship and damaged another. Decima MAS, the Italian special forces unit, in its first operational success, sank the heavy cruiser *York* and a tanker. The Italian submarine *Ambra* sank the light cruiser *Bonaventure*, but three Italian submarines patrolling the passage east of Crete and eight others in the sea lanes south of Crete failed to damage seriously or sink any merchant ships, and recorded just three unsuccessful attacks against warships. At the same time, during March Italy transported almost 93,000 tons of materiel to Africa in 27 convoys that included 80 ships—the highest monthly total of the war to date. The traffic to Albania was even greater, with 530 sailings. Allied submarines were ineffective in opposing this traffic. *Utmost* attacked an inbound convoy and torpedoed two ships, while *Upright* torpedoed a northbound freighter on the last day of the month. In short, during March 1941 the central and eastern Mediterranean teemed with shipping, but hardly any was lost on either side.[16]

Italy's major naval action during this period was the dispatch of a battleship strike force to the waters south of Crete. In the first case of the effective operational use of Ultra intelligence in the Mediterranean naval war, the British received hints that an Italian fleet movement was in the works and immediately suspended traffic between Egypt and Greece. The Italian force, commanded by Vice Admiral Angelo Iachino, chased a British cruiser squadron but only hit the enemy with a few splinters. In return, Iachino stirred a hornet's nest of enemy bombers. Swordfish aircraft eventually torpedoed his battleship, *Vittorio Veneto*, and immobilized a heavy cruiser. This would have been bad enough for the Italians, but the British battle fleet caught up to the damaged cruiser and, in a night encounter, sank her and two other cruisers that had been sent to her rescue, as well as two destroyers. The event, which entered history as the Battle of Matapan, reduced Italy's surface warfare capacity at a critical juncture. It prompted the Italians to limit the use of their capital ships in waters dominated by enemy air, and to regret that they had not made a greater effort to develop radar and aircraft carriers. Italian critics of the operation subsequently complained that it had served no purpose and was forced on a reluctant Supermarina by German pressure, but this was not true. Had the *Vittorio Veneto* and her attendant cruisers merely made an appearance and then successfully returned to port, they would have asserted sea power in the western Aegean by establishing a viable threat. If they had surprised a convoy, the entire program of reinforcing Greece would have been jeopardized. And even after their own victory the British felt the need to deploy battleships to protect convoys from surface threats to the west.[17]

In those eight months, sea traffic to Malta was almost identical to that of the eight months of the Parallel War period, although these later convoys delivered a greater amount of tonnage. Twenty-nine ships were sent and twenty-seven arrived. The Axis sank two (6.9 percent)—including one that sailed independently—and damaged one.

The Axis forces could still not prevent traffic to Malta, although they did better than they had done during the Parallel War period. The British, however, were slowly squeezing traffic to Africa.

Table 1.3. **British Convoys to Malta, March 1941–September 1941**

Operation/convoy	Date arrived	Transports	Loss	From	Tons delivered
MW6	23 March	4	0	West	35,000
MD2	21 April	1	0	East	9,700
Temple*	28 April (Sailed)	1	1 Sunk	West	0
MW7	9 May	6	0	East	41,000
Substance/GM.1	24 July	6	1 Damaged	West	65,000
Propeller*	19 September	1	0	West	5,600
Halberd/GM.2	28 September	9	1 Sunk	West	75,000

*Unescorted.
Source: NSH, *Mediterranean*, 2:xiii, xiv–xv.

Table 1.4. Italian Traffic to Africa, February 1941–October 1941

Month	Convoys/ ships	Ships sunk	Tons sent	Arrived	Percent	Men sent	Arrived	Percent
February	20/57	1	80,357	79,183	98.5	19,557	19,557	100.0
March	29/89	3	101,800	92,733	91.1	20,975	20,184	96.2
April	26/78	6	88,597	71,472	80.7	20,968	19,926	95.0
May	17/58	2	75,367	69,331	92.0	12,552	9,958	79.3
June	16/58	3	133,331	125,076	93.8	12,866	12,866	100.0
July	12/29	3	77,012	62,276	80.9	16,141	15,767	97.7
August	15/47	6	96,021	83,956	87.4	18,288	16,753	91.6
September	18/45	9	94,115	67,313	71.5	12,717	6,630	52.1
October	10/30	7	92,449	73,614	79.6	4,046	3,451	85.3
Total	163/491	40	839,049	724,954	86.4	138,110	125,092	90.6

Discusses the problem of reconciling the number of ships lost as enumerated in various sources. The figures given here for convoys and ships in convoy rely on the various volumes in the *Difesa del traffico* series. Appendix 1 contains a list of all ships displacing more than 100 GRT that were sunk during the period. *Source:* Militär. Forsch, *Second World War* 3:216.

There were also 151 return convoys involving 380 ships, of which five were lost. In total, the African traffic (excluding coastal convoys) that sailed during the period of German intervention totaled 871 commercial vessels, of which 45 vessels (5.2 percent) were lost. Traffic to Albania, Greece, and the Aegean in this period totaled 1,299 commercial vessels, of which 0.3 percent were lost (in terms of GRT).[18]

In March an Axis offensive threw the British out of Cyrenaica, except for an enclave around Tobruk, which then, like Malta, had to be sustained by sea. On 8 April 1941 the Germans, Italians, Hungarians, and Bulgarians invaded Yugoslavia and Greece. On 24 April the British began evacuating Greece. Almost 50,000 troops got out, but the Royal Navy paid a price. Axis aircraft operating over the evacuation ports sank two British destroyers and three transports. In May German paratroopers drove Imperial troops from Crete, forcing another evacuation. During this evacuation the British Mediterranean Fleet suffered crippling losses. Axis aircraft damaged twenty-eight warships, including two battleships and the only carrier, and sank four cruisers and six destroyers. According to British records during the three months that traffic to and from Greece was at its height (March,

April, and May), Axis forces sank or captured 125 Allied and neutral merchant ships displacing 375,080 GRT. Italian submarines did not account for a single vessel. Aircraft sank 102 ships displacing 323,090 GRT. In the same period the Allies lost 37 warships displacing 62,460 tons.[19]

From July through September the British navy's workload decreased, especially after Imperial troops overthrew the Iraqi government in May and finished conquering French Syria in July. Following these achievements, Libya–Egypt was the Middle Eastern command's only active land front. There both sides focused on building up their forces following the defeat of the British Brevity and Battleaxe offensives in May and June of 1941.

British efforts against Axis African traffic were ineffective during the first six months of 1941, apart from the 16 April interception of the five-ship German-Italian *Tarigo* convoy by British destroyers temporarily based in Malta, which resulted in the loss of five merchantmen that together displaced 14,398 GRT. In fact, June 1941 was the second-most-productive month for the Axis, measured in terms of materiel delivered to North Africa. In July, however, British aircraft and submarines finally began chipping away at African traffic.

A close look at July, August, September, and October 1941 shows why British efforts against traffic suddenly became more productive.

The first reason was that the British had better intelligence. To be sure, Ultra initially had many problems in terms of interpretation, confidence, and use, and these are discussed at length in the next chapter. But special intelligence also led to some notable successes. The submarine *Upholder*'s ambush of the *Oceania* (19,403 GRT) and *Neptunia* (19,328 GRT) on 17 September, for example, accounted for a third of the total tonnage lost in transit to Africa in the July–September period. Ultra enabled the British to pre-position submarines, as in the case of *Upholder*, and concentrate reconnaissance aircraft at times and in areas where intelligence indicated traffic would pass. The improvement and greater use of airborne surface vessel (ASV) radar in 1941 amplified the impact of better intelligence by making reconnaissance aircraft more effective, especially at night. The Mark II version had a range of up to sixty miles, although twenty miles was the limit for a destroyer-sized target. ASV-equipped Hudsons, Wellingtons, and Swordfish began operating out of Gibraltar and Malta from mid-1941.[20]

The second factor was a reduction in the British navy's major responsibilities. As Admiral Cunningham fretted in an 18 May 1941 letter to Pound, "This waiting for the Crete attack and having to make dispositions for it is hampering the attack on the Libyan trade. I fear they are running a lot of stuff into Benghazi."[21] After the loss of Crete and the conquest of Syria, the British could focus more attention and resources on attacking Axis traffic.

The third was Malta's increased capacity as a base, especially following the withdrawal of German air forces from Sicily in May 1941. To operate effectively, forces based in Malta needed intelligence and relative security in addition to supplies and weapons. Malta did not begin to realize the advantages of its geographic position until July 1941. The success of the July and September GM.1 and GM.2 convoys, combined with Operation Propeller in September, delivered 145,600 tons of supplies to the island; moreover, 214 Hurricanes arrived through June 1941 and another 58 in September.

By the beginning of August Malta was home to the 10th Submarine Flotilla and 145 operational aircraft. There were 22,000 men and 13 battalions, 330 antiaircraft guns, and 104 artillery pieces for coast defense and field operations.[22] There were five submarines stationed at Gibraltar, of which two were at sea; ten at Malta, with seven at sea; and fifteen at Alexandria, with seven at sea. Allied forces sank 25 loaded cargo ships that collectively displaced 145,059 GRT in transit to Africa in the four months of July–October, of which submarines and aircraft based in Malta accounted for 16, which together displaced 135,694 tons.[23]

To summarize the differences of the July–October period compared to earlier times, the British now could conduct better reconnaissance, and field more strike forces, with better-equipped and more-experienced men. At the same time, a few aggressive submarine skippers in more suitable submarines made a great difference in the overall effectiveness of the entire submarine force. And the supply of better aircraft, particularly ASV-equipped Marylands, allowed the British to attack at night as well as during the day.

The increased effectiveness of British forces caused the Axis commands to howl; nonetheless, 80 percent of the supplies sent to Africa from July through October arrived intact. The land war was static during this period as both sides amassed stocks and prepared to launch an offensive. As Rear Admiral Eberhard Weichold, the German naval attaché in Rome, summarized: "At the end of 1941, both sides in North Africa were striving for definite victory—the Germans and Italians by capturing Tobruk and the British by launching a major offensive aimed at relieving Tobruk and destroying the German and Italian troops in Cyrenaica. Reinforcement and supply efforts on both sides became a race against time in which sea transport was the deciding factor."[24]

Actions Planned

In June 1941 the British Middle Eastern Command consisted of General Archibald Wavell, Admiral Cunningham, and Air Chief Marshal Arthur Tedder. They commanded in consultation one with the other. This "committee" system was in place throughout the period of this work even though, General Alan Brooke, chief of the Imperial General Staff, complained "[t]he committee system is not conducive to firm, decisive and quick action, which is essential to success in war," but was merely "a Council of War, the evils of which have been proved in history."[25] After the July 1941 "Battleaxe" fiasco General Claude Auchinleck replaced Wavell. Auchinleck immediately began reorganizing and gathering reinforcements while planning to relieve Tobruk in an offensive codenamed Crusader. To accomplish this, he activated the 8th Army, under Lieutenant General Alan Cunningham, Admiral Andrew Cunningham's younger brother, stockpiled supplies, and advanced the railhead. The government in London was anxious to launch Crusader as soon as possible. Churchill had high expectations. On 14 October, the prime minister told the director of plans, Major General John Kennedy, that "This battle will have a great effect on the war, if the attack succeeds. It will be the first defeat inflicted on the Germans by the British. It will have a far-reaching influence upon sentiment throughout the world." This meeting with Churchill captured the tension that powered British strategic planning. The wildly optimistic prime minister claimed, "we have been sinking 50 per cent of their shipping," referring to the Axis supplies from Europe to Africa. The mildly pessimistic Kennedy, who remained silent, noted that "my information was that we had sunk only 17 percent." In fact, in September 1941, the month immediately preceding this meeting, the British had sunk 18 percent of the ships engaged in traffic to and from Africa.[26]

After the Crusader offensive the chiefs of staff considered several follow-up operations: Acrobat, the conquest of Tripoli; Gymnast, a movement (by invitation) into French North Africa; and, best of all, Whipcord, an invasion of Sicily. The chiefs concluded, "It is clear . . . there are great possibilities of fruitful action in the Mediterranean and Middle East areas in the near future. The reopening of the Mediterranean would not only be a great prize in itself, but can alone relieve that shortage of shipping which so gravely hampers our overseas operations whichever way we turn."[27]

With respect to shipping, at the end of 1940 the Axis powers in the Mediterranean had available (counting only vessels of more than 500 GRT) 1.981 million GRT of Italian ships and 0.225 million tons of German vessels for a total of 2.206 million GRT—more than sufficient to meet Axis requirements in the Mediterranean.[28] During the summer of 1941 mounting losses on the African route started to worry Berlin and Rome. The Italo-German army in Africa, under the leadership of Lieutenant General Erwin Rommel, was preparing to assault the British enclave at Tobruk. At a 25 August 1941 meeting between Hitler and Mussolini, the Axis leaders agreed that, contingent upon the free flow of supplies, their forces would be ready to attack Tobruk by the beginning of October. This would give the Axis a third port in North Africa, simplify the problem of defending Libya, and facilitate moves toward Suez in 1942. Although Berlin's strategic focus was on Russia, German planners remained absolutely confident that Russia would be defeated and that the war's next phase would include a strategic redeployment toward the Middle East.[29]

As it turned out, Rommel postponed his offensive and complained to Hitler that the Italians were not adequately protecting his supplies. Hitler, therefore, ordered German naval forces into the Mediterranean for the first time, "without taking Italian operations into consideration."[30] In addition, starting in mid-September the German 10th Fliegerkorps in Greece began to protect some traffic.

Apart from a few minor actions, the British and Axis armies in Libya had stood pat for four months, preparing their attacks. Such a delay testified to the logistic challenges they both faced and provided a clear demonstration of the influence of sea power on land operations.

Chapter 2

Communications, Intelligence, Logistics

At the moment of battle, information about the strength of the enemy
is uncertain, and the estimation of one's own is usually unrealistic.
CARL VON CLAUSEWITZ

The line between disorder and order lies in logistics.
SUN TZU

Communications and logistics influence the practice of sea power
in ways both obvious and subtle. Quite obviously, in the case of
the Mediterranean–North African campaign, logistic requirements determined its character, its zones of action, and its objectives,
and it dictated when naval operations were scheduled and how large they
would be. More subtly, in the case of the Regia Marina it even forced ships
to use lower cruising speeds at times when higher speeds would have been
safer. Quite obviously, too, communications is the foundation of all military interaction; yet, it entails misunderstandings and assumptions whose
impact can be subtle indeed.

At its core, communications is the multifaceted ability to transmit
information and instructions quickly, accurately, and securely. Intelligence is a product of this process. First and foremost, it consists of the
collection of information, but it also involves the protection of information, and the application of information to strategic, operational, and tactical activities. Many historians say that intelligence greatly affected the

Mediterranean campaign and that signals intelligence gave Great Britain a decisive advantage over its Axis foes and was particularly significant in the battle against traffic to North Africa. As early as 1977 one historian wrote that Britain's "systematic strangulation of [Rommel's] services of supply" made possible by its knowledge of Axis schedules and convoy routes was a "decisive ingredient of British . . . victory in the Mediterranean." In 1981 Francis Harry Hinsley, the chief author of the British official history of intelligence, wrote: "In the two months up to the middle of December 1941 the combination of high-grade shipping intelligence and the presence of Force K in Malta enabled the British forces to bring about a virtual stoppage of Axis supplies to north Africa."[1]

Such conclusions, reached four decades ago, have stood essentially unchallenged. A close examination of the matter, however, along with an accounting of Axis intelligence and countermeasures, will show that although intelligence often helped Allied operations, it was but one tool of many—and hardly decisive, especially during the period covered in this book. In fact, one expert has asserted that "Axis signals intelligence provided valuable operational intelligence against the [Royal Navy] in the Mediterranean and the British army in Egypt. All told, Britain arguably lost the signals intelligence war in that theatre between January 1941 and May 1942."[2] A quick review of some basic statistics supports this conclusion. This book covers a period when the Italians sailed 188 convoys or single ships to, from, or along the African shore and the British sailed 90 convoys to Malta or between Alexandria and Tobruk (or other ports in Libya). Ultra informed the British of 82 percent of Italian convoys or sailings. The British attacked 49 (26 percent), and inflicted some damage to 30 (16 percent). The Axis powers meanwhile attacked 40 percent of British convoys and inflicted damage to 21 percent.[3]

Ultra

Radio was a fast and convenient way to transmit messages, but it was not secret; anyone could intercept a broadcast. As a result, militaries used codes and other means to protect their radio messages from snoopers. These measures ranged from simple substitution codes, where one letter stands for another, and super-encryption, which involved coded messages of coded messages, to messages that were scrambled randomly through mechanical devices. The problem was that coded messages slow communications and sometimes limit what can be said; a message sent in a complex code can take hours on both ends to encrypt and decrypt. Mechanical and electro-mechanical coding machines offered compelling advantages—relative ease of use, faster speeds, and nearly absolute security—or so it seemed. They became common in the 1930s, and by 1941 all the major powers were using devices such as the German Enigma, the British Typex, the American Sigaba, and the Japanese Purple.

Enigma was an electro-mechanical cipher machine with a keyboard and various complex components such as a series of wired rotors, a fixed reflector, and a plug-board that scrambled the electrical currents that entered and exited the rotor maze. The sender typed in a message and gibberish emerged. The recipient entered the gibberish on a machine with the same rotor and plug settings and the message emerged in readable form. As one expert described the process, "To calculate the total number of possible variables built into the Enigma . . . the cryptanalyst would have to multiply the possible rotor combinations by the possible rotor start-ing positions by the possible notch positions by the possible wirings of the reflector by the possible combinations of plugins." The number of possible combinations, 3.3×10^{114}, was greater than the number of atoms in the observable universe.[4] The German naval interception and cypher unit, B-Dienst (Beobachtungsdienst), knew that Enigma "was vulnerable in theory," but every time it studied the matter, B-Dienst concluded that Enigma enciphered communications were secure. Nonetheless, the Allies (the Poles actually first read Enigma coded messages and the French played a significant role) deciphered Enigma encoded messages by apply-ing resources and talent to the problem, by the mechanization of crypt-analysis, by the physical capture of Enigma machines and codebooks, and last, but in some respects, most important, by exploiting the poor practices of some German operators. By 1940 a British unit based at Bletchley Park, England, and called the Government Code and Cypher School (GC&CS) was generating intelligence summaries based on the content of intercepted and deciphered Enigma encoded radio traffic. The code name for these summaries was Ultra.[5]

The British Middle Eastern Command was an Ultra recipient. Between 20 and 26 October 1941, for example, GC&CS sent Cairo ninety-one Ultra messages, fifty-nine classified as emergency, eighteen as immediate, and fourteen as important. Thirty-five of these concerned convoys and other shipping movements and included information about composition, departure dates, routes, arrivals, postponements, and corrections of previous messages. There were eighteen other naval messages regarding the sailings of warships, policy directives, and navigational matters. Eighteen messages covered the German air force; twelve had to do with logistics, mostly related to the German air force; and eight touched on topics such as order of battle and army movements. The German air force's Enigma machines generated forty of these messages; others came from the German railway system, the Italian air force's C 35, and Italian naval C 38m Enigma. Yet, with an average of thirteen messages a day, this was a light week. From 20 November through 5 December the average was thirty-one messages a day; from 6 December through 18 December it was thirty-five.[6]

Because the British did not want the Axis powers to learn that their most secure cyphering system was compromised, Ultra messages were subject to stringent security. Starting on 20 July 1941 the GC&CS sent items to the Middle East via a Special Communications Unit (SCU) "within four to twelve hours after transmission by the enemy." The SCU sent messages over secure teleprinter lines, or, if it was necessary to use radio, via the one-time pad method using identical pads of tear-off sheets. "Although unbreakable, it was a slow and tedious method of communicating."[7] An SCU operative on the other end received the information and passed it to a cipher sergeant from a GC&CS-controlled Special Liaison Unit (SLU). The sergeant deciphered the message and an SLU intelligence officer—always of relatively low rank to avoid attracting attention—personally delivered the message to the designated recipient in the operational headquarters. Originally, these were Auchinleck, Cunningham, or Tedder. In September 1941, the GC&CS reluctantly included Malta's senior naval officer, Vice Admiral Wilbraham Ford. One SLU officer remembered that "such personal messages as came in for Admiral Cunningham were received by him with great courtesy. Also Air Marshal Tedder always received any 'personal only' messages with appreciation. However, Tedder's outer office assistant . . . was anything but courteous. . . . In general I found a better welcome from the 'top brass' than from their underlings."[8] The recipients, in turn, designated staff members to evaluate the information and recommend action.

Initially the numbers of personnel and procedures used to act upon this mass of information were inadequate. Ralph Bennett, a GC&CS translator who spent time in the Middle East in late 1942 and early 1943, wrote: "the full benefits which flowed from [Ultra intelligence] were long in coming . . . the results of disseminating Ultra intelligence in 1941 must now be judged on the whole disappointing. . . . Intelligence was then not highly regarded, and those who had the power to use it in battle often lacked the will to do so."[9] He noted that only after the August 1942 battle of Alam Halfa were Ultra dispatches regarded as a critical resource. Indeed, the dissemination of such intelligence often was so slow that the information was obsolete by the time it was delivered. As British war historian Hinsley conceded, "Sigint [the military acronym from intelligence gathered by intercepting radio and telephone messages] passing on the SCU/SLU from CG and CS to Vice Admiral Malta and from him operational orders to the Senior Officer Force K, who was not himself an Ultra recipient, was sometimes received too late for action."[10]

Process was one problem, content was another. Some Ultra information was specific and actionable; much was subject to change or proved to be just plain chatter. News that a convoy may leave an unknown port for an unknown destination in a week's time would not result in an interception at sea. GC&CS usually generated paraphrases of deciphered signals—not the actual content—both as a security measure and to give context, and the paraphrases included interpretation and conjecture. As one GC&CS historian admitted in frustration after a British convoy was dispatched into the teeth of an Italian fleet sortie, "Perhaps the rather too copious and conjectural comments made in GC&CS upon individual signals tended to confuse what was in reality a fairly clear picture."[11] Finally, there was the matter of quality. GC&CS worked under tremendous pressure twenty-four hours a day.

According to an internal history, "Complaints on processing errors, were, in the Head of the Z Watches opinion, too frequent, when one considered the enormous bulk of translations which were being turned out daily—Admiralty too, were profuse in criticisms, and lacking in praise." Collectively these issues led to messages that sometimes bewildered rather than enlightened.[12]

The Ultra narrative has it that to preserve secrecy the British prohibited action against any enemy convoy disclosed by Ultra until after the convoy had been found by aircraft or there was some other plausible explanation to account for the attack. Supposedly, the prohibition was to prevent Axis commands from suspecting that their high-level codes had been compromised. This was not true, however, and the narrative contains accounts of many Ultra-enabled attacks on convoys that were not first sighted by Allied aircraft. In fact, because Ultra was seldom precise enough to guarantee contact with enemy targets, the British used reconnaissance aircraft to pinpoint targets. Admiral Cunningham complained about this in a 24 November 1941 letter to Admiral Dudley Pound, the first sea lord: "The movements forecast in MK [a prefix designating an Ultra message] information are all too frequently postponed and communication lags delay appropriate action this end. Air recce [reconnaissance] is too thin to be certain of obtaining confirmation."[13]

The breaking of Enigma was a tremendous accomplishment and has rightly attracted much attention, but the fact that Ultra was kept secret for thirty years after the end of the war has magnified its apparent significance. Put in context, it was one facet of a wide-ranging top-secret intelligence war waged by both sides.

The Axis powers also vigorously attacked Allied communications and codes. While they never cracked the British Typex or the American Sigaba, they achieved notable successes against some high-level Allied naval codes, and routine radio traffic was an open book.[14] Captain Franco Maugeri, the head of the Italian navy's intelligence service, the Servizio Informazioni Segrete (SIS), told British interrogators in 1944 that "The work on the naval tactical codes was relatively easy, and the air code reciphering tables [Syko], though changed every 24 hours, were quite simple, and could be reconstructed after a few messages. The sighting reports sent out by British aircraft could always be completely deciphered at once, and were retransmitted within a few minutes to units sighted."[15] Such immediate and practical information served the Italians greatly in their efforts to fight convoys through the hazardous waters of the central Mediterranean and often diminished the impact of Ultra intelligence. The British realized that low-grade signals were vulnerable, but did not account for the rapidity with which the Italians were able to use such information. The Italians were also successful in deciphering diplomatic traffic. The cracking of the U.S. Foreign Service's Black Code and the cascade of excellent information that resulted from Colonel Bonner Fellers, the U.S. military attaché in Cairo, is a well-known story. The Italians also read British diplomatic codes. The reports of the British naval attaché in Istanbul to the commander of the Mediterranean Fleet provided useful information, especially regarding the movements of Russian tankers.[16]

B-Dienst enjoyed great success in deciphering British naval codes. In the Mediterranean, the British navy used Naval Cypher #2 from September 1941 through 1 January 1942. A British study concluded the "results obtained by [B-Dienst] were so good they were able to read 30–50% of traffic." The introduction of Naval Cypher #4 in January interrupted enemy access to high-level British naval traffic until March, when B-Dienst achieved its first successes against the new code. The Germans and Italians also read the Naval Code #1 from September 1941 through January 1942. This was a less secure system but was useful for the location of major units and administrative matters. During this period the Germans also read the British Inter-service Cypher, Medox, a small ship's code of minimal security, and the Merchant Ship code.[17]

SIS and B-Dienst were linked by a teleprinter and exchanged material, mostly intercepts, and the two organizations shared a daily intelligence summary. However, as one historian noted, "believing that Italians were temperamentally unfit for serious cryptanalysis, the German codebreakers considered their allies very junior partners from whom little could be expected. . . . For their part, the Italians considered the Germans overbearing and patronizing."[18] By January 1942 the two services had begun withholding information from each other.

Littorio during a firing exercise. Italy's modern battleships were fast and well armored, with effective fire control, but by 1942 they lacked fuel even for training. COLLECTION OF E. CERNUSCHI

Logistics

The bulk of the naval action in the Mediterranean from November 1941 to March 1942 occurred as a consequence of efforts to run convoys to North Africa or Malta. Malta lay astride Italian supply lines to Africa—just 60 miles off the shore of Sicily and 840 from Alexandria, 60 hours at 14 knots, but longer in practice due to the need to zigzag and make other diversionary movements. The British also ran traffic in the eastern Mediterranean, with multiple convoys at sea every day, although the only routes subject to regular attack were between the Libyan ports and Alexandria. Almost all supplies and men bound for the Middle East came up the Red Sea, where they were immune to attack during this period.

Sea Traffic to Africa

On 26 October 1941 Italy controlled two ports in Africa—Tripoli and Benghazi—and two anchorages, Derna and Bardia. In 1940 Tripoli theoretically could accommodate five cargo ships or four troop transports and 2,000 tons of materiel a day; Benghazi could hold three cargo ships or two troop transports and 1,000 tons of materiel daily. There also were anchorages that small coastal steamers or—in an emergency—destroyers and submarines could access.[19]

Naval bombardments, air strikes, and weather sometimes decreased these capacities; extra lighters, floating cranes, and labor sometimes increased them. A Supermarina study dated 4 December 1941 calculated that Tripoli could handle between 3,000 and 4,000 tons a day and six or seven larger ships, while Benghazi's daily capacity remained limited to three smaller ships and 1,000 tons. All told, the theoretical maximum amount of cargo that could be unloaded in African ports during any given month, under ideal conditions, was 120,000 tons.[20] Given bad weather and enemy action, however, conditions were never ideal. Moreover, three quarters of Benghazi's cargo was transshipped from Tripoli, which meant that some cargo had to be unloaded twice—once in Tripoli and again in Benghazi (or minor anchorages).[21]

In fact, Italy actually shipped more than 100,000 tons of materiel to Africa in only three months out of the entire war. Between February 1941—when German forces first entered the theater and Tripoli and Benghazi were the major arrival ports—and May 1942, the last month before the Axis captured Tobruk, which also became a supply port, Italian and German ships unloaded 1.204 million tons of cargo in Africa, an average of 75,000 tons a month. Average shipments were 87,000 tons a month.

The number of berths available at Tripoli and Benghazi was a firm limit that dictated the size and timing of African convoys. Ships from one convoy had to be unloaded and to be on their way home before the next convoy could be accommodated. If a convoy were forced to abort or else took losses, it would be at least a week before a replacement ship could arrive, and meanwhile the berth sat empty. Indeed, Admiral Aldo Cocchia, the author of the official Italian histories of the convoy war, wrote: "the Libyan ports at Italy's disposal could hardly absorb more than two million tons of goods"—a reference to the 1.93 million tons landed from June 1940 through November 1942. In other words, taking the campaign as a whole, Cocchia asserted that the Italians could not have landed much more in Libya than they did, even if there had been no British interference. Perhaps Cocchia is right, but he does not mention that if the British had not attacked the ports

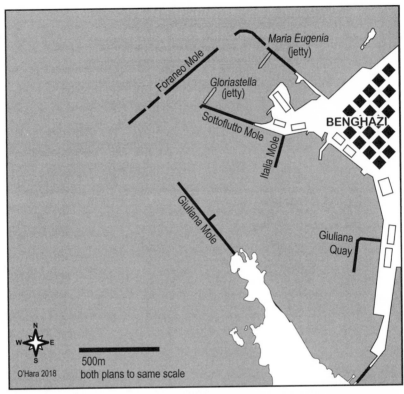

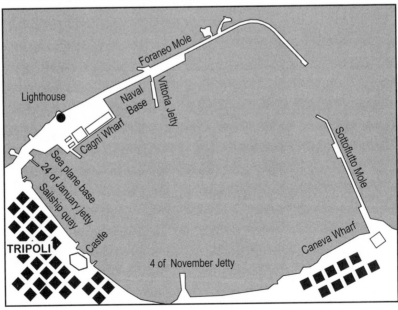

Map 2.1. **Tripoli and Benghazi Harbors**

Italy would have been able to do more to increase port capacity during the war years. He also discounts the element of timeliness. Ammunition, food, and fuel must be available in the necessary quantities when they are needed to conduct operations. Battles were won or lost on Britain's ability to deny the enemy supplies on a timely basis—or on Italy's ability to deliver them.[22]

African traffic during this period consisted of 188 sailings that fell into three broad categories. These categories included:

1. Convoys or single sailings from European ports, most important from Naples and then Brindisi, Bari, Taranto, or Trapani. Naples had the best rail connections with the industrial north and the capacity to load up to fourteen vessels, whereas Bari and Brindisi were limited to five vessels and the other ports less. The problem with Naples, however, was that the sea routes south ran through the Strait of Messina, a vulnerable choke-point and a favorite haunt of British submarines. Piraeus, Greece, was served by a single rail line and, during this period, was rarely an origination point for African convoys.[23]
2. Coastal convoys or single sailings between Tripoli and Benghazi or smaller intermediate ports. Ships on the coastal routes carried supplies forward toward the front.
3. Return convoys or single sailings from African ports to Europe. Ships engaged in this traffic sailed empty or carried prisoners of war, scrap, or commercial goods.

Warships also carried supplies to African ports, generally those close to the front such as Derna or Bardia. There were forty-eight such sailings to and from Africa by submarines (thirty-three missions), torpedo boats (three missions), destroyers (nine missions), and even cruisers (three missions).[24] Forty-three of the forty-eight warships thus used arrived intact.

Italian Fuel Situation

A shortage of fuel impinged upon Italian navy operations during this period. It affected training, limited escort sizes, and in at least one case prevented the Italian navy from contesting a Malta convoy.

The Italian navy began the war with 1,666,674 tons of fuel oil stockpiled. Up through 1 October 1941 it burned 1,465,482 tons—a little less than 90,000 a month—while another 100,500 tons was allocated to industry or lost in combat. Total consumption of 1,565,982 and new supplies of 152,980 left stockpiles of 253,672 tons. Throughout the next quarter, reserves continued to fall.[25]

An accounting compiled on 21 February 1942 showed 51,000 tons held in military and civilian deposits and 43,000 tons aboard bunkers. On 1 April the Italian navy possessed 50,000 tons of fuel oil in tankers and storage facilities and 35,000 tons aboard ships.[26]

Consumption varied according to the requirements of war. In October 1941 Supermarina estimated a monthly average consumption of 75,500 tons.

This was considered a bare-bones allocation and excluded major fleet actions. For example, the fleet sortie against the Halbard convoy consumed 18,000 tons of fuel oil.[27] Additions to inventory came from two sources—the Italian concession of Ploesti in Romania and grants from

Table 2.1. **Oil Situation, October–December 1941 (tons)**

	October	November	December
Beginning inventory	254	212	154
Consumption	66	77	99
Receipts	24	19	53
Ending balance	212	154	108

Source: Supermarina, "Situazione Nafta per Caldaie," 21 February 1942 and 1 April 1942.

Table 2.2. **Monthly Oil Consumption (tons)**

African traffic	22,000
Adriatic/Aegean traffic	11,000
Metropolitan traffic	5,000
Protection of traffic	16,000
Consumption by fleet units in port	9,000
One sortie by a cruiser division	6,000
Training (absolute minimum)	3,000
Routine transit	2,000
Submarines	1,500

Source: CED, "Consume Mensile di Nafta," II/2:1060.

the German navy's reserves. Initial agreements allocated Italy 55,000 tons a month from Romania, but this proved unrealistic. Moreover, some of the oil was unsuitable for the navy's requirements. In December, for example, of 21,000 tons of fuel shipped to Italy from Romania, only 9,000 tons were of a quality that was useful to the navy. Allocations from Germany came from German reserves, but by April these had fallen to 150,000 tons.[28]

Another problem was getting the oil to where it was needed when it was needed. Romanian oil was generally received by train and available at the head of the Adriatic, where it was distributed southward. During this period fuel oil was a major consideration in every action that the Italian navy took. Here is a list of oil depots and the amount of fuel oil stored at each in the beginning and middle of the period studied in this work:

Table 2.3. Oil Depot Levels, 23 October 1941 and 10 January 1942 (tons)

Base	23 October 1941	10 January 1942
Bari	0	1,784
Brindisi	0	1,305
Naples	1,500	2,764
Palermo and Trapani	3,000	1,461
Tripoli	2,000	0
Benghazi	0	0
Cagliari and La Maddalena	9,000	1,832
Augusta	4,500	1,022
Messina and Reggio Calabria	11,000	7,361
Taranto	38,000	11,583
Pola and Venice	0	3,071
La Spezia	0	3,183
Leros	0	1,200
Other	0	9,599
Total	69,000	46,165

Source: AUSMM, "Rifornimento della R. Marina Italiana con nafta," II/2, 1058; AUSMM, "Problema del rifornimento di nafta," 10 January 1942.

Chapter 3

Force K Arrives, October 1941

The most satisfactory and profitable gun actions in the Mediterranean, whether fought by battleships, light forces or submarines, have been fought as nearly as practicable at point-blank range.

MEDITERRANEAN GUNNERY EXPERIENCE, 1940–1941 (REPORT)

On 21 October 1941 the British light cruisers *Aurora* and *Penelope* and destroyers *Lively* and *Lance* arrived in Malta, the first major surface warships to be based there since the previous May. Perhaps the choice of date was meant to imbue the little squadron with some Trafalgar mojo, because the War Cabinet had to prod the Admiralty repeatedly to send the ships. On 3 September 1941 Admiral Pound wrote to Admiral Cunningham: "Personally, I am extremely doubtful whether a weak force of two 6-in cruisers and four destroyers would be able to achieve anything commensurate with their loss in the face of air and surface force attack." Pound considered submarines and aircraft better suited to the task of interdicting enemy traffic. However, Churchill was adamant that warships must operate from Malta. Pound went on record stating that he sent the ships against his wishes because he did not want critics to say that the navy failed to do its utmost if the Crusader offensive were to fail.[1]

The Italians immediately detected the warships' arrival. Supermarina ordered convoys en route to Palermo and Naples to return to Africa, although other convoys bound for Benghazi continued. On 22 October

Admiral Arturo Riccardi, the Regia Marina's chief of staff, met with General Ugo Cavallero, Comando Supremo's chief of staff, and noted that the ships newly based in Malta presented a "considerable threat to our convoys and to the destroyers that are transporting troops." He recommended increasing Italian aerial reconnaissance and bombing the port. At this point, there were fewer than forty Italian bombers in Sicily. Between 21 October and 30 October Air Sicily conducted five night-bombings and two daylight raids—the greatest involving eighteen aircraft, but most with three or four bombers. The most successful action was a daylight assault on the 25th, when four Z.1007bis ignited 850 tons of kerosene in La Valletta and "provoked a vast fire." Several night incursions unsuccessfully targeted Force K.[2]

On 30 October the British flotilla was still at Valletta, and the heads of the navy and air force met with Cavallero to discuss the situation. Riccardi, after complaining vigorously about the Italian navy's fuel situation, advised that cruisers would need to stiffen convoy escorts, but pointed out that the risk would still be great, especially along the western route at night. Riccardi worried that "Nothing could counter the nighttime aerial offense that experience has shown to be particularly effective. It is therefore very likely that our [cruiser] division would be crippled before it would have even been able to perform its task." The eastern route, while safer, posed other problems: "The [cruiser] division cannot, because of range, escort the return convoy of empty ships, which cannot stay in Tripoli along with the incoming convoy." Even if all went well, a cruiser division would cost an extra 2,500 tons of fuel oil along the western route and an added 3,500 tons along the eastern route. The navy could not afford to consume an extra 3,000 tons of fuel on every convoy to Tripoli.[3]

On 25 October two transports, *Capo Orso* (2,449 GRT/10 kts) and the German *Tinos* (2,826 GRT/10.5 kts), escorted by the destroyer *Strale*, left Benghazi for Brindisi. This convoy was the subject of multiple Ultra decryptions, including one that gave the correct itinerary two days before sailing and another that confirmed this information four hours after departure. Based on this intelligence, Force K sortied but could not locate its quarry, and the convoy arrived safely on the 28th. The failure demonstrated that even with the best of intelligence, success was never certain.[4]

Convoy Actions, November 1941

The Regia Marina sent its first convoy to Africa since Force K's arrival when *Capo Arma* (3,172 GRT/10 kts) and *Capo Faro* (3,476 GRT/10 kts), escorted by the torpedo boat *Procione*, departed Brindisi at 1000/29th bound for Benghazi. They were loaded with 6,466 tons of cargo, including 760 tons of munitions and 1,289 tons of fuel. An Ultra message generated at 0140Z/30th warned that they would be at sea that day, on a route unknown, but "probably travelling from Brindisi to Benghazi." At 1012/31st a reconnaissance aircraft spotted the convoy. The Italians intercepted the aircraft's sighting report and Supermarina alerted *Procione*. At 2325/31st four Wellington aircraft from Malta attacked the convoy. The bombers claimed six hits and reported: target "left stationary emitting clouds of black and white smoke." In fact, near misses caused minor flooding on *Capo Arma*, and the pair arrived in Benghazi at 0900/1st with cargo intact.[5]

On 1 November Force K sortied to intercept the steamers *Iseo* (2,366 GRT/11.5 kts) and *Bolsena* (2,352 GRT/11.5 kts), which had departed Benghazi at 1830/1st with *Procione* as escort. An Ultra message disclosed the convoy's departure with thirty-six hours' notice but despite the assistance of an ASV-equipped Wellington both Force K and a Swordfish strike force failed to find it.[6]

At 0900/3rd *Anna Zippitelli* (1,019 GRT) and *Ascianghi* (610 GRT) departed Tripoli bound for Benghazi. Ultra missed this convoy, but routine reconnaissance did not. At 1230/5th eight Blenheim twin-engine bombers caught the two small steamers in the Gulf of Sirte 75 miles short of their destination and assailed them from mast height, sinking *Anna Zippitelli*. The torpedo boat *Calliope* shot down two aircraft. A Wellington assaulted *Ascianghi* again 15 miles short of Benghazi, but she reached harbor safely.[7]

At 2400/6th the steamers *Bosforo* (3,648 GRT/10.5 kts) and the German *Savona* (2,120 GRT/12.5 kts), escorted by the torpedo boat *Pegaso*, departed Brindisi for Benghazi. As early as 29 October Ultra had indicated that a convoy was loading at Brindisi. At 0010Z/8th a message predicted the convoy's imminent departure for Benghazi. This was followed at 1245Z/8th by an emergency dispatch that "There are indications that this convoy, whose sailing must have been postponed from an earlier date, left Brindisi either late on November sixth or early on seventh." There was confusion, because both *Bosforo* and *Savona* had originally sailed on 4 November but foul weather had forced them back to Brindisi. In any case, reconnaissance spotted them at 1030/7th 60 miles southwest of Corfu. Malta dispatched Wellingtons and Swordfish, but they could not find their prey.[8]

The next morning at 1010/8th six Blenheims from Malta had better luck. One aircraft clipped *Savona*'s mast and crashed on her deck, igniting a fierce fire. The crew abandoned ship but then reboarded to fight the fire. At 1326 six more Blenheims appeared, while another six missed the target "owing [to] thick cloud and error in reporting by sighting patrol." The twin-engine aircraft bore in at mast height and released sixteen 250-pound bombs despite intense antiaircraft fire. While this provoked fresh panic on *Savona*, the convoy commander reported, "the wounded vessel was not further damaged thanks to the vigorous action of the torpedo boat that . . . kept shooting down attacking aircraft." Two Blenheims were indeed lost, and the Italians rescued two aircrew members. A British summary noted, "All the aircraft which attacked this convoy were hit by A.A. fire and in many cases seriously damaged."[9]

The crew finally extinguished *Savona*'s fire and, along with *Bosforo*, she continued under her own power, seeking refuge in Navarino. After the detour to that Greek port *Bosforo* reached Benghazi on 12 November and landed 2,748 tons of cargo.

The Beta Convoy

The late October suspension of Libyan traffic forced Axis forces in North Africa to dip into stockpiles intended for a 20 November offensive against Tobruk. This prompted Supermarina to schedule an unusually large convoy to Tripoli. Named the Beta Convoy, it consisted of five steamers and two tankers, including *Duisburg* (GE 7,389 GRT/13 kts), *San Marco* (3,114/10.5 kts), *Rina Corrado* (5,180/11 kts), *Sagitta* (5,153 GRT/10 kts), *Maria* (GE 6,339 GRT/11.5 kts), *Minatitlan* (AO 7,599 GRT/12 kts), and *Conte di Misurata* (AO 5,014 GRT/9 kts). All told, the convoy carried 34,473 tons of cargo (including weight of vehicles), of which 80 percent was intended for Italian forces.

Relying on German commitments to provide extra oil, Supermarina assigned to Beta a powerful escort comprising a close escort, the 10th

Squadron (Captain Ugo Bisciani) destroyers *Maestrale, Fulmine, Euro, Oriani, Libeccio,* and *Grecale*; and a heavy Support Group, the 3rd Division (Rear Admiral Bruno Brivonesi), heavy cruisers *Trieste* and *Trento,* and 13th Squadron (Captain Ferrante Capponi), destroyers *Granatiere, Bersagliere, Fuciliere,* and *Alpino.*

Comando Supremo ordered the air force "to arrange for an aerial escort adequate for all circumstances." Three submarines, *Delfino, Settembrini,* and *Corallo,* patrolled off Malta.[10]

Brivonesi, who had held a shore command at the start of the war, took over the 3rd Division in April 1941. The next month he escorted a convoy of converted ocean liners, from which the British submarine *Upholder* torpedoed and sank *Conte Rosso* (17,897 GRT/19.5 kts), with the loss of 1,279 men. This experience affected the way Brivonesi positioned his ships relative to the Beta Convoy. "The experience during and after the episode of the torpedoing of *Conte Rosso* confirms that a nocturnal close escort of heavy cruisers can provide effective protection if enemy forces are sighted in such a position as to allow the use of guns without the risk of hitting a friendly unit," he wrote in a report, "but it can be a serious danger for the ships in the convoy and for our own cruisers, if, after some alarm, real or false, ships disperse and make sudden course changes that are impossible to signal. Positioning the cruiser escorts ahead of the convoy is too difficult to maintain, in addition to not providing protection in the event of a lateral or aft attack. A lateral position, even though it has some difficulties, leaves one side uncovered." This report concluded that a division of heavy cruisers provided a strong element of security during the day but that, at night "it could be a pure danger to the ships of the convoy, especially at high speeds, which thus does not allow the cruisers to maneuver rapidly."[11]

The Beta Convoy would circle east of Malta, beyond the 190-mile range of torpedo bombers, because experience indicated that these aircraft presented the principal danger at night and that unless the enemy knew the convoy's exact route and speed a surface interception was almost impossible. Brivonesi decided to follow from the convoy's starboard quarter, which he believed would block an enemy force approaching from Malta and enable him to engage without endangering the convoy itself. It would also, in the case of alarm, keep the cruisers separated from the steamers and decrease the chance of collision—a possibility that Brivonesi considered a "grave danger." In all cases, his objective was to maintain freedom of maneuver. The convoy's mean speed of 9 knots forced the warships to maintain position by zigzagging.[12]

Five of the steamers departed Naples at 0500/7th. They reached the Straits of Messina before dawn on the 8th, where *Rina Corrado, Conte di Misurata,* the 3rd Division, and the 13th Squadron joined. The convoy then headed due east to gain separation from Malta. At 1355/8th a Maryland aircraft returning to Malta from its patrol in the Ionian Sea spotted the convoy and reported six merchant vessels and four destroyers forty miles east-southeast of Cape Spartivento, Calabria, heading east at 11 knots. The position and course were accurate, but the speed actually was 8 knots. The escort saw the Maryland, and the SIS intercepted its report to Malta as well. At 1530 Vice Admiral Ford ordered Force K's senior officer, Captain William G. Agnew of *Aurora,* to put to sea, and at 1730/8th the two cruisers and the destroyers *Lively* and *Lance* were threading out the swept passage from Grand Harbor. Agnew started the war skippering an armed merchant cruiser, but had commanded *Aurora* since October 1940 and had led her in a successful night surface attack against a German convoy in Porsanger Fjord, Norway, just two months earlier. He set course northeast toward a point that would intersect the convoy's presumed track by 0200/9th.[13]

Duisburg. This German freighter (7,389 GRT) was sunk by Force K on 9 November 1941. Roughly 15 percent of the merchant ships that the Axis used to carry supplies to Africa were German-flagged vessels caught in the Mediterranean by the outbreak of war. E. BAGNASCO, *GUERRA SUL MARE*

Hinsley's history of intelligence says: "Full details of the route and composition of the convoy . . . were sent out in time for Malta to have it sighted by Maryland reconnaissance aircraft of No. 69 Squadron RAF on the afternoon of 8 November." Hinsley cites three Ultra messages, OL 1847, 1848, and 1849, and four decrypted Italian naval messages, ZTPI 1800, 1803, 1820, and 1829, to support this assertion.[14] ZTPI 1800 and 1803 were the two halves of a message generated in Benghazi that disclosed the route and schedule of convoy "X," to be escorted by the torpedo boat *Pegaso*. Convoy X referred to *Bosforo* and *Savona*—not Beta. ZTPI 1820 is missing from the record. However, the timing of this decryption would have been within a few minutes of 1500Z/8th (1700 local). This was three hours after the Maryland sighting, so ZTPI 1820 and 1829 (decrypted at 2258Z/8th) could not have influenced Malta's assignment of air reconnaissance with respect to Beta. ZTPI 1826, not cited by Hinsley, does concern the Beta Convoy. It is a request from Rome, deciphered at 2049Z/8th, for the Salonica command to remind the German 10th Fliegerkorps of the "extreme importance of reconnaissance flights which have been requested for Convoy *Maestrale*." ZTPI 1829 is an answer from Salonica to Rome asking that 10th Fliegerkorps reserve assets for the convoy. These messages did not contain schedule or itinerary. Bletchley Park transmitted a paraphrase of ZTPI 1826 and 1829 to Malta's SCU in message OL 1847 ("an important convoy will be on its way to Tripoli during November Nine and Ten, during which days the readiness of German air units based Greek area has been requested.") The message incorrectly speculated that "this convoy probably left Naples this morning November eighth." The message was sent three minutes *after Aurora* opened fire. OL 1848 and 1849 were generated later and concern *Bosforo*, not Beta. In short, Ultra had nothing to do with the sighting and destruction of the Beta Convoy.

In fact, Agnew coursed northeast relying on information from a partially erroneous sighting (position and course correct, speed wrong) and the assistance of an ASV Wellington that was supposed to vector him onto his target. The Wellington's radar malfunctioned, however, so Force K had to sail blind. At least the weather cooperated. The night was partly cloudy, with the moon at 84 percent and rising in the east at 2155, with a gentle breeze from the north-northwest. Force K was 135 miles east of Syracuse,

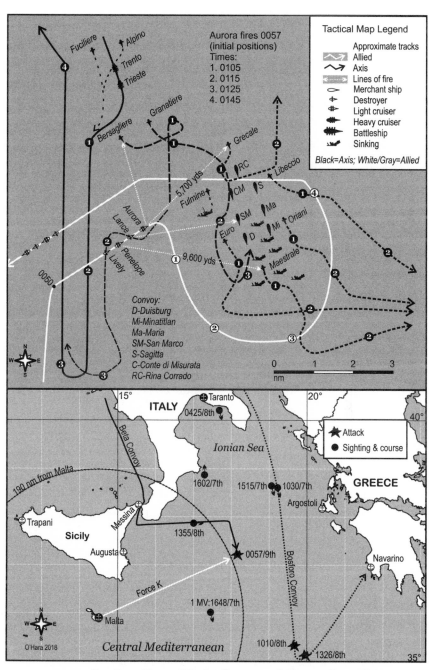

Map 3.1. **Destruction of Beta Convoy, 9 November 1941**

and, as one of *Penelope*'s officers recalled, "getting very near the time for turning homeward, when, at 0039/9th, we suddenly raised a signal from *Aurora* reporting the enemy." The distance upon sighting was 14,000 yards. The SIS intercepted and decoded this report, but not in time to notify the escort that it had been sighted.[15]

Beta sailed south-southeast with its ships in two columns half a mile apart. To starboard *Duisburg* led *San Marco* and *Conte di Misurata*; to port *Minatitlan* preceded *Maria* and *Sagitta*, while *Rina Corrado* sailed behind. *Maestrale* led the escort, while *Euro* and *Fulmine* guarded to starboard and *Oriani* and *Libeccio* to port. *Grecale* brought up the rear. The cruiser force zigzagged at 12 knots some three to five miles off *Grecale*'s starboard quarter. *Trieste* was 4,500 meters northwest of *Rina Corrado*.

Aurora approached, followed by *Lance*, *Penelope*, and *Lively*. The ships were 800 yards apart as they maneuvered to the convoy's starboard beam to silhouette it against the moonlight. At 0050 *Aurora* turned starboard directly toward the convoy and reduced speed to 20 knots. Two minutes later *Aurora*'s lookouts spotted Brivonesi's cruisers looming in the darkness to port. Agnew assessed them as merchant vessels following destroyers, but with his approach already underway he decided to focus on the designated target. Agnew's battle doctrine, which his captains had discussed and practiced, contained four rules:

1. Maintain line ahead formation to "avoid recognition problems and give freedom of torpedo fire."
2. Engage and disable escorts on the near side of the convoy first.
3. While engaging merchant ships always shift fire to any fresh escort sighted.
4. Try to keep escorts fine on the bow until they have been disabled.

These rules were largely defensive. The objective of the last three was "to reduce the danger from enemy torpedo fire as much and as soon as possible." Agnew also stressed the importance of early hits and distributed fire, and instructed his ships to avoid using searchlights or star shell.[16]

The Regia Marina had been rethinking its night surface combat doctrine since the March 1941 disaster at Matapan, but the focus was on a fleet action. As Iachino expressed it: "After the sad experience of Matapan, our ships were prepared to fire at night with their main-caliber guns, which for that reason had been provided with flashless powder . . . [the] cruisers thus held ready during night deployments their 203-mm weapons (in addition to the 100-mm guns), and that night all the guns were quickly used against the enemy." There was, however, no specific doctrine for how flotilla craft acting as convoy escorts were to conduct themselves in the event of a surface action and no doctrine on how a heavy cruiser division was to coordinate with a convoy escort, other than to maintain separation.[17]

Steering east-northeast, *Aurora* laid her guns with her 284 radar. As this was happening, *Bersagliere*, on the 3rd Division's starboard bow, spotted shadows 7,000 meters ahead. She was transmitting an alarm when, at 0057, gunfire erupted. Initially the British line bore straight toward *Grecale*, and *Aurora* blasted the Italian destroyer with her 6-inch guns from 5,700 yards while the 4-inch mounts engaged *Bersagliere*. The 4-inch rounds first fell several hundred yards over and then bracketed, but the first 6-inch salvo struck home. *Grecale*'s captain immediately ordered 25 knots and turned to interpose his vessel between the enemy and the convoy. He had intended to launch torpedoes, but, as he reported, "several shots hit immediately causing serious damage and knocking many personnel from combat." The destroyer lost rudder control and fires erupted. Two minutes into the fight a shell struck Boiler No. 2. *Grecale* was out of action.[18]

Penelope targeted *Maestrale* with her main battery seconds after *Aurora* engaged. The range was 9,600 yards, bearing east-southeast. *Maestrale* reacted by swerving away to port. Captain Ugo Bisciani wrote: "from *Maestrale* we saw two flashes bearing about 280 degrees. No one could see the trajectories; splashes and ships were not visible. We could not even be sure these were enemy shots and not those of the 3rd Division. Nor could an air strike be ruled out. We returned to course 161 degrees and maintained speed trying to comprehend the very obscure situation." *Penelope* shelled *Maestrale* for five minutes, but the cruiser only expended fifty-eight rounds due to a power failure in A turret and then because, after three minutes, Y turret no longer bore.[19]

Lance engaged *San Marco* off her starboard bow, while *Lively*, at the column's rear, snapped off seven quick salvos at 0100, targeting *Duisburg* at the head of the convoy before switching to *Fulmine* two minutes later. *Fulmine* was off the starboard bow of the fast-approaching British column. At 0059 she came to starboard intending to launch torpedoes. *Aurora* responded by turning 50 degrees to starboard and steering toward her. This put the British line on the convoy's starboard side heading east-southeast. The merchant ships reacted to the sudden onslaught by filling the air with antiaircraft fire. Their failure to maneuver flabbergasted the British, but, not knowing the nature or direction of the assault, Bisciani did not order the ships to disperse.

Brivonesi's cruisers had just turned southeast when the firing began. At 0101/9th he ordered a broad swing to starboard, away from the convoy, and accelerated from 12 knots to 18 knots over a ten-minute span. The rear admiral wrote that he maneuvered thus to open gun arcs and clarify the situation. At 0102 *Bersagliere* communicated that the enemy was bearing 155 degrees. By this time the British were pulling away and presenting the 3rd Division with a difficult end-on target.

At 0104 a near-miss from one of *Penelope*'s salvos damaged *Maestrale*'s main antenna and eliminated Bisciani's ability to radio messages. Assuming the 3rd Division had his starboard quarter covered, Bisciani made smoke and circled to the convoy's unengaged side. He did not return fire. *Libeccio* and *Oriani* joined *Maestrale* and thereafter conformed to her movements. With *Maestrale* disappearing *Penelope* engaged *Fulmine* with her A and B turrets over open sights from 2,000 yards (rejecting a radar range of 7,000 yards). A 6-inch round from the cruiser's first salvo smashed into *Fulmine*'s bridge, mortally wounding her captain, and snuffing the destroyer's offensive intention. As *Penelope* came to course 165 degrees she continued to clobber the enemy and at 0106/30, after just six four-gun broadsides, reported, "destroyer seen to turn over on its side and sink." *Lance* launched a torpedo at 0104 and claimed it smacked *Minatitlan*.[20]

At 0103 *Trieste* engaged from 7,000 yards off *Lively*'s starboard quarter, having taken six minutes to select a target—an eternity in a night action. *Trento* followed two minutes later. "Accuracy of aim," an Italian report complained, "was difficult because the English ships, steaming southward in line ahead, were 'end-on' to the cruisers' gunfire; also, the targets quickly disappeared behind the smoke of the burning steamers and their destroyer's smoke screen."[21] Throughout the action Agnew believed the heavy cruisers were destroyers.

Meanwhile, *Euro*'s skipper, Lieutenant Commander Giuseppe Cigala Fulgosi, who in the torpedo boat *Sagittario* had successfully defended a convoy against a daylight assault by British cruisers in May 1941, increased speed and made smoke. At 0101 a shell exploded and sprayed *Euro*'s bridge with splinters, causing casualties and affecting communications but not otherwise harming the ship's fighting ability. By 0109 Cigala, considering that he had accomplished his first task, turned to counterattack. He observed that three or four steamers were burning and that they were shooting into the sky. Then he spotted two large and several smaller units to starboard. He knew this was where the 3rd Division was supposed to be, and, because he was not then under fire despite being clearly silhouetted by burning ships, "it created in me doubt and then the belief that this was the *Trieste* Division which had been staying to starboard of the convoy and was shooting at an enemy that was attacking the convoy's rear." Consequently, he turned away to join *Maestrale* and the other two destroyers to the east, foregoing an opportunity to launch torpedoes.[22]

At 0108 the 3rd Division was steaming due south. The situation remained murky to Brivonesi and *Trieste* lofted star shells to illuminate the scene. After the battle Iachino wrote that "due to an error that is still not well understood, *Trieste* also fired illumination rounds; given that the fall was very short and the good visibility of the moonlit night, instead of helping our units, it hindered their appreciation of the situation and caused considerable confusion."[23] *Aurora* reported shells dropping a hundred yards to starboard at 0110 and *Penelope* said of the 3rd Division's counterattack: "During the following quarter-of-an-hour [from 0115 to 0130], two destroyers engaged *Penelope* and *Lively* from the west at a range of from five to six miles and obtained several straddles. These destroyers fired star shells intermittently, which were all short."[24]

Maestrale noted a near miss at 0114, probably from *Aurora*, which reported engaging a destroyer through smoke at 0115. At the time *Maestrale* was making 20 knots. Captain Bisciani later reported, "I believed nothing could be done to save the convoy, and I thought . . . to gather the destroyers, two of which [*Libeccio* and *Oriani*] were in view in a course very nearly parallel to mine, for subsequent action."[25] Consequently *Libec-cio, Oriani, Maestrale,* and later *Euro* regrouped eastward as the convoy continued onward, still engaging phantom bombers. This enabled Agnew to circle the convoy's head unopposed. One of *Penelope*'s crew wrote, "The ships seemed to make no effort to escape, and it was all too easy; they burst into flames as soon as we hit them. A large tanker was like a wall of flame, and an ammunition ship gave a superb display of fireworks before she blew up with a tremendous explosion."[26] *Aurora* fired three torpedoes to port at 0115 at separate targets and claimed two hits. She also reported engaging *Minatitlan* at the head of the column at 0117, and setting her ablaze. *Penelope* engaged the same target at 0119.

Brivonesi's cruisers were still coming south, working up to 24 knots. At 0123 *Lance* reported many 4-gun salvos falling around her. Agnew ordered *Penelope* to engage this "destroyer" a minute later, and she fired seven 4-inch salvos at *Trieste*. Then the British column turned to port and began to head north. Smoke and then burning ships separated the adversaries. At 0125 the heavy cruisers ceased fire, at a final range of 17,000 yards. Brivonesi turned north four minutes later thinking to intercept the enemy as they withdrew. *Trieste* and *Trento* shot 207 8-inch and eighty-two 3.9-inch rounds in twenty-three minutes and claimed one hit before the enemy vanished.

Steaming up the convoy's port side, *Aurora* engaged the *Maestrale* group as they came into view, but she concentrated on cargo ships. At 0131 *Aurora* observed hits on a vessel "which exploded with tremendous violence and filled the air with burning and exploding debris." This was probably *Rina Corrado* which had the heaviest load of munitions. *Penelope,* targeting the same ship, reported that it "disintegrated" under her fire.[27]

At 0138, concerned about the shortage of 6-inch shells at Malta, Agnew signaled his ships not to waste ammunition, and *Aurora* ceased fire at 0140 as the British passed behind the convoy. *Penelope* shot her final rounds at 0145. Every ship in sight was burning. By 0205 Force K was steering west at 25 knots. The *Maestrale* group finally "counterattacked" as a unit at 0207, making smoke and firing salvos. The British never noticed. Throughout the action *Penelope* shot 259 6-inch rounds and *Aurora* fired 279. *Lively* expended 434 4-inch rounds.[28]

At 0224 *Aurora* exchanged recognition signals with *Upholder*, which had been looking for a convoy expected to be sailing for Benghazi. The submarine had received a message outlining Force K's mission. In fact, the British force had sailed over her and when she surfaced she heard gunfire and was hastening toward that location.[29] At 0230 Force K passed twenty miles astern of Brivonesi's cruisers, which were still—inexplicably—sailing north.

Force K had destroyed the convoy, roughed up the escort, and escaped harm except for splinter damage to *Lively* (near-misses holed her funnel and a steam pipe on the starboard siren). A few splinters came aboard *Penelope*. The British reported that they dodged twelve enemy torpedoes and described some of these incidents in considerable detail. In fact, the Italians did not fire a single torpedo during the action. To add to the Italian misery, the next morning *Upholder* torpedoed *Libeccio* as she was rescuing survivors (the 10th Squadron pulled 693 men from the water). Four S.79s targeted Force K between 0835 and 0920, but the British ships avoided their torpedoes and were back in Malta by 1305 claiming the destruction of ten cargo vessels and four destroyers. Vice Admiral Malta, Commander in Chief Mediterranean, and the Admiralty were all delighted.

According to Ciano, Mussolini was depressed and indignant. Rear Admiral Weichold wrote, "this operation gave rise to widespread criticism of the morale in Italian warships, and of the political reliability of the Italian Armed Forces." Another German admiral more accurately concluded that the failure was due to "absolutely inadequate night training for large and small ships." Iachino excused his admirals, noting that the individual units did their best. He also blamed a lack of training ("you cannot be surprised that the results obtained by inadequately trained destroyers is below expectations"). He only allowed that Admiral Brivonesi was guilty of "tactical appreciation errors."[30]

In retrospect, the heavy cruisers proved to be a handicap because they confused rather than protected. The "rules" for night action in a fleet engagement called for flotilla craft to withhold gunfire and to attack with torpedoes. This was the first reaction of the close escort's destroyers, and it is telling that of the three ships that attempted a torpedo action two were disabled by surface gunfire in the first minutes of their approach

Minatitlan. This Italian tanker (7,599 GRT) was involved in the Beta Convoy battle on 9 November. This image was taken the following morning from an Italian aircraft. She eventually sank. STORIA MILITARE

and the third broke off when it reached position due to confusion about the target's identity. Italian forces lacked situational awareness, and *Maestrale*'s failure to pinpoint the source of the attack is puzzling. The British were using flashless powder which muted but did not completely hide their muzzle blasts. The Type 284 radar that the British cruisers possessed improved their ability to understand the situation, but it gave false ranges. It was not a panacea, nor did it keep Agnew from mistaking heavy cruisers as merchant ships. Instead, as the Japanese were to demonstrate repeatedly in the Pacific, doctrine and training were key to effectiveness in night combat.

The 3rd Division's movements also deserve mention. First, relatively slow-firing heavy cruisers were not the right ships for the job; second, Brivonesi never closed after combat began. His priorities were to avoid friendly fire, to stay clear of the convoy, and to obtain a picture of the events—all of that understandable, but not what the situation required.

Some critics maintained that a more rapid approach would have served better. The way Brivonesi steamed north and let Force K escape behind him was his most inexcusable action of all. For this he was deservedly court-martialed. The court found him guilty of mistakes but did not cite any "elements of criminal fault." He subsequently commanded the naval base at La Maddalena.[31]

Brivonesi's failures stand in great contrast to Captain Agnew's skill and leadership. He applied a well-communicated doctrine. He exploited his advantages of surprise, technology, and position. The units under his command performed well. (It was *Penelope's* first combat action and she had not even test-fired her guns since August. *Lance* and *Lively* were likewise relatively new units, having been commissioned in May and July of that year). Agnew earned a brilliant victory. It is hard, in fact, to think of a better-fought night surface action in the Second World War.

Further Actions: 1–15 November

Two other African convoys departed Italy in the month's first fortnight. The steamers *Sant'Antonio* (271 GRT) and *Tre Marie* (1,086 GRT), escorted by the torpedo boat *Prestinari*, sailed from Trapani on 11 November loaded with civilian cargo. They hugged the Tunisian coast as they made their slow way south. *Sant'Antonio* arrived in Tripoli on 0900/17th. *Le Tre Marie* discharged her cargo in Zuara.

Città di Genova and *Città di Napoli* (both 5,413 GRT/19 kts)—fast motorships armed with a pair of 120-mm guns and a heavy antiaircraft battery—left Taranto at 1830/14th escorted by destroyers *Pigafetta* and *Da Verrazzano*. They docked in Benghazi at 1600/16th delivering 1,219 men and 294 tons of supplies. An Ultra message timed 0100Z/14th accurately disclosed the time of their departure, but not the place. A message generated at 2350Z/14th advised Malta that they had sailed, and another timed 1530Z/16th reported that they were off Benghazi waiting for the fog to clear. Nevertheless, the British did not assail this convoy. Two ships sailed from Tripoli to Benghazi and five from Benghazi to Tripoli. All arrived safely.[32]

On 13 November, as these relatively minor movements were underway or about to start, Cavallero met with Rommel and the German military attaché, General Enno Rintelen, to discuss the offensive against Tobruk.

Cavallero was concerned that not enough supplies had arrived, but Rommel countered that his armored divisions had eight units of fire and enough fuel for extended actions; with the supplies en route, he could attack by the end of the month. The biggest concern was aviation fuel. Cavallero objected that Tripoli would not be available to receive convoys until Malta had been neutralized and that the fuel, ammunition, and food required would have to come in through Benghazi. He worried about not having enough materiel accumulated to withstand the British counterattack anticipated once Tobruk fell. Despite Cavallero's discouraging comments, however, Rommel was hardly out the door before the Italian chief of staff was meeting with Riccardi about sending another convoy to Tripoli escorted by two cruiser divisions.[33]

British Traffic

Along with their focus on stopping traffic to Africa and preparing an offensive out of Egypt, the British had to consider Malta's supply situation. It had been nearly two months since the *Halberd* convoy and the island's offensive activities were burning through the stock of torpedoes, 4- and 6-inch shells, and fuel oil. Thus, the British launched two operations to reinforce the island in the weeks before Crusader started. Operation Astrologer involved sneaking two unescorted ships to Malta from Gibraltar, *Empire Pelican* (6,463 GRT/11.5 kts) and *Empire Defender* (5,654 GRT/11 kts). However, the success of an earlier blockade runner caused the Italians to implement routine air patrols and to station surveillance vessels along the route. A Cant Z.506 reported *Empire Pelican* and on 14 November an S.79 torpedoed and sank her southwest of Galita Island. A pair of S.84s dispatched *Empire Defender* the next day.[34]

Operation Perpetual involved a sortie from Gibraltar by Force H to reinforce the island's air forces. Thirty-seven Hurricanes and a Swordfish flew off the carriers *Ark Royal* and *Argus*. Three Hurricanes failed to arrive. Seven Blenheims also flew in from Gibraltar. As Force H was returning to Gibraltar, the German submarine *U81* torpedoed *Ark Royal* at 1541/13th, just thirty miles short of Europa Point, hitting with one torpedo from a spread of four. The *Ark Royal*'s captain, Loben E. H. Maund, evacuated 1,560 personnel, after which the damage control and steaming

Cant Z.506. This three-engine floatplane, designed as a twelve-passenger transport, entered service in 1936. It had a top speed of 190 knots and a range of 1,100 miles. It was used for reconnaissance and secondarily as a bomber. It remained in service until 1959. A *Navigatori*-class destroyer is visible in the background of this December 1941 photo. USMM

party got to work, but valuable time had been lost, and the contributions of other crewmen, such as shipwrights and electrical staff, were sorely missed. During the night, the flooding overwhelmed the pumps. "At 0600 the flight-deck was vertical and the island lying flat upon the sea. In the dim light before dawn all that the screening destroyers could see was a dark smudge lying in the water." The carrier foundered at 0603/14th. The Admiralty, while noting extenuating circumstances, court-martialed Maund for negligence, promoted him to rear admiral, and sent him to head Combined Operations, Middle East.[35]

In Operation Glencoe at the other end of the Mediterranean, the fast minelayer *Abdiel* and 10 destroyers, under Rear Admiral I. G. Glennie, shuttled 15,000 troops of the British 50th Division from Cyprus to Palestine and replaced them with the 5th Indian Division at a rate of 250 men a ship for each trip. This happened between the 2–8 November full-moon period, so the British suspended traffic to Tobruk. The operation also made fleet actions impossible because there were not enough destroyers to screen the cruisers and battleships.[36]

Traffic into Tobruk resumed on 13 November with Operation Approach. During the moonless nights in September and October, the British had removed the 6th Australian Division from the besieged port, and thus, "supply reserves at Tobruk were below the required limit."[37] On 13 November, *Kipling, Jackal,* and *Encounter* carried materiel into the besieged port. The next night *Abdiel, Hero, Hotspur,* and *Nizam* transported more supplies and a dozen 25-pounder guns. On 16 November *Kipling, Jackal,* and *Decoy* made the run. After this the destroyers focused on fleet operations associated with Operation Crusader.

A snapshot of routine Allied traffic in the Eastern Mediterranean on 13 November showed convoys sailing between

- Port Said–Alexandria, escorted by the corvette *Erica* and the Greek (ex-German) torpedo boat *Niki*;
- Alexandria–Port Said, escorted by the corvette *Snapdragon*;
- Haifa–Port Said, escorted by the corvette *Peony*;
- Haifa–Famagusta, escorted by the corvette *Hyacinth*;
- Port Said–Haifa, escorted by the corvette *Delphinium*;
- Tripoli, Lebanon–Beirut, escorted by the minesweeper *Fareham*.[38]

The British were clearing the decks for the long-anticipated offensive on which Churchill, the War Cabinet, and the Chiefs of Staff were pinning such great hopes.

Chapter 4

The Crusader Offensive, November–December 1941

What's your hand for—if you don't use it?

HERODOTUS—MASSACRE OF THE MAGI *(237)*

On the night of 17–18 November 1942 the British 8th Army launched its long-anticipated Crusader Offensive, pitting the equivalent of six infantry and two armored divisions against three armored divisions (two of them German), two motorized divisions (one of them German), and six infantry divisions—units that were generally two-thirds the size of their Allied counterparts. The 8th Army's XIIIth Corps pinned down the Savona Division and elements of the German z.b.V Division, which guarded Bardia and the frontier at Sollum, while the mechanized XXXth Corps circled the enemy's southern flank. Because most Axis troops were massed around Tobruk, the XXXth advanced without resistance. The weather helped. That afternoon and evening, according to the Italian command's war diary, violent rainstorms had swept the area, "interrupting telephone lines, flooding Benghazi airfields No. 1 and No. 2 . . . submersing some antiaircraft batteries and inundating the region."[1]

The offensive intensified naval activity. On the 16th the British Force H had sortied from Gibraltar to simulate a Malta convoy. Force K sailed at 1900/18th as another red herring. From Alexandria the 7th Cruiser

Squadron (*Hobart, Neptune,* and *Ajax*) with *Kandahar, Hasty,* and *Hotspur* sallied to bombard Sollum on the night of 17–18 November. Finally, in Operation ME4, *Barham,* flying the flag of Vice Admiral Henry Pridham-Whipple, *Queen Elizabeth* and *Valiant,* with the 15th Cruiser Squadron (*Naiad, Galatea,* and *Euryalus*), the 7th Flotilla (*Napier, Nizam, Kipling,* and *Jackal*), the 14th Flotilla (*Jervis, Kingston, Kimberley,* and *Decoy*), and the *Hunt*-type escort destroyers *Avon Vale* and *Eridge,* weighed anchor to support the coastal bombardments. Weather forced the 7th Squadron to abort its mission, but *Naiad* and *Euryalus,* screened by *Kipling* and *Jackal,* blindly lofted 340 rounds into the Halfaya Pass area over the course of twelve minutes, beginning at 2300/18th. The fleet returned to Alexandria by 1100/19th. Axis aircraft shadowed but did not attack.[2]

Italian Convoys

Despite having told Rommel on 13 November that Tripoli was closed, Cavallero recognized that Benghazi had insufficient capacity to support the planned offensive, and spent the next day discussing the situation with Riccardi. The issues included whether to use the safer, but longer eastern route, whether to have several small convoys or one large one, what formation to use in case of night surface attack, and what ships the escort should comprise. After deciding that the newest cruisers, which carried 6-inch guns, were best suited for naval night combat and would give a safe superiority "without using a battleship, which would imply a huge expense of oil," Riccardi agreed to a convoy. "To sum up," Cavallero concluded, remembering the conversation in his diary, "I am pleased to tell our German friends that the navy is preparing to make a generous effort . . . preparing to put men and materials to a task that is very difficult."[3]

Before attempting a new Tripoli effort, however, several previously scheduled convoys sailed. *Bolsena* and *Tinos,* escorted by the torpedo boat *Orione,* left Brindisi bound for Benghazi at 1700/16th loaded with 4,603 tons of materiel and nineteen vehicles. Ultra disclosed their departure, route, and "approximate" schedule in messages timed 1910Z and 2250Z/15th. A strike force of six Blenheims found the convoy ninety miles west-northwest of Navarino at 1445/17th and blitzed it from mast height. There was no preliminary sighting to protect Ultra security. The aircraft reported they left one freighter in flames "with columns of smoke seen thirty miles away." In fact, they damaged both transports lightly, forcing them to divert to Navarino, where they arrived at 0740/18th. Malta dispatched the Polish submarine *Sokol* to blockade the port. On 19 November the *Sokol* fired four torpedoes into the bay and incorrectly claimed that one had struck the destroyer *Aviere*.[4]

On the evening of 21 November *Bolsena* and *Tinos* departed for Benghazi, with destroyer *Strale* reinforcing the escort. Several Ultra messages noted this—including one with the correct itinerary and route generated at 1345Z/21st—but the convoy arrived in Africa unmolested at 0815/23rd.[5]

The *Città di Tunisi* (5,419 GRT/19 kts) and *Città di Palermo* (5,413 GRT/19 kts), escorted by destroyers *Zeno* and *Malocello*, sailed from Taranto for Benghazi at 1400/19th loaded with 195 tons of materiel and 1,453 men. This convoy was the subject of an Ultra message sent at 0225Z/19th that correctly identified departure time and destination but not the departure port.[6] Nonetheless, six Blenheims, again without cover of a preliminary sighting, assailed the well-armed ships at 1425/20th. The Italians zigzagged at high speed and shot down half the strike force. Such losses were unacceptable and, in fact, three months before that Air Marshall Arthur Tedder had warned that daylight mast-height attacks by Blenheims "were likely to involve heavy casualties." That evening *Città di Tunisi* suffered an engine breakdown. She and *Malocello* detoured to Suda while *Città di Palermo* continued to Benghazi, arriving at 1230/21st.[7]

Città di Tunisi. One of the "City" class of passenger liners pressed into service as auxiliary cruisers. They were used to transport men to Libya. Their heavy antiaircraft armament made them difficult targets for aircraft. E. Bagnasco, *Guerra sul Mare*

To make space in Benghazi's constricted harbor for the four transports bound there, *Spezia* (1,825 GRT/11 kts), *Cadamosto* (1,010 GRT), and the motor-sailer *Cora* (349 GRT), escorted by the torpedo boat *Centauro*, departed for Tripoli at 1800/18th. Ultra sent notice of this departure at 2240Z/18th. Five Blenheims struck this group at 1445/19th. The aircraft reported: "Largest M/V seen hit and listing heavily. Schooner also hit and last seen low in the water." In fact, however, the Italian ships arrived unharmed in Tripoli at 0800/21st.[8]

The Tripoli convoy departed Naples on 19 November, with four major components:

- Convoy Alfa: *Ankara* (4,768 GRT/14 kts), *Sebastiano Venier* (6,311 GRT/16.5 kts). Escort (Captain Stanislao Caraciotti): destroyers *Maestrale, Oriani, Gioberti*. Sailed 2000/19th. It would take the longer eastern route.
- Convoy C Section 1: *Napoli* (6,141 GRT/16 kts). *Vettor Pisani* (6,339 GRT/16 kts). Escort destroyer *Turbine*, torpedo boat *Perseo*. Sailed 2000/20th. It would take the western route.
- Convoy C Section 2: *Mantovani* (10,540 GRT/13 kts). *Monginevro* (5,324 GRT/15.5 kts). Escort destroyer *Da Recco*, torpedo boat *Cosenz*. Sailed 0530/21st to join section 1.
- Support Group (Rear Admiral Giuseppe Lombardi): 3rd Division: cruisers *Gorizia, Trieste, Trento*; 8th Division: cruisers *Duca degli Abruzzi, Garibaldi*; 12th Squadron: *Aviere, Camicia Nera, Geniere, Corazziere, Carabiniere*. Sailed 0810/21st.

A British reconnaissance aircraft sighted Convoy Alfa on 20 November soon after the convoy entered the Ionian Sea. Shortly after that, *Maestrale* intercepted radio transmissions from Allied surface warships reporting the discovery. Although the closest British forces were supporting the bombardments of Bardia 500 miles to the southeast, Captain Stanislao Caraciotti, Bisciani's replacement, diverted the convoy to Argostoli, entering there at 0930/21st. Early the next morning the ships returned to Taranto, arriving at 1930/22nd. Although the British sighted Convoy Alfa early, the best Ultra indication dispatched on 2145Z/18th specified only that ships would be at sea on the 20th. A message timed 1220Z/19th advising that Convoy Alfa's departure had been delayed 24 hours confused the intelligence picture.[9]

A series of Ultra messages revealed that Convoy C was preparing to sail and that it would be strongly escorted. Bletchley Park generated the most important message—estimating the convoy's departure time and route—at 1200Z/18th.[10] At 1410/21st, a Maryland aircraft reported the *Napoli* group while it was still in the Tyrrhenian Sea. The convoy's two sections united and entered the Strait of Messina that evening observed by an ASV-equipped Wellington. *Utmost* was lurking south of the strait, and at 2312/21st she aimed two torpedoes at *Trieste*. One struck just abaft the bridge, causing Boiler No. 3 to explode. The ship's captain reported, "The blast of the boiler augmented the effects of the torpedo's explosion but a great mass of steam which was released quickly suffocated the burning fuel oil ending a situation that was extremely dangerous to the ship's safety." The Wellington reported a "terrific explosion." Despite the extensive damage *Trieste* restored power and returned to Messina, escorted by *Corazziere* and *Carabiniere*.[11]

This blow was just the beginning. Shortly after midnight four Albacores and three Swordfish arrived and illuminated the enemy with flares. The convoy, having been forewarned of the incoming torpedo bombers, immediately turned to present sterns toward the lights.[12] *Abruzzi* had almost completed her maneuver when, at 0038/22nd a torpedo struck and blew off her stern. The Albacores concentrated on the merchant ships, but their torpedoes missed. Finally, sixteen Wellingtons made repeated passes at low to medium height, dropping eighty-four 500-pound SAP bombs, targeting by the orange light of their flares. At 0100/22nd Supermarina, concluding that the element of surprise had been lost and the risks of continuing were too great, ordered Convoy C to Taranto. Despite all the claims made by the airmen, *Abruzzi* was the only ship damaged. She steamed in circles at 4 knots until restoring steering control at 0330 and arrived at Messina 1140/22nd.[13]

This was not the result for which Comando Supremo had hoped. The only solace was that the light cruiser *Cadorna*, 3 destroyers, and 2 submarines made several supply runs through the end of the month without loss. Collectively they carried to Africa 608 tons of fuel, 35 tons of munitions, 25 tons of rations, and 996 men.[14]

Fleet Air Arm Fairy Albacore. This aircraft was introduced in 1939 as a replacement for the Fleet Air Arm's open-cockpit Swordfish torpedo bomber. It had a top speed of 140 knots and a range of 820 nm. Albacores of 828 Squadron flying out of Malta conducted many attacks against Axis shipping and also acted as reconnaissance aircraft and as radar-equipped scouts. The type was retired in 1944, although the older Swordfish remained in service. STORIA MILITARE

British Movements

British units were at sea as these events transpired. A convoy consisting of the tankers *Toneline* (811 GRT) and *Gebel Rebir* (1,009 GRT), escorted by the Australian sloops *Yarra* and *Parramatta*, and the antisubmarine trawlers *Sotra*, *Klo*, and *Falk*, left Alexandria for Tobruk on the 18th. Shortly after dark *Toneline* experienced engine problems. *Parramatta* stood by while *Gebel Rebir* continued. *Yarra* shuttled back and forth between the two groups throughout the moonless, rainy night. The next day *Yarra* reported raids by solitary German aircraft at 1303 and 1420/19th and noted that two small bombs exploded 20 yards off her port beam. *Gebel Rebir* made Tobruk on the 20th. Axis shore batteries damaged *Klo* and *ML1048* as they approached the harbor. Meanwhile, *Yarra* returned and found *Toneline* at 0730/20th, anchored ten miles west of Mersa Matruh. She towed the stricken vessel into port, where *Yarra*'s engineer discovered that the tanker's ills were due to "inexperience on the part of the

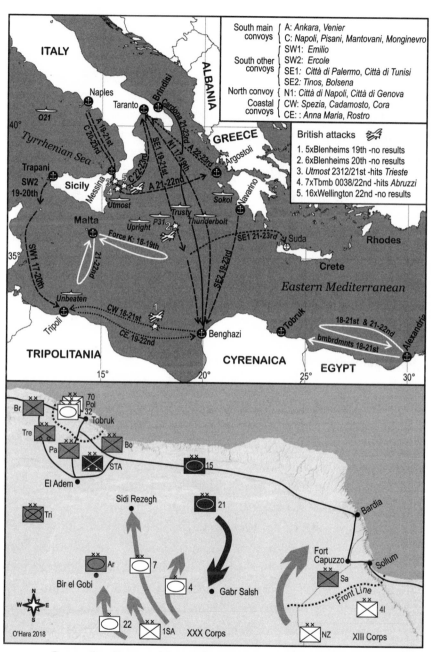

Map 4.1. **Crusader Sea and Land Operations, 18–23 November 1941**

Engine Room Staff."[15] After cleaning various filters and valves, *Toneline* proceeded to Tobruk, arriving there at dawn/23rd.

On the 20th the 7th Cruiser Squadron (*Ajax, Hobart,* and *Neptune)* with *Heythrop* and *Avon Vale* in company departed Alexandria on another foray to bombard Bardia. *Eridge* and *Farndale,* which had been hunting submarines, joined them at sea. At 0800/21st *Barham, Queen Elizabeth,* and *Valiant,* with the 15th Cruiser Squadron (*Naiad, Euryalus,* and *Galatea)* and eleven destroyers of the 7th and 14th flotillas sortied to support this minor operation, even though there was no indication that the Italian fleet, two days' steaming time away, had left base. The cruisers conducted their shoot on the 21st with aircraft spotting overhead, claiming damage to "M.T. and tanks." The Italian high command's war diary did not even record that a bombardment occurred. The 7th Squadron then rejoined the fleet at 1200/21st, and all entered Alexandria at dawn the next day. Finally, at 1300/21st in Operation Landmark, Force K and four freighters departed Malta to "threaten an attack on Tripoli in order to divert the enemy air strength." They returned after dark on the 22nd.[16]

The Ground-Fighting, 18–22 November

The XXXth Corps easily reached its first day objectives. Rommel, newly returned from Rome and focused on his impending offensive against Tobruk, regarded the British advance as a reconnaissance force and failed to react as expected. In the words of the official British history, this left XXXth Corps, "in the odd position of possessing the initiative, and . . . of being uncertain how to use it."[17] On the 19th the 7th Armor Brigade occupied the Italian airfield at Sidi Rezegh, ten miles short of the defensive line encircling Tobruk. But the Ariete Division repulsed a push by the 22nd Armor Brigade, while a battlegroup from the 21st Panzer Division probed south behind the British tank formations. On the 20th German armor struck the 4th Armored Brigade at Gabr Salsh, thirty miles east-southeast of Sidi Rezegh. On the 21st the Tobruk garrison attacked toward Sidi Rezegh but its breakout attempt stalled after a two-mile advance. The German armored divisions approached Sidi Rezegh from the southeast, with the 4th and 22nd armored brigades following. A confused melee among intermixed forces followed. Meanwhile, XIII Corps began to advance. On the 22nd the Germans recaptured Sidi Rezegh, mauling the 7th Armored Division in the process. The New Zealand Division captured Fort Capuzzo and cut the Tobruk–Bardia road.

After four days the decision remained in doubt. Inflated counts of enemy tanks destroyed encouraged Auchinleck and prompted jubilation in London. On 24 November Churchill advised the chiefs of staff that he wanted to telegraph U.S. President Franklin D. Roosevelt: "In view of our victory in Crusader we propose to press on to Tripoli and the frontiers of Tunisia. We also hold ready in Great Britain the forces assigned to Gymnast. The chance to get French North Africa in our hands is 'Now or never.'" The chiefs felt that such a message was premature and Churchill held off.[18]

The Traffic War Continues

With Tobruk now the focus of so much action the British needed to increase the harbor's cargo capacity. Accordingly, on the night of 22/23 November the fleet store ship *Glenroy* (9,809 GRT/18 kts) departed Alexandria for Tobruk loaded with sixteen lighters and two motor launches. The escort included the light cruiser *Carlisle* and the *Hunt*-class destroyers *Avon, Vale* and *Eridge*, as well as fighters patrolling overhead. Nonetheless, at 1620/23rd an S.79 from Rhodes torpedoed *Glenroy* in Hold No. 5, flooding the ship's engine room. *Carlisle* began towing her east, but on the 24th the large supply ship started to founder, forcing *Carlisle* to lodge her on a sandbar west of Mersa Matruh. After emergency repairs, *Glenroy* was refloated and towed to Alexandria. The S.79 achieved this success against a valuable target protected by fighters and three antiaircraft escorts. Torpedo bombers needed to make a low, straight, and relatively slow approach. The optimal dropping point was roughly 1,000 yards from target. These requirements rendered them vulnerable to defensive fire. A British technical assessment noted that "the control systems in themselves were inadequate to enable controlled fire to be brought to bear on low-flying torpedo aircraft and barrage was the normal method of fire used against this form of attack." It was effective. In 1941, of 260 S.79s that attempted torpedo attacks, 14 aircraft were lost and 46 were damaged.[19]

In Italy's mid-month surge to supply Libya, all of the warships used to transport men and materiel successfully reached Africa, but just three of the convoyed merchant ships that attempted the crossing actually arrived. With Rommel loudly complaining about oil supplies, the next surge began on the afternoon of the 22nd, when it appeared that the British fleet was no longer at sea. Sailings included:

- Tanker *Berbera* (2,093 GRT). Escort torpedo boat *Pegaso*. Sailed Brindisi 1730/22nd destination Benghazi.
- *Fabio Filzi* (6,836 GRT/16 kts) cargo 4,000 drums of aviation fuel. Escort: destroyers *Usodimare*, *Saetta*, *Sebenico*, torpedo boat *Centauro*. Sailed Trapani 1900/22nd, arrived Tripoli 1400/23rd.
- *Procida* (1,842 GRT/11 kts), *Maritza* (2,910 GRT/12 kts). Escort: torpedo boats *Lupo*, *Cassiopea*. Sailed Piraeus 1430/23rd destination Benghazi.
- Armed motorship *Adriatico* (1,721 GRT/14 kts, 2x102-mm) sailed Reggio Calabria 1700/23rd destination Benghazi.

Given that four of these vessels were bound for Benghazi, Supermarina generated an urgent signal dated 1232/22nd ordering the harbor cleared of all unessential vessels because "merchant and warships will be sent to your harbour within the next few days." Bletchley Park read this signal and notified Cairo five and a half hours later. In fact, Bletchley Park had been tracking *Procida* and *Maritza* since 3 November from decryptions of Luftwaffe Enigma: "Fliegerkorps Ten are anxious to have sailing of . . . *Procida* and *Maritza* accelerated. They are insistent on the necessity of having three thousand tons of fuel available in [Cyrenaica] before 20 November."[20]

At 2330/23rd November Force K departed Valetta with verbal orders from Vice Admiral Ford to intercept a particularly important two-ship convoy, the *Maritza* convoy, in the belief that it was "the decisive factor" in easing the German shortage of aviation fuel (in fact, *Fabio Filzi* was bringing most of the fuel). Churchill was following events, and wired Cunningham directly to be sure he "had seen the decrypt describing her arrival as decisive." At 0400/24th Force B—*Ajax* and *Neptune* and destroyers *Kimberley* and *Kingston*—commanded by Rear Admiral H. B. Rawlings, departed Alexandria seeking the same target. Cunningham clearly had taken Churchill's hint.[21]

The Italian submarine *Settembrini* detected Force K on her hydro-phones before dawn, and at 0503/24th broadcast that British raiders were at sea. Supermarina promptly ordered ships back to port. This included *Berbera*, which was diverted to Navarino, and *Adriatico*, sent to Argostoli. The *Maritza* convoy, however, was sailing in an area of German respon-sibility. The escort commander, Lieutenant Commander Francesco Mim-belli in *Lupo*, later wrote that "at 1005 we intercepted a top priority radio signal from the control center in Rome to *Freccia*. I tried to decipher it on the presumption that it contained information I would like to know but in vain because it was encrypted with a code not in [my] possession." Thus, Mimbelli sailed blithely unaware that two surface forces and an airstrike were bearing in on him. Had the Axis powers been sharing information effectively, the Germans would have repeated the Italian alarm.[22]

A British aircraft spotted the convoy at 1800/23rd (fifteen minutes after Bletchley Park generated the message about the decisive convoy), when it was barely underway. Another plane updated position, course, and speed at 1040/24th. At 1310 Agnew's ships reached the Piraeus–Benghazi route and began sweeping north-northeast in a line of bearing, each ship five miles apart. They occasionally sighted Axis aircraft; most ignored the British, although *Lively* reported an attack at 1450. At 1523 *Lively* sighted smoke. Force K turned north-northwest and closed at 26 knots. The wind was from the northeast at Force 3; the visibility was 15–20 miles, with clouds and occasional thundershowers.[23]

Lupo was 110 miles off Antikithera when, at 1535/24th, her lookout reported seeing masts. Mimbelli turned in that direction. Because his escort of two Ju.88s had not issued an alarm he hoped to encounter a friendly destroyer. When in fact the horizon revealed first a British destroyer and then a cruiser, he hastily returned to the convoy and ordered *Cassiopea* to make smoke. *Lupo* then dashed up to the steamers and signaled them to separate and head north. Mimbelli reported that "as the two steamships started the turn I saw the enemy open fire and their antiaircraft guns start shooting: our escort aircraft had sighted the enemy formation and turned to attack it. I could not distinguish where the bombs fell: the English flak was of very short duration and for the rest of the battle they, unfortunately, were not harassed by planes." *Penelope* reported that at 1540 a Ju.88

dive-bombed and released four bombs, one of which fell twenty yards off her port quarter. *Aurora*, reporting the same strike, reported that a pair of Ju.88s assailed her at 1544 with bombs dropping a half mile on the port beam and a half mile astern.[24]

Penelope closed the Axis force while *Lively* and *Lance* followed off the light cruiser's quarters to screen her from air strikes and assist if needed. Captain Agnew in *Aurora*—still careful about using ammunition—stood by. At 1548 *Penelope* engaged *Cassiopea* from 20,600 yards and then fired at *Lupo* four minutes later using her forward turrets. Mimbelli wrote that, "upon spotting the enemy force I quickly realized the steamers were almost certainly doomed: there was two hours before sunset; there was no close support group; the coast was far away. I had one hope left: the intervention of German bombers." Therefore, as *Cassiopea* made smoke, *Lupo* approached the cruiser. *Penelope*, however, following Agnew's doctrine, turned bow-on to the torpedo boat. "Because the opponent's countermaneuver left no chance of being able to arrive in a favorable position to launch torpedoes, I desisted from the attack and fell back to the north hiding myself behind smoke. Almost simultaneously, at 1603, estimating the range to be 14,000 meters, I ordered open fire."[25]

Over the next thirty minutes *Penelope* closed alternating salvos between the two torpedo boats. Because of the smoke and haze and their high speed and frequent course alterations, she described them as "very difficult targets." She claimed a hit on the *Cassiopea* at 1607 and in fact splinters lightly damaged the torpedo boat at around that time. At 1613 she shifted to *Lupo* once again, "as this ship was developing accurate fire against *Penelope*." Captain Angus D. Nicholl recorded that "a considerable number of shells fell close to the ship, and the side plating was punctured in several places by splinters."[26]

As the range closed, the Italian warships withdrew northwest. Mimbelli wrote: "when I saw that by now there was nothing more I could do to save the *Maritza* and *Procida* and that remaining in their proximity meant only the loss of the two torpedo boats, I decided to leave the two steamers with their valuable cargoes and their good crews. I never before had to make such a decision so painful."[27] By 1620 the range between *Penelope* and the steamers had dropped to 4,000 yards. As men hurriedly abandoned ship, *Penelope* hammered *Procida*, provoking a massive blaze. She shifted to *Maritza*, and four broadsides left that ship also in flames. At 1624 the *Penelope* targeted *Procida* again "in order to spread the fires." The steamers collided, and then *Maritza* blew up, while *Procida* continued to burn. *Penelope* expended 238 rounds in 57 broadsides. Satisfied with this result, Agnew radioed Malta at 1634: "Both Merchant ships of convoy . . . sunk. Both Destroyers escaped." With his destroyers down to 65 percent of fuel, Agnew ordered Force K back to Malta at 28 knots. Force B, when it received word of the action, turned north, not knowing that the other convoys had headed back. Meanwhile, the 1st Battle Squadron, with Cunningham himself on board *Queen Elizabeth*, and eight destroyers had departed Alexandria at 1600/24th "to form a supporting force in case cruisers got into difficulties and move as far as possible to Westwards during the night." This would be the last time that Cunningham would take to sea in command of a battle force seeking the enemy.[28]

In Mimbelli's opinion, the British fought to minimize risk. His tactics, making smoke and attacking from out of it were standard practice for such situations. *Lupo* expended 116 3.9-inch rounds and *Cassiopea* fired 188, but neither ship launched torpedoes. *Lupo* claimed two hits while *Penelope* reported that several near misses left "the ship's hull and upperworks . . . riddled with splinters hits." She spent a day in dock to repair the many holes and the resulting leaks.[29] Because Malta's stocks of 4-inch shells were low, *Lively* expended only a few rounds; the destroyers otherwise restricted themselves to anti-aircraft fire.

After refueling, Force K returned to sea on 25 November to intercept a convoy reported in the central Ionian Sea. Force B likewise was casting about for targets, but all shipping had vanished from harm's way. Force K returned to Malta at 1700/26th. The only strike by British forces came at 1515/26th, when two Blenheims out of six that took off found *Città di Tunisi* and her escort *Malocello* 18 miles northwest of Homs despite very bad weather. There was actionable Ultra information but no preliminary aerial sighting. The ships had left Benghazi for Tripoli at 1700/25th. The Blenheims landed a few 250-pound bombs, but the damage was minor, and *Città di Tunisi* made Tripoli at 2100/26th. The aircraft incorrectly claimed a hit on *Malocello*.[30]

Bristol Blenheim attacking an Italian destroyer in 1942. Such low-level attacks were effective but often deadly to the aircraft as well. Introduced in 1937 the Blenheim had a top speed of 230 knots and a range of 1,270 nm. Pictured is the Mk V. It sacrificed speed and range for extra armor and a dorsal turret. USMM

Loss of *Barham*

On 12 November *U331* landed a party of saboteurs assigned to cut the rail line between Sollum and Alexandria. Egyptian police quickly captured the raiders, but the submarine remained on patrol between Sollum and Mersa Matruh. At 1430/25th, sixty miles northwest of Sollum, she spotted smoke to the northeast. This proved to be the three battleships and ten destroyers of the British battle fleet, which was providing very distant support to Rawling's cruisers. The ships were zigzagging northwest, and one zag turned them straight toward the German submarine. Helped by the rapidly converging courses, *U331* passed between *Jervis* and *Griffin*. *Jervis* picked up "a loud, raucous and sharp echo," but the extent of the sound seemed so wide that the operator classified it as surface ship. At 1619 *U331* shot four torpedoes from 375 meters toward the middle battleship. Three slammed into *Barham* on the port side between the funnel and after turrets and ruptured the hull over a considerable length. With her vitals exposed to the sea, *Barham* rapidly listed to port. Then there was a tremendous explosion aft. One survivor recalled: "I had reached the railing when she was afloat on her side and was just climbing over when the ship blew up aft. I could see flame and black smoke and much flying material. I was struck on the legs by some of this. I tried to jump clear and must have cleared the splinter shield of No. 1 gun. I was sucked down for a considerable period but managed to get some breaths in two air bubbles. At this time I seemed to be striking through a large number of bodies and a lot of wreckage. When I eventually came to the surface it was completely dark [and I thought] I was trapped under the ship in a pocket of air, but gradually it lightened and I realized that it was a pall of smoke." This man survived, but 861 perished.[31]

After discharging her torpedoes *U331* broached less than two hundred yards off *Valiant's* bow. The battleship steered to ram as the submarine's crew struggled to submerge again—a race that the Germans won. *U331* plunged from view, and there was only time to roil the swirl of water that marked her escape with a few 40-mm rounds. The submarine descended to 250 meters, far below her rated depth, and eventually escaped. *Hotspur* rescued 337 survivors, including Vice Admiral Henry Pridham-Whipple, commanding the 1st Battle Squadron. The other destroyers recovered 120 men.

The Admiralty analysis attributed *Barham's* loss "to a failure on the part of the A/S Screening destroyers." However, it also noted that war duties left the destroyers little time for A/S practice. *Jervis*, for one, had exercised once in ten months. After blaming lieutenant commanders, the court excused the admirals who had set training schedules and who repeatedly had sent their battleships on pointless missions into waters where the only enemies to be found were submarines and torpedo bombers.[32]

The German commander radioed that he had torpedoed a battleship but had no proof of success because he was deep when *Barham* exploded. On 26 November Comando Supremo noted *U331's* claim, but reconnaissance continued to report three battleships at Alexandria as late as 30 December. The British kept the *Barham's* fate a dark secret until finally acknowledging her loss on 27 January 1942.[33]

On the day the *Barham* sank the British sent the merchant ship *Hanne* (1,080 GRT/8.5 kts), escorted by *Paramatta* and *Avon Vale* and the South African trawlers *Southern Isles* and *Southern Maid*, to Tobruk; the heavy expenditure of ammunition and the failure to open an overland supply route had forced this action. At 0016/27th, thirty-five miles short of Tobruk, *U559* loosed torpedoes at the convoy and missed. A half hour later, however, she targeted *Parramatta*. There was an explosion, and the subsequent detonation of *Parramatta*'s after magazine broke the ship's back; she rolled over and sank in just minutes. In the dark and rainy night *Avon Vale* rescued only twenty men. *Hanne*, accompanied by the two trawlers, safely made port.[34]

By the end of December there were twenty-three German submarines in the Mediterranean, but three had been sunk in the Straits of Gibraltar and five during operations, prompting Admiral Karl Dönitz, commander of Germany's submarine forces, to write: "It should, therefore, be investigated whether the value of operations in the Mediterranean and off Gibraltar and prospects of successes by U-boats outweigh those high losses." Dönitz had a point. The Mediterranean rate of 8 boats lost out of 31 deployed (26 percent) contrasted sharply to the rate elsewhere of 2 lost out of 54 deployed (4 percent), as well as to the 6 percent average monthly loss rate in the war up through December 1941. In addition, in November 1941 Allied shipping losses in the North Atlantic were the lowest for any month in the war to date—another consequence of putting submarines in the Mediterranean.[35]

The Dash to the Wire

During the last week in November the ground fighting between Tobruk and Bardia reached a degree of fluidity and confusion seldom seen since the invention of the machine gun. On the 23rd the German Afrika Korps and the Ariete Division counterattacked the British forces to the east of Tobruk and destroyed the 5th South African Brigade, although at the cost of 72 of the 162 tanks remaining to the Germans. Rommel saw this as an opportunity to drive deep into the enemy's rear with his entire armored force, relieve Bardia and Sollum, and incite a British retreat into Egypt. Accordingly, on the 24th the 21st Panzer Division, advancing sixty miles in six hours, crossed into Egypt, brushing aside British forces harassing its northern and southern flanks. The 8th Army's commander, General Alan Cunningham, strongly urged Auchinleck to call off the offensive. Instead, Auchinleck instructed him to maintain the offensive to the last tank. Meanwhile, two New Zealand brigades that had been ordered forward on the 23rd advanced on Sidi Rezegh, oblivious to the Axis armored units far to their rear.

Confused by contradictory orders, disorganized by their long advances, and running short of ammunition and fuel, Axis forces accomplished little on the frontier. Allied resistance was uneven but often sharp and deadly, and the New Zealanders continued to advance. On the 26th Rommel collected his forces and retreated toward Tobruk. On this day the New Zealanders captured Sidi Rezegh. Auchinleck relieved General Cunningham and replaced him with his deputy chief of staff, Major General Neil Ritchie. The German armored divisions counterattacked and recaptured Sidi Rezegh on the 30th, but the British were replacing losses faster than the Axis, and Auchinleck's steady resolution served the British better than Rommel's frenetic dash served the Axis.

Italy Mounts Another Surge

At the end of November, the Italians launched another surge of small, dispersed convoys to Africa. The tanker *Berbera* was scheduled to participate, but Ultra disclosed her presence at Navarino. At 1100/28th five Blenheims flying at mast-height through very bad weather dropped twenty 250-pound bombs. The tanker caught fire and was badly damaged. The hulk was eventually towed to Spalato.[36] The other convoys included:

- *Iseo* (2,366 GRT/11.5 kts), *Capo Faro* (3,476 GRT/10 kts). Escort: torpedo boat *Procione*. Sailed Brindisi 1600/28th destination Benghazi.
- *Sebastiano Venier* (6,311 GRT/16.5 kts). Escort: destroyer *Da Verazzano*. Sailed Taranto 1245/29th destination Benghazi.
- *Adriatico* (1,721 GRT/14 kts, 2x120-mm). Sailed Argostoli 29th destination Benghazi.
- *Mantovani* (10,540 GRT/13 kts). Escort: destroyer *Da Mosto*. Sailed Trapani 1334/30th destination Tripoli.

- *Bolsena* (2,352 GRT/11.5 kts) Escort: destroyer *Centauro.* Sailed Trapani 1815/30th destination Tripoli.
- Cover Group: 7th Division (Rear Admiral Raffaele De Courten) light cruisers *Duca d'Aosta, Montecuccoli, Attendolo*; 11th Squadron *Aviere, Geniere, Camicia Nera.* Sailed Taranto 1300/29th to take position in the central Mediterranean.
- *Duilio* (Rear Admiral Porzio Giovanola), 13th Squadron *Granatiere, Alpino, Bersagliere, Fuciliere.* Sailed Taranto at 1930/29 to join De Courten.
- Light cruiser *Garibaldi* and destroyers *Corazziere* and *Carabiniere.* Sailed Messina 2220/29th to rendezvous with the other support groups.

The British submarine *P31* sighted the 7th Division at 1630/29th some seventy miles south southeast of Taranto. She launched four torpedoes from 4,300 yards and, based upon the sound of explosions, signaled a success at 1720. She received in reply a hearty well-done, but in fact her torpedoes all missed.[37]

On the last day of November, in addition to the five merchant vessels, one auxiliary cruiser, one torpedo boat, twelve destroyers, four light cruisers, and one battleship enumerated above, the Regia Marina also had four destroyers and a submarine at sea in transit to Libya, all carrying gasoline (430 tons), and motorships *Città di Tunisi* and *Fabio Filzi* returning to Italy from Tripoli.

The British Admiralty, meanwhile, calculating that another surface strike group based in Malta would multiply Axis losses, pressured Admiral Cunningham to make it so. Force B, light cruisers *Ajax* and *Neptune*, and destroyers *Kingston* and *Kimberley*, under Rear Admiral Rawlings, packed with extra ammunition and submarine torpedoes, set forth for the island at 0500/27th. *Ajax* fouled the boom leaving port, a navigational error that Rawlings blamed on the "maniac" signalman at the boom hut, who he said "flashed away with such a dazzling light that the seaward arm of the boom could not be distinguished." Alexandria diverted Force B at 2118 to search for an enemy torpedo boat that Ultra had incorrectly predicted would be heading for Benghazi that day. Force B arrived in Malta at 0845/29th and sailed with Force K (minus *Lance*, which docked on 1 December to repair rudder damage) at 0500/30th under Rawlings' flag. His orders were to be 90 miles northwest of Benghazi at dusk on the 30th and sweep north from there along the track of a convoy (actually *Sebastiano Venier*) which Vice Admiral Ford had expected to be in the vicinity, based on a series of Ultra messages. Ford cautioned Rawlings that *Duilio* and the 7th Division were at sea and that he should keep his force concentrated.[38]

The Italian submarine *Tricheco* tried to ambush Rawlings' combined strike force shortly after it sailed, but her three torpedoes missed. Later, an Italian aircraft confirmed the submarine's sighting, prompting Supermarina to order De Courten's cruisers to join the *Venier* group, which was the most important of those at sea.

Conditions were poor in the central Mediterranean that day, with a strong sirocco wind and heavy seas. Malta was receiving multiple reports of shipping from aircraft and submarines. These included the *Capo Faro* convoy, which was laboring south at 6 knots, seriously behind schedule. At 0954/30th six Blenheims from Malta flying an armed reconnaissance mission arrived overhead and dropped ten 500-pound bombs. *Iseo* sustained light damage, but three bombs smashed *Capo Faro* "literally crushing" (and sinking) the vessel. *Iseo* returned to Argostoli arriving at 2230/30th. Another aircraft sighted De Courten's cruisers at 1253 and shadowed them for an hour and a half.[39]

At 1515/30th the *Duilio* joined the *Garibaldi* group, but as they were sailing to meet De Courten the *Garibaldi* suffered a major boiler failure and had to shut down her engines. *Duilio* took the stricken cruiser in tow. Supermarina ordered them north at 1630. During this period the *Venier* group sailed east to distance itself from the British cruisers. It turned south toward Benghazi after dark. *Venier* recorded one aircraft and one submarine strike, but made Benghazi unharmed at 0700/1st. The three support groups were back in Taranto by 1120/1st. *Upholder* sighted Italian cruisers before dawn. After one of the escorts forced her to dive she launched four torpedoes from a depth of seventy feet. All missed.[40]

Meanwhile, Rawlings' four cruisers and three destroyers were coursing east, feeding on a steady stream of aircraft sighting reports. They were themselves shadowed by Italian aircraft most of the afternoon. By 1500/30th Rawlings concluded that the Italian convoys were behind schedule and that there was a battleship and three cruisers between him and his targets. Accordingly, he planned to pass ahead of the convoy after dark and strike with the advantage of the moon after an ASV-equipped Wellington located his target. However, the Wellington did not find enemy vessels where Rawlings expected them. Instead, it reported an unexpected contact to the southeast. At 2320, despite his instructions to remain concentrated, Rawlings detached Agnew and Force K to chase down this contact while he continued north along the enemy's expected track. The British admiral anticipated another night of slaughter.[41]

In November twenty-nine convoys plied the routes between Europe and Africa and fourteen along the African coast (see table 4.1).

Traffic in the Adriatic and the Aegean is included in the table for comparison. The amount of traffic sailing these two seas was about two and a half times that of African traffic, but with a loss rate of just 1.5 percent compared to a 26 percent loss rate on the African routes. Domestic traffic consisted of an average of 33 large ships (each displacing more than 1,000 GRT) at sea on any given day.[42]

Table 4.1. **Axis Traffic for Ships Departing in November 1941**

Type	Convoys	Convoys attacked	Detected by Ultra	Ships sailed	Ships arrived	Ships lost	Ships damaged
Europe to Africa	21	11	17	37	16	13*	5
Africa to Europe	8	0	7	9	9	0	1
Coastal west	5	2	5	11	11	0	1
Coastal east	9	1	6	20	19	1	0
DDs to Africa	4	0		10	10	0	1
CLs to Africa	1	0		1	1	0	0
SSs to Africa	7	0		7	6	0	0
Total Africa**	43	14	35	77	45	14	7
Total Balkans	68	0		119	118	1	0

*Includes two ships sunk on 1 December that departed in November.
**Excludes military sailings. Includes German traffic.
Source: USMM, Difesa del traffico 7:373–84.

Throughout the Mediterranean in November the Allies sank 5 warships of 4,665 tons and 24 commercial or auxiliary vessels displacing 70,967 GRT. Of this total, 18 ships displacing 62,012 GRT were involved in the African campaign—14 were sunk at sea as specified in Table 4.1 and 4 in African ports. Force K sank 9, aircraft 7.5, and submarines 1.5. Malta-based forces accounted for 18 of the 24 ships lost.[43]

Summaries of the Submarine and Air Wars

On 1 November eight Allied submarines were on patrol throughout the Mediterranean. During that month Allied boats sank five merchant vessels displacing 8,684 tons and damaged three more of 9,443 GRT. They also sank one destroyer and damaged one destroyer and one heavy cruiser. This was accomplished in 21 attacks using 64 torpedoes. On 15 November fourteen boats were on patrol.[44]

German submarines entered the Mediterranean in September and scored their first success in October. At the beginning of November there were six German boats in the Middle Sea. Nine more entered during the month and two were sunk, leaving a balance of thirteen at the beginning of December, of which seven were on patrol. They sank a British carrier, a battleship, and a sloop, totaling 55,600 tons. There were nine Italian submarines at sea at the beginning of November. Italian submarines conducted forty-four missions, employing thirty-one boats. These included twenty-five offensive patrols, and eleven transport (and return) missions that carried 561.4 tons of matériel, primarily fuel, to North Africa. Italian submarines expended eight torpedoes in three attacks, sinking a Spanish freighter and damaging a French tanker, both suspected of violating contraband rules.[45]

In the air campaign against traffic, Wellingtons raided Italian ports, especially Benghazi, Tripoli and Naples, but also Brindisi, Palermo, and Augusta. One large raid on Benghazi of twenty-one aircraft on the 25/26th, sank the German steamer *Tinos* (2,826 GRT) and the minesweeper *Zirona* (330 tons); another of twenty-six aircraft on the 28/29th sank the steamer *Priaruggia* (1,196 GRT).

Italian aircraft raided Malta on seventeen days during November, targeting the naval base at La Valletta twelve times and the airfields seventeen times—although only a few aircraft participated on most occasions. A "major" raid conducted during the day on 8 November consisted of four Z.1007bis bombers escorted by eighteen MC.200 and MC.202s. Vice Admiral Wilbraham Ford recorded a total of seventy-six alarms, including forty night raids. German aircraft bombed Suez on the nights of 2/3rd, 3/4th, 6/7th, and 8/9 November.[46]

The combination of surface strike forces and air reinforcements in Malta, an offensive on the North African shore, and actionable intelligence enabled the British to blockade North Africa effectively. These successes had come at a cost, however—with German submarines sinking a carrier and a battleship—but at this point it was a cost that the British could afford. Italian aircraft frustrated the one attempt to send supplies to Malta by ship. Apart from extra ammunition delivered by Force B, the submarines *Porpoise*, *Regent*, and *Olympus*, which arrived with stores and kerosene on 9, 13, and 30 November respectively, brought the only materiel to reach the island during November. Italian air forces and German submarines did not contest traffic to Tobruk effectively; the only loss they inflicted was in sinking one Australian escort vessel. Other British traffic in the Eastern Mediterranean passed without harm.

Chapter 5

Italy's Misery Mounts

A successful attack on a ship in transit by an aircraft [is] worth the effort of fifty aircraft attacking the same cargo once it [is] ashore.

VICE CHIEF OF NAVAL STAFF, QUOTED IN FRIEDMAN,
NAVAL ANTI-AIRCRAFT GUNS AND GUNNERY

On the eve of Japan's entry into World War II in early December 1941, the Axis and Allied coalitions both faced conditions of mixed promise and peril. To the British, it was finally clear that the Soviet Union would not collapse in a single campaign, as France had done. Their position in the Middle East seemed better than at any point since the previous April. The Crusader Offensive appeared to be succeeding, and the Admiralty believed that at long last British forces had seized control of the central Mediterranean. However, this achievement came at a cost to Britain's worldwide position. On 5 December the chiefs of staff concluded: "Over 5 million gross registered tons of shipping are devoted to military purposes alone, mainly for the maintenance of our armies in the Middle East. A great strain has been added to this effort by the practical closing of the Mediterranean since . . . the entry of Italy into the war."[1] Indeed, the global shipping situation would soon become far worse.

In Rome and Berlin, British successes in the central Mediterranean had caused grave concerns. The German Admiralty War Diary for 4 December worried that "it is almost impossible to supply the forces [in Africa] with their most urgent needs. In view of this situation, the Duce does not see how he can replenish the losses of men and material incurred in the fighting or how to ship fresh troops. Neither the use of German submarines, valuable as they are, nor the arrival in Sicily of the II Air Corps could change the transportation situation sufficiently to enable us to keep up with the British in the long run." Mussolini wanted to occupy Tunisia. Cavallero did not think that was possible. All the while Russia remained the theater of decision, and despite the frustration that Germany experienced in its attempt to gain a quick victory, Berlin remained absolutely confident of ultimate success. After 7 December, Japan's thunderous offensives against the British Empire and the United States merely reinforced German confidence; the Reich's naval staff noted that the Japanese assault had brought Germany "great advantage," even while conceding that the German navy lacked the strength to exploit that advantage decisively.[2]

On 14 December, before the British chiefs of staff realized how successful Japan's offensives were going to be, they had reassessed their worldwide naval priorities. The Admiralty confirmed that North Atlantic communications remained the Empire's top priority—after the security of Great Britain itself, of course. The next priority was sea communications in the Indian Ocean. "On the security of these rests our ability to supply our armies in North Africa and the Middle East, to supply Russia through Persia, to reinforce Singapore . . . and to proceed to the assistance of Australia and New Zealand." This new pecking order affected the eastern Mediterranean. Given the conquest of Cyrenaica, which was well underway, the chiefs decided to concentrate most of the Empire's naval strength—including the Mediterranean Fleet's last two battleships, *Queen Elizabeth* and *Valiant*—east of Suez. The Admiralty noted that capital ships in the eastern Mediterranean had three functions—to support offensive operations against Italy, to maintain sea communications inside the eastern Mediterranean, and to support light forces intercepting enemy convoys to Africa.

The global situation no longer permitted offensive operations against Italy, such as a landing on Sicily. As for functions two and three, the Admiralty hoped that airpower could replace the battleships. In other words, the eastern Mediterranean was no longer a top priority for the British Empire. Despite Crusader's apparent success, opportunity had waned—and peril had grown.[3]

War on Traffic: Surface Actions

Rear Admiral Rawlings' Force B spent the night of 30 November and the following morning chasing out-of-date sightings, and finally returned to Malta on the afternoon of the 1st. Force K had separated that evening when Rawlings ordered Agnew to investigate a contact north of Benghazi. *Aurora* twice steered to the reported position only to have the ASV-equipped Wellington supporting her radio that the target was elsewhere. Agnew complained that "the aircraft's reports when plotted showed great inaccuracies in bearing, which not only gave a false idea of the enemy's course and speed but made the correct course to steer extremely difficult to decide."[4] Finally at 0225/1st, under a bright moon that was two days short of full, *Aurora* detected the armed motor ship *Adriatico* twelve miles away, sailing solo from Reggio Calabria to Benghazi.

The light cruiser approached to 5,500 yards, and at 0304 discharged four 6-inch rounds that splashed just short. She then flashed the code for "abandon ship." When the Italian did not respond, Agnew loosed another broadside. One shell hit, and disabled the auxiliary cruiser's aft gun. *Adriatico* then replied with a round from her forward gun. Her captain, Lieutenant Commander Emanuele Campagnoli, stated later that he did not understand the signal and that in any case, once attacked he naturally replied in kind. This provoked a series of rapid salvos from *Aurora*, and *Adriatico* managed only two more rounds before she "quickly caught fire thoroughly." Nonetheless, *Aurora* continued to pump 100-pound shells into the imprudent vessel; Agnew was suddenly not so concerned about wasting ammunition. *Adriatico* finally blew up at 0400. *Lively* picked up twenty-one survivors and then rejoined Force K, which was hastening northeast at high speed, to put some distance between itself and Axis air fields before dawn. This was only the first episode in what would be a long day during which Agnew's command would demonstrate the range and power of a well-handled surface strike force.[5]

Mantovani had sailed from Taranto to Trapani on 26 November, the idea being that all the traffic in the Ionian Sea on 30 November would give the tanker an opportunity to slip unnoticed into Tripoli along the Tunisian route. However, an Ultra message timed 0235Z/29th warned of her departure from Trapani on an unspecified day and gave her general route. Then at 1740Z/30th another message revealed that the tanker could leave any day from the 30th on and included her probable route and schedule. At that time, *Mantovani* was already six hours underway.[6]

A British aircraft sighted *Mantovani* and her escort, *Da Mosto*, shortly before 1000/1st. The destroyer's commander, Lieutenant Commander Francesco Dell'Anno, radioed for reinforcements, but not until 1300 did the torpedo boat *Prestinari* and the tug *Ciclope* leave Tripoli and Zuara respectively. The destroyer *Malocello* followed from Tripoli some hours later.

Force K, en route to Malta, overheard the sighting report. Lacking confirmation that aircraft had sunk the sighted ships, Agnew decided to steer toward this contact. Rawlings had heard the same report, but he awaited orders. When these did not arrive he concluded that Vice Admiral Ford "did not wish me to search for her." Accordingly, Force B turned toward Malta at 1229. However, Rawlings continued, "the Senior Officer, Force K, with what, in retrospect, appears to have been better judgement than mine, stood on toward the tanker."[7]

Three Blenheims assailed *Mantovani* at 1310. *Da Mosto* interposed herself, firing machine guns and special anti-aircraft barrage shells for her 120-mm weapons.[8] Two of the aircraft missed. Before a trio of nearby Italian fighters could intervene, the third released a brace of 500-pound bombs. Dell'Anno wrote, "the action of this sole aircraft was enough; *Mantovani* was hit and immobilized with her engines stopped, rudder impaired and her propeller may be damaged." *Da Mosto* passed a line, but with the tanker slowly settling by the stern, the cable soon parted. "The situation, already very difficult . . . became critical when, at 1650, four more British aircraft became visible at a distance."[9] *Mantovani* was seventy-five miles northwest of Tripoli. The fighter patrol had just departed, and its replacement had yet to arrive. The Blenheims circled to avoid the worst of the destroyer's flak and landed bombs on the tanker's bridge and along her side. The flooding accelerated, and *Mantovani*'s men abandoned ship.

At 1714 *Aurora* spotted aircraft circling above the horizon and turned to investigate. A half hour later masts emerged into view. The aircraft, three CR.42s, buzzed the British warships, but there was nothing that the bi-wing fighters could have done to stop the cruisers. *Da Mosto* was rescuing survivors when her lookouts reported two ships in sight. Hoping to see *Prestinari* and *Malocello*, Dell'Anno suspended the rescue and turned toward the contact.

Aurora settled the question of identity at 1801 when she opened fire from 16,000 yards. As was his practice, Agnew kept end on to present as small a target as possible. *Da Mosto* continued toward the enemy, returning fire and trying to get a good angle for a torpedo salvo. *Penelope* took position on *Aurora*'s starboard quarter and engaged from 11,800 yards. She discharged twelve broadsides from her A and B turrets at ranges that gradually decreased to 8,400 yards, and claimed one hit with her 11th salvo at 1807. The destroyer returned fire, her shells falling in tight groups, and employed standard defensive tactics. At 11,000 yards, she emptied one set of tubes, made what Agnew described as "a very thick smoke screen," and altered course into it.[10]

The cruisers continued coming on so *Da Mosto* emerged from her smoke, closed to 6,500 yards, "steaming in a broad inclination across the bows of Force K," and launched three more torpedoes. Up to this point *Da Mosto* was unharmed. With torpedoes away, Dell'Anno wrote, "I turned the helm to retire into the smoke and definitely escape but as I began the turn I took a broadside astern that detonated No. 3 magazine." Agnew reported that "she was hit heavily and blew up with a tremendous flame and smoke. One minute later, when the smoke had cleared, there was no trace of the ship to be seen." The British assumed that she had sunk with all hands, but this was not the case. Dell'Anno: "Staying at the end of the bridge I found myself, at a certain point, in the sea and I saw the destroyer's bow soar vertically above my head . . . by instinct I swam to a Carley raft I saw nearby and reached it. I saw the two enemy cruisers proceeding in line at low speed about a thousand meters away. One of the two signaled with a red lamp [to] a destroyer that had not participated in the combat. . . . The destroyer rejoined the cruisers through the area of the castaways passing very close to me. I read the distinctive letters

G.40. The destroyer's crew was at attention as the enemy moved away." The Italians assumed that *Lively*'s crew was honoring their gallantry, and perhaps they were, but the destroyer's report says nothing about seeing *Da Mosto*'s survivors.[11]

The cruisers then closed on *Mantovani* and shelled her, setting the foundering vessel ablaze. *Lively* torpedoed the wreck for good measure, and at 1830 Force K turned toward Malta. At 1953 *Mantovani* exploded with "a huge sheet of flame." *Prestinari* witnessed the battle from twelve miles away, and after the British withdrew she rescued survivors. *Da Mosto* lost 138 men and *Mantovani* 73.[12]

British Coastal Operations

On the evening of 1 December the Royal Navy could look with satisfaction upon its accomplishments over the previous two days. Six Italian ships, supported by a battleship, a cruiser division, and a dozen destroyers had been headed for Africa. Force K had sunk two merchantmen, and Royal Air Force (RAF) Blenheims dispatched another. One ship had turned back, and only two of the six arrived. The British also believed they had damaged a cruiser as well as sinking a destroyer. The major concern was a fuel shortage at Malta. After Force K and Force B had filled their bunkers only 7,000 tons remained. Accordingly, Vice Admiral Ford recommended that Force B escort *Breconshire* and three empties from the last convoy back to Alexandria and then return with some tankers.

Concurrent with Force K's successes, the British navy sought to blockade Derna and Bardia. On the night of 30 November–1 December *Jaguar*, *Kipling*, and *Jackal* patrolled off the anchorage without luck. At 1225/1st, three S.79s attacked the formation as it returned to Tobruk. A torpedo slammed into *Jackal* on the port side, opening the steering compartment to the sea and jamming the rudder to port. She made Tobruk at 14 knots, steering by her engines, and was five months under repair. The defensive barrage damaged two of the aircraft. After the action *Jackal* fired a shell to clear a 4.7-inch barrel, with *Jaguar* in the line of fire. The shell hit *Jaguar*'s bridge and killed three men, including her captain, Lieutenant Commander J. F. W. Hines.[13] *Naiad*, *Euryalus*, *Hero*, and *Hasty* patrolled off Derna the next night. This was in response to an Ultra message timed 0125Z/1st that correctly forecast a supply mission by *Maestrale* and *Gioberti*. The blockade-runners arrived at 0800/2nd, as expected, and, in half an hour, offloaded 50 tons of drummed gasoline. The British, however, did not see them. Also on the 2nd, *Napier*, *Griffin*, *Hotspur*, and *Decoy* sailed from Alexandria to operate off the Cyrenaican coast. They likewise saw nothing. Throughout the month, Italian submarines delivered eleven cargoes to Bardia totaling 904 tons. The traffic allowed the enclave to continue its resistance.[14]

After almost two weeks of combat, Italian forces still surrounded Tobruk. Although the RAF had not established air superiority, the British dispatched the first Alexandria to Tobruk Convoy (AT.1) on 1600/30 November. This was the first of thirty-three AT convoys that sailed through the end of March matched by a corresponding number of Tobruk–Alexandria (TA) convoys as ships returned to Alexandria. AT.1 included two steamers, a tanker, an armed boarding vessel, two small lighters, and three larger lighters sailing in slow and fast sections. A destroyer, two Hunts, two sloops, and two trawlers, representing the navies of Great Britain, Australia, Greece, and South Africa, provided the escort. The two sections united on the 2nd as Axis aircraft shadowed overhead. The *Yarra*'s captain, Lieutenant Commander W. H. Harrington, reported, "These made as if to attack at 0930, 0940 and 0947, but being engaged by gunfire, dropped no bombs and made off." AT.1 reached Tobruk on the afternoon of the 2nd. Convoy AT.2 got underway on 4 December also in two sections, arriving at 2300/6th after having been delayed by a sandstorm.[15]

On the 5th the Greek destroyer flotilla patrolled off Bardia while *Breconshire* left Malta, escorted by *Ajax*, *Neptune*, *Lively*, *Kingston*, and *Kimberley*. Convoy TA.1 departed Tobruk at 1800. Three and a half hours later a trio of S.79s jumped the convoy and torpedoed *Chakdina* (3,033 GRT/15 kts). The ship carried 600 men, including 380 stretcher cases and 100 prisoners of war. The torpedo struck in the after hold, and the ship foundered in only three minutes. *Farndale* and the antisubmarine trawler *Thorgrim* rescued two hundred, including Major General Johann Raven-stein, commander of the 21st Panzer Division, who had been captured on 28 November, but four hundred perished, including most of the severely wounded. For example, eighty of ninety-seven New Zealanders on board

Savoia-Marchetti S.79 "Sparrowhawk." This was a three-engine bomber introduced in 1936. Its top speed was 250 knots and its range was 1,400 nm. In the torpedo bomber role these aircraft were Italy's leading antishipping weapons. However, although they enjoyed success they were not as deadly as Italy's leaders believed. Storia Militare.[16]

died. The only surviving stretcher case recalled that the ship rolled after the torpedo exploded and the engine room crew rushed past him, trampling his fingers. He reached the deck just as the ship sank, hearing behind him "a cry, in an agony of terror from the trapped men below." The Italian airmen reported success against two enemy light cruisers.[16]

On 1300/6th Australian light cruiser *Hobart*, with *Galatea*, *Carlisle*, and the destroyers *Griffin* and *Hotspur*, departed Alexandria to meet *Breconshire*, which Force K was escorting from Malta. They met the store ship at 0714/7th, eighty miles south of Cape Lithina, Crete. There Force K turned about for Malta. *Breconshire* reached Alexandria at 0410/8th.

Yarra and *Flamingo* spent the 7th sweeping for submarines east of Tobruk. At 1600, while thus engaged, Axis aircraft struck thirty-five miles northeast of Tobruk. *Flamingo*'s report assessed the enemy force as two groups of sixteen aircraft each, while *Yarra*'s had it as three torpedo bombers and thirty-five Stukas and Messerschmitts. In fact, it was nineteen Ju.87s. The Germans reported they attacked three cruisers and damaged two. In reality, a near miss ruptured *Flamingo*'s hull and disabled her engines. *Yarra* suffered minor damage when a bomb burst close alongside. She towed *Flamingo* to Tobruk, supported by *Hobart*, which joined her from *Breconshire*'s escort. *Flamingo* was not repaired until February 1944. That same evening the armed boarding vessel *Chantala* (3,129 GRT/14 kts) from Convoy TA.2, which *Yarra* and *Flamingo* were scheduled to escort back to Alexandria, struck a mine leaving Tobruk. Her keel snapped, and she sank just inside the entrance channel.[17]

Tobruk was relieved from the land on the 8th; this, and the losses incurred at sea, caused Admiral Cunningham to suspend the AT convoys. He maintained the patrol off Derna, however, with *Euryalus*, *Hero*, and *Havock* doing duty on the 8th. At 1500/10th *Naiad*, *Griffin*, and *Hotspur* bombarded the anchorage, claiming damage to a merchant ship. In fact, they damaged the motor-sailer *Lo Bianco*, and the small motorship *Emilio* (193 GRT). As the force withdrew a single S.79 dropped a torpedo aimed at *Naiad*. The force also reported a strike by Ju.87s. Given that Derna was so close to Axis airbases, the British dispatched two MTBs to assume blockade duties. The two vessels collided in their first sortie on the night of 14 December and *MTB 68* sank. *MTB 215* returned to Tobruk "considerably damaged." On the day before *U431* torpedoed the water carrier *Myriel* (3,560 GRT) enroute to Mersa Matruh in the company of trawlers *Southern Isles* and *Southern Sea*, forty-five miles west of Alexandria. She made Tobruk nonetheless and returned to service in October 1943. Clearly, despite the apparent success of Operation Crusader, the waters between Tobruk and Alexandria remained dangerous.[18]

Italian Reactions

The Regia Marina's failure to deliver desperately needed supplies to Africa provoked a crisis. On the 2nd the German high naval command opined that "The Italian Fleet is incapable of prevailing over even an outnumbered opponent or of gaining temporary control of the seas."[19] Cavallero, painfully aware of German attitudes, not least because the Italians were wiretapping the German embassy's phones, proposed a conference to examine the problem and to seek solutions. The meeting occurred on

4 December and was attended by Riccardi and his deputy, Rear Admiral Luigi Sansonetti, and the air force chief, General Rino Corso Fougier, and his deputy, as well as by the German naval liaison at Supermarina, Rear Admiral Weichold, General Josef Rintelen and Field Marshal Albert Kesselring. Riccardi admitted that for the time being the enemy had "aeronaval supremacy in the Mediterranean's central basin, so much so that our losses have jumped from 30% in October to 80% in the last fifteen days of November." For this situation he blamed the cruisers and destroyers at Malta; the reinforced enemy air forces, including torpedo bombers of greater range; the precise night attacks; and the improved reconnaissance. Riccardi also complained about the fuel situation, noting that monthly consumption was 80,000 tons while telling the Germans that the supply on hand was no more than 60,000 tons and that in November Italy had only received 12,000 tons from Romania. The attendees decided that the emergency required greater efforts. They resolved to strengthen sea and air escorts, and to use destroyers and cruisers to guarantee the delivery of especially important materiel. Kesselring said he would look at organizing air transport from Crete to Cyrenaica, and made several suggestions, such as using routes better protected by aircraft, even if they were longer, and trying to employ radio deception and false convoys, since "English espionage is widespread."[20]

While the navy mustered resources for another major convoy effort to Tripoli, traffic between Benghazi and Tripoli continued. The battle for Tobruk raged on, but British replacements and reinforcements outmatched Axis efforts. By 30 November the Afrika Korps was down to fifty-seven operational tanks. Axis troops succeeded in surrounding Tobruk once again, but the British defeated an attempt on 2–3 December to drive toward Bardia, and on the 4th repulsed a renewed advance by the 21st Panzer Division. Finally, as the 8th Army massed to assault the troops besieging Tobruk, Rommel realized that the battle was lost, and on 7 December he began retreating to Gazala.[21]

The motor ship *Calitea* (4,013 GRT/15 kts), escorted by the destroyer *Freccia*, departed Brindisi at 2010/7th. *Calitea* put into Argostoli on the 8th and then sailed for Benghazi on the 11th. The submarine *Talisman* sank her at 1600/11th with two torpedoes from a spread of five. *Freccia* rescued 230 survivors. Several Ultra messages gave accurate details of her route and destination, but not her departure date. The decisive message finally was decrypted from Luftwaffe Enigma and sent to Cairo at 2245Z/10th. It confirmed that *Calitea* would be at sea on the 11th. This gave *Talisman* time to reach a position astride her known route. However, the unreliability of many Ultra transmissions was demonstrated by a message generated thirteen hours after *Calitea*'s destruction that stated the ship was unloading in Benghazi.[22]

Another victim of British submarines was the motor ship *Sebastiano Venier*. She had arrived in Benghazi on 1 December after a harrowing passage that saw her survive air and submarine strikes. After discharging her cargo in the threatened port, she took on 2,000 prisoners of war, 15 German passengers, including some from the freighter *Tinos* sunk in Benghazi harbor on 25 November, and 167 Italians, including guards and crew. The ship's military commander was a 55-year-old reservist just recalled to the colors, and the return trip was his first voyage in a decade. The torpedo boat *Centauro* escorted the crowded transport, which departed Benghazi for Taranto at 1930/8th. Conditions were bad, with heavy swells and a strong wind from the southwest, and *Centauro* ordered *Venier* to detour to Naravino. *Venier* was five miles off port when at 1430/9th the submarine *Porpoise* surprised her with one of four torpedoes fired from 1,600 yards. The transport came to a stop, and the crew lowered two boats and cast some rafts overboard. Then the captain, some officers, and most of the military personnel abandoned ship. After dropping depth charges, *Centauro* returned and determined that *Venier* was in no danger of sinking. At 1505 the motorship, manned by the chief engineer, two other officers, and most of the crew, requested a tow, but before a tug could arrive from Navarino, *Venier* became stranded on a sandy bottom off Cape Methone. Casualties included 309 POWs and 11 Italians. Saved were 156 Italians, 15 Germans, and 1,691 POWs, many of whom were transferred to shore via a breeches buoy slung between ship and beach. The escort commander thought that *Venier* could have been saved if her officers had not abandoned ship prematurely, and personnel who had done so were arrested. The military commander committed suicide the day before his trial. The submarine *Torbay* finished off the wreck on 15 December.[23]

Battle of Cape Bon

After their meeting on 4 December, Cavallero pressed Riccardi to push supplies to Africa. No navy likes to use warships as transports, but when need compels it the practice is relatively common. The Tokyo Express during World War II is a well-known example; in that instance, the Japanese used warships to deliver personnel, supplies, and equipment to their troops in New Guinea and the Solomon Islands. By the same token, in the Mediterranean conflict, British cruisers, minelayers, destroyers, and submarines brought to Malta everything from canned milk to mail. In the crisis, the Regia Marina assigned its oldest and smallest light cruisers to this duty. *Cadorna* dashed to Benghazi on 21 November and again on 8 December, bringing 273 tons of fuel and lubricants and 522 cases of ammunition. After a notice from the air force that Tripoli was almost out of aviation fuel, Riccardi selected *Di Giussano* and *Da Barbiano* under Rear Admiral Antonio Toscano to bring fuel to Tripoli in advance of the next major convoy operation.[24]

The two cruisers initially departed Palermo at 1700/9th but an ASV-equipped Wellington spotted them at 2057 and shadowed as Malta scrambled seven Swordfish. Rear Admiral Rawlings, leading *Neptune, Aurora, Penelope, Jaguar,* and *Kandahar,* had already departed Malta at 1830/9th. However, the Servizio Informazione Segrete (SIS), the Italian intelligence service, intercepted the plane's radio messages and notified Toscano, who reversed course at 2355/9th. The British strike force returned the next day. Its consumption of precious fuel would affect future operations.[25]

For the next effort, Supermarina reinforced Toscano with the light cruiser *Bande Nere,* but a condenser problem forced her to miss the operation, and a torpedo boat assigned to the escort *Climene* had mechanical problems and could not meet the tight timetable. Meanwhile, Ultra messages generated on 5 December informed Ford that the cruisers were at Palermo, ready to dash to Tripoli. The aborted mission on 9 December was the subject of an Ultra message early the next morning. However, Bletchley Park generated the most crucial of these at 2100Z/11th. It disclosed that the cruisers would be leaving on the evening of the 12th, and gave their course and speed.[26]

On 12 December two cruisers and torpedo boat *Cigno* sailed for Tripoli again. They carried 100 tons of aviation fuel, including 11 tons of drummed fuel stacked on the quarterdeck, 500 tons of fuel oil, 50 tons of ammunition and supplies, and 135 personnel.[27] Air force reconnaissance of the central Mediterranean confirmed that the British cruisers were still in Valletta, but at 1500 a Cant Z.1007bis, one of three aircraft dispatched by Air Sardinia to scour the Western Mediterranean, sighted four destroyers off Algiers heading east at 20 knots. This was the 4th Flotilla, senior officer Commander Graham H. Stokes in *Sikh*, and included *Maori*, *Legion*, and the Dutch *Isaac Sweers*. They were in transit from Gibraltar to Malta to replace the Mediterranean Fleet's Australian destroyers, which the Admiralty was sending to the Indian Ocean as part of the British navy's great shift eastward.

Vice Admiral Ford originally had intended for Rawlings to intercept the Italians ninety miles south of Cape Bon with three cruisers and three destroyers. At 1223/12th he radioed this plan to Stokes and told him to be ready in case the cruisers tried to break back to the north, but otherwise to maintain schedule. Then, at 1645 Cunningham radioed Ford: "Do not use Malta surface forces for attack on cruisers." Cunningham was concerned about Malta's fuel supply, although Ford had earlier estimated that the island would have enough oil for both Force K and Force B to intercept the cruisers, conduct two local operations, and still be able to reach Alexandria from Malta. At 1805 Ford radioed Stokes that where would be no surface foray. Stokes on his own initiative increased speed to 30 knots.[28]

Supermarina allowed Toscano to continue because it calculated that even at top speed the British destroyers could not round Cape Bon before 0300, an hour after the cruisers were supposed to pass. At 2223 it warned Toscano that he might encounter British merchant traffic sailing from Malta to Gibraltar. At 2315 Toscano ordered combat stations, just in case.[29]

As *Cigno* neared Cape Bon, running nearly an hour behind schedule, she heard an aircraft overhead—an ASV-equipped Wellington, in fact— and at 0256 blinkered a report to the flagship. *Sikh*, hurrying along the African shore, saw the flashing light ahead in the distance. At 0302, British lookouts observed ship silhouettes disappearing behind Cape Bon's looming promontory. Altering course from east to southeast at 0316, *Sikh*, followed by *Legion, Maori*, and *Isaac Sweers,* rounded the cape. Stokes believed that he had little chance of engaging. However, at 0320, Toscano, now two and a half miles southeast of the cape, suddenly reversed course. The reason for this action is unclear. *Cigno*'s skipper, Lieutenant Commander Nicola Riccardi, assumed it was because of the aircraft that he had heard half an hour before. A *Da Barbiano* survivor stated that lookouts had sighted a ship off the starboard quarter. Because the aft turret was useless due to the fuel drums stacked around it, Toscano reversed course to attack and warned the other ships by short wave to beware enemy vessels. In any case, his maneuver surprised *Cigno*. She did not come about until 0325, putting her far in the formation's rear.[30]

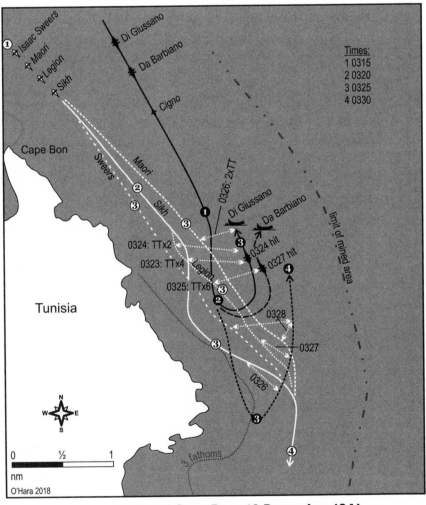

Map 5.1. **Battle of Cape Bon, 13 December 1941**

As Stokes' flotilla steadied on its new course, just a thousand yards off shore, the British commander was startled to see the Italian cruisers rapidly approaching fine off his port bow. He signaled his flotilla, and at 0323 *Sikh* edged starboard and launched four torpedoes to port at *Da Barbiano* from a range that she estimated as 1,500 yards. The run to target at this distance was slightly over a minute. *Da Barbiano*'s senior surviving officer described the scene: "[We] had just spotted at an angle of about 60 degrees two ships I judged to be about 2,000 tons. From their bow waves their speed was about 28–30 knots. The order came from the Admiral's bridge to open fire. Distance abeam from these units was 300 meters. The executive officer, Commander Ghiselli, who was following the enemy's movements, announced 'they have launched.' Captain Giorgio Rodocanacchi quickly ordered the helm hard to port. Ghiselli declared a second time, 'they have launched.' Then there was an explosion at the bow near turret No. 1 followed immediately by an explosion amidships by the forward engine room. At the same moment the enemy units opened fire with machine guns and artillery."[31]

Two *Sikh* torpedoes slammed into the Italian flagship at 0324. As she erupted into flames, the destroyer struck with 4.7-inch batteries and machine guns. By this time *Legion*, following off *Sikh*'s starboard quarter, had two torpedoes running toward *Da Barbiano*. *Legion*'s captain had assumed that Stokes would target the second cruiser, not the first. When he saw this was not the case, he quickly shifted aim and hurled six more at *Di Giussano*. *Maori*, following off *Legion*'s port quarter, fired two torpedoes at 0326. One struck *Da Barbiano* astern. A survivor reported, "The blaze from the gasoline barrels aft propagated itself to the oil that was gushing from the bunkers, igniting a hellish inferno."[32] The ship sank within five minutes just 3,500 meters offshore.

Di Giussano had just assumed her new course, when in the words of Captain Giovanni Marabotto, "a multitude of events occurred in an extraordinarily brief time." Even before *Da Barbiano* exploded, lookouts had reported a dark mass 20 degrees to port. The directors tracked these onrushing shapes, and Marabotto ordered torpedo action to port. The cruiser's forward turrets opened fire. He wrote: "My attention was almost completely focused on the possibility of a torpedo track in the forward

sector. At a certain moment I ordered the helm to port but I quickly centered it for fear of hitting the burning *Da Barbiano* which was drifting to
port. I followed the enemy with heavy machineguns ahead and around to
the side. With the second 152-mm salvo I noted a considerable flame in
the direction I presumed was the enemy. This flame was greeted with joy
by the bridge personnel. Then, from the end of the bridge the navigation
officer warned me that a torpedo track was crossing astern. I put the helm
over hard to starboard but an instant later there came an explosion aft the
port beam. It was around 0330. The blast isolated the bridge and disabled
the rudder, radio, and telephone. Without power the 152-mm guns fell
silent. The machineguns continued for a while but the battle was over."[33]

The rapidly approaching destroyers were a difficult target, and the
cruiser's first salvoes passed overhead. British accounts put the torpedo
impact at 0327; two 4.7-inch shells also struck the cruiser. She swerved 15
degrees to port and began losing way.[34]

Cigno had just reversed course when the pyrotechnics began. As the
Allied ships rapidly passed to starboard, each one took pot shots at the
Italian torpedo boat: *Sikh* at 0326, *Legion* at 0327, and *Maori* at 0328.
Isaac Sweers added four torpedoes, all misses. *Cigno* replied with a hastily launched torpedo and her 3.9-inch guns, incorrectly claiming several
scores. She tried to fire more torpedoes, but the enemy passed too quickly.
The Allied destroyers continued south at high speed, leaving *Di Giussano*
waging a losing fight against an uncontrollable conflagration. The cruiser
finally sank at 0442. Rear Admiral Toscano and 920 members of his division died; *Cigno* rescued most of the 645 who survived.

If Toscano did have offensive intentions against an enemy force that
he realized was tracking him, he played a bad hand poorly. There were
Italian minefields east of Cape Bon that prevented him from doing much
more than confronting the enemy head on. In a meeting action, the Allied
destroyers proved to be the handier vessels and were first to get their
weapons into the water, while the old cruisers were just bigger targets.

The Cape Bon action was the opening act in a series of movements as
Italy launched its next significant effort to force supplies through to Libya.
From the Axis' point of view, the ground situation was rapidly deteriorat-
ing. Italo-German forces at Bardia, Sollum, and a pocket around Halfaya

Pass were now isolated far behind the front line. The remaining Axis divisions established a position at Gazala on 11 December, but British armor was massing to the south. On the 13th the XIII Corps attacked the Gazala line. On 13 December, in this environment of emergency for the Axis and dawning triumph for the Allies, Operation M41 got underway.

Operation M41

This large effort to push supplies to North Africa consisted of four convoys:

- *Del Greco* (6,835 GRT/16 kts), *Fabio Filzi*. Escort: destroyers *Da Recco*, *Usodimare*. Sailed Messina 1030/12th destination Taranto where they were to join other units.
- *Monginevro* (5,324 GRT/15.5 kts), *Vettor Pisani, Napoli*. Escort: destroyers *Pessagno, Usodimare*, torpedo boat *Pegaso*. Sailed Taranto 1900/13th destination Benghazi.
- *Ankara*. Escort: destroyers *Saetta, Malocello*. Sailed Taranto 1700/13th destination Benghazi.
- *Iseo, Capo Orso*. Escort: destroyers *Strale, Turbine*. Sailed Argostoli 1530/13th destination Benghazi.

There were also three support groups that could act semi-autonomously to assist the close escorts of the various convoys:

- Close escort: *Vivaldi, Da Noli, Da Recco, Zeno*. Sailed Taranto 1500/13th.
- Heavy escort: *Doria, Duilio*; cruisers *Duca d'Aosta, Attendolo, Garibaldi, Montecuccoli, Gorizia*; 10th Squadron (*Oriani, Gioberti*); 11th Squadron (*Aviere, Ascari, Camicia Nera*); 12th Squadron (*Corazziere, Geniere, Carabiniere*). Sailed Taranto 1840–1940/13th.
- Heavy support group: (Vice Admiral Iachino) *Littorio, Vittorio Veneto*; 13th Squadron (*Granatiere, Fuciliere, Bersagliere, Alpino*). Sailed Naples 1740/13th.

Eight merchant ships had an escort of four battleships, five cruisers, and twenty-five destroyers. Supermarina's commanders clearly regarded the surface threat as the greatest danger. To meet it, they were willing to draw down their reserves of fuel oil to dangerous levels trusting the Germans to deliver the 40,000 tons promised in early November.

Several Ultra messages alerted the British to the impending operation. Bletchley Park generated the most critical at 1215Z/11th. This specified the itinerary of the support groups and the *Del Greco, Iseo,* and *Ankara* convoys. It also mentioned that another convoy would be at sea that day. This was the *Monginevro* convoy, itself the subject of Ultra messages, although nothing specifically identified route or departure date. In total, these sailings and their escorts were the subject of twenty-one separate dispatches, and while the operation was delayed one day from the time given in the 1215/11th message, the late start enabled commanders to pre-position their submarines; it also proved critical in frustrating the operation.[35]

The destroyer *Antonio Da Noli* in 1942. She belonged to the *Navigatori* class of *esploratori*, a type of large destroyer constructed in the 1920s and envisioned as an intermediate between destroyers and light cruisers. She was rerated as a destroyer in 1938. The class saw hard usage during the war, and all twelve of the *Navigatoris* were sunk but one. The Germans sank *Da Noli* on 9 September 1943. E. Bagnasco

Driven by this tide of intelligence, Force C (Rear Admiral Philip Vian), with light cruisers *Naiad, Galatea,* and *Euryalus* and nine destroyers, left Alexandria after dark 13 December. Vian, who had led a destroyer flotilla in a night action against *Bismarck* and a cruiser force against a German convoy off Norway in September 1941, had assumed command of the 15th Cruiser Squadron on 1 November. *Abdiel* sailed for Haifa to generate radio traffic "giving the impression of the battlefleet being at sea." Forces K and B planned to sortie from Malta, but this proved unnecessary. *Utmost, Upright,* and *Unbeaten* patrolled south of Taranto. At 1034/12th the commander of the 10th Submarine Flotilla ordered them north, advising that "heavy unit may leave Taranto a.m./13 proceeding south." *Urge* and *Unique* were off Messina; *Upholder* and *Sokol* left Malta and rushed to join *P31* and *P34* and establish a patrol line in the southern Ionian Sea; *Truant* guarded Argostoli and *Torbay* Naravino; and *Perseus, Talisman,* and *Porpoise* were all west of Crete. *Perseus* and *Porpoise,* due to return to Alexandria, remained at sea.[36]

M41's first losses occurred at the very start of the operation, when *Utmost* and *Upright* ambushed the *Del Greco* convoy fifteen miles south of Taranto at 0130/13th. *Utmost* discharged four torpedoes from long range and missed, while at 0207 *Upright* launched four from 4,500 yards and hit *Del Greco* twice and *Filzi* twice just when the convoy was changing formation in preparation for entering the port. Both ships sank. *Da Recco* saved 432 of the 649 men on board while *Usodimare* hunted *Upright,* dropping 51 depth charges in a counterattack that lasted 8 hours, according to *Upright*'s account. The explosions distorted the submarine's pressure hull, but she continued her patrol. The Italian wiretap on the German naval attaché's phone line overheard his complaint to the Admiralty in Berlin that it was a disgrace (*schweinerei*) that the Italians could not protect a convoy right outside their port.[37]

On the late afternoon of the 13th Supermarina intercepted radio traffic that led it to conclude that a British force, including three battleships and cruisers, was at sea between Mersa Matruh and Tobruk, heading west (the Axis did not discover that *Barham* had been sunk until 8 January), and at 2000/13th it canceled M41. Although the Italians had more battleships, two of these were older vessels with smaller guns, and Supermarina considered that the lack of air cover and the possibility of a night engagement negated its apparent superiority.[38]

At 1530/13th *Iseo* and *Capo Orso* departed Argostoli. The commander of the British 1st Submarine Flotilla was broadcasting this information to his boats within two hours. At 2250, following Supermarina's order to suspend the operation, the freighters reversed course. However, during this maneuver *Iseo* collided with *Capo Orso*. Both ships were heavily damaged and did not make Argostoli until 0900/14th.[39]

As the various forces returned to harbor, *Urge* torpedoed *Vittorio Veneto* at 0858/14th off Cape dell'Armi, near the southern entrance to the Messina Straits—even though the battleship's escort had been reinforced by the torpedo boats *Clio* and *Centauro* and six aircraft. *Urge* scored with a single torpedo to *Vittorio Veneto's* port side abreast the no. 3 turret. *Littorio* spotted tracks at the last moment and dodged the streaking menace. *Vittorio Veneto* took on three thousand tons of water, but her engines and stability were unaffected and she continued to Taranto. She entered dock on 1 January and was under repair until early March.[40]

Ultra message MK 811 of 0205Z/14th disclosed that the *Ankara* and *Pisani* convoys had turned around. This caused Vice Admiral Ford to radio Alexandria at 1128/14th: "In view of M.K. 811 do you wish Malta force to sail?" The Ultra narrative states that it was expressly prohibited to refer to this top-secret traffic; nonetheless during this period signals such as this, which were subject to interception and decryption, made scattered references to Ultra. In the event, Force K and Force B stayed in port.[41]

A mass operation supported by nearly the entire Italian fleet had failed—foiled by two well-placed submarines. The only recompense for the Axis came as the British squadrons returned to base. At 2359/14th while just thirty miles short of Alexandria the German submarine *U557* torpedoed and sank *Galatea*. The cruiser capsized very quickly. *Griffin* and *Hotspur* rescued 144 men, including Admiral Vian, but there were 470 casualties.

The Regia Marina Hits Bottom

In retrospect, 13 December marked the nadir of Italian fortunes. Riccardi told Cavallero about the losses of the cruisers and two merchant ships. He said the only solution was to open Bizerte to Axis shipping and to assault Gibraltar.[42] The next day Riccardi, Rear Admiral Weichold, and air force representatives met to consider the situation. They recommended three steps—compiling new guidelines for maritime reconnaissance; reviewing the methods of communicating sighting signals between Italian authorities and the German X Air Corps operating in the Mediterranean; and improving liaison and communication between Supermarina, Superaereo (the air force command), and OBS (Oberbefehlshaber Süd), the German high command in the Mediterranean.[43]

Such procedural matters addressed significant problems in the Axis system and were critical for long-term success, but they skirted the real dilemma—that the Axis forces (primarily the Italian navy, supported by the Italian air force, the German air force, and German submarines) had lost control of the central Mediterranean. This was the problem that needed solving, and the navy was getting discouraged. On 15 December Riccardi submitted a memorandum to Comando Supremo entitled "Traffic with Libya." It reviewed the situation and the Operation M41 debacle and concluded, "As things stand and until air superiority can be regained from Sicily and Crete, we can no longer continue, except in exceptional occasions, the traffic with Libya other than with submarines, destroyers and air transport. Otherwise we run the risk of losing the Fleet, without effectively aiding Libya."[44]

The memorandum warned the government that, under current conditions, continuing to use the navy in the battle of the convoys would render the navy incapable of meeting what Riccardi and Iachino saw as its real duty—that of winning a fleet action. That they even submitted this memorandum showed how dire the situation had become. Informants in the service were telling Cavallero that the navy was in grave crisis and "that it was absolutely necessary for a shake up to recover our will to fight the enemy's tactics and materials." He discussed this with Mussolini on the 14th.[45]

Meanwhile, the only solution was to make even greater efforts, although given the damage to the *Vittorio Veneto*, the scale of protection accorded M41 was no longer possible. Ultimately, it was the Italian government's decision, with the Germans a very interested outside party. Through the

middle of December the Regia Marina fought the traffic war under conditions that favored the British. The Axis powers did not realize the extent
to which their radio communications were being compromised. This gave
British air and submarine forces a better chance of engaging targets under
favorable conditions in the wide waters of the central Mediterranean. The
Regia Marina's lack of appropriate doctrine and training, not to mention
radar, had made its surface units virtually helpless against inferior British
forces in night actions, as demonstrated by the Beta Convoy and Cape Bon
actions. The Italian navy had not lost its taste for fighting the enemy, but
it had lost its taste for fighting at a disadvantage. The solution was for it
to win a victory that would change the dynamics of the traffic war. The
Regia Marina needed to fight under its terms. It needed to win a victory
that would nullify the British surface warfare advantage and restore the
confidence of the government, the high command, and the Germans. On
the nights of 17/18 and 18/19 December it won three such victories, and
these transformed the dynamics of the naval war in the central Mediterranean—literally overnight.

Chapter 6

Sudden Victories

When the strike of a hawk breaks the body of its prey, it is because of timing.

SUN TZU (92)

On 15 December 1941 the Italo-German army retreated from Gazala. In the growing crisis, Cavallero flew to Africa and met with Kesselring and Rommel on the 17th. Rommel said he would obey Mussolini's instructions to hold the Libyan port city of Derna, but his troops had only two days' supply of ammunition. If the British struck toward El Mechili, he would retreat to Agedabia to protect Tripolitania.[1]

Fuel was another pressing problem. On the 15th the German air force in Libya had just 103 tons of fuel on hand. Kesselring considered air transport the safest method of delivering more; on the 14th, however, the 37 operational Ju.52s delivered 68 tons—less than the 89 tons consumed by the 116 operational fighters and bombers. Italian transport aircraft delivered 3,728 men and 234 tons of materiel in November and 1,170 men and 835 tons in December. Such totals could not sustain routine air operations, much less an army, and the Axis faced defeat unless the Italian navy could force a major convoy through to Tripoli.[2]

Operation MF1

The British also experienced supply problems, particularly in Malta, where there was no longer sufficient fuel to maintain surface operations.

101

To replenish the island's fuel reserves, Admiral Cunningham decided to take advantage of the recent Italian defeat and rush a supply ship to the island. As he wrote, "it was thought that [the supply ship] *Breconshire* could be got through to Malta before the enemy had re-organized sufficiently to intercept with surface forces or sail the Libyan convoys again." He undertook this action even though Ultra had warned on the evening of the 15th that "there are strong indications [of a] fresh attempt to run ships to Africa." Bletchley Park subsequently criticized the admiral's decision: "C. in C. Mediterranean had been informed currently and in detail of the preparation, postponement and eventual launching of the Italian convoy operation, so that it is difficult in the extreme to comprehend why this moment was chosen for the passage of *Breconshire* to Malta."[3] In any case, the ship, loaded with 5,000 tons of fuel oil, departed Alexandria at 2200/15th. Her escort included Vian's 15th Squadron, the light cruisers *Naiad* and *Euryalus*, the anti-aircraft cruiser *Carlisle*, and Captain Philip Mack's 14th Flotilla (*Jervis, Kimberley, Kingston, Havock, Hasty, Kipling, Decoy,* and *Nizam*). To meet *Breconshire*, the 4th Flotilla (*Sikh, Legion, Maori,* and *Isaac Sweers*) and then Force K (*Aurora, Penelope, Lance,* and *Lively*) departed Malta at 1100/16th and 1800/16th respectively. The 4th Flotilla was to return to Alexandria with Vian after he had delivered *Breconshire* to Force K. *Decoy*, which had collided with a merchant ship in Alexandria and damaged her own bow, was to continue to Malta for repairs. Force B, consisting of *Neptune* and two destroyers, remained at Malta to conserve fuel. Thus, the British and Italians dispatched fleets on intersecting courses within hours of each other.[4]

Shortly after getting underway *Breconshire* suffered a breakdown. *Carlisle* stood by while the supply ship made repairs, and the pair rejoined Vian at 0750/16th. To make up for lost time, Vian steered a straight course, while Axis aircraft flying to Africa periodically passed overhead. The British had fighter cover, but as Vian reported, "these contacts were made at too great a range for successful action by our fighters." Seeking to evade the Axis planes, at dusk the convoy turned south to suggest that its destination was Tobruk. Indeed, the force had been reported by Axis intelligence several times, most recently at 1505, when it was described as comprising three battleships, three cruisers, and four destroyers and was

The British *Tribal*-class destroyer *Sikh* entering Malta on 13 December 1941 fresh from her victory in the Battle of Cape Bon. She also participated in the First and Second Battles of Sirte and the January and February convoy actions. E. Bagnasco, *Guerra sul Mare*

86 miles north-northwest of Mersa Matruh. Later reports clarified that there appeared to be one enemy battleship at sea, while two battleships were at their usual berths in Alexandria.[5]

During the day Ultra messages regarding the transports gathered in Taranto streamed in, but Bletchley Park generated the best indicator of their departure at 1220Z/16th. "Two convoys will leave Taranto sometime this morning and will remain in company until tomorrow evening, seventeenth." However, it added, "Nothing further is known about the extent of the naval forces providing cover." Confirmation of a strong escort arrived eight hours later. "The group which is to meet *Duilio* as above may either be *Doria* Group or *Gorizia* Group or even *Littorio* Group."[6] *Utmost* and *Unbeaten* reported "large number of destroyers, possibly heavy ships" in the Gulf of Taranto at 2245 and 2258/16th. This was followed at 0040/17th by an aerial sighting of two large ships. By 0825/17th reconnaissance had distilled the Italian force to three battleships and seven destroyers, although the position reported was forty miles southeast of their actual location.[7]

Given these changed circumstances, at 1729/16th Cunningham ordered
Vian to stay with *Breconshire* and to seek the enemy convoy after assuring
the transport's safe arrival. Wasting no time, Vian ordered *Carlisle*, *Kingston*, and *Hasty* to return to Alexandria—*Carlisle* because she was too slow,
Kingston because she had developed defects, and *Hasty* as escort. The news
that the Italian battlefleet was at sea also prompted Force B—*Neptune*,
with *Jaguar* and *Kandahar*—to leave Malta at 1500/17th. Cunningham
remained in Alexandria with *Queen Elizabeth* and *Valiant* because there
were no fleet destroyers to screen the battleships.

The night of 16/17 December passed peacefully for the British force,
but the first Axis reconnaissance aircraft appeared overhead at 0625/17th.
At 0800 Vian spotted Force K and the 4th Destroyer Flotilla. He was
roughly two hours behind schedule. The combined formation proceeded
west at 16 knots, with *Naiad*, *Euryalus*, and the 14th Flotilla screening
ahead of *Breconshire* in a "V" shaped formation. The Malta contingent
followed, with the two cruisers off the port quarter and the six destroyers
to starboard. Vian planned that if surface contact seemed imminent, he
would order *Breconshire*, accompanied by *Decoy* and *Havock*, to jog south
and then turn for Malta, while the rest of his force confronted the enemy.

Vian reported that all morning long there were never fewer than two
(and sometimes as many as six) Axis aircraft circling overhead. The
first strike developed at 1255/17th, when the British were two hundred
miles north of Benghazi. Over the next five and a half hours, the rear
admiral estimated that twenty-five torpedo bombers and about ten high-
level bombers attacked his ships. Six times he changed course to dodge
torpedoes. In fact, he faced six Italian S.79 torpedo bombers, six He.111
torpedo bombers, and thirty-seven Ju.88s. A German pilot reported a
heavy cruiser torpedoed at 1349. He observed "a jet of flames." The Axis
aviators also claimed they torpedoed a cruiser or destroyer at 1435 and
near-missed two cruisers and a destroyer. The Italians struck in waves
of three at midday and dusk. They reported having torpedoed a cruiser
and an undetermined vessel. In fact, only *Kipling* was damaged, superficially, when four bombs fell eighty yards off her port side. Nonetheless, at
1735 Vian signaled Cunningham: "Scale of attack has become heavy and
expenditure of ammunition high." A *Jervis* midshipman expressed it more

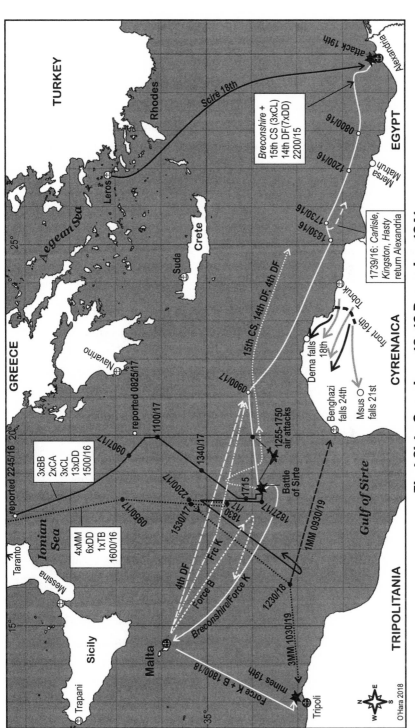

Map 6.1. **First Sirte Overview, 16–19 December 1941**

vividly: "Spent bullets and shell fragments pattered down on the decks and made the sea boil around us while great fountains of smoke capped spray rose into the air as bombs fell wide of their marks."[8]

Vian received an 1122 air report that placed three battleships, two cruisers, and seven destroyers 120 miles north of his position. Having heard nothing more, he turned west by southwest at 1400. At 1630 aircraft warned of fourteen warships sixty-five miles north steering east by south. This sighting led Vian to conclude the enemy would be sixty miles away by dark.[9]

Operation M42

Italy's next major convoy, Operation M42, got underway as soon as the escorts and undamaged merchantmen from M41 could refuel. It had five components:

- Convoy L: *Monginevro, Napoli, Vettor Pisani*; cargo 7,012 tons of materiel, 2,941 tons of fuel and oil, 792 tons of munitions, 192 vehicles including 23 tanks. Direct escort: 14th Squadron/Commodore Amedeo Nomis di Pollone (*Vivaldi, Da Noli, Malocello*), 16th Squadron (*Da Recco, Pessagno, Zeno*). Sailed Taranto 1600/16th destination Tripoli.
- Convoy N: *Ankara*; cargo 3,397 tons of materiel, 345 tons of munitions, 283 tons of oil, and 120 vehicles including 21 tanks. Escort: destroyer *Saetta*, torpedo boat *Pegaso*. Sailed Taranto 1500/16th destination Benghazi.
- Support group: (Vice Admiral Carlo Bergamini) *Duilio*; 7th Division/ Rear Admiral De Courten (*Duca D'Aosta, Attendolo, Montecuccoli*); 11th Squadron (*Aviere, Ascari, Camicia Nera*). Sailed Taranto 1500/16th.
- Heavy support group: (Vice Admiral Iachino) *Littorio, Doria, Cesare*; 13th Squadron (*Granatiere, Bersagliere, Fuciliere, Alpino*); 12th Squadron (*Corazziere, Carabiniere, Usodimare*). Sailed Taranto 1500/16th.
- Scout Group: 3rd Division/Rear Admiral Angelo Parona (*Gorizia, Trento*); 10th Squadron (*Maestrale, Oriani, Gioberti*). Departed Taranto 1500/16th.

At 0800/17th the convoy and close escort were 270 miles east-northeast of Malta. Iachino was roughly sixty miles east of the convoy, with Parona ten miles ahead of him. At 1000, still lacking solid intelligence of the enemy, Iachino ordered *Gorizia* to launch an Ro.43 seaplane to scout ahead. The cruisers and battleships were equipped with this single-engine float plane. The aircraft entered service in 1938 but had several limitations; its endurance was only five hours at 97 knots, and it could not be recovered at sea.[10]

Gorizia's pilot saw nothing and landed at Navarino. At 1024, however, Iachino received word of a battleship, two cruisers, and twelve destroyers steering west at 20 knots. He turned south and then, at 1100, southwest. At 1142 *Littorio* launched an Ro.43 to develop this sighting. By this time, however, the situation had grown obscure. German and Italian air force spotters furnished a flurry of reports that Iachino characterized as "too vague and imprecise to clarify the situation."[11] Then, further confusing the matter, at 1253 *Littorio*'s aircraft, which the admiral trusted the most, misidentified an Italian hospital ship as a British battleship heading north by northwest. It corrected this error twenty-four minutes later. Finally, at 1345 the spotter radioed that the enemy force, consisting of a battleship, four cruisers, and thirteen destroyers, was steering northwest at 22 knots. By 1415 Iachino was pressing forward at 24 knots, *Cesare*'s maximum speed. Then, at 1416, the same plane reported the enemy's course as due west. From this Iachino concluded it would be impossible to intercept before dark. He could have pushed ahead without the slower battleships but elected to keep his force concentrated and continued southwest with the 3rd Division ten miles ahead.[12]

Littorio launched another spotter at 1445, when the first one had to break off, and at 1530 it reported the enemy in a closer position, heading west at 18 knots. This renewed Iachino's hopes of making contact; then, fifteen minutes later, *Oriani* spotted smoke on the horizon. The Italian fleet came to battle stations. *Oriani*'s report proved false, but Iachino pressed on, expecting to encounter the enemy 30 degrees off *Littorio*'s port bow. Then, at 1640 *Littorio*'s Ro.43 reported that the British were now heading due south and had increased speed to 20 knots. This was the last report before the aircraft headed for Benghazi. Iachino concluded that the British had learned of his approach and were avoiding combat. With sunset

Italian battleship *Andrea Doria* on the afternoon of 17 December 1941. *Doria* was a reconstructed dreadnought, originally launched in 1913 and inferior to the reconstructed "superdreadnoughts" of the *Queen Elizabeth* class in all but speed. She participated in several of the battleship convoys as well as in the First Battle of Sirte. E. BAGNASCO, *GUERRA SUL MARE*

just an hour off, contact again seemed impossible. At 1650 he slowed to 20 knots. At 1700 the flagship received an SIS message that enemy aircraft had reported his position, so Iachino decided to reverse course after dark to complicate efforts to find him. This was the situation at 1724, when lookouts spotted smoke from an antiaircraft barrage bursting off the port beam. The Italian formation accelerated to 24 knots, and at 1727 turned east on a line-of-bearing to close the range. Five minutes later *Trento*, 5,000 meters south-southeast of the battleships, spotted enemy ships fine off her port bow. *Maestrale* reported the same at 1740 and, finally, at 1745, just as the sun was setting behind them, lookouts on *Littorio* saw hulls against the darker eastern horizon bearing 120 degrees, distance 35,000 meters. The wind was blowing at Force 2 and there was a slight sea.[13]

The First Battle of Sirte, 17 December 1941

The British warships were dodging bombs when, at 1742, *Naiad* reported masts bearing 300 degrees, range seventeen miles. On board *Decoy* one officer thought it was Force B arriving. "We had been receiving reports all day of a strong Italian battle squadron at sea," he wrote, "but as the last position given for this force was some eighty miles to the north of us there seemed no danger . . . so we examined [these ships] with interest but without excitement . . . As we watched, however, more masts appeared, among them the unmistakable control tower of an Italian eight-inch gun cruiser . . . [T]here was a dim red glow from the leading Italian, like a cigarette end as the smoker draws on it in the dark and then a bunch of tall thin splashes came up round us." This surprise encounter scandalized the GC&CS, which felt that its work was not being properly used. "That the 15th Cruiser Squadron should have been exposed to the hazard of an unexpected collision with the Italian Battle Fleet is also extraordinary," its historian complained. "This can hardly be taken . . . as a classical instance of the application of Special Intelligence."[14]

At 1745 Iachino ordered the battleships to come right 90 degrees and assume a line of file heading due south. With the light rapidly draining from the sky, he wanted to bring as many guns to bear as soon as possible despite the range.[15]

Vian turned south at roughly the same time. *Breconshire* left the formation attended by *Decoy* and *Havock* and continued south at 16 knots while, as noted in Vian's terse report, "15th Cruiser Squadron, Force K, 14th and 4th Destroyer Flotillas moved out toward the enemy." He does not say when he moved toward the enemy, but the British track chart would make it roughly 1748. Italian observations suggest it was later. For example, *Trento* reported: "[At 1752] there was a sighting of enemy destroyers following course 200–220 degrees. . . . At 1755 they came to starboard and headed around to the north on a reciprocal course. The two lead destroyers started laying a smokescreen which proceeded to hide all the destroyers."[16]

At 1754 *Doria* opened fire, followed by *Littorio* a minute later. Iachino ordered each ship to engage her opposite. *Doria* reported that she took a cruiser, the second ship in the enemy formation, whereas *Littorio* targeted what she believed was the enemy battleship, which, if *Breconshire*, would

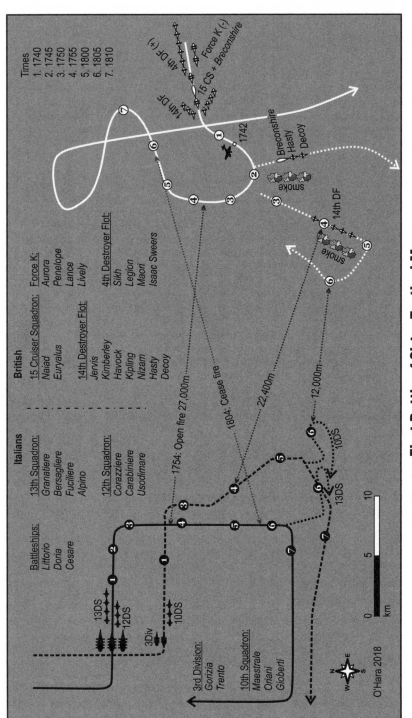

Italians

Battleships:
Littorio
Doria
Cesare

13th Squadron:
Granatiere
Bersagliere
Fuciliere
Alpino

12th Squadron:
Corazziere
Carabiniere
Usodimare

3rd Division:
Gorizia
Trento

10th Squadron:
Maestrale
Oriani
Gioberti

British

15 Cruiser Squadron:
Naiad
Euryalus

14th Destroyer Flot:
Jervis
Kimberley
Havock
Kipling
Nizam
Hasty
Decoy

Force K:
Aurora
Penelope
Lance
Lively

4th Destroyer Flot:
Sikh
Legion
Maori
Isaac Sweers

Times
1. 1740
2. 1745
3. 1750
4. 1755
5. 1800
6. 1805
7. 1810

1754: Open fire 27,000m

1804: Cease fire

22,400m

12,000m

O'Hara 2018

km
0   5   10

Map 6.2. **First Battle of Sirte, Tactical Map**

also have been the second ship. *Littorio* put the range as 32,000 meters, *Doria* at 28,000 meters, while the British had it at 29,000 yards (26,517 meters).[17] In all cases, these were the longest-range opening salvoes fired during the war using optical sights. *Cesare* never used her main battery because vibration confused her rangefinder. Despite the prodigious distance Vian reported that "The fire was accurate."[18] An observer on *Nizam* agreed. "The shell made a 'whoo-ah, whoo-ah' type of roar as it passed over *Nizam*, and exploded with a violent crash 50 yards off the starboard bow. Another geyser of water erupted beside *Kipling* and two more rose close to *Euryalus*." A midshipman in *Jervis* remembered, "we came under unpleasantly accurate fire from the main armament of their battleship for a while." At 1755 *Gorizia* engaged the nearest destroyer from 22,400 meters. *Gorizia* reported a hit and that her target broke in two. In fact, an 8-inch shell burst short 10 yards abreast *Kipling*'s starboard torpedo tubes. Splinters pierced the destroyer's hull, tore away the main wireless antennas, and killed one man.[19]

The British cruisers were out of range but returned fire until a final series of air strikes interfered. Vian complained that "movements were hampered by a well executed attack delivered by the Torpedo Bombers; one torpedo was released within 500 yards of the 15th Cruiser squadron, and three close to the 4th Destroyer Flotilla." His ships scattered as they twisted to avoid the torpedoes. Meanwhile, Captain Mack in *Jervis* pulled ahead, followed by the rest of the 14th Flotilla. *Littorio*'s radio intelligence section intercepted orders for a destroyer attack, so at 1802 Iachino sent his destroyers to counterattack. The 10th Squadron, closest to the enemy, hauled out to the northeast followed by the 13th Flotilla. Although Vian recalled Mack at 1757, the Italians kept coming, closing to within 4.7-inch range. *Maestrale* claimed that she had hit a destroyer. This may have been *Nizam*. The Australian recorded three straddles, but not the type of shell.[20]

Iachino recalled his destroyers when it became clear that the British had turned back. He later described the scene: "To the east, where gathering shadows of night loomed between the vast whitish patches of artificial fog, could be glimpsed the silhouettes of enemy ships, punctuated at times by the flames of guns. Close to us, and more clearly, we could see the English destroyers approaching at great speed, with long trails of mist, and shooting

with their forward guns." However, with twilight ending at 1809, night was
at hand. The Italian ships, one by one, fell silent—*Doria* at 1759, *Littorio* at
1804, *Trento* at 1806, and *Cesare*, which had targeted the British destroyers,
at 1807. *Doria* noted that she saw the 13th Squadron engaging the enemy as
late as 1810. During the short action *Littorio* expended twenty-seven 15-inch
rounds, *Doria* thirteen 12.6-inch, *Cesare* an unspecified number of 4.7-inch,
Gorizia fifty-eight 8-inch, and *Trento* thirty-two 8-inch shells.[21]

At 1807 Iachino ordered a 90-degree turn to starboard from south to
west. He judged that the British, given their radar and superior doctrine, held
the advantage after dark and that it was time to think about protecting the
convoy, but the British were too disorganized to counterattack. Vian wrote:
"By dark I had lost touch not only with the enemy, but with the majority
of the forces acting with me." At 1805 he encountered *Aurora* and ordered
Agnew to escort *Breconshire* to Malta with Force K. Agnew took off south
and west and located *Breconshire* at 1841. Along with *Decoy* and *Havock*,
he continued southwest and then due west at 1900. Although Cunningham
had ordered Force K to "deal with the Tripoli portion of the enemy convoy,"
Agnew reported, "in view of the close proximity of enemy heavy warships
I decided to remain with the 'Breckonshire' [*sic*] steering to the westward."
During the night *Aurora* intercepted signals from an ASV Wellington, but
they did not indicate an enemy force within striking distance.[22]

Force B fruitlessly cast about for targets and then joined Force K at
0750/18th. Hurricanes appeared at 0940 and repelled an incursion by three
S.79s and three Ju.88s that developed at 1120. *Breconshire* made Malta at
1500/18th without further incident.

At 1905/17th Vian began concentrating his scattered squadron. At 2330
it started north in three columns along the anticipated track of the convoy
believed heading for Benghazi. After four hours, having sighted nothing,
Vian turned for Alexandria at high speed. There was a moment of anxiety
at 0843/18th when an aircraft reported the Italian battlefleet just twenty
miles away. Vian increased speed to 29 knots to avoid contact, but then
learned that the aircraft's pilot was reporting his own force in a wrong
position. The British made port at 0100/19th.[23]

Many English-language accounts trumpeted the First Battle of Sirte as
a British victory. For example: "Undaunted by the disparity in strength, the

British cruisers and destroyers moved in to attack, [but the Italians] soon drew off to the north." Yet, Italians also hailed it as a victory: "It was one of the three or four turning points of the war for Italy . . . [T]he route to Libya, red with the blood of Italian sailors, could now be considered open again." Indeed, even Berlin bestowed stiff praise: "It is highly commendable that the [Italian] commander . . . took the risk of proceeding in the darkness in spite of contact with the enemy, so as to complete the mission." The GC&CS assessment cut to the core: "The salient fact remained that the blockade had been broken." Supermarina was pleased by the day's events, but better was to come.[24]

Iachino turned north at 1828/17th. At 2200 the convoy, which had been sailing north since 1830, turned southwest. Iachino was not concerned with Force B, which the submarine *Squalo* had sighted at 1845/17th heading southeast. He believed that *Duilio* and the *Aosta* division were "more than sufficient to repel the attack of two cruisers." Instead, "the major uncertainty was the movements of the enemy formation we had been in tactical contact with." He considered the real threat to be the possibility of night torpedo attacks by its dozen destroyers. His solution was to put his five large units in a line of file and sail them at 18 knots, first southwest and then northeast back and forth parallel to and east of the convoy's route. He deployed the destroyer squadrons to prevent a surprise foray from the southwest and screen the heavy units.[25]

The Italians heard a reconnaissance aircraft shortly after 2000 but held fire. The plane circled at low altitude and flashed a recognition signal at *Littorio*. It finally established that the ships were the enemy by illuminating them. After that the plane stayed high and reported to Malta. Other spotters signaled at 0053/18th and 0110/18th. The SIS intercepted their reports and informed Iachino in near-real time. The Italian formation executed a brief turnabout to make it more difficult for incoming bombers to find it, but reported later that "to our amazement we were never the subject of air attack during this long, endless night." The only negative event was a serious collision between *Granatiere* and *Corazziere*; both destroyers lost their bows. *Gioberti* towed *Granatiere* into Benghazi, and *Oriani* brought *Corazziere* into Navarino.[26]

By 1230 the Italian convoys had entered the Gulf of Sirte, 150 miles east of Tripoli and 205 miles west northwest of Benghazi. Here they separated.

The cruisers turned for home. *Ankara*, escorted by *Saetta* and *Pegaso*, headed southeast for Benghazi, and Convoy L sailed west for Tripoli in three groups, each three miles apart. *Pisani*, with *Vivaldi* and *Pessagno*, led the convoy, followed by *Monginevro* with *Da Recco* and *Malocello*, and tailed by *Napoli* with *Da Noli* and *Zeno*.

Crossing the 100-Fathom Line

At 1345/18th Vice Admiral Ford queried Cunningham on whether he thought forces B and K should intercept the convoy off Tripoli at around 0200/19th. When Ford sent this signal, his best information put the enemy fleet as two battleships, five cruisers, sixteen destroyers, and four motor vessels, 165 miles east by east-northeast of Tripoli. At 1430 a message indicated that the battleships were withdrawing and another at 1514 clarified that three cruisers, six destroyers, and three transports were on course for Tripoli. From this Ford judged that the odds forces B and K would face in a surface engagement had vastly improved, and he ordered *Neptune's* captain, Rory O'Conor, to lead the strike force and intercept. He also arranged for a series of air strikes by Albacores, Swordfish, and Wellingtons. At 1655 Ford advised Alexandria: "Intend torpedo bombers attacking at about 2300B. All available surface forces leaving Malta 1800B and attack about 0200B tomorrow. Special Wellington co-operating. Wellingtons will be mining entrance to Tripoli."[27]

This message crossed Cunningham's 1653 reply to Ford's 1345 message. The commander in chief wrote: "Torpedo bombers only, odds are too heavy for the cruisers." However, Cunningham withdrew his veto at 1809 after he received Ford's 1655 message. *Neptune*, *Aurora*, and *Penelope*, with *Kandahar*, *Lance*, *Havock*, and *Lively* had already weighed anchor, and by 1830 they were at sea to strike the transports nearing Tripoli.[28]

First, six Albacores lifted off. One aborted due to engine problems and the others struck between 2150 and 2217. An Italian account stated: "At 2200 . . . the attack started with the dropping of a single illuminating flare and our steamships, already distant one from the other, tried to hide themselves in a smoke screen. The aircraft attacked equally the two groups furthest astern and succeeded in striking the steamer *Napoli*, which, however, was able to reach Tripoli." In fact, three planes struck the rear formation. A torpedo clipped *Napoli* astern and disabled her rudder. The ship was otherwise unharmed, but while maneuvering *Zeno* plunged through the smoke and collided with *Napoli* forward. *Napoli*'s damage was superficial, but *Zeno* required ten days in dock before she could return to Italy. The other Albacores went against *Monginevro*, but *Da Recco* shot down the flight leader, and another's torpedo missed. The Albacores claimed two ships hit. By this time the weather was deteriorating and strong headwinds prevented five Swordfish dispatched later from reaching their target.[29]

Six Wellingtons raided Tripoli. Three bombed the town while the others scattered six mines around the harbor entrance. Fourteen Wellingtons had been slotted to participate, but a bombing raid on Luqa Airfield kept them grounded. Malta dispatched this information to Force B at 0132/19th, along with the results of a 2210/18th sighting report of two cruisers, three destroyers, and one merchant ship reported 54 miles east of Tripoli. Unfortunately for Captain O'Conor, events had outrun the news.[30]

Forces B and K headed south at 30 knots. By 0100/19th they were 21 miles north-northeast of Tripoli steaming in line ahead. The wind was blowing Force 5 from the southwest with intermittent rain. The sea was rising. They crossed the hundred-fathom line, still in safe waters according to their best information. *Penelope* was operating her echo-sounder to monitor the depth. The formation slowed to 24 knots at 0104 and was preparing to sweep east along the coast. Suddenly *Penelope*'s bridge watch spotted the glow of an explosion at the head of the line. The time was 0106. *Neptune* had detonated a mine on her port side aft. *Aurora* sheared off to starboard, but a minute later she was jolted by "a heavy explosion on the port side." She went down by the bow and took on an 11-degree list. Although the cruiser corrected with counterflooding, the explosion disabled her A and B turrets and severely buckled her hull. *Penelope*'s captain, Angus D. Nicholl, originally believed both ships had been torpedoed. Then "at 0110 there was an explosion abreast the bridge port side, and I realised that we were in a minefield." *Penelope* was streaming paravanes, so the mine only caused structural damage that cost her a month in dock. *Kandahar*, leading the destroyers, turned to port away from danger and then sailed back to the south.[31]

Mines, laid by aircraft, submarines, and from surface ships—silent and indiscriminate—were one of the major ship killers of World War II. Here Italian sailors are manhandling a P.200-type mine over the side. This had a weight of 2,535 pounds, a charge of 441 pounds, and a mooring cable as long as 2,670 feet. E. Bagnasco, *Guerra sul Mare*

At 0116 *Neptune* backed into two more mines, which destroyed her rudder and screws.[32] *Lively* reported that when "When *Neptune* was on the port quarter an explosion was heard and a flash seen on her stern . . . It was thought at first that she had opened fire with her after turrets, but almost immediately it was realized that she had either been mined or torpedoed." *Kandahar* saw a mine explode under *Neptune*'s stern, "blowing a portion of it off." She was three cables from *Neptune* and put the depth at 86 fathoms.[33]

Confusion followed as the ships communicated position and condition. At 0141 *Neptune* advised that she had no power and could not steer. At 0143 Captain Agnew signaled to *Penelope*: "I also am damaged and am returning to Malta. Do what you can for *Neptune* but keep clear of the minefield."[34] *Aurora* struggled back to Malta at 16 knots, escorted by *Lance* and *Havock*. Meanwhile, *Penelope* stood by to tow *Neptune* once she had drifted clear of the field.

Nicholl described his subsequent actions: "I decided that I must not close nearer than 2 1/2 miles until I had more information of the situation. I took my range from *Neptune* by R.D.F. and on closing to 2 1/2 miles patrolled at 9 knots up and down wind. I felt I was justified telling *Lively* to close *Neptune* in order to avoid signaling with bright lights, and in the meantime I hoisted in paravanes and got ready to tow aft. . . . As I was approaching *Neptune Kandahar* hit a mine and I decided that the risk of approaching in closer to *Neptune* must not be accepted. As I was turning away *Neptune* hit a fourth mine. I then took *Lively* under my orders and turned down his plea to be allowed to go to *Neptune* for survivors and started for Malta."[35]

Kandahar detonated the mine at 0318, and it blew off her stern. Her surgeon wrote: "The debris had come down a few seconds after the first crash sounding like all the Thunderbolts of Jove, as Depth Charges, Deck Plating, a Shell Hoist and every sort of solid object descended onto the ship from the height to which they had been hurled . . . [T]he ship rapidly took on a sixteen-degree list to starboard to the accompaniment of the port siren, which continued to wail crazily until the steam was shut off." The destroyer flooded up to the engine room bulkhead but was in no danger of sinking. Meanwhile, at 0400 *Neptune* staggered under a fourth explosion. At the time *Kandahar* was drifting about a mile north of the cruiser. Her captain recorded: "This last explosion caused her to turn over on her Port side and sink slowly."[36]

On *Neptune* only two Carley floats got away. Some men tried swimming to *Kandahar*, but no one made it. One float carried fifteen men and Captain O'Conor, but they died from exposure during the following days. On 24 December the Italian torpedo boat *Calliope* rescued the last man living. The other 762 died.

The deadly mine barrage was called Field D and consisted of 140 German-made EMC mines laid on 1 May 1941 by *Eugenio di Savoia*, *Duca d'Aosta*, and *Attendolo*. The cruisers placed four lines of mines off Tripoli (D, E, F, and I). These fields were unknown to the British. Because the mines were German manufactured and because the field was laid "according to the German specifications," the naval staff in Berlin called it a "gratifying success, which is after all German." Cavallero credited Weichold with the barrage's concept, but the Regia Marina laid the fields according to its own well-tested procedures.[37]

After a quick turnaround in Malta, *Jaguar* set out after dark on the 19th to rescue *Kandahar*'s men, homed in by an ASV-equipped Wellington that was tracking the eastward-drifting destroyer. *Jaguar* established contact at 0420/20th in deteriorating weather. Thirty men jumped from *Kandahar* to *Jaguar* when the destroyer approached bow to stern, but conditions forced *Jaguar* to stand off as the rest of the crew swam for it. *Jaguar* torpedoed the wreck at 0545. She failed to sink as expected, and *Jaguar* continued picking up swimmers until 0605, when she turned toward Malta at 28 knots. "Feared a few survivors not picked up owing to their being widely dispersed and observing ship was about fifteen miles from the Libyan coast and only one hour of darkness remaining." Seven of *Kandahar*'s men were indeed left behind.[38]

In its subsequent investigation, the Admiralty board of inquiry asked: "From plotting the course and speed of the enemy and our own Forces it would appear that there was small chance of interception: was this appreciated when these orders were given?" Ford's staff acknowledged that there had been little chance of interception, but the admiral hoped that an air strike timed for 0100 would scatter the convoy and that this, based on "previous experience and results of air attack on Italian convoys," would give "anything up to two hours delay . . . and allow surface forces to intercept."[39] This rings of hubris. It might be easy to consider the mining of forces B and K as an anomaly or bad luck, but in fact the Malta surface force had been courting risk for nearly two months. It had survived submarine and air attacks; it had dodged surface ship torpedoes and been near-missed by heavy shells. It was only a matter of time—as Admiral Pound knew when he ordered Force K to Malta—before one of the many threats that it faced routinely would exact a cost. The odds of calamity increased when the command ordered high-risk missions with small chance of success.

Ankara entered Benghazi at 0930/19th while the other three transports made Tripoli between 1000 and 1400/19th. The supplies that they carried transformed the ground war. Riccardi, whose job was on the line, received a phone call from Cavallero, who was "delighted by the brilliant action of the navy and by the arrival of the convoy." And this before the greatest success of all.[40]

Man Bites Battleship

The path to Italy's third naval victory won between 17 and 19 December showcased the nation's approach to sea power. In World War I the Italian navy had successfully conducted stealthy raids against Austro-Hungarian naval bases, using small units and special weapons, even sinking the dreadnought *Viribus Unitis* on 1 November 1918 with a two-man attack craft. When the prospect of war against Great Britain arose in 1935, a cadre of naval officers championed this precedent as a way to offset the British navy's battleship superiority. Mussolini and the Italian navy's chief of staff, Admiral Domenico Cavagnari, who himself had participated in a sneak operation against Pola harbor on 1 November 1916, endorsed these proposals and authorized the establishment of a commando-type specialized attack unit called Decima (X) Flottiglia MAS.[41]

The Regia Marina hoped to raid every major British Mediterranean naval base simultaneously on the war's first day before the enemy had any hint of the threat that it faced. However, Italy declared war before Decima MAS was ready. "Given the relative unreliability of the assault equipment and breathing equipment, insufficient numbers, and equipment worn out by intense training, it was not until 10 August . . . that the chief of staff ordered [the first operation]."[42] Instead of a simultaneous, potentially decisive blow, Mussolini's trust in a short war resulted in his commandos' being committed piecemeal and prematurely. The August 1940 effort to raid Alexandria with submarine-carried "manned torpedoes" (Siluro a Lenta Corsa, or SLCs) failed when Swordfish sank *Iride*, the carrier submarine, during a final test. The British sank a second carrier submarine, *Gondor*, as she was returning from an aborted mission in September 1940. On 30 October 1940 an effort against Gibraltar failed due to problems with the breathing apparatuses and the SLCs. In March 1941 Decima MAS achieved its first success, mortally damaging the heavy cruiser *York* and the Norwegian tanker *Pericles* (8,324 GRT) with explosive boats. Weapons and equipment defects scuttled efforts against Corfu in April 1941 and

Gibraltar on 27 May. A major effort against the recently arrived Substance convoy in Malta in July 1941 with SLCs, motor torpedo vessels, and explosive boats failed spectacularly because radar (on which the attackers had no intelligence) alerted the defenders as the force approached. On 20 September 1941 a strike by SLCs against Gibraltar sank two merchantmen and a tanker. This action finally validated the concept and set the stage for a far more important effort against Alexandria—a plan that was intended to neutralize the greatest instrument of sea power (the battleship) with the least (a frogman riding a self-propelled device).[43]

On 3 December the submarine *Scirè* departed Spezia on a purported training cruise. She rendezvoused offshore with a barge carrying three SLCs. The SLC was a motorized two-man sled with a detachable nose. Shaped like a torpedo, it measured twenty-six feet long and twenty-one inches in diameter. An electric motor gave it a range of fifteen miles at 2.3 knots and sprint speed of 3 knots. The nose contained 300-kg of explosives. *Scirè* proceeded to the Aegean base of Leros. En route a British patrol aircraft surprised the submarine on the surface. The Italian crew greeted the plane with large waves and the day's correct recognition signal. The aircraft reported, "A U-boat bearing 'GONDAR2' features was spotted South of CRETE. . . . This particular U-boat was challenged by the aircraft and answered with a green light signal which was the correct signal for the day; she was therefore not molested." The submarine knew the correct signal because the SIS was reading the Royal Navy tactical code that had been used to communicate such information. At Leros the SLC operators joined *Scirè*, and she headed for Alexandria on 14 December.[44]

The submarine arrived off the British base on 16 December, but reconnaissance could not confirm the presence of the battleships. The Italian Aegean air command reported, "The objective was completely covered by clouds, which prevented the aircraft . . . from taking the photographs and carrying out a visual reconnaissance. For the same reason the bombing operation which was arranged for tonight cannot take place." A dawn/17th flyover had better luck, and at 0954/17th the Aegean command signaled Rome that two battleships were in port; at 1234 it confirmed the actual moorings that the battleships were using as well as the fact that the sea was calm. GC&CS bundled these three interceptions into one message generated at 1745Z/17th that stated: "There are indications that an Italian raid intended last night . . . and abandoned because of weather . . . was to be carried out by aircraft of Aegean command." It also reported that "subsequent reconnaissance reports confirmed the presence of two battleships and a calm sea."[45] In this instance the GC&CS interpretation of the original signal was misleading because it specified that an air attack was intended, while the original signals referred only to an "*azione bombardamento*" or bombardment action, not a *bombardamento aereo* or air attack.[46] It did not mention that the Italians were researching specific berths which, taken with an interest in a calm sea, implied that the enemy was considering some other type of operation. As an internal GC&CS history noted, "complaints about Italian translations continued more or less until the Italian armistice." In this instance the CG&CS did not clearly communicate to the threatened point the nuances of the original message.[47]

The Admiralty, however, saw the other possibilities when it warned Cunningham on the afternoon of the 18th that "attacks on Alexandria by air, boat or human torpedo may be expected when calm weather conditions prevail." Frank Wade, a midshipman in *Queen Elizabeth*, recalled that the crew was mustered on the quarterdeck that evening and told to watch for anything suspicious. However, as he recalled, "The reaction in the mess was one of unconcern. How the devil did they think that they could penetrate a harbour as well protected and defended as this one was, with its very substantial entrance boom? We further consoled ourselves with thoughts of proverbial Italian inefficiency, and by ten o'clock had forgotten all about the matter."[48]

Meanwhile, after receiving the latest intelligence, *Scirè* launched the SLCs at 2030/18th. The six operators, riding their three sleds, set off on the surface along the Ras el Tin peninsula to the Alexandria harbor entrance more than six miles away. Their mission was to attach charges to the battleships timed to detonate at 0600. After this, they would scatter incendiary devices set to explode an hour later. The planners hoped that these would ignite drifting oil into a massive conflagration that would damage more shipping and shore facilities. The operators were then to sink their SLCs and make for shore. The submarine *Zaffiro* was to loiter off Rosetta some days hence to give them a chance to steal a small boat and reach her.

There was considerable traffic in and out of Alexandria on the night of 18–19 December. The boom was open from 2122 to 2359/18th so that the tug *Roysterer* could exit and help bring the damaged sloop *Flamingo* into the harbor. The SLCs reached the boom minutes later and saw a large motorboat patrolling and periodically dropping small explosive charges. Lieutenant Luigi Durand de la Penne, commander of the three crews, described this as "rather worrisome."[49] At 0024/19th, as De la Penne was inspecting the defenses, the navigational aids suddenly lit up and the

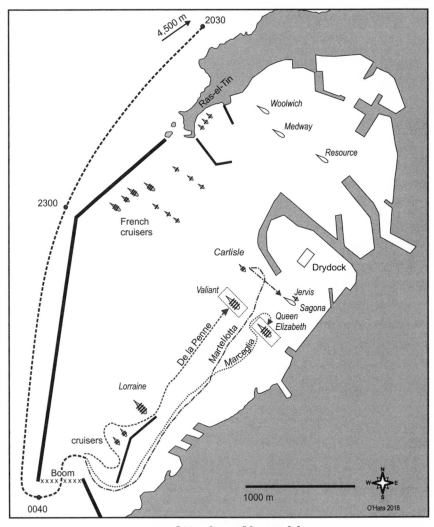

Map 6.3. **Attack on Alexandria**

boom opened again for *Naiad* and *Euryalus* and the destroyers *Sikh*, *Legion*, *Maori*, and *Isaac Sweers*, which were returning from the central Mediterranean. Although SLCs had twice penetrated Gibraltar's boom, De la Penne decided to seize this opportunity and slip in on the surface, despite being tossed about by bow waves as two destroyers passed nearby. The other SLCs—piloted by Captain (Naval Engineers) Antonio Marceglia and assigned to attack *Queen Elizabeth* and Captain (Naval Weapons) Vincenzo Martellotta, assigned to an aircraft carrier but, failing that, a large tanker—also had close calls. Martellotta passed within twenty meters of the patrol boat. Shocks from the explosive charges discomforted the three pilots, but did not deter them. Once inside, the SLCs separated.

Marceglia had to cover 2,200 meters to reach *Queen Elizabeth*. He passed between a line of cruisers and the shore navigating by landmarks such as the French battleship *Lorraine* and reached the net protecting his target. He found a gap and at 0300 plunged his SLC into the darkness. He wrote, "The balance of the device was awkward; the speed of fall increased as we descended, and I could not hold it with the rudders, perhaps because there was not enough forward thrust. I felt a sharp pain in the ear; finally, we touched bottom in 13 meters raising a cloud of mud."[50] From there Marceglia and his copilot detached the explosive charge and suspended it from the hull. There were a few mishaps. They fed air into their SLC to bring it up, but lost control, and it smashed into *Queen Elizabeth*'s hull. Then the copilot got sick (the copilots, occupying the rear seat, spent more time submerged, breathing through their apparatus). Marceglia, however, finished slinging the charge on a cable attached to the bilge keels. At 0325 he set the fuze. The two men escaped along the harbor bottom until Marceglia, concerned about the copilot's condition, surfaced. They scattered their explosive charges, scuttled their craft, and reached land at 0430 after eight hours in the water. They took the train to Rosetta, but police arrested them before they could rendezvous with *Zaffiro*.

Martellotta's SLC slipped between *Valiant* and *Queen Elizabeth*. After finding the carrier berth empty he saw what he believed to be a battleship but then concluded he was looking at a cruiser and that his target did not justify violating his orders. (In fact, the ship was *Carlisle*, whose pronounced control-top gave her a superficial resemblance to an R-class battleship.) He settled upon the large Norwegian oiler *Sagona* (7,554 GRT), although he would have preferred to have targeted the warship. Unable to submerge because of problems with his breathing apparatus, Martellotta held his craft near the ship's stern while the copilot fastened the explosive canister beneath her. He set the fuze at 0255. They then scattered explosive charges, scuttled the SLC, and swam ashore. Police arrested Martellotta and his copilot after they landed, and handed them to the British.

De la Penne's team also had problems. As he approached *Valiant* he encountered a net barrier hanging from a steel cable. After several tries he worked his SLC over the top. "The cable and net got tangled with the clamps and propeller and made a racket. Finally, the [SLC] broke free and I got back on board and headed for the ship's funnel."[51] De la Penne hurried because his rubber suit had torn, letting water leak in and body heat escape. It was about 0200. He submerged and bumped against *Valiant*'s hull, but lost control of the SLC, and it sank to the muddy bottom seventeen meters down. After assessing his position relative to the battleship, De la Penne unsuccessfully tried to start the craft's motor. When he turned to have his copilot check the propeller, he realized that he was alone. De la Penne pulled the SLC to bring it under the battleship's keel, but he made little progress before feeling the effects of breathing pure oxygen at too great a depth. He set the charge, surfaced, and discovered his copilot, who had fainted and inadvertently surfaced, clinging to the mooring buoy. They were noticed and captured a few minutes later. Luckily for the Italians, De la Penne's craft had sunk close enough to *Valiant* to act as a ground mine.

The British detained the two swimmers while an Italian-speaking officer boated over from *Queen Elizabeth*. Then *Valiant*'s skipper, Captain Charles Morgan, and the interpreter took them to the intelligence offices at Ras el Tin. Specialists interrogated the Italians and concluded that their mission had failed. Meanwhile, at 0332 or after, "a general signal was made that the presence of 'human torpedoes' in the harbor was suspected." The signal repeated instructions for patrol boats to drop explosive charges, "if required," and ordered tugs to raise steam. All ships were ordered to pass lines along their bottoms to snag any suspended charges.[52] In his memoirs, Cunningham states that he was wakened at about 0400 with news of the capture. "I at once ordered them to be brought back to the *Valiant* and confined in one of the forward compartments well below the waterline." Midshipman Wade remembered: "we were all rudely awakened at 0400 by the alarm rattlers buzzing us to action's stations and a bugler blowing the alarm." He saw Cunningham, who "had hastened up from his cabin in a raincoat over his pyjamas."[53]

Valiant passed a line along her hull, but because the charge was on the bottom, it encountered nothing. *Queen Elizabeth*'s line snagged, and the crew could not clear it, so the British failed to discover the charge. Both inspections occurred after De la Penne and his copilot had returned to *Valiant*. During this time the British never confiscated De la Penne's large wristwatch. Ten minutes before the blast, he asked to see Captain Morgan and told him his ship would be sinking soon. After the Italian refused to give more information, Morgan returned him below. De la Penne recorded that he heard the loudspeakers ordering the crew to abandon ship as he was returned to confinement.[54]

The charge under *Sagona* exploded at 0547 followed by the one under *Valiant* at 0606, and the third, below *Queen Elizabeth*, at 0610. De la Penne described the moment: "The vessel reared, with extreme violence. All the lights went out and the hold filled with smoke." The blast knocked him off his feet, and he injured his knee. His guard had disappeared, so he quickly made his way to the deck in time to observe *Queen Elizabeth* moored five hundred yards away. "[She] too, blew up," he wrote. "She rose a few inches out of the water and fragments of iron and other objects flew out of her funnel, mixed with oil which even reached the deck of the *Valiant*, splashing every one of us standing on her stern." According to Wade, "there was the low, rumbling underwater explosion and the quarterdeck was thrown upwards about six inches, maybe more. . . . A blast of thick smoke and flame shot out the funnel. Then the ship seemed to settle rapidly." Cunningham wrote: "[I] was tossed about five feet into the air by the whip of the ship and was lucky not to come down sprawling." If he really was literally tossed five feet into the air, he was lucky not to have broken a leg or hip.[55]

The blast ripped *Queen Elizabeth*'s keel plates under B boiler room and damaged an area 190 feet by 60 feet. A, B, and X boiler rooms and the 4.5-inch magazine quickly flooded. Y boiler room "and numerous other compartments slowly flooded up to the main deck level" as 6,500 tons of water entered the ship. The vessel assumed a 4.5-degree starboard list and settled eight feet by the bow and one foot aft. *Valiant* had the port lower bulge structure holed and "blown into the ship over an area of 60 ft. by 30 ft." The lower bulge, inner bottom, shell room, and magazine, along with adjacent compartments, immediately flooded, "forcing her down five feet by the bow." *Sagona* was holed aft, and her shafts and rudder were badly damaged. She was not repaired until 1946. *Jervis* was moored alongside the oiler. George Kean, the signalman on the bridge later recalled that he was hurled "across the compass platform on to the deck. Our bows had jumped up, as I scrambled to my feet they were dropping down again causing me to think for a second or two that our end had come." The blast blew in the plates of the communications mess deck and other compartments, twisted the bow, and ignited the paint stores. She required a month in dock. Some explosive charges that the Italian frogmen had scattered in the water detonated, but failed to ignite any floating oil.[56]

Valiant occupied Alexandria's floating dock until April 1942, when, to free the space for *Queen Elizabeth*, she was moved to Durban, South Africa, to continue repairs. She returned to service with the Eastern Fleet in August 1942. *Queen Elizabeth* emerged from dock on 27 June 1942 and sailed to Norfolk, Virginia, for permanent repairs. She returned to operations in January 1944.

A British priority after the raid was to keep the Axis from learning of its success. *Queen Elizabeth* corrected her list by counter-flooding, and Cunningham remained on board and continued his routine. Axis reconnaissance photographs taken on the 20th showed two submarines alongside one battleship and a tanker and numerous barges clustered around the other, which had its turrets trained to starboard, as if to right a list. Supermarina initially judged that both battleships had been damaged. This was confirmed on 6 January 1942. A bulletin claiming success followed on 8 January. The Germans, however, remained skeptical. Throughout December the German naval staff, still discounting *U331*'s claim that she had sunk *Barham*, believed that the Mediterranean Fleet had three battleships available. The German command first acknowledged the XMAS—the common shorthand for the commando unit—operation on 9 January, calling it a "considerable success." However, as late as 27 January the German Admiralty noted that "radio intelligence reports that there is no confirmation of the intelligence report according to which the *Queen Elizabeth* sank in shallow water in Alexandria. According to the reports from other sources, the battleship had repeatedly been at sea after 18 Dec. while the *Valiant* was undergoing repairs in dock."[57]

Success Must Be Exploited

The British naval strategist Julian Corbett wrote in 1911 that "command of the sea . . . means nothing but the control of maritime communications, whether for commercial or military purposes."[58] The December 1941 victories of the Regia Marina regained command of the central Mediterranean for the Axis. This command is quantified in table 6.1.

The Italian victories of 17–19 December left the British with no counter to Italy's battleship convoys. As Admiral Cunningham wrote to Admiral Pound on 28 December, "The damage to the battleships at this time is a disaster." Rome had claimed sea command and reestablished communications with Africa. These victories also finally enabled Italy to block British communications from Alexandria to Malta. Prior to the Alexandria raid—from August 1940 to December 1941—all thirty-seven merchant ships that departed Egyptian ports for Malta arrived. After the attack and up through the Anglo-American invasion of French North Africa almost a year later, twenty-five merchant ships sailed from Egypt for Malta, but only eight (32 percent) arrived. The intervention of Italian surface units delayed British convoys in February and March, leading to increased losses from air strikes, and in June the Italian fleet repulsed the large *Vigorous* convoy. The threat of battleship intervention prevented any convoys at all from Egypt between late March and mid-June and from

Table 6.1. **Axis Merchant Sailings from Europe to Africa Before and After the December 1941 Victories**

Date	Sailed	Arrived	Percent	Sunk	Percent	Damaged	Percent
21 Oct–16 Dec 41	52	21	40	17	33	7	13
17 Dec–30 Mar 42	63	58	92	4	6	4	6

Source: USMM, *Difesa del traffico*, VII, Appendix 1, 372–409.

June to late November 1942. The convoys from Gibraltar to Malta in June and August 1942 lost twelve of nineteen merchant ships, with another four damaged.[59] Finally, the impact on the Regia Marina's morale cannot be discounted. The French Rear Admiral Raymond De Belot, an impartial observer, wrote in 1951 that "in the dark hours of defeat, when Italy came close to giving way to despair, the memory of such an exploit gave her faith and confidence in her destiny."[60]

The impact of these victories was not immediately apparent as December's final ten days saw a switch from blue-water to brown-water operations while the British army pushed through Cyrenaica. The weather did not help as a series of violent storms swept the region.

The Fall of Benghazi

Sailings from Benghazi increased after the middle of the month as the Axis situation on land deteriorated. The last ships to arrive were *Bolsena* on the 17th, *Ankara* on the 19th, and *Ercole* (5,027 GRT/9.5 kts) on the 21st. *Cadamosto* (1,010 GRT) and the German *Spezia* (1,825 GRT) departed Tripoli for Benghazi at 1900/20th, but both fell victim to drifting mines from an Italian field at 0100/22nd—*Spezia* when she was rescuing survivors from *Cadamosto*.[61]

Ships departing Benghazi after the fall of Gazala included:

- 1600/17th: *Michele, Faro di Levante, Siluro, Tenacemente* (101 GRT);
- 0100/19th: German tug *Max Barendt* (766 GRT) to tow *Granatiere* to Angostoli;
- 1800/19th: *Anna Maria* (1,205 GRT), *San Paolo* (209 GRT), *Ascianghi*;
- 2000/20th: *Emilio* (193 GRT);
- 1800/21st: *Ankara* (with 1,400 British prisoners of war), *Bolsena, Brook, Rita, Nicoló Padre* (66 GRT), *Delfino* (54 GRT), *Fanum Fortunae* (34 GRT);
- 1715/22nd: *Ercole*;
- 2130/22nd: *Polifemo, Labor* (510 GRT), *Raffio* (316 GRT), *Proteo* (399 GRT);
- 0910/23rd: *Tremiti, Porto Levante, Nuova Vicenza*;
- 1900/23rd: torpedo boat *Calliope*.

These ships also evacuated as much material and personnel as possible.[62]

Destruction of port facilities commenced on the 21st. Demolition parties blasted the moles and breakwater on the 23rd and sank a barge to block the channel. A land route south was still open on the 23rd, but it closed the next day. Thirteen Ju.88s mined the harbor on the 24th, the day that the first British forces arrived. The loss of Benghazi left Tripoli as the only major Axis port in Africa.

Ultra said little about the Benghazi evacuation—just a prenotification on the 18th that a tug was about to depart and it mentioned certain arrivals at Tripoli. Although the exodus involved more than two dozen vessels, the British did not intervene.[63]

The first British navy personnel to enter Benghazi reported that "There were no cranes or lighters and more ships had been sunk in the harbour. The piers were damaged." Heavy rain slowed progress, and a clearance party did not arrive until 30 December, a week after the port was captured.[64]

The evacuation of Benghazi was the biggest movement in African waters after the arrival of the M42 Convoy; however, several minor sailings also drew enemy attention. Torpedo bombers out of Malta, guided by an ASV-equipped Wellington, sank the unescorted tanker *Lina* (1,246 GRT) in transit from Pantelleria to Tripoli at 0430/17th. At 1000/17th the steamer *Probitas* (5,084 GRT/10 kts), escorted by the torpedo boat *Climene*, departed Trapani for Tripoli. Three bombers found her 0400/18th south of Cape Bon. One bomb struck and caused minor damage, killing one and wounding three. The ship made Tripoli at 2045/21st.[65]

The Royal Naval Supports Crusader

After the double shock off Tripoli and Alexandria, British naval operations focused on supporting the ground advance and fending off Axis air and submarine forays against traffic to Tobruk. On 13 December RAF fighters began operating out of airbases near Tobruk. They secured air superiority over the port, allowing the AT/TA series of convoys to resume. During the rest of December AT convoys departed Alexandria on the 13th, 17th, 19th, 21st, 23rd, 26th, 28th, and 29th.[66]

On 19 December the British captured Derna, and a navy mission arrived there on the 21st. It reported the port as considerably damaged, but still usable by small ships, and Cunningham ordered the "Western Desert Schooner Force" to implement a shuttle service between Tobruk and Derna. On the 22nd the gunboat *Aphis* and the minesweeping trawlers *Moy* and *Skudd V* departed Tobruk to clear the harbor of mines.[67]

German forces attempted to interfere with these activities. *Hasty* and *Hotspur* located *U79* off Bardia on the 23rd and subjected her to a sustained and successful depth-charge assault. The destroyers rescued the entire crew of forty-four men. However, at 1902/23rd *U559* torpedoed store ship *Shuntien* (3,059 GRT/15 kts) from Convoy TA.5 east of Tobruk; the ship was bringing 850 prisoners back to Alexandria. The corvette *Salvia* rescued a hundred men, but was herself torpedoed by *U568* at 0135/24th, and everyone on board perished.[68]

On the 24th came what the Mediterranean command described as "a series of mishaps to petrol carriers." This began when *Agia Varvara* (2,433 GRT/8 kts) in AT.6 suffered flooding in her engine room and had to return to Alexandria. The Italian SIS heard her distress call and advised the operational commands within minutes of transmission. The French tanker *Lesbos* (1,005 GRT) ran aground between Port Said and Alexandria. The worst "mishap," however, occurred at Haifa, where the French tanker *Phenix* (5,920 GRT/10.5 kts) apparently detonated a mine and exploded while leaving port. Burning oil covered the harbor, forcing it to close, and ignited the Norwegian tanker *Vilja* (6,672 GRT/10.5 kts), which burned out. At one point the entire port was threatened, and shipping had to flee this important oil terminus before the conflagration finally was controlled.[69]

The oiler *Zahra* (821 GRT), fleet tug *St. Issey* (800 GRT/12.5 kts), and a lighter left Alexandria in the afternoon of the 22nd for Mersa Matruh and then Tobruk. *U559* torpedoed *Warszawa* (2,487 GRT/11 kts) at 1430/26th off the coast thirty miles east of Tobruk as she was returning to Alexandria. *Peony* tried to tow her to Tobruk, but *U559* torpedoed her again, and she sank at 2015/26th. Twenty-four men died, but *Burgonet* rescued 309 men and *Peony* the remainder. On the 28th it was the turn of the water stores ship *Volo* (1,578 GRT) from Convoy TA.6, with *U75* the agent. *Kipling* and *Legion* began hunting for the submarine, and sank her with depth charges off Mersa Matruh four hours later. Fourteen men perished and thirty survived to become prisoners.[70]

By the end of December Tobruk's daily cargo capacity was six hundred tons. Traffic into the port was critical because it brought forward matériel that was needed to maintain British mechanized forces on the frontier of Tripolitania. "Even so," as the official history relates, "this did not cover the current needs and at the same time allow for reserves to be built up fast enough."[71]

On 22 December the British launched an operation to bring supplies to Malta and to return to Alexandria some of the accumulated shipping that had been sitting unused and exposed in Grand Harbor. In the first stage the light cruiser *Dido* and destroyers *Gurkha, Zulu, Nestor, Foxhound,* and *Arrow* left Gibraltar at 1730/22nd and arrived in Malta on 24 December. *Ajax,* flag of Rear Admiral Rawlings, and the destroyers *Lively* and *Lance* joined them there. The convoy, ME.8, included *City of Calcutta* (8,063 GRT/15.5 kts), *Clan Ferguson* (7,347 GRT/16 kts), *Sydney Star* (11,219 GRT/16 kts), and the freighter *Ajax* (7,540 GRT/16 kts); it weighed anchor at 1745/26th. At 0630/28th, on the passage to Alexandria, *Carlisle* and destroyers *Sikh, Maori,* and *Nizam* reinforced the convoy's escort. At this point *Lance* and *Lively* returned to Malta. At 1500/28th, when the convoy was north of Bardia, four S.79s from Rhodes attacked. A Martlet (Grumman F4F) fighter flying cover shot down one of them and in turn was splashed by the Italian. The antiaircraft barrage severely damaged the other three S.79s. They claimed a cruiser definitely and a steamship probably hit, but in fact all torpedoes missed. British Fulmar carrier aircraft then intercepted a high-altitude strike by German Ju.88s and forced them to jettison their bombs. *Maori* suffered moderate damage when a stick of four bombs exploded close alongside, driving splinters through her hull and upperworks and igniting fires in two cordite lockers. She was out of action for six weeks. The convoy otherwise arrived safely in Alexandria and Port Said on the 29th.[72]

Italian Sea Traffic Year-End

In the final week of December the Italians ran five small ships into African ports and brought three large ones out. Bad weather complicated these operations. *Rosa* (559 GRT) and *Sant'Antonio* (271 GRT) sailed unescorted from Lampedusa and Tunis respectively, arriving at Tripoli on the 26th. There were no Ultra messages pertaining to their voyage, and they were not attacked. The veteran motorships *Monginevro* and *Vettor Pisani* (with a thousand prisoners of war) departed Tripoli on the 26th and 27th, each escorted by a torpedo boat. Several Ultra messages mentioned these passages. In the case of *Monginevro* a message generated five hours after her departure correctly gave the vessel's itinerary and route, while *Pisani*'s schedule was available to Vice Admiral Ford soon after she sailed. Wellington aircraft mined Tripoli on the 25th and 27th but did not affect these sailings.[73]

On the last days of the month *Achaja* (1,778 GRT), *Gala* (1,029 GRT), and *Sturla* (1,195 GRT) departed ports in Sicily for Africa. These vessels also arrived at their destinations without incident. Only in the case of *Sturla* did Ultra give actionable information, but the British were unable to exploit it. *Ankara* departed Tripoli on the 30th and arrived in Naples on the 1st. Ultra gave notice of her sailing and that she was carrying POWs. She was not attacked.[74]

The loss rate for African traffic was 16 percent, compared to 2 percent for the Balkans.

Table 6.2. **Axis Traffic for Ships Departing in December 1941**

Type	Convoys	Convoys attacked	Detected by Ultra	Ships sailed	Ships arrived	Ships lost	Ships damaged
Europe to Africa	15	5	12	22	12	4	2
Africa to Europe	8	1	6	9	8	1	0
Coastal west	13		7	31	31	0	0
Coastal east	6	1	6	10	8	2	0
Destroyers to Africa	8	2		12	11	0	1
Light cruisers to Africa	2	1		3	1	2	0
Submarines to Africa	14	4		14	11	1	0
Total Africa*	42	7	31	72	59	7	2
Total Balkans	57			83	81	1	1

*Excludes military. Includes German traffic.
Source: USMM, *Difesa del traffico* 7:384–95.

Air and Submarine Summary

In December Malta recorded 169 air raids, 100 of them at night. The Italian air force raided La Valletta ten times and bombed the airfields eight times over a span of thirteen days. The largest strike of fifteen aircraft occurred on the 14th. German aircraft first attacked the island on the 20th. From then until the end of the month German forces bombed Malta ten times. Vice Admiral Ford commented: "A very marked increase in aerial activity is shown during the month." Naples experienced only a few raids and other mainland Italian ports none.[75]

There were sixteen Allied submarines on patrol in the Mediterranean on 1 December and fourteen on 15 December. These boats expended 82 torpedoes in twenty-five attacks, sinking a torpedo boat and five other ships displacing 24,302 GRT and damaging *Vittorio Veneto*.[76]

On 1 December there were twelve Italian submarines at sea. Over the month the Italians conducted forty-one missions involving thirty-six submarines: thirteen were offensive patrols and seventeen were transport missions (which delivered 1,758 tons of fuel, munitions, and supplies to Benghazi, Bardia, and Derna). There also were two special missions associated with the Alexandria operation. Italian boats made three attacks, expending eight torpedoes, with no results. There were thirteen German submarines in the Mediterranean on 1 December of which seven were on patrol on 8 December. Eleven boats entered the Middle Sea and three were sunk, leaving a balance of twenty-one on 1 January 1942. All told, they sank ten Allied and neutral merchant ships, totaling 33,559 GRT, and three warships displacing 6,660 tons.[77]

Intermezzo

A World War

Four months elapse between the time a decision is taken to send reinforcements from the United Kingdom and the time forces can be deployed in battle in the Far or Middle East.

CHIEFS OF STAFF MEMORANDUM, 9 FEBRUARY 1942

The Japanese attack on Pearl Harbor transformed a European conflict into a true world war. If Axis victory did not seem certain in December 1941, as it had in December 1940, the force and fury of Japan's thrust into southeast Asia and Germany's vast Russians conquests made it seem possible.

The new year's imperative for Axis forces in Africa was to stabilize the front at El Agheila and rebuild the divisions that had been battered in the retreat from Cyrenaica. The Axis shipping situation in the Mediterranean was satisfactory. On 31 December 1941 Italy and Germany had 1.844 million GRT of ships grossing more than 500 GRT. This represented a net loss of 361,864 GRT, or 16.4 percent, of the shipping on hand on 1 January 1941. Lost were 130 Italian vessels totaling 503,656 GRT and 26 German vessels totaling 99,643 GRT. New construction and other acquisitions, such as seized Greek and Yugoslav vessels, totaled 77 hulls of 241,435 GRT.[1]

Shipping was one matter, fuel was another. It was significant that on the afternoon of 31 December the Italian chiefs of staff met with Kesselring,

Rintelen, and Weichold, and that fuel was one of the chief items that they discussed. By 1 January 1942, after the heavy expenditures of November and December, the Regia Marina's stockpile of fuel oil had dropped to 108,000 tons. It was clear that Italy needed to find new sources of fuel oil and cut back operations; otherwise stocks would be exhausted by March.[2]

The end of the year saw the British chiefs of staff balancing an array of threats and considering urgent requests to reinforce Ceylon, Java, Burma, India, New Zealand, the Falklands, and Australia. Even the commander of the Shetlands/Orkneys—worried about German paratroopers—petitioned the chiefs for more troops and aircraft. In December the chiefs also reviewed a comprehensive study detailing a German invasion of England in the spring of 1942, indicating that this threat was still on their minds.[3]

Even as the British chiefs worried about events as unlikely as a Japanese landing on the Falklands, they also considered an array of offensive operations, such as invasions of Madagascar, the Azores, the Cape Verde Islands, the Canary Islands, northern Norway, northern France, French West Africa, French North Africa, and Sicily. There were even plans to send ground and air forces to Murmansk and the Caucasus. This required troops, aircraft, warships, supplies, and, most of all, shipping.[4]

The situation confronting the Middle East Triumvirate—Auchinleck, Cunningham, and Tedder—resembled the one that had existed just a year before. Their conquest of Cyrenaica was threatened by new demands, this time from the Far East rather than the Balkans. On 8 January 1942 their representative to the chiefs of staff pointed out, "The immobilization of the two capital ships now in Eastern Mediterranean is likely to entail the loss of our existing control at sea, and urgent steps are thus necessary to remedy the situation."[5] They believed that the Mediterranean should be the nexus of future Allied operations: "The enemy's defences in South Europe are weaker, his communications are worse, and the Balkan peoples are more ripe for revolt and there is ample room for the deployment of American forces in North Africa." They recommended "making our main offensive effort from the Mediterranean through South Europe."[6]

Overshadowing these threats and opportunities was the matter of the United States—at long last a full ally of the British. The Arcadia (or First Washington) conference started on 22 December 1941. At that point

Churchill still believed that "We may expect the total destruction of the enemy force in Libya to be apparent before the end of the year." In 1942 the British hoped to occupy France's North and West African possessions and the whole North African shore from Tunis to Egypt. The goal was free passage through the Mediterranean. Elsewhere, Churchill expected "that Singapore island and fortress will stand an attack for at least six months. In the meanwhile we propose to organize in the Indian Ocean a force of three armoured carriers together with suitable cruiser escort."[7]

However, at the conference such interest as the Americans had for operations in the European-African theater centered on Northwest Africa, not Libya. In the end, the Allied military chiefs agreed upon the following set of priorities:

1. Secure areas of production in the United States, the United Kingdom, and Russia.
2. Maintain or secure both sea and air communications, especially in the North Atlantic.
3. Tighten the ring around Germany by sustaining Russia, reinforcing the Middle East, and occupying the North African coast.
4. Reduce German resistance through bombardment and blockade, revolt in German-occupied territories, and assistance of Russia.
5. Develop land offensives on the continent.

The Allies agreed to an American expedition against French North Africa, as soon as the shipping was available, probably in May 1942. General Alan Brooke, acting head of the Combined Chief of Staff wrote in his diary: "Started new year wondering what it may have in store for us."[8]

Chapter 7

January 1942

I fear I do not look forward to the next few months with much pleasure.
ADMIRAL CUNNINGHAM TO
ADMIRAL POUND, 28 DECEMBER 1941

In January, after six weeks of intense ground combat and mobile operations, the Allied and Axis armies in North Africa raced to resupply before the next lunge.

Front-Line Logistics

The Axis enclave at Bardia fell on 2 January, but Halfaya resisted until the 17th. At El Agheila two weak British brigades maintained a 30-mile front while the rest of the XXX Corps occupied positions ranging all the way back to Tobruk. The troops and airbases operating in western Cyrenaica required a minimum of 1,400 tons of supplies a day, but in early January only 1,150 tons was arriving via the truck convoys working Tobruk and the now-distant railhead south of Sidi Barrani. This was not enough to meet immediate operating requirements, much less to build stockpiles for an offensive against Tripoli.[1] Benghazi was the solution, but progress in opening the port was slow. The British first needed to clear wreckage, repair wharves and jetties, and bring in equipment and lighters. Four minesweepers, including the Great War–vintage coal-fired vessels *Bagshot* and *Aberdare*, reached Benghazi on 29 December and commenced sweeping the next day; the armed boarding vessel *Antwerp* (GRT 2,957), escorted by *Hero* and *Arrow*, carrying three hundred salvage and port-clearance personnel and eighty tons of supplies, arrived on 4 January. AT.11 departed Alexandria on the 3rd and made Benghazi on the 7th. However, gales delayed work and slowed littoral operations in general.[2]

In the first two weeks of January traffic between Alexandria and Tobruk included five AT convoys, which departed on the 5th, 6th, 10th, 11th, and 14th, and an equal number of return convoys. Although the Germans had concentrated *U371, 374, 77, 97, 74, 133,* and *568* to interdict this traffic, only *U77* had a success, when she torpedoed *Kimberley* on 12 January. *Kimberley* had brought *Mausang* (3,372 GRT/11.5 kts) into Benghazi on the 11th and then departed with *Hotspur* and *Hero* on a submarine sweep off Tobruk. At 0240/12th a torpedo from *U77* smashed *Kimberley's* stern and ignited a blaze that gutted the ship's after sections. A tug towed the crippled destroyer to Alexandria and then to Bombay. She returned to service in January 1944. *Unbeaten* sank *U374* the same day east of Cape Spartivento.[3]

In addition to the Tobruk–Derna–Benghazi traffic, which Cunningham estimated at 2,000 tons per day, regular convoy routes in early January also included Port Said–to–Alexandria, at a rate of 2,000 tons per day; oil traffic from Haifa to Alexandria, at 10,000 tons per week; supply to Beirut–Tripoli (Syria)–Iskanderun–Mersin; and supply to Cyprus and other small ports at 500 tons a day. On 2 January Cunningham petitioned the Admiralty for reinforcements, especially antisubmarine escorts, "There are thus 11 ports in the area at present requiring A/S patrols and 3 main traffic routes on which an average of 20 ships a day are moving, in about 5 small convoys."[4]

Ultra and the Convoys

During January forty-seven Axis merchant ships sailed to or from Africa, or along the coast, in thirty-five convoys or single-ship passages. The Allies attacked eleven of these, sinking three ships and damaging two. Yet Ultra gave information on all but three convoys.[5] There were four reasons why the British attacked less than a third of the African traffic in January despite this seeming abundance of intelligence. First, Malta was under increasing pressure from Axis (mostly German) air forces. Second, there was a change in command in Malta. On 13 January Vice Admiral Wilbraham Ford hauled down his flag, replaced by Vice Admiral Ralph Leatham, who assumed his duties on the 19th. During this period both admirals used the rump of Force K more cautiously, mainly to escort shipping, not to hunt surface contacts as Ford had been doing in November and the first half of December 1941. Third, as discussed in previous chapters, Ultra was not always accurate, and although it could be used to pre-position submarines or to schedule air reconnaissance missions, a ship still had to be found before it could be sunk. Italian radio intelligence often frustrated Allied reconnaissance, notifying a convoy that it had been spotted and that a strike was likely or, in some cases, on the way. This enabled convoys to alter course and avoid detection, or at worst, to prepare defenses. Finally, North Africa experienced an unusually wet winter in 1942. Sandstorms, rain, and gales routinely hindered air and sea operations. Germany's transfer of 2nd Fliegerkorps to Sicily in late December also hampered British operations, although as Rear Admiral Weichold noted after the war, "Looking at the matter objectively, it is clear that the change in the Mediterranean situation in favour of the Axis had been brought about even before the first aircraft of the Kesselring Air Force went into action on 21st December 1941."[6]

Italian Operations in Early January

Although the Italian navy delivered a much higher percentage of materiel to Africa in December 1941 compared to November, the total tonnage delivered was still low. Supermarina had no reason to be complacent about Operation M42's success. Although Rear Admiral Luigi Sansonetti, Supermarina's deputy chief of staff, told Cavallero that the escort could be reduced to save fuel, the next operation, M43, was another massively protected battleship convoy.[7] It consisted of these components:

- Group 1: *Nino Bixio* (7,137 GRT/15 kts), *Monginevro, Lerici* (6,070 GRT/16 kts). Escort (Rear Admiral Nomis di Pollone): 14th Squadron (*Vivaldi, Da Recco, Usodimare, Bersagliere, Fuciliere*). Sailed Messina 1015/3rd.

- Group 2: *Gino Allegri* (6,836 GRT/16 kts). Escort: destroyer *Freccia* and torpedo boat *Procione*. Sailed Brindisi 1315/3rd.
- Group 3: *Monviso* (5,322 GRT/15 kts), *Giulio Giordani* (10,535 GRT/13 kts). Escort: torpedo boats *Aretusa, Castore, Antares,* sloop *Orsa*. Sailed Taranto 1500/3rd.
- Heavy escort/Vice Admiral Bergamini: *Duilio,* light cruisers *Garibaldi, Montecuccoli, Attendolo*; 10th Squadron (*Maestrale, Gioberti, Oriani, Scirocco, Malocello*). Sailed Taranto 1600/3rd.
- Cover group/Vice Admiral Iachino: *Littorio, Cesare, Doria*; heavy cruisers *Gorizia, Trento*; destroyers *Carabiniere, Alpino, Da Noli, Pigafetta,* 11th Squadron (*Ascari, Aviere, Geniere, Camicia Nera*). Sailed Taranto 1850/3rd.

Nine submarines screened the convoy's route.

Ultra revealed aspects of the operation but not the big picture. At 0510Z/3rd, the day of departure, a dispatch advised the Middle Eastern Command: "An unknown number of motor vessels are scheduled to leave an unknown port on day two of convoy operation mentioned in 1551." [Message 1551 was a report generated at 0025Z/3rd about escort arrangements for a convoy "that will leave very shortly, or may even have already left."] The British had six submarines watching the approaches to Taranto, but Cunningham complained that other forces were "unable to reach Tripoli area in time to intercept convoy."[8]

Iachino's group had been underway for only three hours when *Doria* suffered an engine-bearing failure. The admiral ordered her back to Taranto, accompanied by *Ascari* and *Carabiniere*, while the rest pressed on. The three convoys united between 0700 and 1100/4th, with the *Duilio* group in close attendance and the *Littorio* group, rejoined by the two destroyers, in distant coverage.

At 1100/4th a Blenheim sighted *Duilio* south-southwest of Navarino and reported one battleship, three cruisers, and destroyers. The Italian SIS deciphered this message and alerted Iachino, who noted that the position broadcast was forty-five miles southeast of his actual location and that the aircraft also had incorrectly reported the force's composition. Then *Littorio*'s lookouts sighted the Blenheim itself at low altitude and at a great

General Ugo Cavallero with Admiral Vittorio Tur inspecting personnel of the Special Naval Force on board the old cruiser *Taranto*. Cavallero, who was appointed chief of staff in December 1940, was considered an outstanding organizer and a brilliant administrator. He was popular with the Germans and in February 1942 General Rintelen reported to Berlin, "He has forced the navy—in spite of opposition from them—to take action in supplying Libya." He died under suspicious circumstances, most likely assassinated by the Germans a few days after the 8 September 1943 armistice. STORIA MILITARE

distance. After it disappeared, Iachino reversed course "to make more difficult the subsequent searching of other scouts, and to separate from the convoy to keep it from being spotted."[9]

Based on the scout's report, Malta dispatched a Blenheim strike force, but it missed the enemy. However, a second aircraft sighted the *Littorio* group at 1730/4th and a third at 0230/5th, while Iachino was returning to Taranto. On the afternoon of the 5th the submarine *Unique* targeted *Littorio* with four torpedoes from 9,000 yards. She reported a possible hit, but in fact all of them missed—not surprising considering the range. At 1000/5th a British aircraft finally pinpointed the convoy itself east of Tripoli, and at 1135 another plane reported nine vessels entering Tripoli. Despite usable intelligence and repeated sightings, the British never delivered an effective strike. After the convoy arrived, twelve Wellingtons from Malta raided the port, but in stormy weather only one dropped its bombs, and the weapons fell errantly.[10]

All told, M43 delivered 2,417 tons of munitions, 10,242 tons of other materiel; 15,379 tons of fuel, benzene, and lubricants; 82 Italian tanks; 62 German tanks; 520 vehicles; and 901 men. Iachino congratulated himself for his evasive maneuvers and observed about his enemy, "the successful outcome of the operation was also due to the low activity and lack of skill shown by the English scouts . . . The sightings made by enemy planes of the Littorio Group and the 3rd Division were very wrong both for position and the type of unit sighted." Cunningham's war diary corroborated Iachino's observation. "The previous day's reconnaissance had apparently not been effective."[11]

Mussolini congratulated Riccardi on the convoy's arrival, but as Iachino noted that "if the actual situation of the British forces of Alexandria and Malta had been known with certainty, we could have avoided using so many valuable ships to escort a convoy of six steamers." On 4 January an Axis survey of British naval forces in the Mediterranean showed one to three battleships in Alexandria, with one presumed fit for action and one heavily damaged. On the 6th Italian photo-reconnaissance of Alexandria observed one battleship in drydock and another berthed at the masonry basin housing the arsenal. On the 7th interrogations of captured pilots finally revealed *Barham*'s fate. On 8 January Cavallero wrote in his diary, "I have news of the serious damage inflicted in Alexandria by our special attack forces. . . . The enemy naval force is in crisis. I ordered Riccardi to push as hard as possible."[12]

Operation MF2

After *Breconshire*'s successful venture to Malta in mid-December, Cunningham was anxious to repeat the process during the January moonless period with the stores ship *Glengyle*, which would sail from Alexandria to

Malta while *Breconshire* returned from Malta to Alexandria. The greatest threat the planners anticipated was air strikes from Crete and Sicily. MF2 consisted of

- MF2 West. *Glengyle* (9,919 GRT/18 kts). Sailed 2030/5th;
- Force C (Rear Admiral Vian): *Naiad, Dido, Euryalus*; destroyers *Foxhound, Gurkha, Kingston, Kipling, Sikh.* (*Dido* fouled her propeller exiting the port, but cleared the problem and caught up);
- MF2 East: *Breconshire*; Force K: *Havock, Jaguar, Lance, Lively.* Sailed 1845/6th.

Force K and Force C met west of Crete on the afternoon of 7 January as planned and traded supply ships. Also, *Sikh* joined Force K, and *Havock* was transferred to Force C. *Glengyle* entered Malta at 1330/8th, while *Breconshire* made Alexandria on the 9th. Although Italian reconnaissance reported cruisers and destroyers off the coast heading west, Axis forces, in a rare intelligence failure, did not otherwise detect the movement of the supply ships.[13]

Operation MF3

Although Malta's last major convoy had been in September 1941, the island's supply situation at the start of 1942 was generally acceptable. Warehouses held flour to last until May, coal to the end of March, benzene and kerosene until the end of April, and aviation fuel to last the summer. Fuel oil and ammunition, however, required replenishment if the island was to continue hosting Force K. Yet, Churchill's desire was not merely to *hold* Malta. He wanted the island to serve as an offensive base as well, and proposed the delivery of 45,000 tons of supplies to the island every month. This was three times Malta's monthly requirement, so three consecutive convoys would accumulate a six-month surplus. The British chiefs of staff endorsed the prime minister's proposal on 5 January. On 16 January 1942 the first such convoy, MW.8, got underway, timed to take advantage of the long winter nights and the availability of fighter coverage from Cyrenaican airfields. Hoping to confuse the enemy, it departed Alexandria in three waves:[14]

- MW.8A: *Ajax* (7,540 GRT/16 kts), *Thermopylae* (6,655 GRT/15 kts), light cruiser *Carlisle*, destroyers *Griffin, Hasty, Hero*, and *Arrow*. Sailed 0815/16th;
- MW.8B: *City of Calcutta* (8,063 GRT/15.5 kts), *Clan Ferguson* (7,347 GRT/16 kts), destroyers *Gurkha, Maori, Legion*, and *Isaac Sweers*. Sailed 1530/16th;
- Force B (Rear Admiral Vian): *Naiad, Dido, Euryalus*, destroyers *Foxhound, Havock, Hotspur, Kelvin, Kingston, Kipling*.

Force B had problems getting underway. It was supposed to sail at midnight on the 17th, but Vian advanced the schedule when an unexpected sandstorm kicked up. *Kingston* fouled the entrance boom in the murky conditions, and *Foxhound* piled into her stern. They both missed the operation. *Hotspur* caught her screws in the protective net, but cleared them in time to continue. The cruisers were also late, with *Naiad* and *Euryalus* out at 0240/17th and *Dido* at 0545, since she needed a tug to clear her berth. She did not catch up until 1440/17th.[15]

Once the convoy was out at sea a strong headwind reduced its speed to 13 knots.[16] At 0735/17th, MW.8B was northwest of Mersa Matruh, sixteen hours into its journey and already three hours behind schedule. The escorts had deployed in case of a dawn air raid, and *Gurkha* was a hundred yards off *City of Calcutta*'s starboard bow when *U133*, one of three boats positioned between Alexandria and Libya, targeted her with a spread of four torpedoes. One blasted a 25-foot-wide hole in *Gurkha*'s hull and caused extensive flooding abaft the engine room.

Legion continued with the two merchant vessels while *Maori* hunted the submarine and *Isaac Sweers* stood by the stricken destroyer. *U133* dove to 160 meters and counted 22 depth charges, "much of which [were] extremely well aimed." On board *Gurkha* oil fuel ignited and, because the fire main had fractured, the crew could not extinguish the blaze, which was spreading on the water from the ship's windward side. A second fire, fed by ready-use ammunition, raged on the after superstructure. By 0820 "the ship was showing definite signs of foundering." A volunteer swam a 9-inch manila line to *Isaac Sweers*, and she towed *Gurkha* clear of the flames, but at 0909 *Gurkha* turned on her beam ends and sank. *U133* heard "the

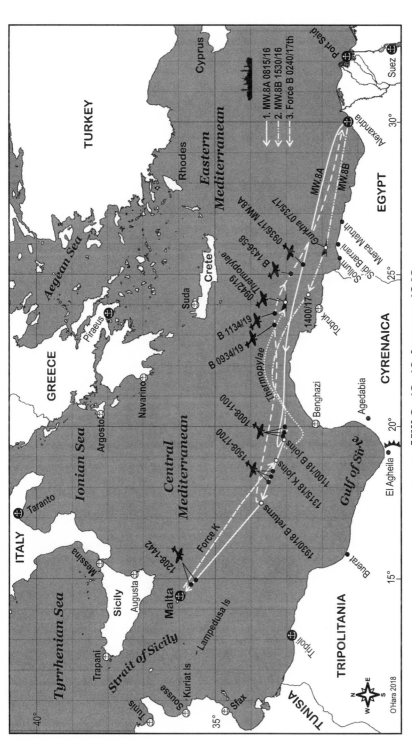

Map 7.1. **MW.8, 16–19 January 1942**

typical noises of a ship sinking, like pebbles falling though water." *Isaac Sweers* rescued the entire crew except for five officers and four of their stewards, who were at breakfast in a wardroom right above the point of impact. *Isaac Sweers* ducked into Tobruk at 1747/17th and landed *Gurkha*'s 236 survivors, weighing anchor again at 1830 and rejoining the escort. *U133* and *U205* were ordered to pursue, but British air patrols kept them down, and by dark the convoys had left the two submarines far behind.[17]

Convoy MW.8A sailed farther offshore than MW.8B. Two Ju.88s attacked at 0936/17th when it was passing Sollum, but otherwise the group proceeded unmolested and kept to schedule. Force K, with *Penelope, Lance, Lively, Jaguar, Sikh*, and *Zulu*, weighed anchor from Malta at 1900/17th. Force B overtook the combined convoy sixty miles northwest of Benghazi at 1100/18th. By this time the British were under assault. At 1023 a single Ju.88 dove out of the clouds and dropped bombs within 50 yards of *Euryalus*. A bomb dropped on *Carlisle* at 1100 missed by 100 yards astern. Then, at 1130, *Thermopylae*, which was already lagging, reported mechanical problems. Two joints had failed on the steering engine, and the workers damaged the rudder while repairing them. Pushing through the heavy seas *Thermopylae* could make only make 10 knots. Vian wrote, "[this] was an unacceptable speed for the operation in hand and there was no expectation that the sea would become less." Therefore, at 1200 he sent the freighter to Benghazi, escorted by *Carlisle, Arrow*, and *Havock*. At 1315 Force K joined MW.8 some ninety miles northwest of Benghazi.[18]

The corvette *Gloxinia* came out from Benghazi to reinforce *Thermopylae*'s escort, but at 1404/18th naval headquarters ordered *Thermopylae* to make for Alexandria, instead recommending a route along the coast to maximize air coverage. *Carlisle*'s captain, Douglas Neame, however, elected to stay forty-five miles offshore, where he believed there would be less danger from submarine attacks. He wrote: "[I] realized that Fighter Protection might not be possible at that distance, although I considered that Beaufighters [aircraft] could well operate as far out as that."[19]

Starting at 1508/18th nine Ju.88s attacked the convoy singly or in pairs for two hours. They claimed direct hits on the three steamships, but actually their bombs fell no closer than 200 yards. In the heavy weather five other aircraft from the same unit could not find the target. After an extensive air search revealed no evidence the Italian fleet had sailed Force B turned east for Alexandria at 1930. *Legion* and *Maori* stayed with Force K, but *Jaguar* left the Malta squadron and joined Force B. On its return Force B experienced scattered strikes by single aircraft at 0934/19th and at 1136, and four between 1436 and 1455. The first plane caught Vian by surprise, and bombs near-missed *Naiad*, but no others fell close, and pilots reported an intense antiaircraft barrage. Force B made Alexandria on the 20th.[20]

At 0942/19th a Ju.88 dropped four bombs on *Thermopylae* from 1,500 feet when the ship was fifty-eight miles north by west of Tobruk; two hit, setting the unlucky freighter ablaze. As the flames spread to holds containing ammunition, the master ordered the crew to abandon ship. *Havock* was nearby and, as her captain, Lieutenant G. R. G. Watkins, reported: "I saw boats being lowered and realized that she was abandoning ship. I approached intending to go alongside the weather side but to my horror saw that men were dropping into the water. I immediately made every effort to stop this by means of Loud Hailer and Lamp. . . . [Finally] I decided I must risk crushing some men and drifted alongside from ahead . . . as it appeared likely that the ship would blow up any minute." *Havock* and *Arrow* rescued 351 men, but 33 perished.[21]

German motor torpedo boats *S31, 33, 34, 35,* and *61* tried to intercept MW.8 off Malta at 0230/19th, but the weather was too rough. Ten Hurricane aircraft from Malta protected the convoy on the morning of the 19th. That afternoon the Germans attempted several sudden attacks from out of the clouds and at 1432 one bomb near-missed *Lance*. The remaining transports passed St. Elmo light beginning at 1530/19th.[22]

The freighters delivered 21,000 tons of supplies (mostly foodstuffs), eight tanks (a dozen were lost on *Thermopylae*), and most of an infantry battalion to Malta. It was a successful action; although German forces accounted for one destroyer and one freighter that had dropped out of formation, the convoy itself encountered light resistance. Cunningham, ever the politician, characterized the air cooperation as "excellent." "Fighter aircraft worked well particularly from forward area under difficult conditions." Vian and Neame were less positive. The reliability of IFF (Identification Friend or Foe) was sporadic, and most escorting groups failed to establish communication. As Neame stated, and Vian agreed that "With no communications fighters may be more of a liability than an asset." and that "The combination of no communication, no I.F.F. and patrolling singly made it only too easy to assume a friendly fighter to be a hostile bomber and vice versa." Bad weather played the biggest role in the convoy's relatively trouble-free passage to Malta.[23]

Benghazi and Tobruk

The first Benghazi convoy, *Harboe Jensen* (1,862 GRT/13.5 kts), and *Crista* (2,598 GRT/10.5 kts), arrived on 7 January, two weeks after the harbor's capture. On the 9th, the Middle East commanders told the chiefs of staff that the drive against Tripoli could begin on 20 January, assuming Benghazi could handle 600 tons of cargo per day. However, the Italians had blasted the breakwater in several spots, allowing waves to break inside the harbor, and severe weather hampered unloading. *Derwentdale* (8,390 GRT/11.5 kts), carrying fifteen landing craft and escorted by the Hunts *Farndale*, *Eridge*, and *Dulverton*, departed Alexandria on the 12th to address this situation. Four Ju.88s dive-bombed her at 1545/14th and missed. She launched the craft off the port at 0100/15th and they motored in under their own power as *Derwentdale* hastily returned to Alexandria.[24]

On 14 January better weather enabled the Allies to unload 1,267 tons of cargo, but by the 17th work was again at a standstill. By the 19th, almost two weeks after arrival, *Harboe Jensen* and *Crista* were still half full. On that day the British discharged 274 tons, and Benghazi's senior naval officer estimated that the ships would not be completely unloaded until the 25th, presuming the weather improved. Instead, a storm blew in that night. *Crista* broke adrift and crashed into *Harboe Jensen* and then *Mausang*. Consequently, nothing was unloaded on the 20th.[25]

Mausang had brought coal for *Bagshot* and *Aberdare*. On the 22nd the coal was still in the hold below ammunition and bombs. However, on the 23rd the weather cleared and stevedores landed 502 tons of cargo, allowing the minesweepers to fill their bunkers. However, just as conditions started to improve, events would force the British to abandon this valuable port.

From the middle of January to the end of the month British traffic to Tobruk and Benghazi consisted of five AT convoys departing on the 18th,

19th, 24th, 28th, and 31st and six convoys back. A sole S.79 from Rhodes attacked and missed AT.18 northwest of Mersa Matruh at 0844/19th. Not all dangers at sea were due to enemy actions, however. On the 21st, while in transit to Benghazi, the freighter *Manoula* (1,966 GRT) and her escort, the corvette *Peony*, ran aground off Ras Aszaz in heavy weather. The tug *St. Monance* pulled them free the next day. *Peony* required docking and returned to Alexandria while *Manoula* made Tobruk undamaged.[26]

Other Axis Traffic to North Africa

After the Italian evacuation of Benghazi in December 1941 only Tripoli could receive large cargo ships. Axis coastal traffic was also diminished, with Buerat, on an open roadstead halfway between Tripoli and El Agheila, receiving the small vessels *Sturla*, *Emilio*, and *Achaja* between the 7th and 15th.

Between major operations African traffic consisted of the following sailings:

- *Delia* (5,406 GRT/10 kts). Escort: torpedo boats *Cigno, Calliope*. Departed Palermo 2350/5th. Arrived Tripoli 8th. Ultra provided no notice of her sailing. Harsh weather forced her to put into Sousse. On the evening of the 8th, two Albacores from Malta attacked while she was nearing Tripoli. They incorrectly claimed a torpedo hit.[27]
- *Bosforo*. Escort: *Da Recco, Usodimare*, and torpedo boat *Cantore*. Departed Messina 2040/12th. Arrived Tripoli 1315/16th. Mentioned in Ultra dispatches, but not attacked.
- *San Giovanni Battista* (5,686 GRT/12 kts). Escort: *Freccia* and, for portions of the voyage, torpedo boats *Papa* and *Calliope*. Departed Naples 2000/12th. Arrived Tripoli 1430/17th. Mentioned in Ultra dispatches, but departure delayed and not attacked.[28]

Sea traffic leaving Tripoli included:

- *Labor*. Escort: motor launch *Arcioni*. Departed 0800/3rd. Arrived Trapani 2145/7th.
- *Bolsena*. No escort. Departed 1100/5th. Arrived Tunis 1600/7th.

- *Perla* (5,741 GRT/12 kts). Escort: Torpedo boat *Cascino.* Departed 1430/5th. Sunk.
- *Leneo* (345 GRT). No escort. Departed 1900/5th. Arrived Tunis 1830/9th.
- *Probitas.* Escort: sloop *Orsa.* Left Tripoli 1430/5th. Arrived Trapini 1700/8th.

Labor, Bolsena, Perla, and *Probitas* were subject of actionable Ultra messages. *Labor* and *Bolsena* were not molested. *Perla* originally departed Tripoli on the 2nd and two Swordfish intercepted her west of Tripoli early on the 3rd. Both claimed hits. *Perla* returned to Tripoli unharmed and made another break north on the 5th. Despite stormy conditions, two Swordfish torpedoed her off Kuriat at 0420/7th. *Probitas,* transporting 350 Allied prisoners, reported a submarine attack on 0915/7th and her escort, *Orsa,* claimed she probably damaged the enemy with depth charges. British records, however, do not mention any such action, and *Orsa* probably hunted a false contact.[29]

Between the 13th and 19th seven more ships cleared Tripoli bound for points north:

- *Monginevro, Monviso.* Escort: *Maestrale,* torpedo boats *Castore, Procione.* Departed 1630 and 1730/13th. Arrived Naples morning/17th. A series of Ultra messages reporting delays and multiple changes in destination confused more than helped efforts to stop these ships.[30]
- *Brook* (1,225 GRT). Escort: Subchaser *Zuri.* Departed 1500/13th. Arrived Palermo 1000/16th. The GC&CS generated a message ten hours after her departure. In response *Zulu, Jaguar, Lance,* and *Lively* teamed with an ASV-equipped Swordfish and sailed after dark on the 13th to sweep the Tunisian shore. They found nothing and were back in port early the next morning. At 1320/14th, however, four Blenheims attacked *Brook* from low altitude. One nicked the ship's mast and crashed, while the escort downed another. The others missed.[31]
- *Giulio Giordani.* Escort: *Da Recco, Usodimare* departed 1700/17th. Arrived Palermo 1300/18th. Ultra provided good information on

her schedule and course. During the night of the 18th she recorded "numerous ineffective air attacks." In fact, Swordfish from Malta reported success against both the tanker and a destroyer in a raid south of Lampedusa at 0250/18th, likely mistaking the protective smoke screen laid by the escort as evidence of damage.[32]

- *Nino Bixio.* Escort: *Freccia.* Departed 1700/18th. Arrived Brindisi 0315/21st.
- *Gino Allegri, Lerici.* Escort: *Da Noli, Saetta,* torpedo boat *Clio.* Departed 1630/19th.

The last two sailings were delayed, which invalidated much of the Ultra information generated before their departure. A message regarding *Bixio* arrived in Cairo with less than an hour's warning. Three Albacores searched the Tripoli-Kerkennah area, but found nothing. In the case of the *Allegri* convoy, the notice came almost ten hours in advance and the course information was accurate. However, the British did not sight this convoy, either.[33]

The Ground War

In January the South African Division reduced the Axis pockets at Bardia and Halfaya Pass. These holdouts were short on supplies and had been receiving inadequate replenishment from aircraft, submarines, and self-propelled barges. After the Savona Division repulsed a brigade assault against Bardia on 16 December, the reinforced South African Division, supported by the 6-inch guns of the cruiser *Ajax* and the gunboat *Aphis*, along with powerful air strikes, forced that town's surrender on 2 January. This left Halfaya Pass as the last Axis enclave on the frontier. *Aphis* had been scheduled to bombard that position on the 7th, but severe weather forced her to cancel. In any case, the Axis forces were ready, having been warned by decryptions of British naval code the night before to expect a bombardment. Halfaya held out until 17 January. In total, the British captured 13,800 Italians and Germans in these two pockets. These last gains of Operation Crusader restored British lines of communication, released considerable forces for other duties, and eased some of the logistical stress, but they came as the British were losing territory they had just captured in western Cyrenaica.[34]

The infusion of supplies brought by the M43 convoy, not to mention 144 tanks, gave the Axis forces at El Agheila superiority over the British detachments that were facing them. In the middle of January, Rommel's staff, benefiting from the ability to read the detailed reports of the U.S. military attaché in Cairo, concluded that this advantage would not last and that the time was ripe for a spoiling attack. In fact, on 21 January Italo-German forces completely ruptured the British position. As General Playfair commented in the official history, "[like the year before] British dispositions had again been such as to invite attack without possessing the necessary strength to meet it. Many people wondered why the British high command had not turned the earlier experiences to better account." Rommel recaptured Benghazi on 29 January and overran the British airbases that had so proved so helpful to the success of the MW.8 Convoy.[35]

Operation T18

On 22 January the Regia Marina commenced Operation T18. This included:

- Convoy 1: *Monginevro, Vettor Pisani, Monviso.* Cargo 13,300 tons of supplies, 342 men, 280 vehicles, 97 tanks. Escort: 14th Squadron, Rear Admiral Nomis di Pollone (*Vivaldi, Malocello, Da Noli*); 11th Squadron, Captain Luciano Bigi (*Aviere, Camicia Nera, Geniere*); torpedo boat *Castore*; sloop *Orsa*. Sailed Messina 0800/22nd.
- Convoy 2: *Victoria* (13,098 GRT/22 kts). Cargo 44 tons of supplies, 720 Italians, 405 Germans. Escort, Vice Admiral Bergamini (*Duilio*); 15th Squadron, Captain Mirti Della Valle (*Oriani, Scirocco, Ascari*). Sailed Taranto 1700/22nd.
- *Aosta* group, Rear Admiral De Courten: light cruisers *Aosta, Attendolo, Montecuccoli*; 13th Squadron, Captain Capponi (*Alpino, Bersagliere, Carabiniere, Fuciliere*). Sailed Taranto 1100/22nd.[36]

The motor ship *Ravello* (6,142 GRT/15.5 kts) was supposed to participate but developed a steering defect and had to drop out. The plan called for Convoy 1 to unite with the *Aosta* group 130 miles south of Taranto at 1800/22nd while *Duilio* and Convoy 2 sailed east of Convoy 1. The two convoys would unite at 1500/23rd some 360 miles south by east of Taranto

The large liner *Victoria* taken from the deck of *Duilio* during Operation T18. This shows the battleship's foredeck, looking forward from the foremost 12.6-inch turret. Her 37-mm antiaircraft weapons stand out. E. BAGNASCO, GUERRA SUL MARE

and 280 miles east-northeast of Tripoli and proceed across the Gulf of Sirte to Tripoli, arriving early on the 24th.

In contrast to its performance concerning Operation M43, Ultra gave the British forces good notice of Operation T18. On the 18th a message warned of an impending major convoy expected to depart for Africa on the 23rd. On the afternoon of the 20th another message revised the start date to the 22nd (which was correct). Over the next two days messages regarding the escort, the route, and schedule flooded in. The British had time to dispatch *Torbay* to cover Taranto while *Urge* and *P36* made for Tripoli. Consequently, T18 had a troubled passage despite its strong escort.[37]

Torbay attacked the *Aosta* group at 1335/22nd seventy miles south of Taranto, missing with six torpedoes fired from 8,000 yards. She reported three cruisers and six destroyers. The Italian SIS deciphered this signal and alerted De Courten that he had been sighted. *Aosta* joined Convoy 1 at 1757/22nd. The united force then headed southeast. Force K, consisting of *Penelope, Maori, Legion, Lance,* and *Lively,* raised steam, but "the enemy was in too great strength to make interception practicable."[38]

That night aircraft searched along the force's anticipated route and reported *Duilio* and Convoy 2 at 2200/22nd and 0105/23rd. *Urge* and *P36*

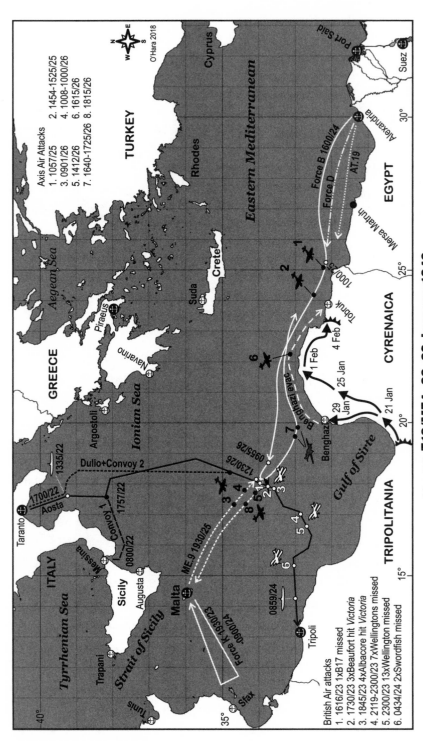

Map 7.2. **T18/MF4, 22–26 January 1942**

Axis Air Attacks
1. 1057/25   2. 1454-1525/25
3. 0901/26   4. 1008-1000/26
5. 1412/26   6. 1615/26
7. 1640-1725/26   8. 1815/26

British Air attacks
1. 1616/23 1xB17 missed
2. 1730/23 3xBeaufort hit *Victoria*
3. 1845/23 4xAlbacore hit *Victoria*
4. 2119-2300/23 7xWellingtons missed
5. 2300/23 13xWellington missed
6. 0434/24 2xSwordfish missed

O'Hara 2018

were alerted. After dawn a Blenheim aircraft, operating from a base near Benghazi, established contact and shadowed *Duilio*, making reports at 0945, 1100, and 1405/23rd. Another plane reported Convoy 1 at 0950 and 1055. *Aosta* joined *Duilio* at 1500/23rd at a point about 200 miles east by south of Malta. British aircraft reported this junction and appraised the enemy force as comprising one battleship, four cruisers, fifteen destroyers, and four motor vessels.[39]

At midday six Blenheims took off from Cyrenaica but failed to make contact. Of two B-17s from Egypt, one found the convoy and reported missing a battleship by a hundred yards and a merchant ship by fifty. The Italians recorded this strike at 1616. Six Blenheims unsuccessfully bombed the *Aosta* group in the face of intense antiaircraft fire. Then, at 1730, three Beauforts skimming the sea approached the heavily escorted column of ships from the west with the sun low in the sky behind them. This was the first appearance in the Mediterranean of this two-engine torpedo bomber, which had entered operational service in the North Sea in April 1940. The escort assumed they were Blenheims, and not until *Vivaldi* saw two torpedoes streaking toward her did she appreciate the attack's true nature. The destroyer turned to meet the threat head-on, and her crew watched one torpedo pass close to starboard and another to port. She signaled the convoy to make an emergency 90-degree jog to starboard, but it was too late. At 1731 a torpedo exploded on *Victoria*'s starboard side as she was turning, throwing a column of water high into the air. The liner gradually skewed to a halt with a slight list. The swiftness of the strike caught the escort of a dozen Ju.88s by surprise and they ineffectively counterattacked after the damage was done. Four Blenheims sent out at dusk failed to locate the convoy.[40]

Aviere steamed into the midst of hundreds of men who had been thrown overboard by the blast and began pulling people from the water. *Ascari* and *Camicia Nera* joined as the convoy gradually drew away. *Aviere*'s captain considered towing the large ship, but the sea was rough with a long swell and a strong sirocco wind was blowing. The wind was quickly scattering the crowded rafts and floats and the water was very cold. He decided to focus on rescue, since *Victoria* seemed to be in no immediate danger of sinking. He also shuttled small boats between the liner and the destroyer to evacuate men still on board.

By 1840/23rd the waters were clear and *Aviere* came alongside to rescue men from *Victoria*'s deck. At that moment, another alarm sounded. Two aircraft were bearing in from the east, the darkest area of the horizon, with the troop ship's silhouette outlined against the setting sun. *Aviere* and *Camicia Nera* opened fire with all guns and tried to interpose themselves between the intruders and *Victoria*. The planes, two Albacores out of seven that had taken off from Berka, near Benghazi, dropped torpedoes at 1,500 meters. One missed. The other passed a hundred meters ahead of *Aviere* and exploded harmlessly. The aircraft observed a "violent explosion" and claimed a hit. The destroyers shot down the flight leader.[41]

Five minutes later two more Albacores approached from the east, and this time one planted a torpedo directly into *Victoria* amidships. With the deck now only a few feet above water, the three Italian destroyers immediately came alongside and at 1900 *Victoria* sank stern-first. The destroyers combed the area until 0300; they ultimately rescued 1,046 of the 1,453 troops and crewmembers and delivered them to Tripoli.[42]

Force K, comprising *Penelope* and four destroyers, weighed anchor at 1930/23rd. "Being unable to attack the main enemy force [it] put to sea . . . to intercept a northbound convoy, reported in the Kerkennah area." The only convoy to depart Tripoli northbound was *Raffio* (316 GRT) and *Sant'Antonio* (271 GRT), which sailed without escort at 1900/23rd. Force K was chasing a false alarm and returned to port at 0900/24th.[43]

Seven Wellingtons from Malta harassed the main convoy between 2119 and 2300/23rd. Flying at two thousand feet, they dropped flares and then twenty-one 500-pound and forty-one 250-pound bombs, claiming two large explosions on the liner, and "probably hits on 2 other merchant vessels and on a warship believed to be a cruiser."[44] After that they strafed the Italian vessels. In fact, by this time the liner had sunk, and the Wellingtons caused no harm to other vessels. *Urge* spotted the flares, but was unable to close. Next, Malta dispatched seven Swordfish and two Albacores, but six aborted due to the weather and the other three missed the target. A second wave of six Swordfish followed. A pair returned with engine problems, but two pressed on and at 0434 claimed probable hits. In fact, they missed as well. Finally, thirteen Wellingtons from Egypt bombed the Italian formation and claimed two near misses. The escort commander, Rear

Bristol Beaufort. This aircraft came into operation in January 1940 and first appeared in the Mediterranean two years later, catching the Italians by surprise and distressing them knowing that they now had to face such a relatively fast (236 knots), long-range (1,400 nm) torpedo bomber. Storia Militare

Admiral Nomis di Pallone, reported that the Wellingtons had dropped flares to mark the route of the vessels and later the path of the torpedoes that were threatening the cruisers, but there was absolutely no damage, which the Italian admiral described as "testimony to the effectiveness of the active defense made by the naval units of the escort and the validity of the techniques used (smoke and maneuver) to frustrate the aggressive aerial enemy." Indeed, the British aircraft reported that "smoke screen very effective throughout attack A A very intense."[45]

At 0859/24 *P36* discharged a salvo from 4,500 yards at what she believed was a group of cruisers (but which actually was the convoy) and incorrectly notched a hit. In turn, destroyers counterattacked with thirty depth charges. The freighters began filing into Tripoli's harbor at 1415/24th. Weichold's report to the German admiralty noted that "disposition and performance of enemy reconnaissance planes, submarines and bombers, as well as the execution of their operations from bases on Malta, and partly also from Alexandria, were remarkably good." Given the scale, skill, and persistence of the attacks, Italian losses could have been far worse.[46]

Operation MF4

The 24th of January was a busy day. As the T18 convoy entered Tripoli, the British prepared to evacuate Benghazi, even as ships frantically continued to discharge cargo. Some 420 tons were unloaded that day. The trawlers *Wolborough* and *Hailstorm* sailed on the 24th, while the *Hunt*-class destroyers *Heythrop*, *Southwold*, and *Dulverton* hurriedly departed Alexandria for Tobruk to support an evacuation should one be necessary. AT.19 headed out for Tobruk while *Farndale* and *Eridge* left Tobruk for Alexandria escorting returning transports. Finally, to maintain the schedule of arrivals and to move valuable fast transports sitting uselessly in Malta under the bombs of an ever-increasing air offensive, the British launched operation MF4. The components of this operation included:

- MF4 West: *Breconshire*. Force B: *Naiad, Dido, Euryalus, Carlisle*, destroyers *Griffin, Kelvin, Kipling, Arrow, Kingston, Jaguar, Hasty, Isaac Sweers*. Sailed Alexandria 1600/24th;
- ME.9 *Glengyle, Rowallan Castle* (7,798 GRT/16.5 kts); and Force K: *Penelope*, destroyers *Lance, Legion, Lively, Maori, Zulu*. Sailed Malta 2000/25th.

The two escort forces would meet as usual in the central Mediterranean northwest of Benghazi and swap convoys.

At 1415/25th the army ordered Benghazi evacuated and all ships, lighters, and auxiliaries departed at midnight. *Heythrop, Southwold*, and *Dulverton* escorted *Crista, Harboe Jensen, Mausang, Bagshot*, and *Aberdare*. Another convoy included four large barges, while a third group consisted of eleven small lighters. A naval demolition party remained to wreck the partially repaired facilities. Axis reconnaissance reported this traffic at 1130/26th and again at 1645, prompting strikes by two waves of Libyan S.79s. *Heythrop, Southwold*, and *Dulverton* reported raids at 1715/26th, when they were 50 miles west northwest of Derna. *Heythrop* reported that five torpedo bombers dropped eight torpedoes against the convoy but all missed, and one of the aircraft was damaged. The aviators reported that they observed one cruiser sinking, while another was damaged. In fact, all the vessels, save one lighter that ran aground just short of Tobruk, arrived at Tobruk on the 27th. Most of the force, less *Dulverton* and the mine-sweepers, continued to Alexandria.[47]

Fighters covered Force B from 0745 to 1740/25th. Nonetheless, a Ju.88 began shadowing at 0935/25th. A solitary Ju.88 bombed *Breconshire* at 1057 and missed well astern. Four Ju.88s (four others had to abort due to engine problems) bombed in two waves between 1454 and 1521 when the British were thirty miles northwest of Tobruk. The Germans reported that two bombs struck a cruiser. "The cruiser was stopped and white smoke seen. Less than a minute later three or four explosions were felt." In fact, no bombs fell close and Hurricanes downed one of the Junkers.[48]

On the morning of the 26th a Ju.88 spotted ME.9 in the central Mediterranean heading away from Malta. The plane bombed *Glengyle* at 0901 and missed well ahead. Reacting to this sighting, forty-six Ju.88s, two He.111s, five Cant Z.1007bis, and three S.79s departed Sicily in successive waves. However, only ten Ju.88s and the He.111s located targets. One group delivered four shallow dive-bombing attacks between 1125 and 1136 just before Force K joined. A near miss disabled *Legion*'s asdic submarine-detection equipment. When the convoys met at 1230 there was a moment of excitement when an unknown vessel appeared to the south, but it proved to be the Italian hospital ship *Augusto*, which was searching for survivors from *Victoria*'s sinking several days before. Vian allowed her to proceed unharmed. *Kingston* left Force B and joined Force K, while *Lance* left Force K and joined Force B.[49]

Force K and *Breconshire* were bombed twice on the return trip. At 1412 a single Ju.88 missed badly and at 1545 four Ju.88s came in from astern. One landed bombs "fairly close to *Penelope*." By this time the wind was blowing Force 7–8 and the seas were increasing. Meanwhile, Force B recorded a series of strikes between 1640 and 1725 as it approached the 19th parallel. Six S.79s flying out of Sicily delivered these attacks, reporting a force of a battleship, three cruisers, and ten destroyers. They claimed: "one cruiser hit by three torpedoes, considered sunk. Other cruiser hit and seen abandoning ship." The British observed several torpedoes being dropped, but none came close to target. *Breconshire* and Force K made Grand Harbor at 1030/27th while Convoy ME.9 and Force B reached Alexandria at 1038/28th.[50]

Other Italian Activities

By the end of the month a shortage of fuel oil was seriously cramping Italian naval operations. On 26 January Riccardi reported insufficient fuel for destroyers to carry out a routine minelaying operation in the Sicilian Straits. Taranto was completely out, and depleted bunkers kept the *Aosta* group, which had just returned to port after escorting the T18 convoy, from contesting the MF4 operation.[51] Instead, Italian naval activity after T18 focused on the protection of traffic. This included the arrivals in Tripoli of *Tembien* (5,653 GRT/11 kts) on the 25th, *Ariosto* (4,116 GRT/10.5 kts) on the 27th, and *Bengasi* (1,567 GRT/11 kts) on the 30th. *Tembien* was the subject of one Ultra message generated four days after she arrived in Africa that forecast her departure from a Sicilian port "almost certainly Palermo" on the 29th. She clearly slipped under the radar. However, Ultra accurately pegged *Ariosto*'s route and departure date the day before she sailed. Nonetheless, like *Tembien*, *Ariosto* and her torpedo boat escort enjoyed an untroubled passage. Ultra intelligence concerning *Bengasi* was ambiguous. A message timed 2040/26th advised that she would be leaving some Sicilian port on the 27th, with "route very uncertain." Then, on p.m./27th, another message stated her departure had been delayed twenty-four hours. She indeed left Palermo at 2100/28th. The next night four Swordfish from Malta jumped her seventy-five miles northeast of Tripoli in gale force winds. The aircraft claimed two torpedo strikes and suffered one plane shot down. *Bengasi* made port unharmed at 0800 that morning.[52]

The British also interfered with traffic from Tripoli. *Sant'Antonio* sailed unescorted and arrived in Tunis on the 31st. She was not molested. *Napoli* and *Monginevro* left on the 29th and 30th respectively, each escorted by a torpedo boat. *Monginevro* docked in Naples on 1 February, but on the 3rd the submarine *Umbra* ambushed *Napoli* and torpedoed her thirty miles east of Sousse. *Napoli* ran aground, and Swordfish aircraft finished her the next day. *San Giovanni Battista* also sailed from Tripoli on 30 January, escorted by *Orsa* and *Calliope*. These vessels were all the topic of Ultra alerts of varying quality. One dispatch mentioned *Sant'Antonio*, stating that she had already departed Tripoli that day. *Monginevro* was misidentified, although her route and departure information was correctly related hours before her departure. *San Giovanni Battista*'s departure was the subject of several

Table 7.1. **Axis Traffic for Ships Departing in January 1942**

Type	Convoys	Convoys attacked	Detected by Ultra	Ships	Ships arrived	Ships lost	Ships damaged
Europe to Africa	15	5	13	22	21	1	0
Africa to Europe	15	6	14	18	15	2	2
Coastal west	1	0	1	1	1	0	0
Coastal east	4	0	4	5	5	0	0
Destroyers to Africa	0	0		0	0	0	0
Light cruisers to Africa	0	0		0	0	0	0
Submarines to Africa	5	1		5	4	1	0
Total Africa*	35	11	32	47	42	3	2
Total Balkans**	89			136	134	1	1

*Excludes military sailings. Includes German traffic.
**Excludes German traffic.
Source: USMM, *Difesa del traffico,* 7:392–97.

timely and accurate Ultra messages.[53] On the night of the 30/31st, when the convoy was seventy miles northwest of Tripoli, four Swordfish found and torpedoed *San Giovanni Battista,* leaving her dead in the water with a heavy list. The destroyer *Da Noli* left Tripoli to stiffen the *San Giovanni Battista's* protection, while *Calliope* brought the survivors to Tripoli. On 1 February the ship was taken under tow and *Calliope,* with assistance from *Da Noli,* brought her to Tajura, just east of Tripoli, where she arrived at 1800 on 2 February. The ship was repaired and not sunk for good until 1943.[54]

In January Italy's extensive commitments in the Tyrrhenian, Ligurian, Ionian, Adriatic, and Aegean seas continued to require greater resources than traffic to North Africa. Every day an average of thirty-one commercial vessels greater than 1,000 GRT plied metropolitan waters.[55]

The loss rate for ships involved in African traffic was 6 percent, down from 16 percent in December and 26 percent in November.

Air and Submarine Summaries

Axis aircraft raided Malta every day during January (1,973 sorties for the month by all types of aircraft), but weather often turned the Sicilian airfields into quagmires and the scale of attack was not what the Axis envisioned. The official Italian history complained that "The intensified attack was delayed much later than expected and in the months of January, February and in the first fortnight of March 1942 the II CAT forces, with slight Italian contribution, conducted only what [Kesselring] described as harassment raids." Indeed, in January Italian forces conducted only two night and one day operation. The British sent small groups of Wellingtons against Tripoli nearly every night.[56]

On 1 January seventeen British submarines were on patrol and at mid-month there were eleven. Throughout the Mediterranean British submarines made nineteen attacks firing sixty-nine torpedoes, and sank three submarines, an auxiliary, and five merchant vessels displacing 21,106 GRT. They damaged nine other vessels that totaled 5,300 GRT. The Italians conducted nineteen offensive and scouting patrols and six transport missions using twenty-two submarines. They did not attack any enemy units and lost two boats. The Germans started January with twenty-one boats in the Mediterranean. Two more entered and three were sunk. Eight boats were on patrol on 1 January and seven at mid-month. Despite heavy traffic along the Egyptian and Cyrenaican coast, German submarines enjoyed little success there, severely damaging *Kimberley*, while sinking *Gurkha* and the minesweeping trawler *Sotra* (313 GRT).[57]

Italy failed to exploit its December victories fully; it did not effectively impede enemy convoys to Malta, and the navy squandered oil using battleships to escort traffic. The scale of attack mounted against Italy's T18 Operation, and the relatively easy passage to and from Malta enjoyed by the MF2, 3, and 4 operations demonstrated the impact of Britain's passing possession of Cyrenaica. On the other hand, Italy delivered 99.9 percent of the material that it shipped to Africa in January. What both adversaries failed to do during the month was to use surface forces to attack shipping. The lack of this vital element helps explain why traffic on both sides was relatively successful.

Chapter 8

February 1942

After the conclusion of our counter-offensive . . . serious difficulties arose over supplies. The blame for this . . . lay with the half-hearted conduct of the war at sea by the Italians. The British Navy, in contrast, was very active in the early part of 1942, and the R.A.F. was also extremely troublesome.

ROMMEL (ROMMEL PAPERS, 191)

The Axis counteroffensive in Cyrenaica petered out in early February and the front line stabilized near Gazala, forty miles west of Tobruk. After capturing Benghazi on 29 January, Italy rushed minesweepers and auxiliaries to that port and hastened to repair its battered infrastructure. A 4 February meeting between the Italian and German commanders highlighted how the protection of traffic dominated the navy's activities. Rear Admiral Sansonetti told the group that commitments to maintain Crete, deliver oil, and feed the army and civilians in the Balkans required "34 ships per day. For the direct protection of these, we have 10 escort ships and 12 torpedo boats, of which 5 or 6 are normally in maintenance. . . . So, the escort is extremely poor. Libya absorbs all available destroyers. For Sardinia's traffic in coal and salt and [to supply] 100,000 men there are only five escort vessels available of which one is in maintenance and one resting. In the Aegean, daily traffic is five steamships and five torpedo boats for escort, which must also undertake war missions."[1]

The fuel oil situation had reached the point where the navy was draining oil from battleships to fuel destroyers and port depots were running
dry. On 7 February the navy's undersecretary of state complained, "Only
yesterday, with the arrival of a tanker in Palermo, was it possible to refuel
the destroyers of the *Aviere* Squadron. . . . However, Palermo had to supply
other units in transit and is again without oil. . . . Also, in Taranto the
Attendolo division has not yet been refueled with Romanian oil since its
return from Operation T18."[2]

In London, the British chiefs of staff concluded on 9 February that
the 8th Army could not advance beyond Cyrenaica in 1942, and that
"the risks are less immediate in the Middle East and must be accepted in
this theatre rather than elsewhere."[3] However, despite a concerted effort
to reinforce Singapore—at the cost of resources that otherwise would
have gone to or remained in the Middle East—the Asian bastion fell to a
smaller Japanese force on 15 February, rocking the British Empire, especially east of Suez.

British sea traffic in the Eastern Mediterranean remained heavy.
Freighters and tankers ran under escort between the Egyptian ports
and Tobruk, Haifa, Cyprus, and Beirut. Fleet destroyers conducted antisubmarine sweeps routinely, and in conjunction with special operations.
The fall of Benghazi and the withdrawal from Derna on the night of 2–3
February simplified the Mediterranean Fleet's tasks west of Tobruk. The
navy successfully evacuated most of the lighters and all shipping and auxiliaries from these ports despite "uncertainty and confusion."[4]

AT convoys departed on the 2nd, 3rd, 8th (two), 17th, 20th, 23rd, and
25th, with TA convoys running regularly in the other direction. Axis forces
attacked several of these. On the afternoon of the 5th, northeast of Tobruk,
a pair of S.79s approached an eastbound convoy of empty storeships
escorted by *Heythrop* and *Hurworth*. Only one plane dropped its torpedo;
it claimed leaving a freighter in flames. In fact, the only damage suffered
was that done to both aircraft, which were badly shot up, with one dead
and three wounded. On 1610/9th two S.79s from Rhodes raided AT.26.
They claimed one certain hit and one probable hit on a cruiser. The British
recorded unsuccessful strikes against *Heythrop* and *Antwerp*. At 1846/9th
German aircraft bombed *Farndale*, one of AT.27's escorts. A bomb passed

through the *Hunt*-class destroyer and burst in the water alongside. There were no casualties, but both of her boiler rooms flooded and *Gloxinia* towed her to Mersa Matruh. *Hurworth* came up in support and was bombed in turn at 0953/10th, although this time the Germans missed. A pair of S.79s from Rhodes attacked an eastbound convoy northeast of Mersa Matruh at 1145/14th. Their torpedoes missed, but the aviators claimed the sinking of one steamer of medium tonnage and probable damage to another.[5]

AT.29 was off Sidi Barrani on the 22nd when Ju.88s flying out of Crete appeared overhead. They bombed *Bintang* (2,779 GRT/10.5 kts) at 0930. There was "a great ball of fire" and in "less than a minute, she was blazing from stem to stern." The escort rescued twenty-seven men. At 1410 three more dive-bombed *Hanne* (1,080 GRT) and detonated her cargo of ammunition. Just twenty crewmen survived. Only *Alisa* (1,072 GRT) made it to Tobruk. Axis aircraft raided Convoy AT.31 after its 27 February arrival in Tobruk. A near-miss damaged *Southern Sea* and a bomb holed *Harboe Jensen*, forcing her to run aground to keep from sinking.[6]

Restoration of Benghazi

The Italians had devastated Benghazi's harbor in December 1941. The British had partially repaired it and then damaged it again when they evacuated in January. The Regia Marina assessed its condition in early February and concluded that it would need to reconstruct the unloading quay and the wooden jetty near the customs house. There were five easily repaired breaks in the Giuliana Mole, and, fortunately, no fresh damage to the Foraneo, Italia, or Sottoflutto moles. The Italians were gratified to find the naval headquarters building and barracks, semaphore, lighthouse, wireless station, electric power station, and a 5,000-ton fuel tank, all undamaged. There were no new obstructions in the harbor, and the retreating British had abandoned supplies like fuel containers and tires. Comando Supremo remarked with amazement: "while opening the port of Benghazi we recovered artillery for which we have the breeches."[7]

The first convoy from Tripoli arrived on the 18th, and included auxiliary minesweepers *Eritrea* (which struck a mine entering port) and *Tenacemente* (101 GRT), and the water-carrier *Tanaro*. The recovery vessel *Falco* (325 GRT) arrived the same day and the German steamship *Sturla* on the 24th. Using military engineers from all three services and civilian labor, the Italians quickly repaired the moles and restored the damaged quays and piers. By March Benghazi was back to full capacity.[8]

After a pause forced by stormy weather, the first vessels to leave for Tripoli in February were the German steamer *Trapani* (1,855 GRT/11 kts) and the tanker *Rondine* (6,077 GRT/9 kts), escorted by the destroyer *Premuda* and the torpedo boats *Castore* and *Polluce*, all from Palermo, on the 4th and 5th respectively. The small steamer *Bolsena* left Tunis for Tripoli on the 5th. All were the subject of multiple Ultra messages that detailed itineraries but not departure dates. *Trapani* and *Bolsena* had untroubled voyages. The British submarine *Upholder* missed *Rondine* off Cape San Vito, Sicily at 1345/5th. The sloop *Orsa* and torpedo boat *Aretusa* intervened and unsuccessfully hunted the submarine. At 2150/6th an ASV Wellington reported *Rondine* off the Tunisian coast. Two Swordfish attacked at 0100/7th. The escort shot one down and the other reported a "violent explosion followed by large red fire." In fact, its torpedo missed as well. *Rondine* safely made Tripoli at 1700/7th. The motor ship *Monviso*, escorted by destroyer *Da Noli* and torpedo boat *Cantore*, left Tripoli for Messina at 1800/5th. An ASV Wellington reported the convoy at 2030/6th; four Albacores found it off Cape Passero at 0100/7th. The Albacores reported one certain and one probable hit and that the ship was stopped

Tripoli harbor, 27 February 1942. This photo shows from left to right the destroyer *Strale*, a small motor-sailer, the steamship *Tembien*, the motorship *Unione*, the torpedo boat *Pallade*, and the motorships *Monviso* and *Ravello*.
STORIA MILITARE

amid columns of black smoke. They were probably seeing the defensive smoke screen, as the convoy was unharmed.[9]

Lively and *Zulu*, working with an ASV-equipped Wellington, sortied from Malta at 1530/7th to hunt the ships that had been reported damaged in the previous night's airstrikes. Italian reconnaissance spotted and followed them and Supermarina had time to suspend or divert most traffic. However, the Wellington led the destroyers to "two 4,000 ton steamers." The first proved to be the armed trawler *Grongo* (316 GRT), in passage from Lampedusa to Pantelleria. The destroyers closed to 1,500 yards, and at 2216/7th smothered the small ship with gunfire and left her burning. *Grongo*'s seven survivors from her crew of seventeen fought the blaze until 0900 the next morning, when *MAS 577*, sailing from Lampedusa, rescued them. The drifting wreck foundered that afternoon. The motor-sailer *Aosta* (494 GRT), in transit from Pantelleria to Tripoli with a load of ammunition, ran afoul of the raiders at 0130/8th. The destroyers illuminated the scene from only 500 meters and a flurry of shells smashed aboard. At 0300 *Aosta*'s cargo exploded, and she quickly sank. *MAS 560, 563,* and *574* out of Pantelleria rescued twenty-five survivors from her crew of forty-one. This was to be the last successful strike by surface warships operating out of Malta until December 1942. Significantly, Ultra had not mentioned either of these vessels. In a meeting on the 8th with Cavallero and Riccardi, Kesselring admitted that German aircraft had sighted the British destroyers before *Grongo* and *Aosta* had sailed, but were unable to act against them due to "radio disturbance." Sansonetti asked Kesselring if it was possible to expedite communications. "If they had known, they would not have sailed." Kesselring promised to have technicians investigate the matter.[10]

During this period coastal traffic included *Emilio* and *Achaja*, which left Tripoli for Buerat on the 5th and 6th; and *Delia*, which departed Tripoli for Tunisia on the 8th. *Sturla* and *Emilio* returned to Tripoli from Buerat on the 10th and 11th. Shipping activity spiked on the 13th. *Argentea* (3,302 GRT/12 kts), escorted by *Calliope*, left Palermo for Tripoli; the *Eritrea* convoy to Benghazi, described above, got under way; *Anna Maria* sailed unescorted; and the German *Atlas* (2,297 GRT/10 kts) and *Ariosto* (4,116 GRT/10.5 kts), escorted by *Premuda* and *Polluce*, departed Tripoli for Palermo. There were many Ultra messages, and although none of them provided concrete information, the volume of radio traffic was enough to justify an air search of the area. At 2245/13th an ASV Wellington reported enemy ships, and in response four Albacores and two Swordfish took off to hunt them down. At 0327/14th the Albacores reported striking a destroyer and two 3,000-ton merchant vessels a hundred miles northwest of Tripoli, saying that they had left one vessel listing and ablaze. This was the *Atlas* convoy, which reported being delayed by "persistent air attacks that had, however, no consequences." The defensive smokescreen had deceived the Swordfish. However, at 2203/14th submarine *P38* intercepted the convoy as it continued north and torpedoed *Ariosto* off Cape Afrika, Tunisia. The ship sank with 410 men on board, of whom 294 were prisoners. The escort rescued 252. Of the 158 men lost, 132 were prisoners.[11]

Operation MF5

The Malta convoy operation MF5 followed the template that had been established in December and successfully applied in January. Four empty cargo ships in Malta formed Convoy ME.10 bound for Alexandria escorted part way by Force K; three vessels from Alexandria formed Convoy MW.9 bound for Malta. MW.9 was to sail in two sections "to arrive off Tobruk at dusk, in the hope of deceiving the enemy into thinking that Tobruk was the actual destination." ME.10 and MW.9 would swap escorts in the central Mediterranean, 170 miles west by south of Crete.[12] The convoys included these elements:

- Convoy MW.9A: *Clan Campbell* (7,255 GRT/16 kts), *Clan Chattan* (7,262 GRT/16 kts). Escort: *Carlisle*, destroyer *Lance*, *Hunt*-type destroyers *Avon Vale*, *Eridge*, *Heythrop*. Sailed 1600/12th;
- Convoy MW.9B: *Rowallan Castle* (7,798 GRT/16.5 kts). Escort: Hunts *Southwold*, *Beaufort*, *Dulverton*, *Hurworth*. Sailed 1700/12th;
- Force B (Rear Admiral Vian): *Naiad*, *Dido*, *Euryalus*, destroyers *Arrow*, *Griffin*, *Hasty*, *Havock*, *Jaguar*, *Jervis*, *Kelvin*, *Kipling*. Sailed 0300/13th;
- Convoy ME.10: *Breconshire*, *Ajax*, *City of Calcutta*, *Clan Ferguson*. Escort: *Penelope* (Captain Nicholl), destroyers *Decoy*, *Fortune*, *Legion*, *Lively*, *Sikh*, *Zulu*. Sailed 1900/13th.

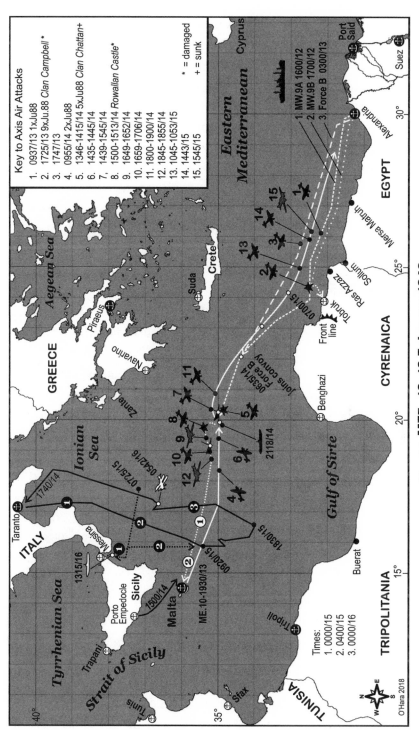

Key to Axis Air Attacks
1. 0937/13 1xJu88
2. 1725/13 9xJu.88 *Clan Campbell**
3. 1747/13
4. 0955/14 2xJu88
5. 1346-1415/14 5xJu88 *Clan Chattan*+
6. 1435-1445/14
7. 1439-1545/14
8. 1500-1513/14 *Rowallan Castle**
9. 1649-1652/14
10. 1659-1706/14
11. 1800-1900/14
12. 1845-1855/14
13. 1045-1053/15
14. 1443/15
15. 1545/15

* = damaged
+ = sunk

Map 8.1. **MF5, 12–16 February 1942**

O'Hara 2018

Axis aircraft sighted MW.9A as it passed Sidi Barrani. At 0938/13th a Ju.88, on an armed reconnaissance mission out of Libya, suddenly dove out of the sun and dropped a stick of four bombs off *Clan Chattan's* starboard quarter. Then at 1014 *Carlisle* spotted a pair of S.79s. The light cruiser engaged them at 10,000 yards, and they circled away because their pilots judged the steamships to be of small tonnage and "therefore an objective of scant importance." Torpedoes were another necessary item of naval warfare that the Italians needed to husband and expend only with care. The aircraft reappeared half an hour later and fighters chased them off.[13]

MW.9A and 9B were to have rendezvoused north of Tobruk at 1800, but nine Ju.88s flying from Crete jumped them a half hour before despite their cover of eight fighters. *Carlisle's* Captain Neame complained, "At this time the plot was considerably confused by the presence of 8 to 10 fighters, not all in communication with *Carlisle.* . . . [T]here was no means of telling whether they were hostile or not until they came within sight." Diving out of the clouds and through heavy flak, "with little or no R.D.F. warning," a Ju.88 struck *Clan Campbell* at 1725/13th. One bomb landed in a coal bunker and another passed through the ship and exploded beyond. The freighter's speed dropped and Neame sent her to Tobruk, accompanied by *Avon Vale* and *Eridge*. She arrived at 0300/14th and the *Hunts* turned around to rejoin MW.9. The Germans claimed, "one steamship and one destroyer probably sunk and one destroyer damaged."[14]

Force B also had a troubled passage. The shadowing started at 1415/13th, and between 1747 and 1838 single Ju.88s bombed Vian's cruisers through the gathering twilight at low altitude and achieved only several "close misses." Force B sailed through the night and joined MW.9 at 0635/14th. The convoy then steamed northwest, staying equidistant between enemy airbases in Greece and Cyrenaica.[15]

Convoy ME.10 departed Malta at 1915/13th in two columns, zigzagging at 15 knots, bothered only by a pair of Ju.88s at 0955/14th. The escort was to have been stronger. The light cruiser *Cleopatra* with the destroyer *Kingston* had left Gibraltar on the 10th. The Italian submarine *Aradam* spotted them enroute to Malta, and on the morning of the 11th 9 Ju.87s and 15 Ju.88s lifted off from Sicilian air fields. The Ju.87s failed to make contact in bad weather, but Ju.88s dive-bombed the cruiser at 1035/11th just off St. Elmo Light. A 1,000-pound bomb passed through the fore-castle deck and detonated in the water alongside, damaging the keel and flooding several magazines. The next day in Grand Harbor German aircraft sank *Maori*, another scheduled participant. A bomb struck the destroyer's upper deck and exploded in the gearing room. The oil tanks ruptured, feeding a large blaze that quickly enveloped the ship's after end. After forty-five minutes a magazine exploded, breaking the ship in two. In almost four months of attacks, this was the first major warship in Malta to be destroyed by bombing.[16]

Axis aircraft began shadowing MW.9 at 0700/14th, but the air raids did not begin in earnest until the two convoys approached their rendezvous. At 1346 one of five Ju.88s flying out of Greece bombed *Clan Chattan* in a hold filled with munitions, igniting a fierce fire. As antiaircraft ammunition began exploding, the vessel's master ordered his crew to abandon ship. *Southwold* came alongside at 1405 and in ten minutes rescued 69 crewmembers and 227 passengers. *Beaufort*, *Dulverton*, and *Avon Vale* retrieved others who had jumped overboard. *Southwold* continued to stand by as the rest of the force steamed to meet ME.10. Meanwhile ten He.111s and five Ju.88s from Sicily were hastening to join the action. At 1413 a Ju.88 released bombs that fell close to *Naiad* while others dropped ordnance outside the screen.[17]

At 1445/14th the convoys met 160 miles north of Benghazi with, as Vian commented, each "attended by own bombers." Captain Nicholl reported that "A heavy bombing attack developed on both convoys as they approached and during the changeover of escorts between 1435 and 1445." *Eridge*'s captain wrote that "cruisers and destroyers were criss crossing each other's tracks, or making drastic alterations of course, while steaming to their new screening positions. The sea was choppy and a stiff breeze was driving low clouds across the sky. Aircraft, either singly or on [sic] small groups, were frequently crossing breaks in the clouds and the guns were in almost continuous action. . . . It soon became difficult to spot the aircraft amongst the ever-increasing black puffs of exploding anti-aircraft." The four transports of ME.10 passed to the protection of Force B while Force K took *Rowallan Castle*. *Decoy* and *Fortune* continued to Alexandria with Force B while *Lance* rejoined Force K.[18]

Air strikes on the crossing convoys were largely ineffective. After *Clan Chattan* the closest any ordnance fell was within a hundred yards of *Clan Ferguson* at 1444 and near *Kelvin* at about 1450 (splinters killed one and wounded another member of her crew). However, at 1514, with the exchange barely complete, five Ju.88s descended in shallow dives and planted a stick of bombs alongside *Rowallan Castle*. A crewman wrote: "An enormous wall of water rose, then swamped the boats and deluged the Oerlikon gunners on the boat deck. It felt as though the ship had taken a leap in the water." A fuel line fractured, and after emergency repairs the ship could only creep along at four knots. *Zulu* passed a line to the crippled ship. Nicholl hoped the freighter could make repairs, and indeed she signaled to *Penelope* that she might to be able to restore some speed within an hour. At 1545 the intervention of four Beaufighters from Malta, still 250 miles away, gave the convoy a respite, but with the action happening so far from the island they could linger only half an hour.[19]

After the convoys separated and the Beaufighters withdrew at 1615, attacks on both the eastward and westward coursing formations continued. Moreover, three Axis naval formations sortied on the 14th. At 1500 eight German S-Boats left Porto Empedocle in Sicily and headed southeast to lurk off Malta. More worrisome, at 1840 Vice Admiral Carlo Bergamini in *Duilio* with the 10th Squadron (*Maestrale, Grecale,* and *Scirocco*) departed Taranto, followed at 1945 by Rear Admiral De Courten's 7th Division (*Aosta* and *Montecuccoli*), and the 13th Squadron (*Alpino, Bersagliere, Carabiniere, Fuciliere*) from Taranto. From Messina came Rear Admiral Angelo Parona's 3rd Division (*Gorizia* and *Trento*) and the 11th Squadron (*Ascari, Aviere, Camicia Nera, Geniere*). They departed at 2315/14th. *Duilio* was hardly underway when at 1955 Supermarina ordered her back because it had concluded that the British formations did not include capital ships.[20]

Parona and De Courten were to have met at 0800/15th seventy miles east of Malta. Their movements were calculated on Supermarina's faulty premise that two convoys were bound for Malta, the first of two merchant ships, one or two cruisers, and five or six destroyers, while the second was three steamers with two cruisers and three destroyers. Supermarina believed the first convoy would arrive at the point where Parona and

De Courten were to meet at about the same time. German and Italian aircraft kept station overhead and the flagships carried German radio operators to improve ship-to-air communications. German aircraft had bombed Malta's airfields hard the night before to reduce the island's retaliatory power. With the wisdom of hindsight, Vice Admiral Iachino later noted critically that Parona's departure had been delayed, and that if he had sailed at midnight/13th he could have caught the British during the critical period when the convoys were being passed one from one group of escorts to the other.[21]

Vian started back to Alexandria, shaping his course to pass *Clan Chattan*. At 1530 he saw the merchant ship, "afire aft and right down by the stern," and ordered *Decoy* to sink her. *Decoy*'s first torpedo was errant, but she dispatched the burning freighter with her second. The destroyer then closed on *Southwold* and at 1615 took off half the personnel that *Southwold* had rescued. The two destroyers, along with *Carlisle*, steamed east to rejoin Vian.[22]

At 1650 two S.79s from Libya approached Force K and claimed they "hit a 10,000-ton ship, which was subsequently seen to sink, and a destroyer which ... must be considered severely damaged." The British reported that

The British freighter *Clan Chattan* burning, with *Southwold* standing by. She was bombed by Ju.88s at 1346/14th February and a hold full of ammunition caught fire, prompting her master to order abandon ship. She was torpedoed and sunk by *Decoy* two and a half hours later. STORIA MILITARE

planes dropped torpedoes at long range and that tracks were sighted at a distance. Eight other S.79s from Sicily failed to find the convoy.[23]

As dusk approached Force B/ME.10 encountered more adventures. These started at 1750, when one of *Carlisle*'s steam pipes fractured. The cruiser stopped to repair the damage as *Eridge*, *Heythrop*, and *Beaufort* stood by. Five minutes later ten Ju.88s began harassing this stationary target, followed at 1804 by six He.111s. A pair of 550-pound bombs straddled the cruiser amidships and inflicted minor damage; four smaller bombs bracketed her astern. At 1840 *Eridge* "was near missed by four small bombs" that fell just ahead. Her captain wrote that she "staggered as if she had collided with a stone jetty, teetered on the edge of the crater, then tumbled in: tons of water crashed onto the upper deck. . . . The ship struggled in the maelstrom before rising, with water gushing over the sides, as if she was a dog shaking itself after an unexpected immersion." On her return *Eridge* needed to be docked to repair the damage.[24]

Carlisle fixed her pipe by 1853, and, in company with the three Hunts, rejoined Vian at 2215. In addition to the strikes against *Carlisle*, Vian recorded that aircraft dropped bombs at 1800, 1807, 1812, 1825, 1830, 1844 (800 yards off *Naiad*), 1850 (200 yards off *Naiad* and *Euryalus* and near *Dido*), and 1855 (100 yards astern of a destroyer and 100 yards ahead of *Dido*). The final and closest attack occurred at 1901 when a bomb landed 50 yards off *Euryalus*' bow.[25]

At 1734 eighteen Ju.88s struck Force K/MW.9 and claimed two hits on *Rowallan Castle*, although in fact they missed.[26] But this did not matter. At 1718/14th Cunningham signaled to scuttle *Rowallan Castle* if she could not make 10 knots. Nicholl queried *Rowallan Castle*'s master about his prospects of reaching this speed. The news that the Italian fleet was at sea did not come until 0121/15, when Parona's force passed *P36*, but the possibility was on everyone's minds as when *Zulu* queried Nicholl, "In the event of surface attack am I to slip *Rowallan Castle*?" At 1910 the merchant ship answered that she was making 8 knots, to which Nicholl replied two minutes later: "I do not feel justified in accepting the risks for the whole force which will result from your best speed. Regret you must be sunk . . . Very sorry." After *Lance* removed the crew *Lively* torpedoed the transport. Force K then sped for Malta—without *Sikh* and *Zulu*, which headed east for Alexandria. The two destroyers passed the submarine *Topazio* at 2118/14th. The Italian boat sighted a large, two-funnel destroyer and tried to maneuver into a launch position. When a second destroyer came up *Topazio* quickly submerged and launched a single torpedo at *Zulu* that missed. At 0700/15th *Zulu* and *Sikh* eventually joined Force B sixty miles north of Tobruk.[27]

The Italian surface forces united at 0920/15th, seventy miles south by southeast of Malta under the cover of a strong air umbrella. De Courten had already received word from the German S-Boats that the first convoy was too close to Malta to be intercepted. However, he proceeded south at 20 knots, hoping to cut off the second convoy he thought was at sea. Naturally, he sighted nothing, and the disappointed admiral turned back to Italy at 1830/15th.[28]

In the early hours of 16 February Supermarina alerted De Courten that, based on a decrypted sighting report, a British airstrike was incoming before dawn. As a result, the squadron was prepared when flares suddenly illuminated it at 0444/16th. The ships immediately made radical turns and emitted smoke. By 0532 the force of five Albacores had dropped the last of four torpedoes. They claimed three definite and one probable hit. "Fires seen on four ships. One [cruiser] seen to be well alight at stern." In fact, all torpedoes missed. However, *P36* torpedoed the destroyer *Carabiniere* south of Messina at 1345/16th, blowing off the vessel's bow despite an enhanced escort that included a torpedo boat, two MAS boats, and seven aircraft. The submarine claimed a heavy cruiser. The badly damaged destroyer made Messina under her own power.[29]

Force K entered Grand Harbor on the morning of the 15th. Axis bombers raided ME.10 two more times, with aircraft identified as He.111s bombing *Dido* and *Breconshire* at 1053/15th. At 1520 a pair of S.79s in company with other bombers from Rhodes attacked when the convoy was passing north of Tobruk despite British fighter coverage that shot one aircraft down. They claimed to see "a ship in the process of sinking." Vian detached *Carlisle, Beaufort, Dulverton, Hurworth,* and *Southwold* to Tobruk at midnight. *Clan Campbell* had made temporary repairs, unloading and then reloading her cargo. Escorted by *Southwold*, she joined *Carlisle* and the other Hunts at 0629/16th and, under heavy fighter

The destroyer *Carabiniere* had her bow blown off by the submarine P36. Here she is returning to port under her own power. Comparison with the image of a sister destroyer to the left clearly shows the damage that *Carabiniere* suffered. Storia Militare

protection, all arrived in Alexandria at 1830/16th. Force B and *Breconshire* made Alexandria at 0130/16th, while the other three transports of ME.10, escorted by five destroyers, continued to Port Said.[30]

MW.9 was the first Malta convoy to be completely stopped by Axis forces. The 15th Cruiser Squadron expended 3,700 rounds of 5.25-inch ammunition, even though it was involved in only five of fifteen separate attacks that Axis air forces delivered. Of these fifteen, only three were effective, but that was enough. However, based on typically inflated aviator reports, the Germans tallied losses of two steamers sunk and four steamers, three cruisers, and three destroyers damaged. The German admiralty noted uncritically that, combined with losses claimed by Italian flyers, "the enemy shipping in the central and eastern Mediterranean must have been seriously impaired."[31]

RAF fighter coverage disappointed the Royal Navy, which submitted a memorandum stating that "There is still much room for improvement in the co-operation of fighters working with the Fleet." Also, "The Air Ministry have been requested by signal to hold a Meeting to discuss the local control of H.M. Ships of R.A.F. short range fighters. They have not agreed to this in the past, but appear likely to do so now." A handwritten comment on this further observed: "It is astonishing how unreliable R/T [ship-to-aircraft radio] still is. This failure deprives the Fighter Protection of half its value."[32]

Operation K7

The major Italian convoy operation in February was code-named K7. As the assigned transports gathered in their departure ports there were two other sailings to Tripoli. On 15 February *Bravo* (1,571 GRT) weighed anchor from Pantelleria, and the next day *Tembien* left Trapani. They arrived on the 19th and 18th respectively. Ultra's only notice of *Bravo*'s passage was word of her arrival. Preliminary information about *Tembien* was unhelpful. "A convoy, composition unknown, escorted by torpedo-boat *Saetta* had orders to steer from eighteen hours Tuesday seventeenth for a point probably about 33d10m by 12d05m." This message was received four hours after the ship had passed the specified point. During that week coastal traffic—*Rosa* (559 GRT) to Buerat, *Labor* to Tripoli, and *Bolsena* to Buerat—all transited unmolested.[33] K7 involved two convoys, each of three ships.[34]

- Convoy 1: *Monginevro, Unione* (6,071 GRT/15.5 kts), *Ravello*. Cargo: 8,451 tons of materiel, 1,758 of munitions, 1,804 of oil and lubricants, 84 tanks and 363 vehicles. Direct Escort: 14th Squadron/ Rear Admiral Amedeo Nomis di Pollone (*Vivaldi, Malocello, Zeno, Premuda, Strale*). Torpedo boat *Pallade* joined at sea at 0955/22nd. Sailed Messina 1730/21st;
- Convoy 1 Support Group: 3rd Division/Rear Admiral Angelo Parona (*Gorizia, Trento, Bande Nere*) 13th Squadron/Commander Ferrante Capponi (*Alpino, Da Noli, Oriani*). Sailed Messina 1830/21st;
- Convoy 2: *Lerici, Monviso, Giulio Giordani*. Cargo: 3,108 tons of materiel, 752 of munitions, 13,643 of gasoline, oil, and lubricants, 49 tanks, and 212 vehicles. Direct Escort: 15th Squadron/Captain Enrico Mirti della Valle (*Pigafetta, Usodimare, Pessagno*, torpedo boat *Circe*); 10th Squadron/Captain Riccardo Pontremoli (*Maestrale, Scirocco*). Sailed Taranto and Brindisi p.m./20th. *Lerici* had steering problems, but all arrived at Corfu. Sailed Corfu 1330/21st;[35]

- Convoy 2 Support Group/Vice Admiral Carlo Bergamini: *Duilio*; 11th Squadron/Captain Gastone Minotti (*Aviere, Geniere, Ascari, Camicia Nera*). Sailed Taranto 1600/21st.

Convoy 1 and the *Gorizia* group united at 2315/21st and angled southeast to pass 190 miles east of Malta. *Duilio* joined them at dawn on the 22nd and Convoy 2 hove into view at 1245/22nd, a little behind schedule. Ju.88s and Bf.110s from Sicily formed overhead from early dawn. The convoys maintained separate formations in a one-by-four-mile rectangle heading south at 14 knots while the support groups guarded the rectangle's starboard side, expecting that surface threats, if any, would materialize from this direction.

As early as 13 February signals intelligence warned the British that Convoy 2 was to gather at Corfu, but there was no concrete information about the operation itself—just hints that Bletchley Park passed along as "No details available [but] may be connected with important convoy mentioned [earlier]."[36] The first actionable information regarding Operation K7, timed 1550Z/21st, was that Convoy 2 was getting under way. The message said: "Now definitely known that an important convoy escorted by destroyers and cruisers and supported by a battleship will be at sea in Central Mediterranean Sunday Twenty second to reach Tripoli morning of Twenty third." Information about the escorts arrived after they were at sea.[37]

Battleship support was a sure sign of something big, and the British scrambled to respond, but conditions over the Ionian Sea that day were miserable. Moreover, Axis forces were pounding Malta's airfields. On the night of the 21st/22nd there were "almost continuous intruder" alerts, and two aircraft were damaged. On the 22nd repeated raids on Hal Far airfield destroyed two Albacores and damaged three Albacores, three Swordfish, a Maryland, and an ASV Wellington. Nonetheless, at 0135/22nd a Malta-based ASV Wellington reported a battleship, two cruisers, and four destroyers eighty miles west of Zante. Five Albacores took off, but were recalled an hour later when another sighting put the same group of warships eighty miles east of the position originally reported. The SIS intercepted the sighting reports, and the forewarned fleet awaited an attack, which never came.[38]

At 0925/22nd a Maryland reported three merchant vessels, two cruisers, and ten destroyers 210 miles east southeast of Malta. By this time several strikes from Egypt were inbound. Two B-17s had taken off at 0900 and five torpedo-armed Beauforts left the airfield at 0920. One escorting Bf.110 damaged a B-17, while the other scattered ordnance in *Duilio*'s vicinity at 1440. Bergamini requested aerial reinforcements and "the request was promptly accepted after a very fast connection." The Beauforts aborted when they reached the limit of their range without spotting the enemy.[39]

During the daytime Marylands maintained contact with the convoys. Supermarina noted, "[sighting reports] occurred at quite frequent intervals up to 1500 then they became fewer and at 1600 ceased completely." Bu Amud airfield, just east of Tobruk, dispatched three Blenheim strikes. Four aircraft flew off at 1220/22nd. The SIS was listening in; Supermarina's war diary recorded, "at 1240, based on interceptions we learned that English air attacks would begin shortly. Appropriate arrangements were made, German fighters sought." Rear Admiral Nomis di Pollone positioned the destroyers expecting that the enemy would come from out of the sun.[40]

These arrangements were not tested, however. One Blenheim returned with engine problems and the others could not find the target. The second strike at of six aircraft returned at 1335 after the leader's radio malfunctioned. Finally, the last group of seven aircraft, which took off at 1420, had four planes abort due to engine problems, and the other three reached the limit of their range without contact. Shortly after noon Vice Admiral Leatham designated *Penelope* and *Legion* to "intercept possible shipping on westward route" at dusk, but he rescinded this order seven hours later because of unfavorable weather.[41]

At dusk an ASV-equipped Wellington left Malta to maintain contact, but engine problems forced its return. Air raids had damaged the island's other two ASV Wellingtons, so ground crews quickly repaired the original aircraft. It took off again, but did not report until 0310/23rd. Of three torpedo-armed Wellingtons that left Malta only one found the enemy, at 0410. The Italians reported that the British dropped eleven flares between 0410 and 0518 and the escort covered the convoy in smoke.

The Wellington's strike was ineffective. Indeed, the escort reported, "we were not able to verify any air attack." Leatham considered it too late to dispatch Albacores.[42]

Based on a false alarm, the Mediterranean command had previously ordered submarines *P34*, *P38*, *P39*, and *Una* to gather off the Libyan coast to intercept a convoy. However, when confirmation about K7 came in on the 21st they reestablished a patrol line off Tripoli. Malta also dispatched *Upholder*, *Unbeaten*, *P35*, and *P36*, but they could not arrive in time. It was hazy on the morning of the 23rd. The convoy proceeded in two groups about eight miles apart. At 0820 CR.42 fighters appeared overhead. At this time the convoy started passing through the submarine concentration. *Circe*, the only Italian vessel equipped with an echo-location device, picked up a contact at 1015. As the formation maneuvered around the danger, she and *Usodimare* hunted and dropped depth charges. At 1030 *P38* breached the surface. *Usodimare* engaged, and the submarine immediately submerged, mortally wounded. Her crew of thirty-two men perished. Two torpedo boats from Tripoli reinforced the escort at 1130. At 1149 *P34* launched four torpedoes on the inshore side from 4,500 yards. A CR.42 spotted the tracks and radioed an alert. The convoy immediately turned, and *Unione* observed torpedoes passing "a few meters astern and ahead." The convoys arrived at their destination between 1545 and 1750/23rd.[43]

Operation K7 was a complete success. The British had good intelligence; they mounted repeated air strikes and concentrated a strong submarine force at the right time and place. None of this availed. Weather favored the Italians, but the escorts, both in the air and at sea, deployed new technologies, such as sea-to-air radio links and sonar, which proved effective. Bergamini identified several other reasons for his trouble-free passage: the British loss of the Western Cyrenaican bases; the suppression of Malta's airbases; and he was especially enthusiastic about the air support, reporting, "I will only observe that this was the first time an air escort functioned truly excellently. It failed to keep the enemy reconnaissance entirely away but this cannot be expected; it did create a significant obstacle." He lauded the cooperation and noted that *Duilio*'s ship-to-air radio link "gave a sense of security."[44]

The Value of Malta

On 21st February General Auchinleck wrote to the chiefs of staff: "Of the seven ships forming the Jan. and Feb. convoys three have arrived Malta. . . . It appears useless to try to pass in a convoy until the air situation in Malta has been restored and the military situation in Cyrenaica improved. Recommend policy of reinforcement of Malta be reconsidered."[45] On 24 February the War Cabinet duly reconsidered. They noted that the stocks of "certain vital items" would be exhausted in two months' time and other essential commodities would then be "in very short supply." Admiral Pound recommended against attempting convoys from the eastern Mediterranean, "even if we are prepared to accept very heavy shipping losses." However, an escort of battleships "strong enough to deter the Italians from attempting a fleet action" would be required for a Gibraltar–Malta convoy.[46] Despite these problems, and notwithstanding Auchinleck's recommendation, the chiefs decided that "Malta is of such importance both as air staging point and as impediment to enemy reinforcement route that the most drastic steps are justifiable to sustain it." They told Auchinleck that they could not supply Malta from the west and urged Cunningham to attempt a convoy during the March period of darkness and that "no consideration of risks to ships themselves need deter you . . . it should be regarded as our primary military commitment."[47]

Italian Conclusions

On 16 February the Italian high command reflected on its activities in the war to date and summarized its perception of Great Britain's naval strategy. "Except for the traffic war, the British have rarely undertaken offensive actions (like the bombardments of Genoa and Tripoli which were of practically no significance and seemed intended to win prestige rather than secure results of a military nature) [strategically] the British have followed a rather prudent course aimed at conserving a perfect balance between air and naval elements, which has allowed them to maneuver safely avoiding decisive battles, and exploiting only opportunities that are favorable." The study concluded that "The British have so far sought resolution of the maritime war not in a decisive fleet action based upon their initial numerical superiority but in the war on enemy traffic and protection of their own traffic; that is, on a war of attrition and exhaustion." About itself Supermarina commented that "fleet activities since the beginning of the war have been directed mainly at keeping open the necessary lines of communication for our armed forces and possessions and to countering the enemy's lines of communication," saying that "The maintenance of our communications is a very heavy burden because we need food by sea for considerable occupation forces and civilian population in Dalmatia, Albania, and Greece, as well as the fighting forces and the people of Libya. This task has absorbed all the surface forces and in some cases also some submarines. . . . The scarcity of fuel had greatly limited the fleet's activities."[48]

The report showed that Supermarina still considered the main purpose of the battle force to be a fleet action, and that the miles that had been steamed by the destroyers, cruisers, and battleships in protecting the vital lines of communication were not the best use of ships and fuel. Such a conclusion seems curious in that the only purpose of a fleet action, in any case, is to secure maritime lines of communication. Nonetheless, whether it was the hard way or the easy way, whether it was according to the wishes of the high command, or not, whether it was a task for which the navy had trained and acquired ships or not, the Italian navy fought the war with which it was faced, rather than the war that it wanted—even to the point of using their precious, fuel-starved battleships as convoy escorts.

Traffic to the End of the Month

After K7 the only Axis transport to reach Africa during the rest of February was the German ship *Wachtfels* (8,467/13 kts) which, escorted by *Polluce*, departed Palermo on the 22nd and docked in Tripoli at 1630 the next day. She was the subject of six separate Ultra messages, but none provided actionable information. In any case, at this time British resources were focused on stopping the K7 convoy.[49]

Between 22 February and 27 February *Beppe* (4,859 GRT/10 kts), *Argentea*, *Bengasi*, *Vettor Pisani*, and *Tembien* departed Tripoli for Italian harbors. Ultra provided intelligence on all of them. On the night of the 24th three Albacores attacked the *Bengasi* convoy west of Malta without result. *Argentea* recorded an air strike at 0200/26th, but no

Table 8.1. **Axis Traffic for Ships Departing in February 1942**

Type	Convoys	Convoys attacked	Detected by Ultra	Ships	Ships arrived	Ships lost	Ships damaged
Europe to Africa	10	3	9	14	13	1	0
Africa to Europe	10	5	10	11	10	2	0
Coastal and Inter-Island*	13	1	10	15	14	1	0
Submarines to Africa	1	0		1	1	0	0
Total Africa**	33	9	29	40	37	3	0
Total Balkans***	84	0		154	153	1	0

*Includes *Grongo* from Lampedusa to Pantelleria and four convoys from Tripoli to Benghazi.
**Excludes military sailings. Includes German traffic.
***Excludes German traffic.
Source: USMM, *Difesa del traffico,* 7:398–403.

British accounts mention such an event.[50] Finally, the submarine *Upholder* waylaid *Tembien* three hours north of Tripoli. Two torpedoes fired at 1906 from 2,800 yards smashed into the freighter. She sank in twenty minutes. Of 654 men, including 498 prisoners of war, 497 men, including 419 prisoners died. *Strale,* the escorting destroyer, dropped eight depth charges and then rescued survivors.[51]

Table 8.1 shows Axis traffic to Africa during February 1942. Of fourteen ships dispatched to Africa, only one small vessel was sunk. Of the tonnage dispatched 99.2 percent (58,965 of 59,468 tons) arrived. On any given day during the month there were an average of thirty-five merchant ships displacing more than 1,000 GRT plying domestic waters.[52]

Air and Submarine Summaries

The weather in early February was bad. There was a four-day pause in Axis sailings to Africa, and departures from Tripoli were suspended on the morning of the 3rd. Malta reported gales and heavy rain. Nonetheless, German bombers raided the island every day but one, while Italian bombers conducted raids on four separate days. The British struggled to maintain air strength. On 25 January there were 142 aircraft on the island, but only 60 were operational, including 16 bombers and 39 fighters. The bombers conducted 63 sorties during the following week. By 8 February there were 137 aircraft of which 47 were operational, including

17 bombers and 24 fighters. The bombers conducted 48 sorties in the following week.[53]

On 1 February eleven Allied submarines were on patrol and at mid-month there were nine. *Turbulent*, *Porpoise*, and *Olympus* brought stores, aviation fuel, and kerosene to Malta on the 2nd, 13th, and 20th respectively. Allied submarines conducted twenty attacks during the month, expending sixty-four torpedoes and sinking seven ships of 29,752 tons. They also damaged two destroyers, a merchant vessel, and a trawler. Italian forces sank *Tempest* and *P38*.[54]

Italian submarines conducted thirty-one missions using twenty-four boats, of which one mission brought 147.5 tons of supplies to Tripoli. Twenty German submarines operated in the Mediterranean in February. Seven were on patrol on the first and six at mid-month. Although German boats claimed success in thirteen attacks, in fact during February they inflicted no damage whatsoever.[55]

February's activities marked a complete reversal from the situation in November. The only benefit that the British had accrued from their Crusader offensive was the restoration of a land link to Tobruk. Still, London was not ready to concede control of the central Mediterranean to the enemy. On 24 February General Alan Brooke considered Malta's supply situation and concluded that "clearly we must, in spite of the difficulties, transport to Malta what is really indispensable for the continuance of operations and the maintenance of civilian morale. [Otherwise] we must face the fact that operations will probably cease after the end of June."[56] Brooke's staff appended an inventory of supplies on hand. Items that would be exhausted before 1 May included aircraft torpedoes and 500-pound bombs, benzene and gasoline, fodder, and some types of food (canned fish, coffee, bacon, sausages, and jams). Stocks of naval fuel oil, coal, submarine diesel oil, and cement would be nearing exhaustion. Given these conditions, the imperative was clear, and the chiefs agreed that there was "no reason to abandon as yet attempts to pass supplies to Malta by convoy from the Eastern Mediterranean."[57]

Chapter 9

Sirte Preliminaries

That which depends on me, I can do; that which depends on the enemy cannot be certain.

Sun Tzu

On 8 March 1942 Japan captured Rangoon, the capital of Burma. Java surrendered on the 10th, just eight days after Japanese troops invaded the island. In Russia, the 1941–42 winter counteroffensives were petering out with the Soviets' failing to recapture the Crimea. At sea the Allies had lost 679,632 GRT of shipping worldwide in February, two-thirds of it in their most vital maritime corridor, the North Atlantic. The figures for March would be even worse, with 834,164 GRT sunk, almost double January's losses.

The Anglo-American powers had agreed to invade French North Africa (Operation Gymnast) in May 1942 if conditions and the availability of shipping permitted. Just five weeks after this agreement the chiefs of staff concluded, "Operations such as 'Gymnast', which require large quantities of shipping, are at present out of sight."[1] In fact, the Americans already were regretting this project, and were developing other plans that called for a buildup in England and an invasion of France in 1943—or even in 1942, should Russia appear in danger of being defeated. The British clung to their Middle East–Mediterranean focus, but could not ignore the threats to India or Australia—a fact vividly demonstrated on 1 March, when eleven transports departed Suez for the Far East. The movement was just the tip of the iceberg, with twenty-one more transports gathering to carry the 70th and 9th Australian divisions east.[2]

On 27 February, in response to a query from the War Cabinet in London, General Auchinleck summarized the position in Libya. He pointed out that the 8th Army had established a strong defensive position between Gazala and Tobruk, that supply levels had improved, and that he recognized Malta's dire situation and the need for "recovering landing grounds in Cyrenaica." However, he conceded, "it is clear we cannot have reasonable numerical superiority before first June and that to launch major offensive before then would be to risk defeat in detail and possibly endanger [the] safety of Egypt." He intended to strengthen defenses, accumulate supplies, advance the railhead to the vicinity of Tobruk, and seize the opportunity to launch a limited offensive, should such an opportunity arise.[3]

This was not what Churchill wanted to hear. He complained that Auchinleck's assessment appeared to be one of "indefinite stalemate at the best" and that it seemed to demand a reconsideration of "our strategy which has been based on an offensive in Libya." To Auchinleck himself, Churchill was almost abusive. "Armies are expected to fight, not stand about month after month waiting for a certainty which never occurs." "The delays you contemplate will seal the fate of Malta."[4] The debate between the Middle East commanders and London about when to attack persisted for another three months, and in the end Rommel struck first.

From the Axis point-of-view, the situation at the beginning of March was promising: supplies were arriving regularly, and constant air raids were eroding Malta's strength. Rommel flew to Berlin on 17 March to seek reinforcements and promote his idea that the Mediterranean was a theater of "immense importance." He advocated the capture of Tobruk in May and then a push to the Nile Valley. Comando Supremo, however, envisioned Axis forces stopping at the Egyptian frontier while Malta was captured and then advancing to Cairo that autumn. Comando Supremo thought that to take the island would require a strong amphibious force supplemented by paratroopers, but Kesselring and his airborne generals believed that nine paratroop battalions—six German and three Italian—could do the trick.[5]

Grand Admiral Erich Raeder, commander in chief of the German navy, distributed a naval staff memorandum to Hitler outlining his service's belief that "a successful early offensive against the Suez Canal . . . and later the establishment of a direct sea connection with Japan will have a devastating effect on Anglo-American warfare. These steps are therefore of *decisive importance to the outcome of the war.*" The Japanese concurred, at least in principle. On 11 March a Japanese general proclaimed that this was the time to finish off Great Britain, in cooperation with Germany and Italy, "who will occupy Suez and Gibraltar in the near future." In practice, however, the Axis powers did little to realize a joint strategy. Throughout 1941 only three German raiders and one heavy cruiser operated in the Indian Ocean, and collectively they sank just ten Allied merchant vessels and the light cruiser *Sydney.* After Japan entered the war, only three submarines operated beyond the immediate waters of the Dutch East Indies, sinking fourteen Allied commercial vessels through the end of March 1942.[6]

British Sea Traffic

Preparations for the next Malta convoy began in early March, after the chiefs of staff instructed Cunningham, "The passage of a convoy should be treated as the primary military commitment." On 4 March a snapshot of British traffic throughout the Eastern Mediterranean showed convoys underway from Alexandria to Port Said, Port Said to Alexandria, Beirut to Port Said, Haifa to Port Said, Port Said to Tripoli, Port Said to Famagusta, and Beirut to Famagusta. The traffic to Egypt via the Red Sea was immense. The German Admiralty War Diary reported that on 8 March aerial photographic reconnaissance found forty-five commercial vessels of approximately 260,000 GRT in the Suez area, thirty-one vessels of 160,000 GRT in Port Said, and three steamers and various barges transiting the canal itself.[7]

Convoys left Alexandria for Tobruk on the 2nd, 10th (two), 16th, 25th, and 27th. Because the front lines were static and close to Tobruk the traffic was not as crucial as it had been during the height of the Crusader offensive. Moreover, Axis air forces were raiding the port more frequently. Auchinleck noted, "Enemy action against our shipping in and out of Tobruk is causing us some anxiety but generally our maintenance situation is strong now that railway has reached [Sollum]."[8] Convoy AT.32 arrived on the 4th. On the 7th Ju.87s bombed the ships as they were unloading and damaged the tanker *Cerion*, causing the loss of 800 tons of fuel. Two Beaufighters and two Hurricanes jumped a pair of S.79s from Rhodes that had been trying to attack TA.27 on afternoon of the 13th and badly damaged both. AT.34 was not so lucky. *U83* torpedoed *Crista* on the 17th. She was brought back into Alexandria still on fire after a difficult salvage operation. German bombers damaged *Destro* on 19 March.[9] The worst loss of all came on the 26th, when the small tanker *Slavol* (2,623 GRT/12 kts) was enroute to Tobruk. The British destroyer *Jaguar*, the Greek destroyer *Vasilissa Olga*, and the trawler *Klo* escorted this valuable ship. *U652* spotted the convoy— the escorts in line abreast ahead of the tanker. She was going to submerge and attack from behind when *Jaguar* zigged north and presented a better target. *U652* fired four torpedoes at 0227/26th from three thousand meters and hit *Jaguar* with two. The ship broke in half and sank in just four minutes. The other two escorts returned to rescue the survivors, pulling just fifty-three of *Jaguar*'s men from the water and leaving *Slavol* to continue alone. When *Jaguar*'s senior surviving officer was pulled aboard *Klo* and discovered this error, he dispatched *Vasilissa Olga* to her support, but too late. *U205* torpedoed and sank *Slavol* at 0510/27th.[10]

Italian traffic in the first week of March included several convoys to Africa:

- *Salona* (936 GRT), *San Giuseppe* (108 GRT). Sailed Trapani 2 March and arrived Tripoli on the 7th after a stop in Sfax. There was no escort and this minor operation went unnoticed by Ultra;
- *Petrarca* (3,329 GRT/10 kts). Escort: *Saetta*. Sailed Taranto 2 March, arrived Benghazi on the 9th. Ultra accurately disclosed details of her voyage but British forces did not attack;[11]
- *Marin Sanudo* (5,081 GRT/12 kts). Escort: torpedo boats *Procione*, *Cigno*. Sailed Trapani 1940/4th destination Tripoli.

Ultra had mentioned *Sanudo* in a 17 February message, but had not done so since. Nonetheless, at 1230/5 she ran afoul of the British submarine

P31 south of Lampedusa. The submarine hit *Sanudo* squarely with three torpedoes from a salvo of four fired from 800 yards. The freighter capsized and sank in just a minute. *Procione* rescued 155 men, while *Cigno* saturated the area with thirty-eight depth charges. *P31* went deep and sustained minor damage in what her captain characterized as a "fairly accurate counter attack." She had been patrolling the area based on a 1944/2nd signal from Alexandria that it was a likely route for northbound traffic. This showed how Ultra could result in unintended consequences. A series of messages had predicted that the tanker *Giulio Giordani* would be heading north through the area. The predictions were wrong, but they put the submarine in the right place to sink *Sanudo*.[12]

The Axis began using motorized barges (*marinefährprahm*, or MFPs) on the coastal routes. These 220-ton, 10-knot vessels proved effective for carrying small amounts of critical supplies, such as gasoline and ammunition, to front-line destinations. On 7 March they transported 84 tons of gasoline to Derna from Benghazi.[13]

Operation V5

The major Italian operation in early March consisted of four southbound and two northbound convoys sailing over a two-day span. The idea, once again, was to spread the risk and confuse the British with multiple targets. Because Malta's striking capability was much reduced, Supermarina decided that one convoy could sail within range of the island's airbases in full daylight, trusting its air escort for protection.[14] The convoys included:

- Convoy 1: *Nino Bixio, Reginaldo Giuliani* (6,830 GRT/16 kts). Escort: *Pigafetta, Scirocco*. Sailed Brindisi 1230/7th;
- Convoy 2: *Gino Allegri*. Escort: *Da Noli, Bersagliere*. Sailed Messina 0500/7th;
- Convoy 3: *Monreale* (6,968 GRT/12.5 kts). Escort: *Vivaldi, Fuciliere, Castore*, torpedo boat *Circe*. Sailed Naples 0130/7th;
- Covering Group/Rear Admiral De Courten: 7th Division (*Garibaldi, Eugenio di Savoia, Montecuccoli*); destroyers *Aviere, Ascari, Geniere, Oriani*. Sailed Taranto 1330/7th;

- *Ravello, Unione, Lerici, Giulio Giordani.* Escort: *Strale*, torpedo boats
  Procione and *Cigno.* Sailed Tripoli 2100/8th. The first two carried
  470 Allied prisoners and *Lerici* had 110 civilians being deported
  from Libya.

Along with these two large groups scheduled to pass east of Malta there
was traffic along the Tunisian coast:

- *Luciano Manara* (8,396 GRT). Escort: *Usodimare*, torpedo boat
  Polluce. Sailed Trapani 9th, destination Tripoli;
- *Monviso.* Escort: destroyer *Da Noli*, torpedo boat *Pallade.*
  Sailed Tripoli 1930/9th, destination Palermo.

The plan called for the *Garibaldi* group to cover the *Bixio* convoy until
it picked up the northbound ships near the western end of the Gulf of
Sirte, protecting them as they returned to Taranto. The Axis air forces
set up a shuttle to cover the convoys continuously and scheduled raids to
suppress Malta's airfields.

Preparations on this scale generated a lot of radio traffic. An Ultra message timed 1250Z/6th correctly forecast convoys to Tripoli by the eastern
and western routes, a northbound convoy from Tripoli, and predicted that
the *Garibaldi* division would cover. A message regarding the *Bixio* convoy
arrived at 2245/7th, but gave an 8 March departure date when certain
units actually had been at sea for fifteen hours. Ultra provided the first
indications of the northbound convoy a week in advance, and a message
generated an hour before its departure (1750Z/8th) provided good schedule and route information. *Luciano Manara*'s sailing was the subject of
actionable Ultra information, but for *Monviso* the picture was hazy, with
messages incorrectly predicting her departure and then reporting that
she had already sailed almost ten hours after the fact. In any case, at one
point on 9 March the Italians had five transports at sea heading south,
five heading north and three light cruisers, fourteen destroyers, and five
torpedo boats covering them.[15]

Rear Admiral Alberto Da Zara sailed in *Eugenio* to observe the
operation before assuming command of the 7th Division. He had led

a cruiser division in 1940 and was curious to see how conditions had evolved since his last stint at sea. He found that due to fuel restrictions "even during combat navigation there was reluctance to maintain the high speeds that are an excellent protection against submarines; exercises at sea are very rare and firing practice is usually conducted moored between two buoys."[16] These were handicaps that the oil-rich Allied navies could scarcely imagine. In fact, in the middle of one operation, Vice Admiral Sansonetti noted: "The fuel situation requires serious consideration . . . Taranto does not have the means to supply all the units from V5 that return tonight. It is necessary to discharge oil from *Doria* which is in refit for another twenty days, but that is not enough. To fill all the destroyers and bring the cruisers to at least 2/3rds full, we must also use *Littorio*'s oil. . . . The first arrival of fuel oil in Taranto is scheduled for the 16th and it is not much."[17]

Convoys 1 and 2 united p.m./7th and Convoy 3 joined them on the morning of the 8th. The combined force and its escort proceeded south at 15 knots, staying roughly 190 miles from Malta. During the day two Cant Z.1007s and six German aircraft flew cover.

De Courten recorded that "During the convoy's outward navigation it was not, in all likelihood, spotted by enemy air forces: this exceptionally favorable result must be attributed in part to the systematic hammering of Malta, which left it with very limited aerial efficiency, and in part to the conditions of [poor] weather and [heavy] sea on the day of the 8th." Indeed, according to Vice Admiral Leatham, there were heavy raids on 8 March that left "enormous craters [on the] Aerodrome and taxy [sic] tracks" and damaged many buildings at Luqa and Hal Far airfields.[18]

At 1100/9th a Maryland aircraft spotted the northbound convoy 200 miles southeast of Malta, reporting three cruisers, five destroyers, and four merchant ships. The 10th Submarine Flotilla ordered *Thorn* and *Torbay* to intercept the cruisers on their return to Messina and *Sokol*, *Una*, and *P31* to patrol off Tunisia. Another Maryland spotted the southbound convoy at mid-day on the 9th. Eight Beauforts and one B-17 departed Egypt's Bu Amud airfield to hit this target, but instead at 1630 they found the northbound group. They attacked through an escort of four German aircraft and claimed "1 cruiser, 1 destroyer, hit 1 merchant ship 10,000 [tons] set on fire." In fact, however, all their torpedoes missed. A Bf.110 damaged the B-17 at 20,000 feet and forced it to abort.[19]

That afternoon the southbound ships turned west toward Tripoli. Of this important convoy Cunningham's war diary ruefully noted: "[it] had evidently escaped a full reconnaissance of the Taranto-Messina to Tripoli route on 7th and 8th." The motor ships began entering Tripoli at 1730.[20]

After dark sixteen bombers and three torpedo Wellingtons from Egypt searched for *Luciano Manara*. Two bombers and one torpedo aircraft made contact and (incorrectly) claimed a possible hit. At 2135/9th two Swordfish from Malta, supported by two ASV-equipped Wellingtons, found *Manara* near Pantelleria. One (incorrectly) claimed a hit. Three Albacores arrived over the same target at 2310/9th, dropping flares before lining up for their strike. The escort made thick smoke as two aircraft dropped torpedoes from just 600 yards. The third time proved the charm as one torpedo struck *Manara* in the bow. However, the ship remained afloat and returned to Palermo, attended by the tug *Nereo*. *Una* spotted the *Monviso* convoy, but broke off her approach when *Pallade* intervened. At 0930/10th the torpedo boat radioed that the motorship had maneuvered around a torpedo and was hunting a submarine. *Monviso* arrived at Palermo at 0215/11th.[21]

Force K, comprising *Penelope*, *Cleopatra*, and *Kingston* steamed to a point fifty miles south of Pantelleria and swept north from there until 0300/10th searching for cripples but sighting nothing. It was back in Malta by 1000/10th.

At 0400/10th, acting on aerial reports of three damaged enemy vessels, Cunningham ordered Vian with *Naiad*, *Euryalus*, and destroyers *Kipling*, *Kelvin*, *Lively*, *Sikh*, *Zulu*, *Hasty*, *Havock*, and *Hero* to sally from Alexandria "on chance of pickings."[22] There were no cripples to find but Vian's excursion did give *Cleopatra*, which had completed repairs from her 11 February bombing, an opportunity to join his squadron. As a result, *Cleopatra* and *Kingston* sailed from Malta on the afternoon of the 10th and met Vian on the morning of the 11th. On their return Axis aircraft shadowed and bombed Vian's force. The Germans deployed twenty-nine planes and recorded (incorrectly) one hit. Pairs of S.79s out of Rhodes launched torpedoes at 1603/11th and 1815. The first claimed (incorrectly) one certain hit on a cruiser. Beaufighters arrived and covered the force, doing "excellent work." They shot down one Ju.88, but two Beaufighters crashed on their return to base. Despite the failure of the Axis air actions, the cruiser sortie proved costly when *U565* torpedoed and sank *Naiad* at 2031/11th on the return to Alexandria. Vian wrote: "The torpedo exploded in the exact spot in which a single hit would sink a cruiser of the *Dido* class, that is, on the bulkhead between the two engine-rooms . . . the water pressure set up in the engine-rooms burst the bulkhead into the boiler-rooms; the ship at once heeled twenty degrees, and within twenty minutes turned right over, and sank." Eighty-two men perished. *Zulu* sighted the submarine and counterattacked to no avail.[23]

Rear Admiral Philip Vian greeting Canadian officers with an intense stare and a firm grip. Vian started the war as a captain commanding a reserve destroyer flotilla. By the time he took command of the 15th Cruiser Squadron in the Mediterranean in November 1941 his feats included freeing captured British mariners from the German supply ship *Altmark*, which he stopped in neutral waters; leading a destroyer flotilla in a night attack against *Bismarck*; and shooting up a German convoy in the Arctic. He went on to become second in command of the British Pacific Fleet. This photo was taken during that period. Canadian Department of National Defence M2318

In Operation V5 nine of ten transports involved reached their destination. Malta-based air units made just two interceptions and registered the only British success, but the Beaufort strike from Egypt caused concern. De Courten called it "dangerous," especially because it occurred during the day and on the eastern route, which had been considered safe before. "The intervention of long range torpedo aircraft from eastern air bases shows that even without taking Cyrenaica, the enemy can act offensively with aviation against naval units at sea from both Malta and the east."[24]

Subsidiary Movements

Italy conducted several subsidiary actions through the middle of the month. At 2100/9th *Wachtfels*, escorted by *Bersagliere* and *Castore*, left Tripoli for Lampedusa. From there *Bersagliere* continued to Palermo while the others headed for Naples. *Castore* reported torpedo aircraft attacks on the night of the 11th, which she frustrated with smoke. However, the British war diaries do not record any actions against convoys on this night even though Ultra gave useful information. *Wachtfels* arrived in Naples on schedule.[25]

The small motor-sailers *Maria Immacolata* (248 GRT), *Maria Camali* (196 GRT), and *Daino* (167 GRT), all loaded with non-military cargo, left Trapani without escort on the 10th bound for Tripoli. They called at Pantelleria on the 11th, but at 1200/13th on their way south from there they ran afoul of *Una*. The submarine surfaced and engaged *Maria Immacolata* with her deck gun. The motor-sailer replied with her 20-mm weapon but there was only one possible outcome—*Maria Immacolata* was sunk. The other two ships escaped and made Susa on the 13th.

On the 10th *Sant'Antonio* departed Tunisia for Tripoli, arriving on the 12th. She was unescorted, and Ultra gave no notification of her sailing. Finally, at 1600/13th the German steamer *Trapani*, escorted by the torpedo boat *Cantore*, sailed north from Tripoli bound for its namesake port. *Una* intercepted *Trapani* off Kerkennah Bank on the 14th, but missed with a volley of three torpedoes, and the ship arrived safely on the 16th. An Ultra message generated at 2315Z/12th correctly reported the date of departure and probable route; another one confirmed *Trapani*'s departure.[26]

As an exercise for the upcoming Malta convoy, and to shake the bad taste of *Naiad*'s loss, the 15th Squadron accompanied by six destroyers bombarded Rhodes on 15 March. *Dido* and *Euryalus* each flung 150 6-inch rounds at a flour mill and workshops, starting at 0130/15th, while *Sikh*, *Zulu*, and *Lively* shot a hundred rounds each at the harbor. *Hero, Havock*, and *Hasty* "provid[ed] minesweeping protection." Albacores dropped flares to illuminate targets, but low clouds rendered these ineffective and the ships fired blind. Wellingtons raided the harbor in conjunction with the naval bombardment. Italian shore batteries targeted British gun flashes during the 15-minute action. The gunboat *Sebastiano Caboto* joined in, shooting eighty-six 76-mm rounds. *MAS 536* and *545* had been on patrol but "the dark night did not allow our MAS to trace the attacking formation." The British squadron returned to port undamaged. The subsequent press release claimed that the port was "heavily and accurately bombarded" and that "the enemy failed to make any effective reply." Rome recorded some houses hit, seven civilians killed, and ten civilians and three soldiers wounded.[27]

As the British prepared to reinforce Malta, the Italians sent another surge of shipping across the central Mediterranean.

Operation Sirio

Operation Sirio involved the passage over a two-day span of four ships from Italy to Africa, three ships from Tripoli to Italy, and three ships from Tripoli to Benghazi. The convoys included:

- *Bosforo* cargo: 2,121 tons materiel, 481 tons fuel, 103 tons munitions. Escort: *Saetta*. Sailed Taranto 2250/15th, destination Benghazi;
- *Assunta de Gregori* (4,219 GRT/9 kts). Escort: *Premuda*. Sailed Palermo 0230/16th destination Tripoli;
- *Reichenfels* (7,744 GRT/16 kts). Escort: torpedo boat *Polluce* and then *Lince*. Sailed Naples 1945/15th destination Tripoli;
- *Vettor Pisani*. Escort: 14th Squadron/Captain Ignazio Castrogiovanni (*Vivaldi, Malocello, Pessagno, Zeno*), torpedo boats *Pallade, Sirtori*. Sailed Messina 1600/16th destination Tripoli;
- Cover Group/Rear Admiral DaZara: *Duca d'Aosta*, destroyers *Scirocco* and *Grecale*. Sailed Taranto 1815/16th.[28]

Cargo for Tripoli consisted of 7,000 tons of coal, 2,623 tons of fuels and oils, 3,501 tons of materiel, 314 vehicles, and 103 men. Delayed oil deliveries from Germany forced Supermarina to cut the escort to the bare minimum. On the evening of the 16th *Reichenfels* joined *Pisani* near Messina and the two completed their trip together.[29]

The other elements of the Italian convoy-swarm consisted of four groups leaving Tripoli:

- *Salona* (936 GRT), *Achaja*. Escort: torpedo boat *Calliope*. Sailed 2000/17th destination Benghazi;
- *Reginaldo Giuliani*. Escort: torpedo boat *Perseo* and two MAS boats. Sailed 2130/17th destination Benghazi;
- *Gino Allegri*. Escort: torpedo boat *Circe*. Sailed 2200/17th destination Palermo;
- *Monreale, Nino Bixio*. Sailed 1930/18th destination Naples. They picked up the 14th Squadron as their escort.

A series of Ultra dispatches referenced various portions of the operation. The first, sent at 1240Z/16th, stated that a German air force operation scheduled for the 19th resembled a previous convoy-support operation and correctly forecast that a convoy would arrive in Tripoli on the 18th. At the time this message was received in Malta, *Reichenfels* was already on her way to meet *Pisani*. Bletchley Park dispatched a more urgent message eight hours later at 2220Z/16th. This indicated that *Allegri* and *Giuliani*, escorted by three torpedo boats, would be leaving Tripoli at 1800/17th, possibly to meet a southbound convoy 160 miles east of Tripoli at 0500/18th. This was actionable information, but storms limited Malta's air operations on the night of the 16th and the lone Albacore that was sent on shipping search sighted nothing.[30]

Unbeaten encountered the *Reichenfels-Pisani* convoy off Messina and at 1706/16th launched four torpedoes at *Pisani* from 4,000 yards. The Cant Z.501 flying coverage spotted the wakes and dropped two 160-kg bombs on the submarine's position. British records say that one torpedo hit but failed to explode. The Italian history says the ships arrived "without damage or loss." *Sirtori* and *Malocello* dropped four and sixteen depth charges respectively in an eighty-minute counterattack.[31] *Unbeaten* had better luck the next morning when she torpedoed the submarine *Guglielmotti* from 2,000 yards. MAS boats responded with twenty-four depth charges, but the submarine escaped again.

A Maryland out of Egypt, one of three searching along the convoy's presumed route, sighted the *Reichenfels/Pisani* group at 0900/17th before being driven off by an escorting aircraft. Based on this report nine Blenheims departed Egypt but could not locate the enemy.[32] Malta, meanwhile, was processing a sighting report generated at 1044/17th showing an enemy cruiser and three destroyers two hundred miles east of Malta heading south at 15 knots and another timed 1110 reporting four destroyers and three small merchant ships also heading south at 12 knots. At 1131/17th Vice Admiral Leatham alerted submarines on patrol. *Unbeaten, Una,* and *P34* were all clustered around the Straits of Messina or Taranto. After receiving *Unbeaten*'s report, Malta instructed *Una* and *P34* to watch for the return of the enemy covering force.[33] Meanwhile, Bletchley Park generated a flurry of emergency messages. One, timed 1915Z/17th indicated that a convoy mentioned twenty-three hours before would shortly be departing Tripoli, and gave the route as being west of Pantelleria, not east as expected. In fact, Bletchley Park had confused the *Giuliani-Allegri* convoy with the *Monreale* convoy, which was to meet the 14th Destroyer Squadron east of Tripoli for the trip north. Other messages concerned schedule changes and routing information. Before these reports arrived, Malta had already dispatched two strikes. Five Albacores (one ASV) unsuccessfully searched for the *Reichenfels-Pisani* convoy off Cape Misurata. Three Swordfish (one ASV), meanwhile, headed for Tripoli. The strike followed an Ultra message dispatched at 1435Z/16th that reported that *Achaja* and *Salona* would be departing Tripoli at 1800Z/17th for Benghazi.[34]

Salona and *Achaja* and their escort did indeed get under way at 2000/17th. The Swordfish jumped them just out of Tripoli and claimed one hit on a 2,000-ton merchantman that set her "completely ablaze."[35] In her defensive maneuvers, *Achaja* strayed outside the swept channel and blundered into a defensive mine field. The explosion ignited her cargo of fuel, and she burned fiercely before finally sinking at dawn. *Calliope* shot down one of the attackers and rescued the ship's crew. *Salona* continued to Benghazi, arriving at 0800/20th. That the Swordfish arrived at the right spot at exactly the right time, just outside an Italian port, again demonstrated the British use of Ultra information without a conventional explanation for the attack.[36]

The *Reichenfels-Pisani* convoy followed the customary route taking a wide swing to the east of Malta and then crossed the Gulf of Sirte to reach Tripoli without incident at 1515/18th. *Assunta de Gregori* arrived the next day at 0730 after an untroubled voyage.

Upon their return to Malta four Albacores and two Swordfish rearmed and took off again to hit the northbound convoy. At 0232/18th they found *Giuliani* and *Allegri* forty-five miles south of Lampedusa. One Albacore and one Swordfish dropped torpedoes, the others being frustrated by low clouds and bad visibility. They claimed their target was "hit once, possibly twice, large blue flash followed." In fact, the ships made Palermo undamaged by 2330/18th.[37]

Ultra also had much to say about the *Bosforo* convoy. A message generated at 2216Z/14th gave her time of departure, route, and speed. However, this information while correct when generated, proved misleading because *Bosforo*'s escorting destroyer encountered engine problems and

Reginaldo Giuliani (6,837 GRT). She was one of the fast motorships that were the workhorses of the Naples-to-Tripoli run. Others included *Fabio Filzi, Del Greco, Allegri, Unione,* and *Napoli.* E. BAGNASCO, *GUERRA SUL MARE*

the little convoy made an unscheduled stop at Navarino at 1900/17th. *Bosforo* arrived at Benghazi unmolested at 0950/21st after spending the night anchored outside the port while minesweepers cleared the channel.[38]

Operation Sirio demonstrated how the pendulum of sea power had slowly but surely swung. The Italians—with the assistance of some German aerial escorts and air raids on Malta—undertook a complex operation involving four ships to Africa and three ships back to Italy without damage or loss, although one of three transports engaged in coastal traffic was sunk over a "friendly" minefield. During the balance of the month eight more small convoys engaged in African traffic sailed. This included four coastal convoys and three from Italy to Africa: *Brook*, *Saturno* (4,909 GRT), and *Argentea*. The British attacked only the convoy that was heading north, which resulted in *Proteus* sinking *Bosforo* on the last day of the month.

Mining Operations

Italy began mining the waters around Malta in September 1940 (fields M1 and M2) and continued in October 1940 (M3), May 1941 (M4 and M4bis: 100 mines total), and September 1941 (M6 and M6bis: 100 mines total). These fields seriously damaged the destroyer *Imperial* on 10 October 1940. The newly arrived German S-Boats of the 3rd Flotilla, based at Porto Empedocle, undertook several mining offensives against Malta, putting down the first field on 16 December 1941. They laid four small fields in December and one in January 1942. On 15 March they began a second offensive with a field off Xghajra. The next night six boats laid another barrage off Sliema. More fields went in on 17 and 19 March off Marsaskala and St. Andrews respectively. Between 16 December 1941 and 17 May 1942 S-Boats laid 557 mines and 416 buoys in twenty-four minefields. These fields required constant sweeping and made every arrival and departure from Malta an adventure in precision navigation.[39]

Reinforcements to Malta

It took the British War Cabinet two years to send its best fighter—the Supermarine Spitfire—to Malta. The first attempt occurred on 27 February, when Force H, the battleship *Malaya* (Rear Admiral Edward N. Syfret), the aircraft carriers *Argus* and *Eagle*, the light cruiser *Hermione*, and nine destroyers departed Gibraltar. *Argus* provided fighter cover while *Eagle* carried seventeen Spitfires. Syfret aborted the mission, however, just hours before takeoff when flight engineers determined that the newly designed 90-gallon auxiliary fuel tanks that the aircraft needed to reach the island were defective. When he got the news "[Syfret] nearly exploded" and took Force H back to Gibraltar with the Spitfires still embarked.[40]

On 6–8 March, after flying in the system's designer to supervise repairs, Syfret tried again with substantially the same force and delivered fifteen Spitfires (two had engine troubles and did not attempt the journey). Four Blenheims from Gibraltar led the fighters on the four-hour flight to Malta, where they arrived without incident.

The Spitfires found Malta a dangerous place, and by 20 March four had been shot down, two destroyed on the ground, and seven damaged. On 20 March Force H departed Gibraltar once again to bring more reinforcements. The operation was only partially successful. Nine Spitfires, led by two Blenheims, arrived on the 21st. One pilot commented that "The weather was lousy. . . . We formed up on the leader and began our 700-mile trip. We were right down on the deck all the way, flying through rainstorms and patches of thick mist." A flight of seven Spitfires had to be canceled when its Blenheim guide did not appear. It finally made it to Malta on 29 March.[41]

These reinforcements represented one element in the next significant effort to supply Malta. Another was to reduce the number of Axis forces available to contest the convoy. To this end, the Long-Range Desert Group raided air fields at Barce, Benina, and Benghazi, and artillery shelled the Martuba and Timini landing fields. On the 24th Cunningham cabled the Admiralty that this "undoubtedly reduced scale of air attack."[42]

The loss rate for March was 8 percent of the ships and 18 percent of the cargo. Supermarina suspended sailings from 21 to 26 March due to a combination of harsh weather and the British convoy operation to Malta. Traffic in domestic waters consisted of a daily at sea average of thirty-seven ships totaling more than 1,000 GRT.[43]

Table 9.1. **Axis Traffic for Ships Departing in March 1942**

Type	Convoys	Convoys attacked	Detected by Ultra	Ships sailed	Ships arrived	Ships lost	Ships damaged
Europe to Africa	16	3	13	20	17	2	1
Africa to Europe	11	4	10	16	15	1	0
Coastal west	5	0	1	7	7	0	0
Coastal east	3	2	3	5	4	1	0
Total Africa*	35	9	27	36	32	3	1
Total Balkans**	93			196	195	1	0

*Excludes military and coastal sailings. Includes German traffic.
**Excludes German traffic.
Source: USMM, *Difesa del traffico*, 7:404–9.

Air and Submarine Summaries

The Germans and Italians continued to hit Malta with daily attacks that increased in scale as the month progressed and by nuisance raids at night. During the month there were 185 daylight raids and 90 that were conducted at night.[44] In the beginning of March Wellingtons still operated offensively from the island. On the night of 1–2 March six Wellingtons bombed Tripoli. Then, on the next night, sixteen Wellingtons surprised a convoy assembling in Palermo. Bombs detonated the German ammunition ship *Cuma* (ex-*Australien* 6,652 GRT), and debris from the massive explosion damaged the freighters *Gino Allegri*, *Securitas* (5,366 GRT/10 kts), *Tricolore* (179 GRT), and *Tre Marie*; the destroyers *Folgore* and *Strale*; the torpedo boats *Abba* and *Partenope*, and a yard tanker.[45] That same night Axis aircraft raided Suez, dropping mines into the canal and hitting the Kabret airfield. They destroyed four Wellingtons, damaged six others, and cratered the runways. Heavy Axis raids on Malta on the night of 3–4 March caused some damage and on the night of 4–5 March only three Wellingtons bombed Tripoli. Four Wellingtons hit Tripoli on the night of 6–7 March and three struck the same target the next night, but the steady raids on Malta's airfields were telling, and this was the last bomber attack until the night of 13–14 March, when a single Wellington appeared over Tripoli. By the time of this raid Malta's operational air assets consisted of three Wellingtons, two Marylands, two Beaufighters, fourteen Hurricanes, and nine Spitfires. There were also some Albacores and Swordfish.[46]

At the beginning of March, the Allies had nine submarines patrolling the Mediterranean. They made twenty-six attacks during the month, with guns and torpedoes. They sank eight small vessels displacing less than 300 tons, mostly in the Aegean; three submarines; and four larger merchant vessels displacing in total 21,981 GRT. This included *Martin Sanudo*, as described, *Maddalena G* (5,212 GRT) at Corfu on the 5th, *Galilea* (8,040 GRT) south of Corfu on the 28th, and *Bosforo* on the 31st. During March *Thunderbolt, Porpoise, Olympus,* and *Pandora* made supply runs to Malta.[47]

On the debit side, Axis air raids strongly affected Malta's submarine force. Conditions grew so bad that boats had to spend daylight hours under water. On 8 March *P35* holed her hull when she submerged on top of a mooring buoy's clump-block. A compartment flooded and she was eleven days in dock. *Sokol* was damaged on the 17th and the 19th. The incessant bombing, which only intensified after the arrival of the MW.10 convoy ultimately made operations impossible to sustain. On the 26th a direct hit broke *P39* in two. *P36* and the recently arrived *Pandora* were sunk in air raids on 1 April.[48]

Italian operations included twenty missions involving nineteen boats. They engaged in six actions expending nine torpedoes and three with guns only, sinking a French motor-sailer suspected of transporting fuel to Malta. The British sank three Axis submarines. There were three German boats on patrol on the beginning of the month and six at mid-month. German boats sank *Naiad, Heythrop,* and *Jaguar* and one merchant vessel and damaged another.[49]

Convoy MW.10

Implementing London's directives, the Mediterranean Command began gathering the shipping that would be required to run a Malta convoy from Alexandria during the mid-March new moon. Cunningham petitioned the chiefs for six fast merchant ships capable of at least 17 knots. They replied on 9 March, asking whether ships of 14 knots would do, and what would be the latest date acceptable for beginning loading.[50] Time was pressing: with the full moon on 1 April, the operation had to get underway no later than the 3rd week of March. Otherwise, it would

Table 9.2. **Operation MG1 Cargo**

Description	Breconshire 9,776 GRT/18 kts	Talabot 6,798 GRT/14.5 kts	Pampas 5,415 GRT/15 kts	Clan Campbell 7,255 GRT/16 kts	Total
Military stores (tons)	957	2,534	2,611	2,319	8,421
Ammunition (tons)	245	500	448	419	1,612
Civil and government stores (tons)	6,660	6,373	4,796	4,387	22,216
Fuel oil (tons)	5,000	0	0	0	5,000
Personnel	91	49	48	36	224
Vehicles	3	6	1	7	17
Total (tons)	12,862	9,407	7,855	7,125	37,249

Source: ADM 223-548, 22.

have to wait till mid-April. Finally, *Breconshire* and three freighters were assigned to this task and loaded with 37,249 tons of supplies, ammunition, and fuel.

Contrary to past practice, the plan for this convoy called for the groups to sail as a single unit. The 5th Flotilla would head out a day early and search for submarines along the route. The close escort would consist of the light cruiser *Carlisle* (Captain D. M. Neame) and Captain J. A. Micklethwait's 22nd Flotilla (*Sikh, Hasty, Havock, Hero, Lively, Zulu*). Rear Admiral Vian's 15th Squadron (*Cleopatra, Dido, Euryalus*) and Captain A. L. Poland's 14th Flotilla (*Jervis, Kelvin, Kingston,* and *Kipling*) would provide support. Force K, reduced to just *Penelope* and *Legion*, would meet the convoy in the central Mediterranean and bring it into Malta, reinforced by the Hunts of the 5th Flotilla as required.

This was the plan.

Chapter 10

Second Battle of Sirte, 22 March 1942

It's only those who do nothing who make no mistakes.

JOSEPH CONRAD

Operation MG1 began when the 5th Flotilla's seven *Hunt*-class destroyers, *Southwold* (Commander C. T. Jellicoe) *Avon Vale*, *Beaufort*, *Dulverton*, *Eridge*, *Heythrop*, and *Hurworth* left Alexandria at 1130/19th March 1942 to sweep for submarines along the convoy's route.

The *Hunts* searched to Sollum and back to Mersa Matruh without incident. From there they turned for Tobruk to refuel before joining the convoy. The 20th dawned a "cold, blustery morning with an overcast sky and choppy sea. Conditions were at their very worst for submarine detection." At 1030/20th, *U652*, one of three submarines operating between Alexandria and Tobruk was about forty miles northeast of Bardia when she saw the British destroyers zigzagging toward her. Her captain, Lieutenant Georg-Werner Fraatz, hardly needed to maneuver. At 1054 he launched four torpedoes from an estimated one thousand meters. *Southwold*'s Commander Jellicoe watched a torpedo pass fifty feet ahead of his ship. It had a "bright polished shell, dark blue warhead and a conical shaped pistol." *Heythrop*'s lookouts spotted two passing off her port quarter. But the officer on watch had barely shouted "hard to starboard" when one exploded against the destroyer's port side. From

204

Eridge it seemed as though "*Heythrop*'s quarterdeck had vanished into a mass of mangled, twisted metal."[1]

Eridge stood by to tow *Heythrop* while *Hurworth* screened and the other ships hunted the German. *Dulverton* dropped six depth-charge patterns between 1130 and 1252 while *Southwold* attacked at 1142 and 1245. Fraatz wrote: "The first depth charges are not very well aimed but thereafter we are overrun several times with a fair degree of accuracy, though without damage." At 1300 Jellicoe broke off because he thought his ships were bombing their own patterns and the squadron still needed to refuel in Tobruk before joining the convoy. He therefore ordered *Dulverton* and *Hurworth* to screen *Eridge* as she slowly towed *Heythrop* toward Tobruk, while he headed out with the other three *Hunts*.[2]

The squadron had hardly separated when at 1430 a pair of Italian S.79s appeared on the horizon and turned toward *Eridge* and *Heythrop*. *Eridge*'s Lieutenant Commander Gregory-Smith wrote that the initial salvos from his ship's 4-inch guns "burst immediately in front of the leading aircraft, which jerked violently to one side. . . . A wall of shell burst clearly weakened their determination, persuading them to fire their torpedoes at long range." The Italians reported that they sank a 2,500-ton warship. In fact, both torpedoes missed, and the aircraft returned undamaged.[3]

Eridge labored on through rising winds and seas. Finally, at 1600/20th *Heythrop* started to settle by the stern. *Eridge* removed the crew while *Dulverton* and *Hurworth* hastened toward Tobruk. *Heythrop* capsized at 1615, having lost fifteen men.

Jellicoe arrived at Tobruk at 1830. *Southwold* and *Avon Vale* came alongside *Chantala*'s wreck, which was serving as a mole, to refuel and load depth charges. *Beaufort* approached next, but a berthing wire fouled her screw. Jellicoe found the fueling process frustratingly slow, with a transfer rate of twenty tons an hour instead of the fifty he expected. *Dulverton*, *Hurworth*, and *Eridge* appeared at 2000, but *Southwold* and *Avon Vale* only finished fueling at 0100/21st. Jellicoe realized there was no time for the others, and when the 5th Flotilla sailed at 0235 to join the convoy, *Dulverton*, *Hurworth*, and *Eridge* carried only 60 percent of their fuel capacity and *Beaufort* was still clearing her screw.[4]

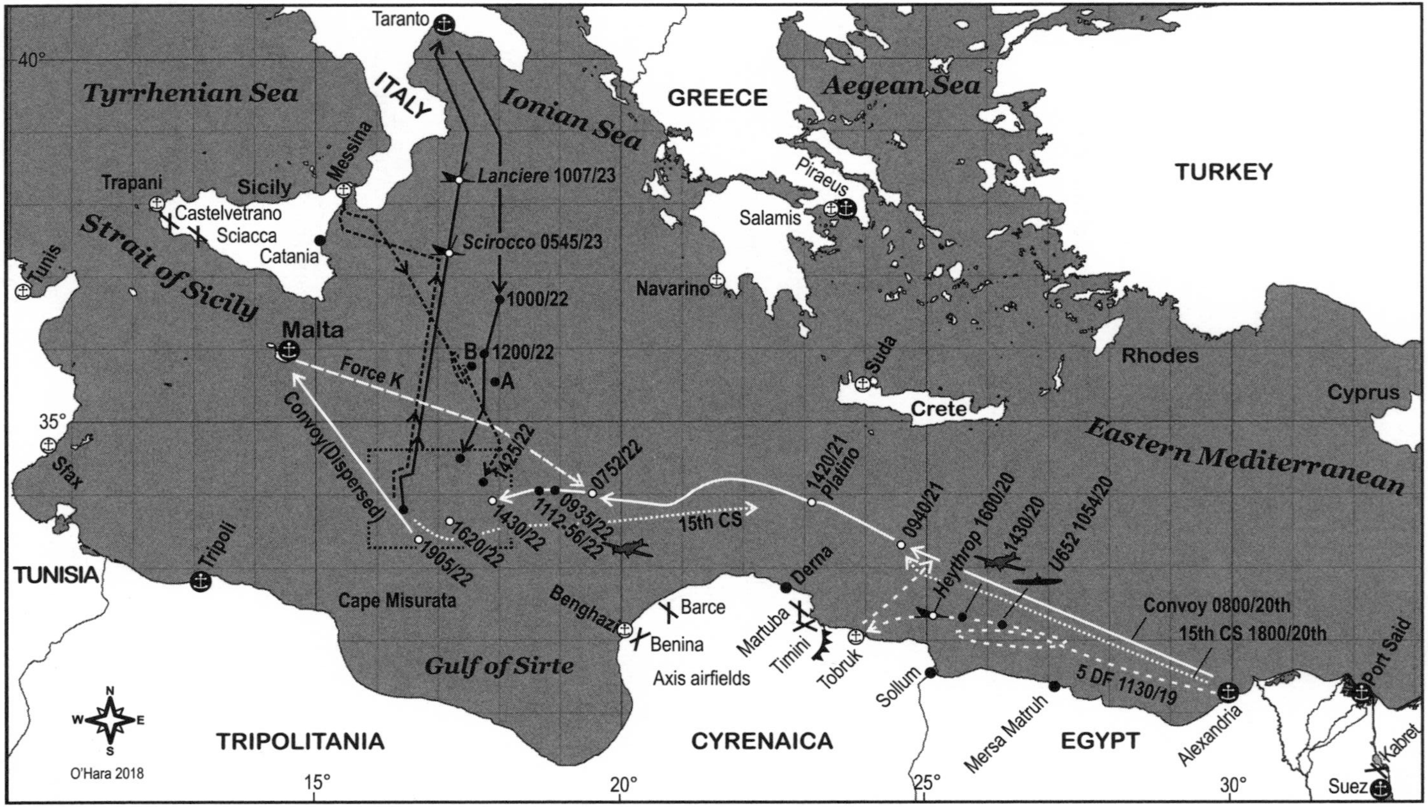

Map 10.1. **MG1, 19–23 March 1942**

The Convoy's Progress

The convoy, accompanied by *Carlisle* and the 22nd Flotilla, got underway at 0800/20th. The 5th Flotilla without *Beaufort* joined at 0655/21st. Vian's 15th Squadron and the 14th Flotilla, which sailed at 1800/20th, hove into view at 0940/21st, eighty miles north-northeast of Tobruk. The combined force zigzagged west-northwest at 13 knots through thick weather. The fleet destroyers and cruisers screened four thousand yards ahead, while the *Hunts* closely guarded the flanks and rear. It seemed that every convoy had a laggard, and *Clan Campbell*, unable to maintain the required speed, quickly claimed that role. She finally steered a straight course to keep up. Flights of Beaufighters and P-40 Kittyhawks shuttling in from North African bases provided air cover from just past dawn to dusk on the 21st. At 2000/21st Force K left Malta to meet the convoy in the central Mediterranean.

At 1705/21st the British sighted a flight of northbound Ju.52s. Vian wrote: "Attempts made to direct Beaufighters by informative methods were not successful." Because there was no ship-to-plane radio link, this probably meant firing in the enemy's direction. The admiral was positive that the German aircraft had reported him (they did at 1658, but it took eight hours for word to reach Supermarina) and he ordered various course alterations of up to 50 degrees to change his future plotted position.[5]

Other German aircraft had reported three cargo ships and four destroyers forty miles north of Sidi Barrani at 0905/20th (the 5th Flotilla). Analysis of radio traffic and decrypted signals, along with *U652*'s report, suggested that a major enemy movement was under way off the Egyptian coast. Supermarina believed that these signified a Tobruk convoy, but considered a Malta operation possible. An Italian report complained, "Reconnaissance by X CAT (Fliegerkorps 10) south of Crete on the 21st would have clarified the situation." That morning, however, no news arrived, so Supermarina assumed that the destination had been Tobruk. Only later did Supermarina learn that the Germans had been unable to conduct reconnaissance on the 21st.[6]

The submarine *Platino*, patrolling the passage between the western end of Crete and the Libyan bulge, provided the first news that a Malta convoy was indeed at sea. At 1420/21st her hydrophones picked up a cacophony of propeller sounds. As the convoy passed she was unable to attack, but at 1630 the submarine reported a cruiser, four destroyers, and three steamers. This news electrified Rome.

Italian Reactions

At 1830/21st Rear Admiral Luigi Sansonetti, Italy's deputy naval chief of staff and operational head of Supermarina, conferred with Vice Admiral Pietro Barone, chief of the Sicilian naval district. Sansonetti said that Supermarina believed a Malta convoy was underway and was suspending the next African resupply surge. He said that the convoy's escort seemed weak considering its importance, and he wanted the 3rd Division (*Gorizia*, flagship of Rear Admiral Angelo Parona; *Trento*; and the light cruiser *Bande Nere*) to sortie from Messina as quickly as possible. Escorting them would be the 13th Squadron (*Alpino, Fuciliere, Bersagliere, Lanciere*). Sansonetti would ask the Germans for air cover. In addition, Supermarina was pondering whether to send *Littorio* from Taranto.[7]

An hour later Sansonetti was on the scramble phone again, this time with Iachino. He briefed the fleet commander and ordered *Littorio* to follow Parona. "There will be naturally . . . a new oil crisis but I'm sure that OKM [the German high command] will supply a little more as they always have when we undertake an initiative of this nature." Iachino told Sansonetti that his force and the 11th Squadron (*Aviere, Grecale, Ascari, Oriani*, reinforced by *Geniere* and *Scirocco*), would weigh anchor shortly after midnight. He would proceed to a position designated as "Point A" (see map 10.1) and from there would act as the situation required. Parona would head for a position called "Point B" and await Iachino's instructions.[8]

The objective was to prevent the convoy from reaching Malta, either by forcing it to turn back, or better, by destroying it. The navy would cooperate with Italian and German air forces to achieve this objective. Several details emerge from these exchanges. First, Supermarina did not set the degree of risk that Iachino could take or tell him how to conduct the mission. Second, Supermarina needed to request air support from both the Germans and Italian air force, and they had better prospects of obtaining it from the Germans (Sansonetti to Iachino: "I will ask OBS to try and give some air escort to the *Littorio* Group considering that the

[Italian air command] cannot assure us this.")[9] Finally, the fuel situation was so dire that Supermarina could only undertake a critical operation on the assumption of future German largesse.

Iachino departed Taranto at 0027/22nd. Parona cleared Messina at 0100/22nd, an hour behind schedule because strong winds impeded *Gorizia*'s departure. This delayed Parona's scheduled arrival at Point B from 0800 to 0900. Machinery defects prevented *Geniere* and *Scirocco* from leaving until 0250. Iachino ordered them to catch up at 28 knots.[10]

As ships sped to sea, Superaereo deployed to Sicily the total torpedo-bomber strength available in the central and western Mediterranean. Air Aegean and the 5th Air Fleet in Africa prepared their torpedo bombers, and Air Sicily readied land bombers as well.[11]

The Italians believed that their naval deployments were undetected, but while this was true of Parona's cruisers, *P36* noted *Littorio*'s passage at 0131/22nd. At 0518 Vian received *P36*'s report of "three destroyers and hydrophone effect of heavier ships," and at 0600 he adjusted course to 250 degrees. Most important, the Italian SIS did not intercept *P36*'s message, so Iachino had no idea that he had been detected so early.[12]

Signals Intelligence

To have any impact on a fast-moving action, intelligence had to operate in minutes, not hours, and provide information that would be germane either at the moment or in the very near future. In this operation the most important information for both British and Axis forces was the enemy's location. The major instrument for providing that information was the airplane, although in this case submarines provided the first notice that each side received of the enemy's actions.

Malta was supposed to deploy eight Marylands, but when the action began only one was available. Rear Admiral Vian complained in his report that "No air reconnaissance from Malta proved practicable." He received just one message, generated at 1052, saying that the convoy had been sighted by enemy aircraft at 0940 and 0953, but there was nothing to indicate the location or progress of the Italian fleet, which found him several hours before he expected. The fact he was thus surprised not once but twice ranks as a failure of the first order for British intelligence.[13]

Table 10.1. **Sightings of MW.10 by Date and Agent**

Day (March 1942)	Total	By Italian submarines	By German submarines	By Italian aircraft	By German aircraft
20	2	0	1	0	1
21	3	2	0	0	1
22	14	0	0	7	7
23	13	1	0	0	12
Total	32	3	1	7	21

Source: AUSMM, Supermarina, SIS Notiziario Speciale, 17–19.

The Axis powers had far greater resources. Aircraft flooded the convoy's zone of transit and from 0220/20th through 1732/23rd, the Italians logged thirty-two separate sightings of the British units at sea.

Signals intelligence benefited the Italians more than the British. With an average time of almost five hours from interception to message, Ultra often was old news when it arrived. For example, at 0925Z/22nd a message warned that "Italian naval forces were . . . intending to intercept British convoy bound for Malta. Composition of Naval Forces Unknown"—confirming *P36*'s sighting of four hours earlier. At 1400Z/22nd, 1510Z, and 1520Z messages predicted that torpedo aircraft and bombers would raid the convoy. Considering that the attacks were already under way, Vian hardly needed special intelligence to know this. At 2311/22nd information arrived that at 1835 Supermarina had ordered its naval forces to return to base. By this time the battle was long over.[14]

On 22 and 23 March the SIS intercepted seventy-seven radio and wireless messages pertaining to Operation MG1 generated by Alexandria, Malta, and the ships at sea. It could not read messages generated in naval cypher and those in naval code were decoded only in part. Fifty-six of the seventy-seven interceptions—those sent in plain language, using Syko, a simple device with sliding bars to facilitate use of a substitution cipher, where one letter stood for another—were read immediately. Some important messages were not intercepted, especially several referring to planned air strikes. Nonetheless, the timeliness of the information had value. In addition, an SIS interception and decryption team on board *Littorio* fed Iachino information directly.[15] For example, Rear Admiral Vian signaled his sighting of Parona at 1431; Iachino's SIS liaison handed the Italian admiral a translation at 1433. This told Iachino that Vian thought he was facing three battleships. Finally, just to be sure of the matter, Supermarina forwarded the same information to Iachino at 1455.[16] At 1648/22nd Vian signaled to Malta that he had sighted an enemy force, the composition of that force, and his own position. Iachino read Vian's signal at 1651. Supermarina followed up with the same information seventeen minutes later. Throughout the course of the action *Littorio* was reading most British tactical messages within minutes.[17]

British Reactions

News of the Italian sortie was worrisome, but not unexpected. Cunningham's operational orders provided that "Enemy surface may endeavor to intercept the convoy. . . . Should this occur it is my general intention that the enemy should, if possible, be evaded until darkness, after which the convoy should be sent on to Malta with destroyer escort, being dispersed if considered advisable, and the enemy brought to action by Force 'B'." Vian's orders resembled those that had been issued in his past Malta operations: they organized the cruisers and destroyers into divisions and provided for either offensive or diversionary tactics, using smoke to cover the convoy's escape if confronted by an enemy squadron. He also noted, "The convoy, if it were to reach Malta at all, must arrive within a very few hours of daylight." After learning that the Italians had sortied, Vian steered a direct course "as it was considered essential to make the best speed." He also noted that if a surface encounter did result, "it was clear that the enemy must be driven off by dark since, if involved in night operations to the Westward, the oil situation for the return passage to Alexandria would be most difficult."[18]

Cunningham remained ashore at Alexandria, and issued periodic, mostly informational, messages. He had already praised Vian's "great skill" in his handling of the mid-December operations and clearly trusted the rear admiral's judgment. As a result, he made no effort to direct the operation once the ships were at sea.[19]

Air Actions

Force K joined Vian at 0752/22nd north-northwest of Benghazi. Axis air strikes commenced after 0935/22nd as the convoy sailed beyond the range of RAF fighter coverage. Four S.79s from Libya that had taken off three hours before attacked 140 miles northwest of Benghazi. A fifth plane crashed en route. One pilot remembered: "We were really worried because we feared the mission would turn into a disaster due to the stormy seas. The High Command didn't share our point of view, insisting we had to attack. . . . Immediately after takeoff, under the rain, we closed up our formation, flying at a height of just 50 m. We felt like we were on a roller-coaster." According to British accounts, the planes dropped torpedoes outside the destroyer screen. Flak severely damaged one of the intruders. Another four S.79s dropped their torpedoes between 1112 and 1156, in the face of heavy anti-aircraft barrage that left two damaged. All missed. The aviators claimed success against a cruiser and a destroyer in the first sortie: "A large fire at once broke out . . . and dense smoke was seen." The second strike claimed two cruisers and a large merchant ship. Such fantastic pronouncements were common among airmen on all sides. The problem came when commanders accepted such reports uncritically. A few solitary Ju.88s attacked shortly after noon as the convoy hastened west through steadily deteriorating weather.[20]

Progress of the Italians

Ju.88s appeared above Parona's cruisers at 0625/22nd, and Iachino had Italian aircraft overhead half an hour later. At 0733 *Gorizia* catapulted a floatplane to search along the cruiser's course, but engine problems forced it to abort almost immediately. *Bande Nere* launched another at 0816. It probed out to a distance of 120 miles without contact before breaking off to land at Augusta. There was a light sirocco wind from the southeast, with moderate sea swells. According to Iachino, "Weather conditions, on the morning of the 22nd continued good, but grew worse progressively." A cold front was moving in, but there was no indication that conditions would deteriorate so severely during the day.[21]

Gorizia passed point B at 0911 and continued southeast at 20 knots. At 0948 Parona reversed course and returned north past Point B as he

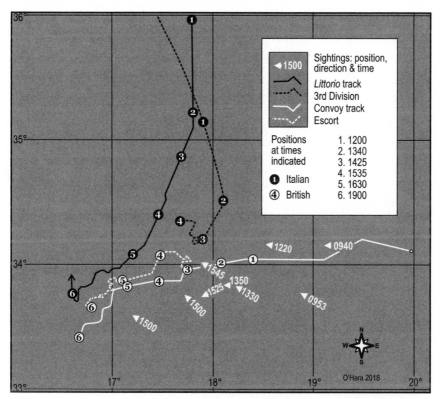

Map 10.2. **Advance to Combat: Relative Sightings, 22 March 1942**

awaited information on the enemy's location. Iachino, meanwhile, was growing anxious as the morning passed without word of the convoy, despite vast efforts by German and Italian aircraft to pinpoint its location. Finally, at 0953 Iachino received a 0940 report from one of the S.79s of "a considerable naval force" 130 miles north-northwest of Benghazi, heading due west at 14 knots. The admiral rang up 28 knots and came to 190 degrees. At 1009 he radioed the course and position to Parona. A second sighting report, made at 0953, arrived on *Littorio*'s flag bridge at 1013. It told of 5 cruisers, 7 destroyers, and 7 steamships, course 300 degrees, speed unknown, 27 miles southwest of the position that had been reported at 0940, with a 30-degree difference in course. These discrepancies were serious enough to worry Iachino. He ordered Parona to advance toward the enemy at 30 knots and establish visual contact, but to avoid becoming enmeshed in combat until he arrived. Alexandria intercepted this message and at 1052, an hour after the 0953 sighting radioed Vian: "Your force was probably sighted by enemy aircraft at 0740 and 0753 G.M.T." *Cleopatra* logged this message as received at 1105. By 1036 Parona was pressing south by east, into the teeth of growing winds and heavy seas. *Trento* launched a spotter at 1101.[22]

At 1107 Iachino received news of the successes claimed by the torpedo planes, which he considered encouraging. At 1212, as the winds increased to 20 knots, Parona reduced speed to 28 knots so that his destroyers could keep up. Then, at 1239 *Trento's* Ro.43 reported five cruisers, five destroyers, and four merchant ships heading west by north at 16 knots. It modified this report fourteen minutes later to a count of eight destroyers and seven streamers. The enemy bore ninety miles south by east from Parona's squadron. Iachino adjusted *Littorio's* course from 190 degrees to 180 degrees to hasten contact. Parona pressed on, although at 1332 deteriorating conditions forced him to shave another 2 knots from his speed. He altered course at 1340 to 210 degrees, anticipating an imminent sighting of the enemy.[23]

At 1300 British lookouts saw aircraft gathering on the horizon. One of these reported the British location almost fifty miles southwest of where *Trento's* aircraft had placed it an hour before. At 1331 several British ships reported a Ju.88 dropping four red flares—"a probable indication that enemy surface forces were in the vicinity—though it was not thought that they should make contact before 1630 or 1700." At 1418 a single Ju.88 dive-bombed the convoy.[24]

Meanwhile, to the north, Iachino had to decide how and where to engage. From the positions being reported, which clearly had a large margin of error, he would have at best two hours of light and twilight to effect a result (see map 10.2). Conditions were worsening even as he weighed his options. The wind was now blowing from the southeast at 25 knots. Visibility was steadily dropping. Iachino calculated that if he maintained his present course the enemy would appear to the southeast. This was good, since it would place him between the convoy and its goal. It was bad because the wind would be blowing directly toward him, facilitating the enemy's use of smoke and degrading his gunnery. He could bend his course to the east and attempt to come up behind the convoy.

This was good because the escort would then be unable to use smoke to hide (although it could still cover the convoy in smoke), and shooting would be easier. It was bad because he would have to sail into the teeth of the storm to get downwind of the convoy—a factor that would significantly delay contact. His squadron's effective speed was just a few knots faster than the enemy's reported speed of 16 knots (the convoy actually was making only 12 to 13 knots, but Iachino had to base his decision on the information that he was receiving). This maneuver would push the convoy toward its goal, and it seemed doubtful that once he attained the downwind position he would have time to force a decision before dark. He did not consider fighting at night, given British advantages in radar and doctrine. He also believed that the enemy was superior in torpedo tubes, having 112 to his 42 (in fact the British had 89 tubes). "For these reasons," Iachino reported to Mussolini, "while realizing the drawbacks of fighting a position to leeward of the enemy I felt it proper to persist in the more secure maneuver intended to block the route of the convoy and push it toward the south."[25]

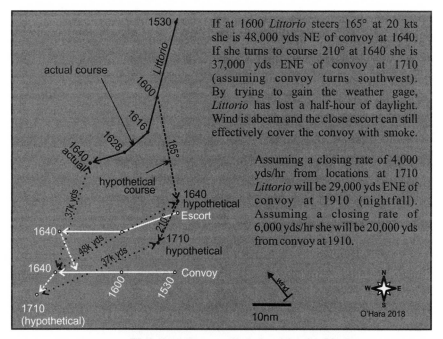

Map 10.3. **Fighting Downwind: Iachino's Choice**

Iachino had had too many actions go bad to risk giving the enemy a chance to escape. He wanted to force combat in the limited time available, and the only way he could guarantee that was by placing his ships between the British and their destination. A review of the times and distances (see map 10.3) indicates that he made the proper choice.

The Cruiser Action

At 1422 Parona sighted the enemy twelve miles off the port bow as his ships labored southwest on a line of bearing. British sightings followed quickly, with *Euryalus* reporting three ships at 1424. Vian admitted that contact had come "much earlier than was expected." His concern over the enemy's early arrival was compounded by an overestimation of its strength, signaling at 1432 that he had sighted "3 battleships bearing 010 degrees distance 12 miles course unknown."[26]

The escorts' organization for surface action consisted of six divisions and a close escort (see map 10.4). At 1429 Vian's flagship, *Cleopatra*, broke out the signal ZLG: "Carry out diversionary tactics, using smoke to cover the escape of the convoy." This was a well-practiced evolution covered in the *Fighting Instructions* and *Fleet Signal Book*. The division leaders turned northeast as subordinate units fell in behind them. Vian complained that *Penelope* had caused a delay by not realizing that *Dido* belonged in her division. "This should have been clear from my signal timed 0805 of 22nd March to *Penelope* and *Legion*." But *Legion* was confused as well and joined the First Division. In fact, Vian's 0805 signal just stated that *Penelope* and *Legion* formed the sixth division in Organization No. 3 or the second division of striking force in Organization No. 4. It did not mention *Dido,* so confusion in Force K seemed reasonable.[27]

As the six divisions headed north, the convoy and *Hunts* turned south-southwest. At 1433 *Euryalus* started spewing black funnel smoke. Three minutes later the 1st Division did the same. At 1432 Parona turned starboard and *Gorizia* engaged at 1435 from 21,000 meters. However, the Italians continued to circle to the north away from the British, who were now steaming east by northeast. Parona wrote that "to comply with *Littorio*'s orders I turned to starboard to disengage, but during successive maneuvers I brought the formation back towards the enemy and I began shooting as

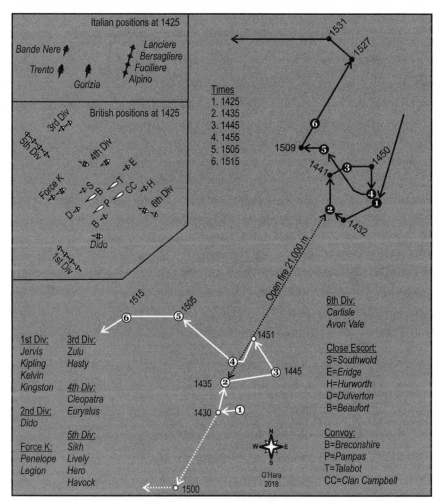

Map 10.4. **Second Sirte Tactical Map, First Phase: 1425–1530**

soon as the shape of a cruiser appeared in the curtain of smoke." *Cleopatra* reported that the Italian shells had fallen short and to the right. *Trento* was not able to join in until 1440 due to a lack of visible targets, and even then she only managed two salvoes.[28]

At 1441 Parona turned east to parallel the enemy; four minutes later the British responded by turning hard aport to the northwest. At 1445 Vian ordered "Negative close screen. Turn toward enemy." By 1447 all the British divisions were generating smoke. *Littorio*'s Ro.43 No. 2 had been catapulted off the battleship at 1430. It overflew the battle at this time and accurately reported to Iachino that four cruisers and nine destroyers had engaged the 3rd Division. It also provoked "a violent burst of antiaircraft fire," forcing the plane to bank sharply away.[29]

At 1450 Parona turned south, causing *Cleopatra* to turn south by southwest a minute later. Nonetheless, Vian signaled Jellicoe to steer the convoy west as he concluded that the Italian ships, which he now realized were cruisers, did not seem intent on pressing an attack. He then bent west at 1453 to open the distance. At 1455 Parona turned west as well and then northwest. At this time *Cleopatra* and *Euryalus* tried to concentrate their guns against *Gorizia*—a maneuver that enables two ships to engage the same target with one acting as control vessel—but their rate of fire was too slow. *Euryalus* took over from *Cleopatra* as control vessel at 1459. "During this part of the engagement the observation of fall of shot was extremely difficult owing to the long range, the hazy conditions due to spray blown up by the high wind, and the smoke screen being laid by *Cleopatra* and *Euryalus*." *Sikh*, leading the 5th Division off *Cleopatra*'s bow, noted that "throughout the action little was seen of any other ships." At 1456 she caught sight of the enemy through a gap bearing 025 degrees, distance 16,000 yards. Nevertheless, "Smoke interference prevented fire being opened and accurate recognition of the types of enemy ships." *Zulu* observed several 6-inch salvos fall within 500 yards. Trento recorded that from 1455 to 1505 she shot with all turrets against *Euryalus*, which periodically came into view through the smoke at a range starting at 19,500 meters.[30]

At 1459 *Carlisle* and *Avon Vale*, which were north of the convoy but south of the other five divisions, started making smoke. Shortly afterward a Ju.88 bombed *Carlisle*. When the aircraft released its ordnance, the light cruiser altered to port. Smoke smothered *Avon Vale*, and the destroyer struck the cruiser's port side "a glancing blow." The cruiser was superficially damaged, but the small destroyer crumpled her stem and suffered "serious damage to main structural strength." Permanent repairs would require four weeks. Two more Ju.88s attacked immediately afterward but "the bombs fell harmlessly some distance from the ship."[31]

At 1500, the convoy resumed its westerly heading. To the north the dance of the cruisers continued. Parona turned due west at 1505 and so did the British. At 1509 Parona turned sharply to port to head north by northeast. The Italian admiral, mindful (perhaps *overly* mindful) of his mission, wrote that "while the convoy was rapidly hidden with curtains of smoke, the enemy cruisers advanced decidedly towards the Division: in obedience to the orders received, I conformed to the enemy maneuver taking a northerly course in order to lead the cruisers towards the Littorio Group, which indeed happened." In fact, Vian continued west and the range rapidly opened. *Euryalus* ceased fire at 1507, followed a minute later by *Cleopatra*. At 1511 *Bande Nere* dropped a salvo between *Cleopatra* and *Euryalus*. *Cleopatra* replied at extreme range, but could not see the fall of her shot. After that the two forces lost contact.[32]

Parona had pushed the convoy south for half an hour. He clearly could have done more by maintaining a southwesterly course, but this would have also delayed *Littorio*'s arrival, and his mission was to facilitate the battleship's intervention, not retard it. At 1020 Iachino had radioed him "establish contact and communicate without becoming engaged." According to Iachino's report, he was to "maintain contact without committing [this division] deeply," and this task he "brilliantly performed." He had "maneuvered to maintain contact with the enemy and had sought, in the meanwhile, to attract it toward *Littorio*."[33]

As the cruisers swapped slow salvos, Ju.88s and a dozen S.79s from Catania sought the convoy. Fifty-two German bombers had lifted off, but in the stormy conditions only thirty-eight made contact. Weather grounded the guide units of the Ju.87s scheduled to participate so the Stukas bombed Malta's airfields instead. Jellicoe reported that from 1445 the convoy was under "heavy and sustained air attack." The *Hunts* and *Carlisle*'s 4-inch guns foiled the initial Ju.88 strike in a barrage that Vian later described as "resembling continuous pom-pom fire." The warships were also harassed. At 1453 a solitary Ju.88 buzzed *Euryalus*. At 1510 *Euryalus*, *Cleopatra*, and *Dido* all reported attacks.[34]

At 1535, with the Italians over the horizon, Vian signaled Cunningham: "Enemy driven off." By 1605 the convoy was seven miles to the southwest and by 1640 the units of the striking force were steaming west five miles north of the freighters. The wind, which was coming from the port quarter, was blowing more than 30 knots (Force 7). The sea was churning. Vian

Bande Nere during the Second Battle of Sirte. By March 1942 she was the only surviving cruiser in her class, *Di Giussano* and *Da Barbiano* having been sunk in December 1941 at the Battle of Cape Bon and *Colleoni* by the Australian cruiser *Sydney* in July 1940. This picture shows how camouflage distorted her silhouette. COLLECTION OF E. CERNUSCHI

checked with Neame and Jellicoe and learned that *Carlisle* had expended a third of her ammunition and that *Southwold* had only 40 percent left. Consequently, at 1631 he ordered the 1st Division to join the close escort and cover the convoy "from air and surface attack from the southward."[35]

The Main Action

At 1512 Iachino suffered his first casualty when *Grecale* reported a rudder failure caused by having pounded into the heavy seas at high speed—a disquieting sign of hard usage and deferred maintenance. *Grecale* immediately reduced speed because she needed to steer by hand. In turn Iachino cut the squadron speed to 25 knots—course still 200 degrees—not wishing to lose more destroyers as conditions worsened. Despite this setback, expectations on the battleship's flag bridge were high and at 1520 Iachino ordered crews to battle stations.[36]

Vian's force had hardly dropped below the horizon to the southwest when, at 1520, Parona's lookouts reported *Littorio* looming to the west. Ten minutes later Parona was in a line of file five thousand meters east of Iachino. The three remaining destroyers of the 11th Squadron, which were four thousand meters ahead of the battleship, deployed from a line-of-bearing to a line-ahead formation. At 1531 *Littorio*'s Ro.43 No. 2 radioed that that four enemy cruisers and nine destroyers were steaming south at 28 knots. Immediately after that Iachino received news that *Grecale* could not repair her defect, so he ordered her back to Taranto. The rough conditions made station-keeping difficult, particularly for the destroyers, and, given this loss, at 1549 Iachino reduced speed to 22 knots—"the maximum sustainable under present sea conditions."[37]

At 1547 Ro.43 No. 2 spotted the convoy twenty miles off, beyond the enemy's cruisers. At 1604 it reported that the cruisers had joined the convoy and the whole force was steaming southwest. Seven minutes later a land-based reconnaissance aircraft confused the matter by signaling that the convoy was thirty miles south-by-southwest of *Littorio* and steering west-southwest. This report suggested that the enemy was crossing ahead of *Littorio*. At 1616 *Littorio* came 15 degrees to starboard to prevent the convoy from slipping past.[38]

At 1628 *Littorio*'s lookouts reported "confused shadows on the horizon" off the port bow. Iachino ordered the 11th Squadron to increase speed to 25 knots and to veer starboard to clear his probable line of fire. Then came word of a *Dido*-type cruiser, and at 1631 the battleship's floatplane reported: "steamships ten miles bearing 240° from the [enemy] cruisers, course west." This information placed both the escort and the convoy. Iachino finally had the certainty that had been lacking in so many of his previous actions, particularly the one involving the September 1941 *Halberd* convoy. The trouble was that certainty came with just two hours of daylight left and in horrendous conditions that were growing worse, and with the enemy farther west than he expected.[39]

Although the British forces believed that the surface threat had been defeated, their lookouts remained vigilant, and at 1637 *Zulu* reported four ships 18,000 yards to the northeast. After *Euryalus* confirmed that at 1640, Vian turned north with four of his divisions—the 4th (*Cleopatra*

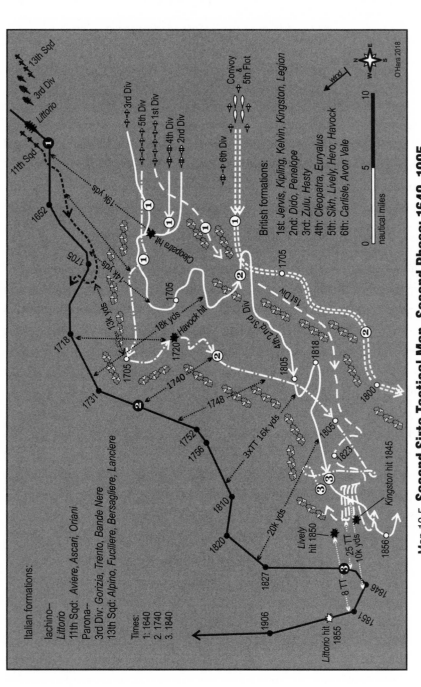

Map 10.5. **Second Sirte Tactical Map, Second Phase: 1640–1905**

Italian formations:

Iachino—
Littorio
11th Sqd: *Aviere, Ascari, Oriani*
Parona—
3rd Div: *Gorizia, Trento, Bande Nere*
13th Sqd: *Alpino, Fuciliere, Bersagliere, Lanciere*

Times:
1: 1640
2: 1740
3: 1840

British formations:

1st: *Jervis, Kipling, Kelvin, Kingston, Legion*
2nd: *Dido, Penelope*
3rd: *Zulu, Hasty*
4th: *Cleopatra, Euryalus*
5th: *Sikh, Lively, Hero, Havock*
6th: *Carlisle, Avon Vale*

O'Hara 2018

nautical miles

0   5   10

and *Euryalus*); the 2nd (*Dido* and *Penelope*); the 3rd (*Zulu* and *Hasty*); and the 5th (*Sikh*, *Lively*, *Hero*, and *Havock*). The 1st Division (*Jervis*, *Kelvin*, *Kingston*, and *Kipling*, with *Legion* tagging along) headed southwest to reinforce the convoy's escort. Captain Poland had received a garbled signal and, unsure of the enemy's precise location, he decided that Vian's orders of 1631 still applied, although he took station on the engaged side rather than the far side and made smoke. Vian assessed his foe as two 8-inch and two 6-inch cruisers, followed by a battleship and two more cruisers to the east. Once again he was exaggerating the enemy, this time mistaking destroyers as cruisers. Even after the battle he stubbornly maintained: "There is no confirmation that any destroyers were present nor is it considered now at all likely that there were."[40]

Iachino turned west at 1641 as the British began belching smoke. Three minutes later the battleship engaged *Cleopatra*, "the only target visible." The British replied almost simultaneously. *Cleopatra* had been steering course 010 degrees to gain separation from the convoy, but when shells started flying she quickly swung west to parallel the enemy. Vian judged the range to *Gorizia* as 21,000 yards and *Littorio* as 26,000 yards, but he clearly had the two ships confused. *Littorio* calculated the distance as 19,000 yards. *Euryalus* recorded that she obtained "some snap ranges of targets" "as they came in view through gaps in the smoke screen. These ranges varied between 19,400 yards and 18,500 yards." After that, it was a matter of flinging a few random shots because "*Euryalus* was unable to see any targets owing to the smoke screen."[41]

Within a minute, despite the long ranges, the ships' plunging, rolling motion, and the wind-whipped smoke, a 6-inch shell struck *Cleopatra*'s bridge "wrecking the Air Defence Position and starshell sights, bringing down all except one aerial and one set of halyards and radio." The blow killed fifteen men and wounded five. A shell from another salvo fell alongside and drove splinters through the hull, killing one man. The British attributed these blows to *Bande Nere* but, as stated, Vian had confused the position of the *Littorio* and *Gorizia* groups. Iachino credited *Littorio*'s 6-inch secondary armament. He reasoned that *Bande Nere* was the most distant of the cruisers, and that her primitive fire control could not have acquired a target so quickly. Meanwhile, the 2nd (*Dido*) Division conformed to the 4th (*Cleopatra*) Division's maneuvers. *Dido's* captain reported that "The smoke was at that time extremely dense, 15 inch guns could be heard firing at no great distance, occasional large splashes were seen . . . a very exciting period ensued." At 1644 *Dido* engaged an enemy vessel but found that the spray and smoke made accurate gunnery impossible. *Penelope* discharged ten salvos between 1647 and 1652. She identified her targets as a light cruiser and then a battleship or heavy cruiser at ranges that averaged 15,000 yards. Clearly she was targeting *Aviere* and then *Littorio*. Smoke hid the fall of most salvos and *Dido* and *Penelope* saw very little of the enemy.[42]

The Italians engaged as they were able but without success, except at 1649 when *Littorio* straddled *Euryalus*. Fifteen-inch shell fragments hurled into the cruiser, including one of more than two hundred pounds, which sliced through nine bulkheads. At 1645 *Littorio* spotted *Sikh* off her port bow. Iachino assumed that the destroyer intended to attack with torpedoes from out of the smoke and ordered the 11th Squadron to intervene. *Sikh* aimed at "what was thought to be two destroyers on a westerly course." *Aviere* had a more limited view. At 1647 she distinguished smoke fine off her port bow and turned her guns in that direction waiting for shapes to emerge from the murk. At 1650 she engaged. Spray and pounding seas made her fire-director useless, so she aimed by eyeball. *Aviere's* Captain Minotti reported later that the enemy had turned to starboard and he came to a reciprocal course, closing the range to seven thousand meters. "*Aviere* continued to be bracketed by numerous enemy salvoes of which some fell right alongside." He swerved his ship starboard to avoid this accurate shooting. At 1655 he reported one torpedo passing astern, although no British ships launched torpedoes at that time.[43]

The duel between *Sikh* and *Aviere* was the most vigorous action during this period. Elsewhere, gunnery petered out within ten minutes as smoke separated the antagonists. The 2nd, 3rd, and 4th Divisions—the four cruisers, with *Zulu* and *Hasty* acting as one unit—moved west to maintain the smoke while at 1655 Vian ordered the convoy to turn due south. Vian reported that "There was . . . an enormous area of smoke which lay well in the existing weather conditions of a 25-knot wind from southeast." From Iachino's perspective, "At the moment of sighting the visibility conditions were already very bad and they continuously got worse, aggravated by the presence of a vast mass of smoke being extended by the English units . . . we could partially glimpse hulls only periodically and the apparent horizon was extremely confused."[44]

Nonetheless, both sides fired whenever targets emerged into view, however fleetingly. Between 1701 and 1712 as the 4th Division headed south it targeted the flash of Italian guns 14,000 yards to the north. In turn shells splashed near the cruisers. *Dido* shot nine broadsides at a heavy cruiser between 1703 and 1710. She claimed two hits (which *Zulu* confirmed). *Trento* reported that "from 1650 to 1711 [she] fired on targets one after the other as they became visible, changing target four times." From 1711 to 1716 she shot four salvoes from her stern turret.[45]

As the Italians pressed on in a southwesterly direction the 5th Division stayed ahead of the enemy. At 1700 *Sikh*'s course was west-southwest, with a speed of 20 knots, but at 1704 she turned northwest. *Havock*'s captain, Lieutenant Commander G. R. G. Watkins, wrote that "The enemy, consisting of a battleship and three 'Alfieri' destroyers were plainly visible at about 13,000 yards. Their cruisers were astern. . . . The enemy destroyers turned away when straddled and we shifted target to the battleship. The latter was occupied with our cruisers at the time, which was appreciated. But I speculated as to when his secondary armament would 'wake up' and return our fire." The view from *Littorio* was less distinct. "Through the curtain of smoke we could fleetingly glimpse the cruiser formation while two destroyers 10 to 15 degrees off our port bow suddenly emerged on an opposite course and bracketed *Aviere*'s squadron with their fire."[46] The Italian destroyers pressed forward, although only *Aviere* could see to shoot back. She reported that at 1702 destroyers suddenly emerged from the smoke on an opposite course just five thousand meters away. *Aviere* also reported a cruiser on a parallel course 7,500 meters south. She was reporting the 5th Division after its turn to the south and beyond the 4th Division, also heading south. The destroyer's torpedo alert of 1655 confirmed Iachino's fears, although despite her best efforts *Sikh* never reached a suitable firing position. At 1705 Iachino ordered the 11th Squadron to disengage and turn north. At 1709 *Aviere* launched two torpedoes from her stern mount at "an enemy cruiser," range seven thousand meters. She then swung north as ordered.[47]

When *Aviere* vanished and with *Littorio* looming before him, *Sikh*'s Commander Micklethwait ducked south to shelter in his own smoke. *Havock* was the last ship in line. Watkins wrote that "By 1710 the ship was steadied on course 190 degrees. . . . [I]t was about this time the incensed enemy battleship took action and straddled us with his main armament using 15″ H.E. . . . beyond feeling the shock of the splinters hitting us, I did not realise much had happened until I found that the ship was slowly coming to a standstill. It was a paralyzing sensation." Large shell fragments had perforated the destroyer's engine room and all three boiler rooms. "We were rolling gunwales under at the time and both No. 1 and No. 2 [boiler rooms] were flooding." Energetic damage control stemmed the inrush of water, and after five minutes the destroyer could make 12 knots. She steered south and took refugee behind the convoy.[48]

Iachino, meanwhile, assumed that *Sikh*'s turn away signified that more torpedoes would be coming. At 1707 the *Littorio* and *Gorizia* groups swung to 290 degrees to avoid danger waters and then, after a few minutes, came to course 270 degrees. This opened ranges, especially since the three divisions led by Vian were now heading southeast, and by 1716 all Italians guns were silent. "All the enemy units were completely hidden inside a dense shroud of smoke." At 1718 *Littorio* came to course 240 degrees and reduced speed to 20 knots as Parona's cruisers fell into line behind her. The 13th Squadron stayed tucked in with cruisers since the heavy seas left no margin for independent operations. *Alpino* fired three salvos during this period—one at 17,800 meters and the other two at 14,300. Her report noted: "navigation difficult due to strong wind and sirocco sea." The 11th Squadron kept to *Littorio*'s disengaged side "to be ready for any other counterattack action." Crewmembers on the battleship looked skyward as flights of Axis aircraft droned by overhead. An officer on *Littorio* observed above the wall of smoke "the bursts of shellfire from an intense antiaircraft barrage." Ship recognition had vastly improved since July 1940, when Italian aircraft had relentlessly bombed their own fleet.[49]

The convoy, meanwhile, labored south in two columns with the rising gale on its port beam. *Breconshire* led the starboard column and *Pampas* the port one. *Southwold* and *Beaufort* guarded to starboard and port respectively, while *Dulverton* led and *Eridge* and *Hurworth* followed on the starboard and port quarters. Air strikes, mostly delivered by small groups of Ju.88s, started at 1445. The Hunts greeted every intruder with an intense barrage even though spray and breaking seas drenched the gun crews. *Eridge*'s Gregory-Smith wrote: "Each time speed was increased, the bows plunged deeply into the short, steep seas and flung solid green water across the focs'le and bridge, drenching everyone. . . . At each alteration of course, the ship heeled sharply and cross-seas swept hungrily along the low waist, turning it into a seething cauldron of turbulent water."[50] On *Breconshire*, the convoy commodore, Captain Colin Hutchison, tallied sixteen bombing runs between 1445 and 1820. Jellicoe estimated that about sixty bombers attacked between 1445 and 1800 in formations of three to nine aircraft. At 1730 five Ju.88s dived simultaneously; two bombs near-missed *Breconshire*, but did no damage. At 1724 Ro.43 No. 2 confirmed that the convoy was heading south—its last communication before breaking off to land in Libya. The aircraft had reported accurately for two hours under difficult conditions. Iachino had retained *Littorio*'s third Ro.43 to spot his gunfire, but by the time he needed it, the storm was too intense to launch. Hutchison was concerned about reaching Malta after dawn and at 1730 he ordered the cargo ships to steer west. Jellicoe, who as the senior escort officer had authority over the convoy commodore, overruled him and turned the convoy back south. At 1745 *Breconshire* turned southwest, and at 1800 Jellicoe again ordered her to steer south.[51]

1729–1759

At 1729 *Littorio* engaged *Sikh* when the destroyer briefly appeared off her port beam. Scattered four-gun salvos from *Cleopatra* and *Euryalus* had been falling around the battleship since 1727. According to *Cleopatra*'s report, she was periodically targeting a cruiser from 18,000 yards when the ship was visible through the smoke. *Littorio* could only discern gun flashes in the murk. At 1731 *Littorio* swung to port to course 200 degrees in order to close range.[52]

At the same time that Iachino decided to close Vian turned southeast with the four cruisers and *Zulu*'s division "in search of two enemy ships not accounted for and which I thought might be working round in the rear." Given that Vian believed that every Italian ship engaged was at least a cruiser and the fact that the 11th Squadron was on *Littorio*'s far side, he likely lost track of these destroyers. He left *Sikh, Lively,* and *Hero* to oppose the entire enemy fleet. Vian later acknowledged that it was "a serious tactical error." Even the official British naval historian, Stephen Roskill, concedes, "This nearly gave the Italians their chance."[53]

Vian's report does not document when he reached the easternmost point in his investigation. In any case, when he learned that the Italians were closing to leeward, and seeing nothing to windward, he reversed course and plunged back through his own smoke. The time was approximately 1745. At this point Iachino was 25,000 yards northwest of the convoy.[54] At 1742 *Cleopatra* reported firing a few rounds from maximum range at an enemy battleship (most likely *Trento*), bearing 315 degrees. When *Cleopatra* turned from east to west, *Zulu*, which was near the rear of the column, ran through the smoke and sighted "Two Trento Class cruisers and three destroyers . . . to the north." At 1748 *Cleopatra* was near enough to the convoy to observe bombs falling between *Carlisle* and *Clan Campbell*, and her aft turrets were "engaging aircraft bombing convoy."[55]

At 1740 *Littorio* engaged "a formation of enemy cruisers that appeared through the smoke."[56] This was clearly *Sikh*'s division, and the destroyer answered the battleship, estimating the range as 16,000 yards. Smoke masked the two destroyers that were following her and they did not engage. *Littorio*'s report noted sporadic return fire after 1740, and at 1744 her lookouts reported damage to an enemy cruiser. *Trento* targeted a ship identified as a cruiser and at 1748 likewise claimed a hit. *Sikh* reported that she was straddled at just this time. Mickelthwait, believing that he was risking fatal damage "and in the hope of making the enemy turn away," discharged two of the four torpedoes that armed his large *Tribal*-class ship. The Italians did not spot this launch, although at 1752 Iachino ceased fire and bent his course to 220 degrees, giving Mickelthwait some of the relief that he sought. About this maneuver Iachino wrote, "Realizing we could not use our weapons due to the impossibility of seeing the enemy targets, I decided to withdraw a little from the screen to make the enemy fire less precise." The gunnery he was trying to confuse was coming from mainly just a single destroyer. He added, much later, that this was a happy inspiration because it enabled him to avoid

Sikh's torpedoes without realizing it.[57] In fact, Iachino's moment had arrived, but the admiral focused on difficulties instead of opportunities. "The gunnery action had assumed a twilight character, and this had rendered uncertain the fire of our vessels. Moreover, the great inundation of seawater coming aboard our ships shrouded the fire control optics so that both measuring instruments (inclinometers and rangefinders) . . . were practically useless." At 1756 *Littorio* shifted course 30 degrees to starboard. Lookouts spotted a low-flying S.79 approaching the convoy and then, through a gap in the smoke, they saw bursts of antiaircraft, but "it was absolutely impossible to see the units firing." Nonetheless, Iachino was slowly blocking the convoy from its destination. In fact, at 1758 Micklethwait radioed to Vian, "Emergency: 1 Battleship 1 Cruiser bearing 330 degs. 8 miles from convoy."[58]

1800–1850

Between 1745 and 1810, the 2nd, 4th, and 3rd Divisions sped west-by-south, spewing smoke and closing in on the battleship. At 1759 *Cleopatra* signaled: "Prepare to fire torpedoes under cover of smoke." At 1802 *Cleopatra* burst through the smoke and sighted *Littorio* to the northwest. The cruiser engaged and at 1806 turned away to port and launched three torpedoes from her starboard tubes "as the battleship disappeared behind drifting smoke." *Euryalus*, one of two British ships equipped with Type 284 Fire Control Radar (*Penelope* was the other, but she only fired briefly on four widely separate occasions and never used her radar) got her first radar range of the action on a target 16,000 yards to the northwest on the other side of the smoke screen. She reported this to *Cleopatra* by radio and shot blind "zig-zag groups" through the smoke. The *Dido* and *Zulu* divisions held their torpedoes because no targets were visible.[59]

At 1810 Iachino edged 30 degrees to starboard to avoid *Cleopatra*'s torpedoes. Meanwhile, Vian swung east once again with four cruisers and two destroyers. He wrote that it was "evident that the enemy's most effective course of action was to pass to windward of the [convoy] and that all his force was not with the battleship so that some cruisers might be taking this course of action." Again, he left just three destroyers to face the battleship and three cruisers that were visible. He continued east for ten minutes until 1818, when he concluded that it was "evident that by this time 2 or 3 of the enemy 6" cruisers must have retired from the battle."[60]

At 1808 Captain Poland, commanding the five destroyers of the 1st Division, received *Sikh*'s 1758 emergency broadcast. Acting on his own initiative, Poland headed northwest to intervene. At 1823 four S.79s attacked and he turned south to avoid their torpedoes, resuming a northwest course six minutes later. At 1832 he swung due north.[61]

Meanwhile Iachino steered 280 degrees until 1820, when he came to 220 degrees. At 1827 he pointed his ships due south. In his words, "In order to overcome the serious fire control difficulties [presented by the weather] and to achieve a decisive result at any cost, I stubbornly maintained contact with the enemy ships, decreasing the range even into the enemy's torpedo waters." This was unquestionably the correct action, and it would have been better done half an hour earlier. [62]

The Italian column resumed fire at 1831, and at 1834 Poland's division spotted *Littorio* twelve thousand yards northwest. One British sailor recalled, "Looking through my gunlayer's telescope, we seemed to be right alongside the battleship." Poland vigorously tried to draw Vian's attention to the danger, making enemy reports at 1834, 1837, 1839, and 1840. Meanwhile, the destroyers carried out a concentrated shoot using their forward guns, and Poland believed that he saw two shells strike home. He also said that the Italian gunnery was "very erratic and it was impossible to tell at whom he was firing." At the end of the line *Legion* engaged at 1839 from eight thousand yards and also claimed several hits.[63]

The Italians were firing every gun that could bear. *Legion* disappeared into a forest of giant geysers as 15-inch shells churned the water around her. Italian and British sailors alike were astonished to see the destroyer emerge on the same course and speed. Her captain reported that several splinters came onboard but caused only negligible damage. However, splashes drenched the bridge and soaked binoculars and telescopes "so we were unable to see Captain (D)'s signals, and I could not tell which way he was going to turn."[64]

At 1846, according to her clock, a shell rocked *Kingston*. She described it as 15-inch, but an 8-inch round is more consistent with the damage inflicted. *Trento* reported at 1845: "I clearly saw the second enemy destroyer on the right hit by a broadside of mine near the aft mast where a lasting fire began." In any case, the shell "passed through the whaler at the starboard foremost davits, through the No. 2 boiler room intake and the S.R.E. room and exploded under the port Oerlikon platform." It severely damaged "the pom-pom and Oerlikon structures and the upper deck in the vicinity of the burst." Splinters tore through the engine and gearing rooms and disabled three torpedo tubes. A blaze erupted in the engine room. The ship lay stopped as heavy seas washed over her upper deck. The blast killed fifteen men and wounded twenty-one.[65]

As *Kingston* lost way she swung to port and discharged two torpedoes before drifting to a dead stop. Damage control parties fought flames and plugged holes with hammocks and duffel coats. The chief engineer and two other crewmen, working in darkness and escaping steam, isolated the damage on the port side and restarted the starboard engine. By 1905 *Kingston* could make 16 knots. She eventually reached Malta independently.[66]

At 1841 with the range at six thousand yards, all of Poland's destroyers but *Legion* swung starboard to launch torpedoes; she turned port so as to not lose bearing or foul the rest of the division. *Jervis, Kelvin,* and *Kipling* shot their full load of five torpedoes. *Legion*'s eight torpedoes were away at 1844 from a range of 4,400 yards. She then started to make smoke.[67]

At 1846 Iachino turned 110 degrees to starboard and reduced speed by two knots. Lookouts spotted a torpedo passing ahead of *Littorio,* and others streaked between the Italian ships. As the British flotilla retired east "the results were difficult to see owing to the smoke." However, *Kelvin* claimed one certain strike on the battleship and an underwater explosion was heard indicating another. An officer saw a "column of water that obliterated funnels." Another, "Great flame followed by cloud of spray higher than masts." It was all wishful thinking. At 1848 *Sikh* led the 5th Division past *Kingston,* which was burning and dead in the water. Then, at 1851, Micklethwait reported a violent explosion on the battleship "which could only have been caused by one of the torpedoes, fired by the 14th Destroyer Flotilla." More wishful thinking.[68]

As Poland attacked, Vian's four cruisers and two destroyers rushed toward the enemy. At 1831, once she had closed to twenty thousand yards, *Cleopatra* fired "almost continuously," engaging *Littorio* when that ship was visible and *Gorizia* at other times. Vian's narrative states that *Cleopatra* continued in to ten thousand yards by 1847. The light cruiser claimed two scores at 1841, "one of which started a considerable fire on the battleship's quarterdeck and appeared to put her after turret out of action and further hits observed after she had turned away at 1845." At this time the blast from *Littorio*'s aft 15-inch turret ignited the Ro.43 on her stern catapult. This undoubtedly caused the fire that Vian took as evidence of a hit.[69] Of the Italian gunnery Vian said it was "erratic and it was hard to say who was the target." *Euryalus*' captain, E. W. Bush, had no such doubts. At 1841 "I saw flashes from [*Littorio*'s] fifteen-inch guns rippling down her side as she fired a salvo at us . . . *Euryalus* shuddered and shook and then rocked so violently that I thought the topmast would come down, while fragments of shell screamed through the air to bury themselves in our ship's sides." The cruiser discharged twenty-one six-gun salvos between 1839 and 1856 and claimed "some direct hits."[70]

Sikh's division, seeking to launch torpedoes, pressed west through smoke laid by Poland's unit. On the way in, *Lively*'s funnel caught fire "caused by the unavoidable accumulation of soot." The wind was coming from the port quarter and blowing the flames toward the starboard bow. This prevented the destroyer from turning since the blaze would have overwhelmed either the bridge or the after gun and torpedo tube crews. *Sikh* and *Hero* tried to launch but "smoke interfered and prevented an aim." *Lively* increased speed and forged on, her forward mounts hammering at the enemy. "Hits were seen." *Littorio* replied with her aft turret. A 15-inch shell landed beside *Lively* and a large fragment holed the destroyer to port near the waterline; other splinters caused more damage. *Lively* turned at 1851 and discharged eight torpedoes at an estimated range of seven thousand yards. She then rejoined *Sikh*, her two forward mess decks flooded and speed reduced to 20 knots.[71]

At 1851 Iachino turned northwest and increased speed to 26 knots. He wrote that "after the last enemy torpedo attack, led with great courage . . . when the sun had already set and darkness was rapidly adding to the haze on the horizon to cover the whole scene of the action in shadow . . . I pulled out with my ships to avoid being hit."[72]

At 1855, a 4.7-inch shell struck *Littorio* on the aft portion of her starboard deck. This parting shot was, despite all the claims and eyewitness accounts, the only hit that the British scored during the entire battle. *Cleopatra* turned south at 1856. Italian guns fell silent at 1858. *Zulu* and *Hasty* plunged through smoke seeking to use their torpedoes. *Zulu* reported that several salvos fell close and that her aerials were shot away. At 1905 she finally spotted the enemy to the northwest six miles away, steaming north at high speed, but there was no opportunity to launch torpedoes.[73]

At 1911 the British striking divisions concentrated and at 1920 turned south to close the convoy. At 1940, Vian wrote, "the convoy not being in sight and dark fast approaching, it was decided . . . to turn Force 'B' for Alexandria." He also ordered the convoy to disperse. In fact, Hutchison had already decided the convoy would disperse at 1900. This was Operation "B" in the orders, and called for the slowest ship to immediately sail directly for Malta. "Other ships are to be opened out at the discretion of the Commanding Officer of the escort, so that ships are about 5 miles apart." The intent was for the convoy to reunite at dawn just outside Malta's swept channel, where *Carlisle*, the *Hunt*s, and fighters from Malta could combine to protect the entire force. However, it also kept the fastest ships from heading directly for Malta at their best speed. Originally, the baseline course was to have been west by north (280 degrees) but at 1858 Hutchinson signaled that the course would be west by south (260 degrees) because the Italians still presented a potential threat.[74] Accordingly, *Clan Campbell*—the force laggard—peeled off for Malta first. *Breconshire* did not turn northwest until 2100. Had she immediately gone for Malta at 17 knots, she would have arrived two hours earlier than she did.

The *Hunt*s were attached to Force K for the run to Malta, and the damaged *Havock* and *Kingston* likewise headed for the island. *Carlisle's* Captain Neame signaled Vian that he was returning to Alexandria due to a shortage of ammunition, but at 2000 Vian ordered *Carlisle* to remain with *Breconshire*. The cruiser came about and found the store ship at 2145.

German aircraft delivered the day's last air raid at 1925. Throughout the surface action, the merchantmen had recorded twenty-eight attacks by Ju.88s and S.79s. The Axis flyers claimed three steamers damaged and one sunk. The escort expended most of its munitions frustrating their attacks. Over the entire day the Germans lost one Ju.88 and the Italians three S.79s.[75]

The Voyage Home

The weather continued to deteriorate as Iachino steered for Taranto. At 2000 he ordered course north-northeast at 20 knots. At 2026 he altered this course 15 degrees to port. Reports of difficulties started arriving on the flag bridge almost immediately. At 2027 *Bande Nere* asked permission to follow a different heading. *Scirocco* signaled at 2045 that she had to reduce speed to 14 knots, and, later, that her port engine had failed. *Lanciere* indicated problems at 2030. At 2245 the destroyer stopped to repair machinery and requested assistance from *Alpino* half an hour later. At 0355 *Fuciliere* radioed that she had lost an engine. Indications that *Scirocco* was in distress came at 0539. *Geniere* attempted to assist but could not find her and *Scirocco* probably foundered around 0545. Only two of her crew survived. Both were below deck, and suddenly found themselves swimming for their lives; the destroyer likely broke in two. At 0910 *Oriani* also reported damage. At 0958 *Lanciere* radioed an SOS and at 1007 reported that she was sinking. The only surviving officer later recalled that "Her speed started falling because water had got mixed with the fuel. The ship engineers worked like hell, but all the attempts to restore a proper pressure level failed. . . . It was a very long night. On the next morning, the ship power was inexorably dropping; she no longer answered the helm, was full of water, and was laying on her beams to leeward. . . . Then a wave which to me looked enormous fell over the stern and went inside. The ship trimmed and began to sink by the stern, with her stem upwards. I was on the bridge overhang when I suddenly found myself in the water."[76]

Littorio entered Taranto at 1842. Beyond the two destroyers sunk, ships damaged included *Bande Nere, Trento, Geniere, Fuciliere, Ascari, Oriani,* and *Grecale*. Riccardi wrote Iachino on 27 March asking whether the courses that he had ordered contributed to the disaster. The unspoken implication, at least in Iachino's eyes, was that slavish insistence that all ships maintain station exacerbated the problem. Iachino replied, "The

Littorio pushing through heavy seas on her return to Taranto on the afternoon of the 23rd. Conditions were rough for the battleship, but the destroyers, two of which were lost, had it much worse. E. BAGNASCO, *GUERRA SUL MARE*

vast majority of our units did not, in fact, have difficulty in following the course of 10 degrees, and found it quite suitable to the sea conditions existing at that time. On the other hand, the units that, for one reason or the other, asked to follow different routes, were definitely authorized to do so." Iachino blamed the problems on sub-par maintenance due to the loss of skilled workers and the constant wear and tear of so much time at sea spent escorting convoys.[77]

Force B returned to Alexandria with the seas on the starboard bow, although conditions improved the farther east it went. Still, the formation reduced speed to 18 knots at 2130 and then to 15 knots at 0325/23rd. All the destroyers except *Sikh* had to reduce speed even further and all were lagging by dawn on the 23rd. "Most of them had suffered damage from the weather." For example, *Lively* reported that, "the breakwater, supporting stanchions for 'B' Gun deck flare and 'A' gun ready use lockers were torn from the deck and caused bad flooding of the upper messdecks." On *Kelvin*, "the whole ship was completely flooded and the mess decks feet deep in water." On *Kipling*, "it was a ghastly night for the ship was being shaken from stem to stern by the high seas." On *Hero*, "it was abominably rough and we were continuously falling with tremendous crump into holes where the ocean was entirely missing. The shield of our foremost gun was ... wrapped round the gun and training gear so tightly that nothing could be moved." *Zulu* suffered extensive structural damage to the forecastle.[78]

On 24 March Cunningham listed these estimates for the times that it would take to repair the damage that the destroyers had suffered from bad weather and battle: *Zulu* and *Lively*, six to eight weeks; *Jervis*, *Kelvin*, and *Kipling*, one week; *Hero* and *Hasty*, four or five days.[79]

At dawn the weather was slightly improved, and at 0756 Force B had coverage from a pair of Beaufighters. At 1610/23rd, however, six Ju.87s dive bombed *Lively*, which was straggling. At 1810 three S.79s dropped torpedoes and claimed strikes on two cruisers and probably a destroyer (in fact, all missed). The antiaircraft barrage damaged the lead plane. By 2200/23 the worst of the storm was over and Force B arrived at Alexandria at 1230/24th. By that time disaster had already struck in Malta.[80]

Chapter 11

After the Battle

The wheel of fortune's sphere is a marvelous thing; What proud head
will it next to the lowly dust bring?

HAFIZ

A t 1900/22nd March 1942 the transports of MW.10 began going
their separate ways. With the wind astern, they rolled and yawed
in the massive following sea. Axis aircraft, lacking anything like
ASV radar, lost touch within an hour. Anxious to reestablish contact as
early as possible, 2nd Fliegerkorps allocated fifteen armed Ju.88s to scour
the waters east and southeast of Malta beginning at dawn. Bombers lined
the runways pending their reports. Meanwhile, on Malta, the British had
fourteen Spitfires and eleven Hurricanes operational, including the newly
arrived Spitfires, whose crews had hurriedly calibrated their guns. The
fighters would operate in pairs, taking off at half-hour intervals—half to
defend the island and half to protect the incoming ships.[1]

The first sighting came at 0703/23rd, when a Ju.88 reported four
merchant ships and two destroyers. Conditions were so bad that many Axis
air units assigned to the operation could not participate. This included
nineteen Italian bombers at Sciacca airfield, which had an unpaved runway,
and all of 2nd Fliegerkorps' Ju.87s. The turbulent sea state rendered low-
level torpedo operations perilous, grounding the eight S.79s at Catania.
Thirteen reconnaissance planes and sixty-nine Ju.88 bombers took off, of

which just forty actually bombed a target. Bf.109s, serving as fighters and fighter-bombers, also participated.[2]

Pampas was initially escorted by *Hurworth*. Just before she turned northwest at 2100/22nd, the cargo ship suffered a steering defect and, while it was being repaired, *Hurworth* disappeared. After that *Pampas* sailed alone. She recorded an attack at 0715 by a solitary Ju.88 that dropped two bombs. One damaged the forward derricks and then bounced over the side; the other dented the funnel and continued into the water. Neither exploded, but the damage would prove significant later. Shortly after that a second Ju.88 released a bomb, which exploded alongside and caused flooding aft. Other planes strafed the ship, but despite the attention that her solitary status invited, *Pampas* continued and at 0830 encountered *Talabot* and her escort.[3]

Havock received orders to stick with *Talabot*. With *Dulverton* astern and the damaged destroyer ahead, *Talabot* steamed at 16 knots west by south until 2100, when she turned northwest. *Havock* had some touch-and-go moments. At midnight Lieutenant Commander Watkins even signaled the freighter to stand by, anticipating that he would need to abandon ship. "That night was a nightmare," he wrote. "The wind was fine on our port quarter until 2100 and then on the starboard quarter. . . . The wind was force 7. . . . We were rolling gunwales under and shipping more water though our big hole. . . . When the ship yawed on several occasions the lower bridge touched the water. I expected her to capsize."[4] The first bombers struck after 0700 and shook the ship with a stick that exploded just off the bow. At 0800 Malta came in view and two Hurricanes appeared overhead. Although they "seemed to have difficulty seeing the enemy aircraft despite frequent 'indicating salvoes' from the destroyers," they discouraged further attack. Shortly after that *Pampas* joined the little convoy. They entered Grand Harbor soon after 0900 to the acclaim of crowds gathered along the waterfront, serenaded by the sirens of the ships in port.

On receiving the dispersal order *Clan Campbell* immediately turned northwest, escorted by *Eridge*. Only then did the master inform *Eridge*'s captain, Lieutenant Commander Gregory-Smith, that a near-miss that afternoon had damaged his rudder and he could only make 10 knots.

Nonetheless, throughout the night *Clan Campbell* stuck to the little destroyer "yawing and wallowing in our wake . . . like some great, ungainly sea monster."[5]

At dawn *Clan Campbell* was sixty miles from Malta. Planes shadowed her for two hours as Germans bombers focused on closer targets. After *Pampas* and *Talabot* reached port, *Clan Campbell* still was two hours out. Then the raids started in earnest. *Eridge* began the day with only twenty rounds of high-explosive ammunition and these went quickly. At 1030, with *Eridge* shooting practice rounds and smoke shells, a file of Ju.88s pressed in. The last aircraft skipped a bomb into the merchant ship's side, rupturing the hull. The Hunt signaled Malta that the freighter's engine was flooded, adding that "I have no ammunition left or towing arrangement." The tow did not matter; *Clan Campbell* sank within minutes, still twenty miles offshore. Over the next two and a half hours *Eridge* rescued 112 survivors. *Legion* was approaching to help when a bomb exploded close alongside and ruptured the destroyer's hull. The ingress of water exceeded *Legion*'s pumping capacity, and at 1133 she signaled Malta: "Am in danger of sinking." She barely reached shore at Marsaxlokk, and was towed into port the next day.[6]

Southwold and *Beaufort* accompanied *Breconshire*. *Carlisle* joined them at 2145. Single Ju.88s attacked at 0755 and 0817 without effect but at 0920, just twenty-five minutes from St. Elmo Light, three Bf.109s buzzed the ship at low altitude, strafing and dropping 100-kg bombs. Three of them exploded along the port side, knocking out electrical power, jamming the steering, and flooding the engine room. Ten minutes later a Ju.88's bombs fell close alongside, shaking the large vessel, and her main engines stopped. Finally at 0940 another pair of Ju.88s "came in low, almost feathering the sea, half hidden by the drifting belts of mist." One dropped two bombs that exploded beneath *Breconshire*, and "With a sickening crash she bit deep into the crest of a wave then she yawed broadside on and, turning slowly in circles, started to drift toward the shore."[7]

Penelope arrived shortly after. By 1117 she had secured a 6.5-inch wire between the vessels but, "there was a heavy swell from the East-Southeast and [*Breconshire*] was riding heavily with a draught of forty feet." At 1126 the tow parted. At 1215, with waves and winds pushing her toward shore, *Breconshire* dropped her anchors a mile shy of Zonkor Beacon. For the rest of the day *Beaufort, Southwold, Hurworth,* and *Dulverton* took turns providing anti-air protection, supplemented by *Penelope* or *Carlisle.* *Breconshire* rode out the night hoping that the winds would abate the next day and tugs could bring her into Malta.[8]

These raids, although more effective than those delivered the days before, were made under more difficult conditions. A German pilot recalled: "Since yesterday there has been a fantastically heavy storm which made heavy attacks on the island almost impossible. But we have to fly in fog, storm and rain as the convoy is now sailing into Valletta . . . and so with 100kph squalls and visibility of four kilometers, our crews and bombers have to attack and if possible sink the ships." During the day, the Germans lost six Ju.88s and one Bf.109.[9]

The Goods Are Not Delivered

With the anchoring of *Breconshire* so close to shore, it may be said that Convoy MW.10 had arrived. However, the point of the operation was to deliver supplies to Malta, not ships, and in this the British authorities failed.

Talabot moored to No. 6 buoy in the middle of Grand Harbor at 0915. She carried 9,407 tons of cargo. At 0931 *Pampas* berthed at the oil fuel wharf at Marsa. Her cargo totaled 7,462 tons. Despite their early arrival, nothing was unloaded the first day. Vice Admiral Leatham explained: "The strong wind, swell and air raids caused difficulty and delay in securing M.V.'s *Talabot* and *Pampas* and placing lighters between them and the shore to form a gangway to the rock shelters. The crews of all ships were extremely tired. On going aboard *Pampas* it was found that her derrick gear and winches at all hatches had been damaged by [bomb] splinters. Repairs were put in hand at once (but it was not until the evening of 25th that all holds could be worked)."[10] Moreover, Leatham, in consultation with the sea transport officer, decided to rely exclusively on civilian labor. He calculated that civilian stevedores could unload ships at twice the rate of service personnel; however, he also noted that the job would go on only "provided air raids are not too severe." Also, because civilian workers took cover during the night whenever the warning siren was sounded, Leatham

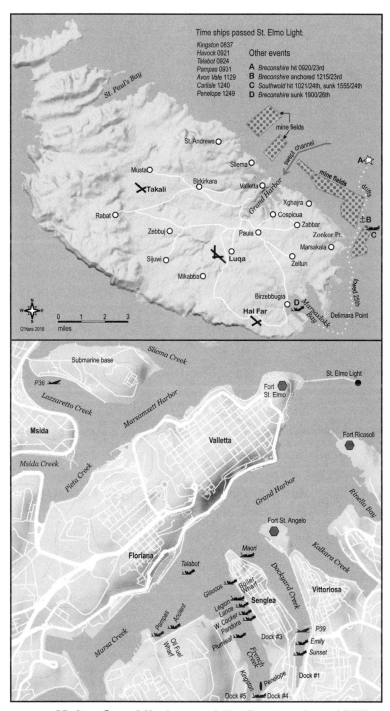

Time ships passed St. Elmo Light:

Kingston 0837
Havock 0921
Talabot 0924
Pampas 0931
Avon Vale 1129
Carlisle 1240
Penelope 1249

Other events

A Breconshire hit 0920/23rd
B Breconshire anchored 1215/23rd
C Southwold hit 1021/24th, sunk 1555/24th
D Breconshire sunk 1900/26th

St. Paul's Bay

mine fields

swept channel

St. Andrews

Sliema

A

Musta

Birkirkara

Valletta

mine fields

drifts

Takali

Grand Harbor

Xghajra

Rabat

Cospicua

±B

Zebbuj

Paula

Zabbar

C

Sijuwi

Luqa

Zonkor Pt.

Marsakala

Mikabba

Zeitun

towed 25th

Birzebbugia

D

Delimara Point

Hal Far

Marsaxlokk Bay

N W E S

0   1   2   3
miles

O'Hara 2018

Submarine base

Sliema Creek

St. Elmo Light

P36

Lazzaretto Creek

Marsamxett Harbor

Fort St. Elmo

Msida

Valletta

Fort Ricasoli

Msida Creek

Pieta Creek

Grand Harbor

Rinella Bay

Fort St. Angelo

Floriana

Maori

Kalkara Creek

Talabot

Dockyard Creek

Glaucos

Boiler Wharf

Vittoriosa

Legion

Senglea

Lance

Pampas

Ancient

W. Cooker

Pandora

P39

Marsa Creek

Plumleaf

Dock #3

Emily

Oil Fuel Wharf

French Creek

Sunset

Dock #1

Kingston

Penelope

Dock #5

Dock #4

Map 11.1. **Malta, Grand Harbor, and the Destruction of MW.10**

added: "taking all things into consideration I decided that unloading should be done by day only (0630 to 1900)." In fact, Leatham focused more on *Breconshire* than on unloading the cargo ships that had arrived. "During the two following days the chief anxiety was caused by the weather which prohibited 'Breconshire' being towed into Grand Harbour. . . . Air attacks during this period were heavier than usual but the visibility was poor and as in the past they failed to cause any vital damage to the dockyard or the merchant ships in harbour."[11]

On the 24th the weather over Malta improved slightly and starting at 1142 fifty-eight German bombers struck the harbor, the dockyards, the collection of ships at Marsaxlokk, and the airfields, dropping seventy tons of bombs. Leatham wrote that unloading *Talabot* and *Pampas* (by hand) "proceeded as fast as possible," with 807 tons landed during the day.[12]

Outside Marsaxlokk Bay the swells had moderated only slightly, with heights of fifteen feet and intervals of fifty yards. The trawler *Beryl* attempted to come alongside *Breconshire* to remove her passengers, but that proved impossible. Worse, the anchors had dragged and *Breconshire* was now on the edge of a minefield. *Southwold* approached to evacuate the passengers by breeches buoy, but, at 1021, when she was maneuvering three hundred yards astern of the supply ship, a mine—probably laid by the Germans on 15 January 1942—detonated, opening the destroyer's engine room to the sea. Escaping steam killed five men, but the ship's two 20-ton pumps kept pace with the flooding. After two hours, Jellicoe wrote that "at this stage the situation appeared to be well in hand." While *Abingdon* swept the area for mines the tug *Ancient* passed a line to *Southwold*. At 1258 the tug had taken up slack and was just beginning to tow *Southwold* when the sudden strain snapped the ship's back. She sank to deck level amidships, with the two buoyant ends keeping her afloat and the upper deck plating holding her together. Nonetheless, Jellicoe did not give up, and by 1330 *Ancient* was slowing pulling *Southwold* toward the harbor channel. Her progress was not unhindered, however, and Ju.88s attacked three times. Finally, a bomb exploded thirty feet from the port side and the concussion caused both ends to begin flooding. The cable parted at 1530 and *Southwold* yawed to starboard and sank at 1555. *Dulverton, Ancient,* and *Beryl* rescued the thirty-nine men still on board.[13]

At 0200/25th *Ancient* and *Robust* secured lines to *Breconshire*. She slipped her anchors and began slowly moving toward Marsaxlokk; given the conditions, Grand Harbor was an impossible destination. They drew her away from the minefield towing off either bow "at a steady knot and a half." Troubles began, however, when the tugs tried to swing *Breconshire* around to the south. This put the swell abeam, and the wallowing supply ship "took on a vicious malevolence . . . she started to yaw and dip and plunge, striving continually to swing her head into [the] wind." Finally *Robust's* line parted. By dawn *Breconshire* seemed in danger of grounding on the Delimara Point reef. Leatham ordered *Eridge* and *Beaufort* out to provide gunnery support. Gregory-Smith arrived to find that "the leading tug was trying to pull *Breconshire* to starboard but, each time she started to turn, the wind caught her and pushed her back again. To help, the other tug had taken a hawser from *Breconshire's* port quarter and was pulling her stern in that direction. But with only one small tug towing the heavy ship quickly became unmanageable and began to wallow helplessly in the trough of the swell." *Penelope's* Captain Nicholl, who was supervising the operation from *Ancient*, ordered *Eridge* to secure a cable and lend a hand—and to "make it snappy. We've got to berth her before heavy raids commence." Despite an exciting moment when the supply ship's heaving mass and the line from *Ancient's* tow almost trapped *Eridge*, they successfully brought *Breconshire* into Marsaxlokk Bay by midday/25th. Captain Hutchison noted that "[*Eridge*] was very well handled by her captain."[14]

On the 25th a heavy assault against Grand Harbor started at 1300. Bombers near-missed *Penelope* and *Talabot* and the two ships only unloaded 539 tons during the day. *Carlisle, Hurworth, Dulverton, Eridge,* and *Beaufort* sailed at 2050 for Alexandria, "just as the sirens were wailing for the first of the night's raids." For two days, Leatham stuck to his plan. The stevedores did not work on the night of 25th even though they had unloaded only 8 percent of the stores carried and the scale and fury of the air attacks was increasing. Throughout the day the Germans deployed eighty-four Ju.88s, Ju.87s, and Bf.109s over Malta and dropped seventy-five tons of bombs.[15]

The 26th proved decisive. Even though the German Admiralty staff incorrectly believed that "Doubtless the steamers had already been unloaded to a large extent before the air attacks of 26 March," 2nd Fliegerkorps mounted

Table 11.1. **Cargo Unloaded from MW.10, 23 March to 13 April 1942**

Date	Pampas	Talabot	Breconshire	Total
Total cargo	7,855	9,407	12,862	30,124
Unloaded on 23 Mar	0	0	0	0
Unloaded on 24 Mar	310	497	0	807
Unloaded on 25 Mar	209	330	0	539
Unloaded on 26 Mar	280	145	0	425
Unloaded on 27 Mar	603	0	0	603
Unloaded on 28 Mar	588	0	0	588
Unloaded on 29 Mar	325	0	0	325
Unloaded on 30 Mar	422	0	0	422
Unloaded on 31 Mar	158	30	0	188
Unloaded 1-13 April	1,075	48	0	1,123
Total cargo unloaded	3,970	1,050	0	5,020
Percent of load	50.5	11.2	0.0	16.7

Source: ADM 116/4559, 38.

a sustained effort to sink the shipping remaining in the harbor. Throughout the day 126 bombers deployed against the harbor. Eighty of them dropped a total of 106 tons of bombs. Another twenty-nine concentrated on the antiaircraft defenses dropping thirty tons of bombs. Six Bf.110s and 182 Bf.109s also participated. The Germans lost only one Ju.88.[16] At 1230 two bombs struck *Talabot*, one near the bow and the other in the engine room. The blast ignited leaking fuel oil. The blaze spread to hold numbers 3 and 4, while another bomb struck in Hold No. 1, which was filled with drummed kerosene. Hold No. 4 also contained ammunition, so Leatham ordered the ship scuttled to prevent an explosion—no easy matter, given the intense blaze. Even so, the hulk continued to burn for two days. At 1430 a bomb exploded in *Pampas*' engine room. Hold No. 4 flooded and the ship sank by the stern. The aft superstructure burned all day. A bomb hit *Ancient* while she was fighting *Talabot*'s fires, and she beached to keep from sinking. Two bombs struck *Legion*, which was docked at the boiler wharf—detonating her forward magazine and killing eleven. The destroyer's remains sank with only the mast above water. A bomb exploded beneath *P39*; it killed two men and caused flooding, but the submarine remained afloat. The tanker *Plumleaf* (5,916 GRT/12 kts) took a hit in the forward cargo tank. Fuel oil gushed out and covered French Creek. Captain Hutchison emerged from the operations room at Marsaxlokk to see "a stick of bombs fall all round *Breconshire.*" Flames erupted from No. 4 hatch.[17] Four more bombs smashed into the store ship at 1740. *Beryl, Swona,* and *Robust* pumped water on the blaze and had it under control by 1955, but their efforts caused additional flooding. *Breconshire* was listing 15 degrees and seemed on the point of capsizing, so the crew abandoned ship. A near-miss holed the light cruiser *Aurora,* which was in dock completing repairs of the mine damage inflicted in December 1941. Bombs near-missed *Penelope* at 1230 and 1700. The last cracked the lower keel plate and flooded "all compartments below the two foremost mess decks and a number of compartments aft, and also [put] A and B Turrets out of action [and] lifted all the decks forward, resulting in the straining of most of the watertight doors." A small bomb ventilated *Avon Vale* with splinters. "But the most serious thing was that No. 2 Dock Caisson was damaged and *Lance* was thereby locked in dock." Stevedores unloaded just 425 tons during the day. *Talabot's* loss finally stirred Leatham to order unloading day and night and to assign a hundred troops and a party of naval ratings "to augment and give heart to the stevedores in *Pampas* which was the only ship where work could at present proceed."[18]

In the early hours of the 28th *Breconshire's* smoldering fires flared up and her list increased. Hutchison got Leatham's permission to sink the ship on an even keel. He flooded a boiler room and tried to open the stern with a depth charge. "Unfortunately the depth charge was wrongly set for the depth of water and did not explode." As a result, the ship settled on her beam with ten feet of her starboard side above water. This rendered the oil and stores inaccessible although eventually "some hundreds of tons of oil fuel were pumped from her hull."[19] On this day the raids were not as severe, and the stevedores and soldiers unloaded 603 tons from *Pampas.* Dockyard workers and crews worked feverishly to ready *Aurora* and *Penelope* for sea.

Aurora and *Avon Vale* escaped Malta on the 29th bound for Gibraltar. Leatham wrote that "under normal conditions neither ship would have been considered fit for such a passage."[20] *Penelope* occupied *Aurora*'s vacated drydock, but the dockyard superintendent estimated that he would need a month to complete repairs. Captain Nicholl observed that the "system is to carry on working regardless of the sounding of the General air raid alarm until a red flag is hoisted in Valletta. . . . Unfortunately, while the move to the shelters is carried out with alacrity, the return to work afterward is a very different matter and it is usually twenty minutes to half an hour before work is again going in full swing. On a day of frequent raids therefore the amount of work done is extremely small." He further complained that it was worse at night. With his ship in danger, Nicholl saw that "the only hope was to complete the job in record time with the ship's staff of shipwrights and artificers." The dockyard gave permission and things started to happen.[21]

On the 31st renewed strikes against the harbor damaged *Penelope*, *Lance*, and *Sokol*. Leatham concluded that "owing to the prolonged and constant heavy air raids, little work was being got out of the Maltese stevedores. I decided . . . to dispense with their services from a.m. 1st April and to continue the unloading of *Pampas* with Service personnel only. . . . It was agreed that work should continue day and night regardless of air alarms except in the heaviest attacks directed on the harbour." They were able to take off another thousand tons through April 13th before recovery efforts ended. Leatham wrote, "there must remain in my mind the grief that such a large portion of what had been fought so successfully through to the shores of Malta was lost after its safe arrival in harbour. We just were not strong enough." Indeed, much more would have been unloaded if the policy of using service personnel only that was adopted on 31 March had been in place from the first. Leatham was right that the island's defensive capabilities were not strong enough, but a greater sense of urgency would have mitigated this weakness.[22]

Heavy air attacks against the docks continued in April. The submarines *Pandora* and *P36* went down permanently on the 1st. An attempt to recover oil from *Breconshire*'s wreck that night failed because *Boxol* (2,410 GRT), the ship dispatched, was so slow that "she had to leave almost as soon as she arrived and nothing was achieved."[23] On the 4th the Greek submarine *Glaucos* fell victim, while *Lance* and *Penelope* sustained additional damage.

On 5 April *Lance,* one of the original members of Force K, received her coup de grâce when a bomb exploded in No. 2 dock and ruptured her sides. The blast knocked the ship off the blocks and partially submerged her. Multiple near-misses caused splinter damage to *Kingston's* hull and upper works. *Havock* sailed for Gibraltar, but hit a sandbank off the Tunisian coast at 30 knots and became a total loss; the French interned her crew. A bomb clobbered *Penelope,* inflicting fresh damage, not to mention "many hundreds of small holes." A near-miss on an adjacent building blasted large pieces of stone on to the upper decks. After that "It was a matter of all hands to remove 'rock garden' from decks." This caused Captain Nicholl to appeal to the army for welders to help speed repairs. Five responded and "their work was invaluable."[24]

As dangerous as it was, the air assault also quickly became numbing. *ML126* and *130* arrived at the island on 21 March after a harrowing passage from Gibraltar. One launch's skipper recalled that on his first day in port he had tea at the Malta Union Club. "The sirens wailed and soon we could hear

Havock, the last destroyer to flee Malta, ran aground at speed off the coast of Tunisia. This photo, taken from an Italian MAS boat, shows her on fire shortly after the crew scuttled her and took to their boats. COLLECTION OF E. CERNUSCHI

aircraft overhead. Bombs whistled down and went off nearby, but no one made for the shelters down below. And then one bomb chipped a hole in the corner of the ceiling of the hall and exploded outside. Still no one moved. They went on drinking tea. I was not sure I liked it." However, after just a week the raids had become entertainment, "The MLs [motor launches] were grandstand seats. At gin time before meals we lounged in deck chairs and looked up at the lines of Junkers streaming down upon Valletta and the dockyard cities through a sky pock-marked with tracer and shell bursts."[25]

The 6th saw one concentrated strike, but *Penelope's* repairs progressed, greatly assisted by the army welders. The 7th, however, was a "difficult day," as Captain Nicholl described it. There were four severe raids. "Bombs fell all round the ship and it was extraordinary that not one bomb hit." Given the inevitability of fatal damage, Nicholl decided to sail on the 8th, come what may. Indeed, the departure was difficult. Both the oiler and the lighter meant to fuel her in dock were damaged. At 0815 the Germans attacked for two hours, landing one bomb forward that made hundreds of holes on the starboard side. Only the most serious could be patched, and workers plugged the balance with wooden pegs. "The ship looked rather like a porcupine when she sailed." One officer rigged a loudspeaker and broadcast an appeal for help in loading 4-inch ammunition, of which the ship had none. "Survivors from destroyers and trawlers sunk in the recent raids, soldiers of the Cheshire Regiment billeted in the Canteen and dockyard officials lent us a willing hand. A precious five hundred rounds and some pom pom ammunition were embarked." *Penelope* finally slipped at 2115. Nicholl was not sure whether she was sufficiently watertight to make Gibraltar.[26]

Penelope's departure ended the saga of Force K at Malta. The sinking of *Kingston* in drydock on the 11th, when a direct hit broke the battered destroyer's back, was the final blow to the destroyers from the Battle of Sirte. Axis airpower eliminated another weapon in Great Britain's sea control arsenal when the incessant bombing forced the 10th Submarine Flotilla to begin leaving the island on 25 April, with *Una*, the last boat, clear by 4 May.

In the three weeks from 24 March to 12 April the island experienced 2,159 bomber sorties, which dropped 1,869 tons of bombs. Sixty-eight

Kingston capsized in dock. This large destroyer was severely damaged at
1846/22nd March by a shell variously attributed to *Littorio*, *Gorizia*, and *Trento*.
She had to seek shelter in Malta rather than return to Alexandria with her unit,
and there she was damaged in air raids on the 5th and 7th of April and finally
destroyed on the 11th, when she capsized while drydocked. COLLECTION OF
J. ROBERTS

men died and ninety-two were seriously injured. Ships sunk included
Legion, *Lance*, *Kingston*, *P39*, *P36*, *Glaucos*, *Pandora*, *Breconshire*, *Plumleaf*, *Talabot*, *Pampas*, the trawlers *Jade*, *Abingdon*, *Andromeda*, *Emily*,
West Cocker, and the drifters *Girl Margaret* and *Sunset*.[27]

Impact and Assessment

In the Second Battle of Sirte both sides partially met their goals. The Italians delayed the convoy and inflicted light damage to one cruiser and
three destroyers, moderate damage to a cruiser, and heavy damage to two
destroyers. The British successfully protected the merchant ships during
the surface actions, despite the heavier guns that were facing them. They
could not prevent the convoy's delay and did no damage to the enemy.
Admiral Iachino made some questionable decisions and missed his best

opportunity to bring the convoy itself under his guns. Nevertheless, he secured a positive result. Vian also made some poor decisions, but independent actions by his subordinates, particularly Captain Poland, saved the effort. The greatest single factor in the battle's outcome, however, was the weather. The persistent, violent gale determined the direction of the attack; it degraded the accuracy of the weapons on both sides; and it influenced every action, and every decision on all sides.

Churchill and Cunningham accorded the Second Battle of Sirte a place in the British pantheon of great naval victories. Cunningham called it "one of the most brilliant actions of the war, if not the most brilliant."[28] However, given the imbalance in the damage inflicted and the fact that the Italians achieved at least their minimal objective, it seems odd to call it a victory at all, much less a great victory. In fact, Cunningham and Churchill authored a mythical Battle of Sirte—one that proved that the Royal Navy had retained the Nelson's Touch and one where resolute men and brilliant, aggressive tactics enabled a vastly outnumbered force to rout a craven enemy. It happened like this: On 25 March, shortly after Vian's return to Alexandria, Cunningham, who, against his wishes, was about to be replaced as commander in chief of the Mediterranean Fleet by (Acting) Admiral Henry Harwood, who had started the war as a mere commodore (and whose promotion Cunningham had opposed), sent a long wire to the Admiralty.[29] In this he described "a brilliant delaying action" in which the enemy "was attacked through a smoke screen" and in which "a torpedo hit [was scored] amidships on a Littorio Class battleship . . . [which] was seen to be blazing aft. One enemy cruiser was also seriously damaged, and another was hit. The effect . . . was to hold the enemy off convoy until dusk when enemy retired." There was no mention of the convoy's subsequent fate. There was no mention of the weather. He exaggerated the air action, stating that 150 bombers had been involved. He accepted every claim that his captains made, boasting of imaginary damage inflicted and ignoring damage suffered.[30]

Churchill found this cable agreeable, and that same day instructed Pound to convey to Admiral Vian his admiration for "the resolute and brilliant action by which the Malta convoy was saved. That one of the most powerful modern battleships afloat attended by two heavy and four light cruisers and a flotilla should have been routed and put to flight with severe torpedo and gunfire injury in broad daylight . . . constitutes a naval episode of the highest distinction."³¹

Thus, Vian was only one day back in port when his commander in chief and the head of his government were lavishing him with praise and the compliments of the British nation. Churchill released his statement to the press that same day. Yet, Cunningham and Churchill both jumped the gun before they checked their facts. They inflated the enemy force, acclaimed imaginary damage, distorted the battle's conditions (broad daylight), and failed to mention that most of the supplies failed to arrive (although this was only just becoming clear).

Why was this done? In wartime, exaggeration and propaganda are normal. A series of calamities had befallen Imperial forces in the Mediterranean, starting with the loss of *Ark Royal* and *Barham* in November and *Queen Elizabeth* and *Valiant* in December, followed by the destruction of a Malta convoy in February. The British clearly could not use the central Mediterranean, and a series of major Italian convoy successes in January, February, and early March demonstrated that neither could they deny the enemy from using it. Disasters elsewhere exacerbated this unpalatable situation. In December Japanese aircraft sank *Prince of Wales* and *Repulse*. In February the Germans sailed the battleships *Gneisenau* and *Scharnhorst* though the English Channel. Singapore had fallen. The Dutch East Indies had just surrendered. Burma was being overrun. The nation was desperate for good news and, at long last, it seemed the Royal Navy had delivered.

Once the British claims were published, the Axis press furiously disputed them. It called the British liars and claimed their force had suffered no damage at all. In turn, the Italians published their own set of exaggerations. In its own way, the propaganda battle was as intense as the actual shooting, and once wild claims had been made and then defended there was no honorable way for Churchill or Cunningham to admit that news of a Nelsonian victory had been premature; thus, the British dug in their heels and perpetuated the legend of the great naval victory. The sea lords were presented with a list of 125 awards, and although there was some grumbling by the Second Sea Lord—who complained that the number was especially excessive given "the negative results of the action so far as enemy losses are concerned"—the medals were presented and could not be rescinded.[32]

Since the end of the war, official and popular British histories have repeated the enthusiastic excesses of Churchill's 25 March telegram. Roskill called the Battle of Sirte "a classic example of the ability of a weaker force, handled with skill and determination, to parry the intentions of a far stronger enemy." General Playfair's official history is more circumspect, admitting that to the extent of delaying the convoy "the Italian manoeuvres succeeded," but also asserting that "by skill, boldness and bluff the British ships had prevented their much heavier opponents from coming within range of the convoy." In a 1993 work one author writes: "What decided the day, however, was not gunnery but resolution, and Vian richly merited the knighthood that was bestowed upon him." Correlli Barnett takes this to the point of nonsense: "Yet whenever possible the little British ships went for the Italians: first for the 8-inch gun cruisers and then, from 1700 onwards, for *Littorio* herself, even starting a fire abaft her after 15-inch turret. It was a majestic display of tactical skill and sheer aggressive seamanship absolutely true to the tradition of Hawke and Nelson; and it dominated and daunted the enemy."[33] In truth, Second Sirte was a battle in which the British navy fulfilled its minimum objective: sheltering the convoy from direct harm. Had it avoided delay by driving off the Italian fleet with an effective torpedo attack shortly after the start of combat, then indeed it would have been a victory. Had it also inflicted major damage to the Italians in so doing, then the battle would have been the type of victory that Cunningham and Churchill claimed it was. Instead, the British fought cautiously and at long range, employing standard destroyer tactics. Despite the massive advantage conferred on them by the smoke, they never came to grips with the enemy until the very end, after Iachino had already achieved his minimum objective. Even then, their attack was ineffective. The Italians withdrew not because of enemy action but because they had run out of daylight. The Battle of the Barents Sea in December 1942 and the Battle of Leyte Gulf in October 1944 provide much more impressive examples of weak forces frustrating much stronger aggressors for much longer periods of time in conditions that favored the attacker, not the defender.

Admiral Arturo Riccardi (*center*), with Vice Admiral Angelo Iachino on his left, visiting Taranto on 25 March 1942 to congratulate the men who served in the Second Battle of Sirte. Riccardi was naval chief of staff from December 1940 through July 1943. Iachino was fleet commander from December 1940 through April 1943. COURTESY OF E. BAGNASCO

Although Iachino never engaged the merchantmen, the Italians shot much better than the British (1,480 Italian rounds expended and seven ships damaged, compared to 2,807 British for one minor hit) and forced the convoy to detour south so that even *Breconshire*, the fastest freighter, was a half hour from port when she was decisively damaged. The push south cost her forty nautical miles, more than two hours' delay. And because the escorts had expended most of their antiaircraft ammunition while the fleet units fought the surface engagement, these extra air attacks were particularly effective.

Supermarina drew certain lessons from the action. Iachino sought battle with high hopes of a decisive result due to Axis air superiority and gunnery strength. Weather, a lack of time, and his own deliberateness, frustrated his expectations. He wrote that "the tactic of the smoke screen, which the British have studied and developed with great care and with undeniable skill, we can counter only, if in a future meeting, we will have many hours of daylight before sunset, or a large mass of cruisers, destroyers, and possibly MAS boats launched within the curtain of fog to fight a type of night melee without worry of losses that the forces might incur."[34]

The best measure of victory, however, is to see which side best asserted control of the central Mediterranean following the action. It would be three months before the British attempted another Malta convoy—three months despite the failure of MW.10 and Malta's desperate need for provisions and the growing possibility of an Axis invasion. The sortie of Iachino and Parona established a credible threat. The Italians had bigger and stronger weapons, and they were willing to use them in any conditions, even at significant risk. This threat kept the British in port for three months—a result that did not cost the Italians a drop of fuel oil. This threat caused Vian and the June 1942 *Vigorous* convoy to retreat without a fight when confronted by a possible interception by Italian battleships. The British would not run another convoy to Malta from the east until November 1942, after the Allies had landed in North Africa. These results were the true confirmation that the Italians did indeed win the Battle of Sirte and that the fruit of that victory was control of the central Mediterranean.

Chapter 12

Conclusion

SIX VICTORIES

There has never been a protracted war from which a country has benefited.

SUN TZU

In November 1941 the British established maritime superiority in the central Mediterranean. The triumphant congratulations sent to Force K on the morning of 9 November, after it claimed two destroyers and ten merchant men sunk, symbolized this superiority. "Attack . . . carried out with great skill and determination, reflects the very greatest credit."[1]

During Force K's 171-day tenure in Malta, it sortied fourteen times against Italian shipping and made five interceptions. It sank thirteen merchant ships or auxiliaries displacing 57,825 GRT, as well as two destroyers. It helped protect seven Malta convoys and fought in the first and second battles of Sirte. This seems a good return on investment. Yet, although Force K accounted for a fifth of the African traffic sunk during its time in Malta, it was only one factor in the complicated formula that the British used to achieve their success. Also key was the focused application of air, sea, and undersea forces, assisted by good intelligence. So was effective doctrine, applied by aggressive leaders such as Rear Admiral Philip Vian, Captain William Agnew, and Captain Albert L. Poland. So were superior technology, such as radar (especially ASV), and plentiful supplies of the wherewithals of naval warfare, such as fuel oil.

In the end, however, even all of this was not enough. On 13 December 1941 British destroyers sank two Italian cruisers that were transporting fuel to Tripoli. Over the next two days British submarines frustrated Italy's most strongly defended convoy effort of the war to date, sinking a pair of merchant ships and torpedoing a battleship. On 15 December 1941, the Italo-German army abandoned the Gazala position and began a long retreat west. Despite deep discouragement and a growing sense of doom, the Italian navy persisted, and the next convoy to Africa commenced as fast as ships could refuel. Simultaneously, the British launched a supply operation to Malta. The two forces clashed in what history calls the First Battle of Sirte. The Italians believed that they had intercepted and repelled an enemy fleet that had been hunting their convoy; on the next night the Malta strike force tried to intercept the convoy as it entered Tripoli. The raiders sailed straight into a minefield: two were damaged and two sank. Simultaneously, Italian frogmen penetrated Alexandria harbor and disabled two battleships, damaged a destroyer, and crippled a tanker.

With these Italian victories, the British lost the superiority that they had worked so hard to establish—even if this was not completely apparent at the time. How did this happen? The British had discounted the Regia Marina's capabilities and assumed that it would not mount another major resupply effort so hard on the heels of failure. They sent the Malta strike force on a risky mission with faulty intelligence. Finally, they disregarded their enemy's ability to adapt and to deploy innovative weapons of its own. But the sudden transformation in the balance of sea power was more about what the Regia Marina did when in a crisis. The Italian navy persisted with its routine tasks while deploying its special weapons, and it used the advantages that it possessed, which included its central position, its possession of greater forces in-theater, its support from increasing German reinforcements, and intelligence windfalls of its own.

After transforming the campaign's dynamics, Axis air forces asserted a blockade of Malta, powerfully complemented by the appropriate use of Italy's battle fleet. On 22 March, in the Second Battle of Sirte, the Italian navy demonstrated that the operational and strategic implications of a proper and successful use of naval force can far outweigh the short-term tactical results. In this case, the Italians delayed the convoy and roughed up the escort, but more important, they established a powerful and credible threat that crimped British operations for the next six months.

Statistics demonstrate the impact of Italy's three December victories. From 1 July 1941 to 17–18 December, 1941 British forces sank 74 merchant ships, displacing 266,738 GRT, engaged in traffic to Africa. From 17–18 December, 1941 to 30 June 1942 they sank 20 merchant ships totaling 85,968 GRT. In the first period, one of sixteen Allied ships convoyed to Malta failed to arrive. In the second period twenty of twenty-nine ships convoyed to Malta failed to arrive. Statistics also suggest that Ultra did not greatly affect operations. The British attacked 49 (26 percent) of 188 Axis convoys or single-ship sailings to, from, or along the African coast undertaken between 1 November and 31 March 1942, even though Ultra provided warning of 154 of them (82 percent). Thirty of these attacks (16 percent of sailings) resulted in a ship sunk or damaged. In the Axis war against British traffic during the same period, Axis forces attacked 26 of the 78 convoys that passed between Alexandria and Libyan ports (mainly Tobruk), and 10 of the 12 convoys (or sailings) to or from Malta. The Axis attack rate of 40 percent was higher than the rate achieved by the Ultra-assisted British. The Axis conducted eleven successful attacks against Tobruk traffic at sea and eight successful attacks against traffic bound for Malta, for a total success rate of 21 percent, again better than the Ultra-assisted British.

The Axis powers maintained maritime superiority in the central Mediterranean until November 1942, when Anglo-American forces from outside the theater invaded French North Africa.

Sea power is a fragile thing; it cannot be taken for granted. The lessons that the Mediterranean campaign teaches are that everything is important. Big ships and big victories matter, but so do doctrine, morale, training, and persistence. Navies do not prosper by believing what they wish to believe. Reading the enemy's mail is a good thing, but it is better to do things right. In many cases good communications between services or allies beats knowledge of enemy intentions.

History matters. The conditions that the Allied and Axis powers faced then in the central Mediterranean—intersecting lines of communication, strong enemy forces, and narrow seas—are conditions that are still present in the Mediterranean, as well as in the straits of Malacca, Singapore, and Hormuz; in the Baltic; and in the South China Sea. The lessons learned then apply today. The principles of success do not fade with time.

By May 1942 *Vittorio Veneto* was back in service. These images, taken from *Vittorio Veneto*, show *Littorio* conducting gunnery practice in the Gulf of Taranto on 13 May 1942. The following month the Italian fleet exercised sea power by forcing a very large convoy from Alexandria bound for Malta to turn back. STORIA MILITARE

Appendix 1

SHIPS SUNK AND DAMAGED

Table A1.1. **Summary of Ships Sunk, November 1941–March 1942**

Losses	Mercantile	GRT	Warships	Tonnage
Allied losses to Italians	5	12,547	7	28,606
Allied losses to Germans	18	104,239	18	88,180
Total Allied losses	23	116,786	25	106,786
Allied losses supplying Malta	9	63,021	2	2,100
Axis losses	70	243,837	19	27,984
Axis lost supplying Africa	35	151,632	7	16,938
Axis lost to forces based in Malta	44	166,440	9	11,041
Axis lost in supplying Africa due to forces based in Malta	27	123,800	4	5,065

See Tables A1.6 and A1.7 for details of ships sunk.

Only merchant vessels larger than 100 tons GRT or warships with standard displacement greater than 100 tons are listed here. These statistics include all losses in the Mediterranean.

This table shows that half of all Axis mercantile losses were involved in supplying Africa and that forces based in Malta inflicted three quarters of those losses. Table A1.2 specifies the nature and degree of the threats facing Axis traffic in the period of November 1941 through March 1942.

Table A1.2. **Axis Losses, by Agent**

Agent of loss	Mercantile	Tons	Warships	Tons
Aircraft	17	58,853	2	1,080
Submarines	33	114,265	9	9,661
Surface ships	13	57,825	8	17,243
Mines	7	12,894	0	0
Total	70	243,837	19	27,984

See Tables A1.6 and A1.7 for details of losses.

Submarines were the deadliest agent, accounting for almost half the vessels and gross tonnage sunk, but they were generally less effective against the most important and heavily defended traffic. Moreover, their ability to venture deep into enemy-controlled waters enabled them to prey on softer targets. Aircraft and surface ships based in Malta were the most effective killers of African traffic during this November 1941 through March 1942 period, but their impact diminished after Italy's mid-December 1941 victories and the German bombing campaign that began in January 1942.

Table A1.3. **Allied Losses, by Agent**

Agent of loss	Mercantile*	Tons	Warships*	Tons
Aircraft	3/9	70,289	0/3	4,419
Submarines	0/8	29,907	0/12	72,560
Surface ships	0	0	3/0	2,920
Mines	1/1	9,036	2/3	11,620
XMAS	1/0	7,554	2/0	702
Total	23	116,786	25	92,221

*By Italians/Germans
See Tables A1.6 and A1.7 for details of losses.

Looking at Allied losses, it is interesting to observe that aircraft were the most efficient killers of merchant ships, but they were relatively ineffective against warships. Submarines enjoyed more successes against Allied warships than against commercial vessels, reflecting the type of campaign and the nature of the targets available to Axis forces. Italian submarines failed to deliver a single effective attack on a British commercial or military vessel during this period.

Counting ships sunk is a way to keep score in much the same way as counting tons of supplies delivered, but damaging a warship (as in the case of the battleships at Alexandria) may have an impact almost as great as sinking the vessels outright. The final tables consider warships significantly damaged or sunk during November 1941 through March 1942. "Significantly damaged" is used here to describe vessels that required three or more months in repair.

Table A1.4. **Italian Warships Significantly Damaged, 1 November 1941–31 March 1942**

Agent	Number	Tons
By submarines	3	52,730
By aircraft	1	9,440
By surface ships	2	2,615
Total	6	64,785

Table A1.5. **Allied Warships Significantly Damaged, 1 November 1941–31 March 1942**

Agent	Number	Tons
By Italian aircraft	1	1,690
By Italian surface ships	2	3,060
By Italian special forces	2	62,600
By Italian mines	1	5,250
Total Italian	**6**	**72,600**
By German aircraft	3	3,160
By German submarines	1	1,690
Total German	**4**	**4,850**
Grand total	**10**	**77,450**

Table A1.6. **Allied Vessels Sunk by Enemy Action in the Mediterranean, 1 Nov. 1941–31 Apr. 1942**

For nationality/type and agent abbreviations see Abbreviations.

Merchant ships

Date	Name	GRT	Nationality/type	Agent	Location
14 Nov	*Empire Pelican*	6,463	BR MM	IT AC	Cent. Med
15 Nov	*Empire Defender*	5,649	BR MM	IT AC	Cent. Med
2 Dec	*Fjord*	4,032	NO MM	GE SS	Western Med
2 Dec	*Grelhead*	4,274	BR MM	GE SS	Western Med
5 Dec	*Chakdina*	3,033	BR ABV	IT AC	Eastern Med
7 Dec	*Chantala*	3,129	BR ABV	GE mined	Tobruk
19 Dec	*Sagona*	7,554	NO AO	IT XMAS	Alexandria
19 Dec	*Varlaam Avanesov*	6,557	SU MM	GE SS	Aegean
21 Dec	*Hellen*	5,289	NO MM	GE SS	Western Med
23 Dec	*Shuntien*	3,059	BR MM	GE SS	off Egypt
24 Dec	*Phenix*	5,907	FR AO	IT mined	Hafia
26 Dec	*Warszawa*	2,486	PO MM	GE SS	off Egypt
28 Dec	*Volo*	1,587	BR MM	GE SS	off Egypt
19 Jan	*Thermopylae*	6,655	BR MM	GE AC	Cent. Med
13 Feb	*Rowallan Castle*	7,798	BR MM	GE AC	Cent. Med
13 Feb	*Clan Chattan*	7,262	BR MM	GE AC	Cent. Med
22 Feb	*Bintang*	2,825	BR MM	GE AC	off Libya
22 Feb	*Hanne*	1,360	BR MM	GE AC	off Libya
22 Mar	*Clan Campbell*	7,255	BR MM	GE AC	Cent. Med
24 Mar	*Talabot*	6,798	BR MM	GE AC	Malta
24 Mar	*Pampas*	5,415	BR MM	GE AC	Malta
26 Mar	*Breconshire*	9,776	BR MM	GE AC	Malta
26 Mar	*Slavol*	2,623	BR AO	GE SS	off Libya

Naval vessels

Date	Name	GRT	Nationality/type	Agent	Location
13 Nov	*Ark Royal*	22,600	BR CV	GE SS	Western Med
25 Nov	*Barham*	31,300	BR BB	GE SS	Eastern Med
27 Nov	*Parramatta*	1,060	AU DS	GE SS	off Libya
1 Dec	*Perseus*	1,475	BR SS	GE mined	Cent. Med
11 Dec	*Lady Shirley*	477	BR AMT	GE SS	Western Med
11 Dec	*Rosabelle*	525	BR PC	GE SS	Western Med
15 Dec	*Galatea*	5,220	BR CL	GE SS	Eastern Med
19 Dec	*Kandahar*	1,750	BR DD	IT mined	off Libya
19 Dec	*Neptune*	7,175	BR CL	IT mined	off Libya
24 Dec	*Salvia*	955	BR DC	GE SS	off Egypt
31 Dec	*Triumph*	1,290	BR SS	IT DC	Aegean
17 Jan	*Gurkha ii*	1,920	BR DD	GE SS	off Egypt
19 Jan	*Erin*	394	BR AMT	IT XMAS	Western Med
19 Jan	*Honju*	308	BR AMT	IT XMAS	Western Med
30 Jan	*Sotra*	313	BR PC	GE SS	off Libya
12 Feb	*Maori*	1,959	BR DD	GE AC	Malta
13 Feb	*Tempest*	1090	BR SS	IT DC	Med
22 Feb	*P38*	540	BR SS	IT DC	Med
11 Mar	*Naiad*	5,450	BR CL	GE SS	Med
20 Mar	*Heythrop*	1,050	BR DE	GE SS	off Libya
24 Mar	*Southwold*	1,050	BR DE	GE mined	Malta
26 Mar	*P39*	540	BR SS	GE AC	Malta
26 Mar	*Legion*	1,920	BR DD	GE AC	Malta
26 Mar	*Jaguar*	1,690	BR DD	GE SS	off Egypt
13 Mar	*Zoodochis Pigi*	170	GK AMT	GE mined	Eastern Med

Table A1.7. Axis Vessels Sunk by Enemy Action in the Mediterranean, 1 Nov. 1941–31 Mar. 1942

Ships in **bold** sunk by forces based in Malta. Ships underlined engaged in supplying Africa. For nationality/type and agent abbreviations, see Abbreviations.

Merchant ships

Date	Name	GRT	Nationality/type	Agent	Location
1 Nov	*Marigola*	5,996	IT MM	AC	Cent. Med
2 Nov	*Balilla*	2,469	IT MM	SS	Cent. Med
5 Nov	*Anna Zippitelli*	1,019	IT MM	AC	off Libya
6 Nov	*Maria Bruna*	246	IT MM	AC	Benghazi
8 Nov	*Sant'Antonio*	271	IT MM	AC	Brindisi
9 Nov	*Conte di Misurata*	5,014	IT AO	SURF	Cent. Med
9 Nov	*Rina Corrado*	5,180	IT MM	SURF	Cent. Med
9 Nov	*Maria*	6,339	IT MM	SURF	Cent. Med
9 Nov	*Sagitta*	5,153	IT MM	SURF	Cent. Med
9 Nov	*Minatitlan*	7,599	IT AO	SURF	Cent. Med
9 Nov	*Duisburg*	7,389	GE MM	SURF	Cent. Med
9 Nov	*San Marco*	3,073	GE MM	SURF	Cent. Med
10 Nov	*Ithaka*	1,773	GE MM	SS	Aegean
24 Nov	*Maritza*	2,910	GE MM	SURF	Cent. Med
24 Nov	*Procida*	1,842	GE MM	SURF	Cent. Med
24 Nov	*Unione*	216	IT PC	SS	off Libya
24 Nov	*Attilio Deffenu*	3,510	IT AMC	SS	Cent. Med
24 Nov	*Heracles*	632	IT Tug	SS	Crete
25 Nov	*Tinos*	2,826	IT MM	AC	Benghazi
25 Nov	*LVII*	300	GE MM	SS	Aegean
28 Nov	*Berbera*	2,093	IT AO	AC	Navarino
28 Nov	*Priaruggia*	1,196	IT MM	AC	Benghazi
30 Nov	*Capo Faro*	3,476	IT MM	AC	Cent. Med
30 Nov	*Speranza*	445	IT AO	AC	Benghazi
1 Dec	*Adriatico*	1,976	IT MM	SURF	off Libya
1 Dec	*Iridio Mantovani*	10,540	IT AO	SURF	Cent. Med
4 Dec	*Eridano*	3,586	IT MM	SS	Cent. Med
9 Dec	*Sebastiano Venier*	6,311	IT MM	SS	Cent. Med

(cont.)

Date	Name	GRT	Nationality/type	Agent	Location
11 Dec	*Calitea*	4,013	IT MM	SS	Cent. Med
13 Dec	*Carlo del Greco*	6,836	IT MM	SS	Cent. Med
13 Dec	*Fabio Filzi*	6,836	IT MM	SS	Cent. Med
17 Dec	*Lina*	1,235	IT AO	AC	Cent. Med
30 Dec	*Campina*	3,032	GE AO	SS	Aegean
31 Dec	*Bagnoli*	246	IT Tug	mined	Navarino
22 Dec	*Spezia*	1,825	GE MM	mined	off Libya
22 Dec	*Cadamosto*	1,010	IT MM	mined	off Libya
1 Mar	*Egitto*	3,329	IT MM	mined	Cent. Med
5 Jan	*Città di Palermo*	5,413	IT MM	SS	Aegean
7 Jan	*Perla*	5,741	IT MM	AC	Cent. Med
10 Jan	*Fedora*	5,016	IT MM	SS	Aegean
17 Jan	*Rampino*	301	IT Aux	SS	off Libya
18 Jan	*Città di Livorno*	2,471	IT MM	mined	Aegean
24 Jan	*Victoria*	13,098	IT MM	AC	Cent. Med
25 Jan	*Dalmatia*	3,320	IT MM	SS	Cent. Med
28 Jan	*Ninuccia*	4,583	IT MM	SS	Adriatic
30 Jan	*Fertilla*	986	IT MM	SS	Adriatic
31 Jan	*S Giovanni Battista*	5,686	IT MM	AC	off Tripoli
1 Feb	*Absirtea*	4,170	IT MM	SS	Aegean
3 Feb	*Lanciotto Piero*	180	IT PC	SS	Aegean
3 Feb	*Napoli*	6,142	IT MM	SS/AC	Cent. Med
7 Feb	*Grongo*	316	IT AMT	SURF	Cent. Med
8 Feb	*Aosta*	494	IT PC	SURF	Cent. Med
8 Feb	*Duino*	1,334	IT MM	mined	Adriatic
9 Feb	*Salpi*	2,710	IT MM	SS	Western Med
1 Feb	*Giuseppina*	392	IT MM	SS	Cent. Med
1 Feb	*Lucania*	8,106	IT AO	SS	Cent. Med
15 Feb	*Ariosto*	4,116	IT MM	SS	Cent. Med
27 Feb	*Lido*	1,243	IT MM	SS	Cent. Med
27 Feb	*Tembien*	5,584	IT MM	SS	Cent. Med
3 Mar	*Cuma*	8,260	GE MM	AC	Palermo

(cont.)

Date	Name	GRT	Nationality/type	Agent	Location
3 Mar	*Securitas*	5,366	IT AO	AC	Palermo
3 Mar	*Tricolore*	179	IT MM	AC	Palermo
5 Mar	**Marin Sanudo**	5,081	IT MM	SS	Cent. Med
5 Mar	*Ottavia*	260	IT PC	SS	Aegean
5 Mar	*Maddalena G*	5,212	IT MM	SS	Cent. Med
13 Mar	**Maria Immacolata**	248	IT MM	SS	Cent. Med
17 Mar	**Achaja**	1,778	GE MM	AC	off Libya
27 Mar	*Oreste*	2,679	IT MM	mined	Adriatic
29 Mar	*Galilea*	8,040	IT MM	SS	Cent. Med
31 Mar	*Bosforo*	3,648	IT MM	SS	Aegean

Naval vessels

Date	Name	GRT	Nationality/type	Agent	Location
9 Nov	**Fulmine**	1,220	IT DD	SURF	Cent. Med
9 Nov	**Libeccio**	1,615	IT DD	SS	Cent. Med
16 Nov	*U433*	750	GE SS	DC	Western Med
25 Nov	**Zirona**	330	IT GB	AC	Benghazi
28 Nov	*U95*	750	GE SS	SS	Western Med
1 Dec	**Da Mosto**	1,900	IT DD	SURF	Cent. Med
11 Dec	*Caracciolo*	1,653	IT SS	DC	off Libya
11 Dec	*Alcione*	670	IT TB	SS	Aegean
13 Dec	*Di Giussano*	5,110	IT CL	SURF	Cent. Med
13 Dec	*Da Barbiano*	5,110	IT CL	SURF	Cent. Med
24 Dec	*U79*	750	GE SS	DC	off Egypt
28 Dec	*U75*	750	GE SS	DC	off Egypt
15 Jan	*U577*	750	GE SS	AC	off Libya
5 Jan	**St. Bon**	1,653	IT SS	SS	Cent. Med
12 Jan	**U374**	750	GE SS	SS	Cent. Med
30 Jan	*Medusa*	650	IT SS	SS	Adriatic
14 Mar	**Millo**	1,653	IT SS	SS	Cent. Med
17 Mar	**Guglielmotti**	1,000	IT SS	SS	Cent. Med
18 Mar	**Tricheco**	920	IT SS	SS	Adriatic

Table A1.8. Allied Warships Suffering Significant Damage, 1 Nov. 1941–31 Mar. 1942

For nationality/type and agent abbreviations see Abbreviations.

Date	Name	Type	Tons	Agent	Months of damage
1 Dec	Jackal	DD	1,690	IT AC	5
7 Dec	Flamingo	DS	1,060	GE AC	25
19 Dec	Queen Elizabeth	BB	31,300	IT XMAS	20
19 Dec	Valiant	BB	31,300	IT XMAS	8
19 Dec	Aurora	CL	5,250	IT mine	7
12 Jan	Kimbereley	DD	1,690	GE SS	24
9 Feb	Farndale	DDE	1,050	GE AC	6
22 Mar	Kingston	DD	1,690	IT SURF	Sunk before repaired
22 Mar	Havock	DD	1,370	IT SURF	Sunk before repaired
22 Mar	Avon Vale	DDE	1,050	GE AC	3.5
Total			77,450		

Table A1.9. Italian Warships Suffering Significant Damage, 1 Nov. 1941–31 Mar. 1942

Ships in **bold** sunk by forces based in Malta. Ships underlined engaged in supplying Africa.
For nationality/type and agent abbreviations, see Abbreviations.

Date	Name	Type	Tons	Agent	Months of damage
9 Nov	**_Grecale_**	DD	1,615	Surface	4
9 Nov	**_Euro_**	DD	1,070	Surface	3
21 Nov	**_Trieste_**	CA	10,340	Submarine	8
22 Nov	**_Abruzzi_**	CL	9,440	Aircraft	8
14 Dec	**_Vittorio Veneto_**	BB	40,700	Submarine	5
16 Feb	**_Carabiniere_**	DD	1,690	Submarine	11
Total			64,855		

Appendix 2

Alexandria Convoys

Westbound

- Operation Approach (13–14 Nov. 1941): DD *Kipling, Jackal, Encounter* carrying supplies.
- Approach (14–15 Nov.): ML *Abdiel*, DD *Hero, Hotspur, Nizam* carrying supplies.
- Approach (16–17 Nov.): DD *Kipling, Jackal, Decoy* carrying supplies.
- Operation Aggression (18–20 Nov.): *Toneline* (811 GRT), *Lesbos* (1,005 GRT). Escort: DS *Yarra, Parramatta*, AMT *Sotra, Klo. Toneline* broke down and arrived 22nd.
- Aggression (22 Nov.): *Glenroy* (9,809 GRT/18 kts). Escort: CL *Carlisle*, DDE *Avon Vale, Eridge, Farndale. Glenroy* torpedoed by S.79.
- Aggression (26–27 Nov.): *Hanne* (1,080 GRT). Escort: DDE *Avon Vale, Parramatta*, AMT *Southern Isles, Southern Maid*.
- Aggression (28–29 Nov.): DD *Hasty, Nizam* carrying supplies.
- Alexandria to Tobruk (AT).1 (30 Nov.–2 Dec.): ABV *Chakdina* (3,033 GRT/15 kts), *Kirkland* (1,361 GRT/10 kts). *Elhis* (3,651 GRT/9.5 kts), tug *St. Issey* (800 GRT/12.5 kts) plus 5 lighters. Escort: DD *Kondouriotis*, DDE *Heythrop, Avon Vale*, DS *Yarra, Flamingo*, AMT *Southern Star, Calam*. Sighted, but not attacked.
- AT.2 (4–6 Dec.): ABV *Chantala* (3,129 GRT/14 kts), *Crista* (2,590 GRT/10.5 kts), *Lesbos, Darien II* (459 GRT) plus 3 lighters. Escort: DDE *Heythrop, Avon Vale*, DS *Yarra, Flamingo*, AMT *Southern Maid, Southern Isles, Wolborough, ML1023*. Sighted, but not attacked.

- AT.3 (13–15 Dec.): *Zealand* (1,433 GRT/10 kts), *Rodi* (3,320 GRT), *Hanne* plus two lighters. Escort: DD *Hero, Hasty*, DDE *Farndale*. Sighted. Aircraft slightly damaged *Rodi* after arrival.
- Alexandria to Mersa Matruh (13–n/a Dec.): *Myriel* (3,560). Escort: AMT *Southern Isles, Southern Seas*. *Myriel* torpedoed by *U431* and returned to Alexandria.
- AT.4 (17–19 Dec.): *Bantria* (2,402 GRT/9 kts), *Gibel Kebir* (551 GRT). Escort: DD *Hero*, DDE *Heythrop, Avon Vale*, AMT *Wolborough, Southern Isles, Cocker*.
- AT.5 (19–21 Dec.): *Shuntien* (3,059 GRT/15 kts), *Kirkland, Eocene* (4,206 GRT/10 kts). Escort: DD *Hasty, Hotspur*, DDE *Heythrop*, DC *Salvia*.
- AT.5.1 (21–22 Dec.): *Prince Baudouin* (3,050 GRT/15 kts). Escort: *Farndale, Eridge*.
- AT.6 (23–25 Dec.): *Warszawa* (2,487 GRT/11 kts), *Agia Varvara* (2,433 GRT/8 kts), *Alisa* (1,072 GRT). Escort: DD *Kipling, Legion*, DDE *Avon Vale*, DC *Peony*, boom defense vessel *Burgonet* (530 tons, 1x76-mm). *Warszawa* sunk by *U559* at 1430/26th. *Varvara* broke down and returned.
- AT.7 (26–29 Dec.): Convoy? Escort: DD *Griffin, Hasty*, DDE *Eridge*, AMT *Southern Sea*.
- AT.9 (28–31 Dec.): *Prince Baudouin*. Escort: DD *Sikh, Hero, Hotspur*. Alexandria to Tobruk, then to Benghazi with MS *Bagshot, Aberdale*, AMT *Hailstorm, Sotra*.
- AT 9.1 (28–31 Dec.): Petrol carrier. Escort: DDE *Heythrop*. Attacked by torpedo bombers 1446/30th.
- AT.10 (29–31 Dec.): Convoy? Escort: DD *Kipling, Legion*, DDE *Farndale*, AMT *Southern Isle*.
- Alexandria to Benghazi (2–4 Jan. 1942) *Antwerp*. Escort: DD *Hero, Arrow*.
- AT.11 (3–4 Jan. to Tobruk; 5–7 Jan. to Benghazi): *Harboe Jensen* (1,862 GRT/13.5 kts), *Crista* (2,598 GRT/10.5 kts). Escort: DD *Kimberley, Hasty, Griffin, Hotspur*. Sighted. Combat between attackers and air escort.
- AT.12 (5–7 Jan.): *Robert Maersk* (2,290 GRT/14 kts). Escort: DD *Legion, Isaac Sweers*, DDE *Eridge*, 2xAMT. Sighted.

- AT.14 (6–8 Jan.): *Toneline*, tug *St. Monance* (800 GRT/12.5 kts) plus barge. Escort: DDE *Southwold, Avon Vale*. *Toneline* broke down 7th.
- Alexandria to Benghazi (9–11 Jan.): *Mausing* (3,372 GRT/11 kts). Escort: *Kimberley, Hotspur*.
- AT.15 (10–12 Jan.): *Bintang* (2,779 GRT/10.5 kts), *Alisa, Flora Nomicou* (2,012 GRT/8 kts). Escort: DD *Hero, Arrow*, DC *Peony*, DDE *Heythrop, ML1051, ML1023*.
- AT.16 (11–14 Jan.): Convoy (composition unknown). Escort: DD *Griffin, Hasty*, DC *Peony*.
- Alexandria to Benghazi (12–15 Jan.): *Derwentdale* (8,390 GRT, 11.5 kts), *Malines*. Escort: DDE *Farndale, Dulverton, Eridge*. Attacked 14th by German aircraft.
- AT.17 (14–16 Jan.): Convoy (composition unknown). Escort: DDE *Avon Vale*, ABV *Antwerp*, AMT *Southern Maid, Soika*.
- AT.18 (18–20 Jan.): *Cerion* (2,588 GRT/10.5 kts), *Empire Patrol* (3,334 GRT). Escort: DDE *Heythrop, Hyacinth*. AMT *Southern Sea*. Attacked by S.79s.
- Alexandria to Tobruk (18–22 Jan.): *Manoula* (1,966 GRT/2.5 kts). Escort: *Peony*. Both grounded 21st, refloated 22nd.
- AT.18.1 (19–21 Jan.): *Eocene*. Escort: DDE *Farndale, Eridge*.
- AT.19 (24–27 Jan.): *Robert Maersk*. Escort: DDE *Avon Vale*, ABV *Malines*, AMT *Vikings*.
- AT.21 (28–30 Jan.): *Athene* (4,681 GRT/10.5 kts). Escort: DD *Hero*, DDE *Farndale, Eridge*.
- AT.22 (31 Jan.–3 Feb.): Convoy (composition unknown). Escort: DD *Hasty*, DDE *Southwold, Dulverton*. Italian air attack aborted due to weather.
- AT.23 (2–5 Feb.): Convoy (composition unknown). Escort: DDE *Avon Vale*, DC *Hyacinth*.
- AT.25 (3–5 Feb.): Convoy (composition unknown). Escort: DDE *Heythrop, Hurworth*.
- AT.26 (8–10 Feb.): *Bantria* (2,402 GRT/9 kts), *Cerion, Antwerp*. Escort: DDE, *Heythrop, Hurworth*. AMT *Southern Maid*. Attacked by S.79s.
- AT.27 (8–10 Feb.): *Popi* (2,083 GRT/8.5 kts). Escort: DDE *Farndale*, DC *Gloxina*. *Farndale* damaged by German aircraft 1849/9th.

- Alexandria to Mersa Matruh and Tobruk (11–13 Feb.): *Brigand* plus other ships. Escort: DC *Snapdragon*, AMT *Southern Sea*.
- AT 28 (17–23 Feb.): *Empire Patrol, Robert Maersk*. Escort: DD *Decoy*, DDE *Hurworth, Southwold*, DC *Hyacinth*.
- AT.29 (20–23 Feb.): *Bintang* (2,779 GRT/10.5 kts), *Hanne, Alisa*. Escort: DDE *Eridge, Beaufort*, DC *Gloxinia*. *Bintang. Hanne* sunk by German aircraft 1410/22nd.
- AT.30 (23–25 Feb.): Convoy (composition unknown). Escort: DDE *Dulverton, Hurworth*.
- AT.31 (25–27 Feb.): *Harboe Jensen* plus one ship. Escort: DD *Jervis, Lively, Zulu*. AMT *Southern Sea. Harboe Jensen, Southern Sea* damaged 27th by aircraft.
- AT.32 (2–4 Mar.): *Cerion, Heron* (2,374 GRT/12 kts). Escort: DD *Hasty, Havock*, DDE *Dulverton, Hurworth*, DC *Gloxinia. Cerion* bombed and damaged 7th.
- AT 33 (10–12 Mar.): *Toneline, Destro* (3,553 GRT/10 kts), *Amalia*. Escort: DDE *Dulverton*, DC *Hyacinth*, 2xAMT.
- AT 33.1 (10–12 Mar.): *Vulcan* plus small craft.
- AT 34 (16–18 Mar.): *Crista* (2,590 GRT/10.5 kts), *Destro, Katie Moller* (3,100 GRT/9.5 kts). Escort: DDE *Avon Vale, Beaufort*, DC *Peony, Gloxinia*, AMT *Protea, Boksburg. Crista* torpedoed by *U83* 17th. Salvaged. *Destro* damaged by German bombers.
- Alexandria to Tobruk (25–n/a Mar.): AO *Slavol* (2,623 GRT/12 kts). Escort: DD *Jaguar, Vasilissa Olga*. AMT *Klo. Jaguar, Slavol* sunk by *U652* and *U205* respectively.
- AT 35 (27–28 Mar.): *Empire Patrol, Robert Maersk*. Escort: DD *Hero, Vasilissa Olga*, DC Peony, *Hyacinth*. Attacked by German bombers.

Eastbound

- Tobruk to Alexandria (TA).1 (5–7 Dec. 1941): *Chakdina, Kirkland*. Escort: DDE *Eridge, Farndale*, AMT *Thorgrim, Sotra. Chakdina* sunk by S.79s 2130/5th.
- TA.2 (10–12 Dec.): *Darien II, Lesbos*. Escort: DDE *Eridge, Farndale*, AMT *Sotra, Wolborough*.
- TA.3 (13–15 Dec.): Empty store ships. Escort: DD *Hasty, Hero*.

- TA.4 (22–23 Dec.): *Prince Baudouin*. Escort: *Farndale, Eridge*.
- TA.5 (23–25 Dec.): *Shuntien*. Escort: DD *Hasty, Heythrop, Hotspur*. DC *Salvia*. *Shuntien, Salvia* sunk by *U559* and *U568*.
- TA.6 (27–29 Dec.): Convoy *Volo* plus others. Escort: DD *Kipling, Legion*, DDE *Avon Vale*, DC *Peony*. *Volo* sunk by *U75*. Escort sank *U75*.
- TA.7 (29–31 Dec.): *Eocene, Kirkland*. Escort DD *Griffin, Hasty*, DDE *Eridge*, AMT *Southern Sea*.
- TA.8 (3–5 Jan. 1942): Empty stores ships. Escort: DC *Peony*.
- TA.9 (7–9 Jan.): Empty stores ships. Escort: DD *Legion, Isaac Sweers*, DDE *Eridge*. Escort attacked submarine en route.
- TA.10 (10–13 Jan.): *St. Monace, Toneline*. Escort: DDE *Avon Vale*, DC *Hyacinth*, AMT *Southwold*.
- TA.11 (10–13 Jan.): No details.
- TA.12 (14–16 Jan.): Empty stores ships. Escort: DD *Griffin, Hasty*, DC *Peony*, 2xAMT.
- Benghazi to Port Said (15–18 Jan.): *Derwentdale*. Escort: DDE *Farndale, Dulverton, Eridge*, ABV *Malines*.
- TA.17 (17–18 Jan.): *Robert Maersk* plus others. Escort: ABV *Antwerp*, DDE *Avon Vale*.
- TA.18 (20–22 Jan.): Empty store ships. Escort: DC *Hyacinth, Gloxinia*.
- TA.19 (24–26 Jan.): Empty store ships. Escort: DDE *Farndale, Eridge*.
- Benghazi to Tobruk and Alexandria. (26–28 Jan). *Crista, Harboe Jensen, Mausang, Bagshot, Aberdare*. Escort: DDE *Heythrop, Southwold, Dulverton*. Attacked by S.79s.
- TA.20 (27–29 Jan.): *Bantria, Cerion*. Escort: DC *Gloxinia*.
- TA.21 (27–29 Jan.): *Empire Patrol, Havre* (2,073 GRT), *Robert Maersk*. Escort: DDE *Avon Vale*, DC, *Hyacinth*, ABV *Malines*. *Havre* and *Malines* collided.
- TA 21.1 (29–31 Jan.): Empty store ships. Escort: DC *Gloxinia*, AMT *Vikings, Sotra*. *Sotra* sunk by *U431* 2146/29th.
- Tobruk to Alexandria (31 Jan.–1 Feb.): Empty store ships. Escort: DD *Hero*, DDE *Farndale, Eridge*.
- Tobruk to Alexandria (3–5 Feb.): Empty store ships. Escort: DD *Hasty*, DDE *Southwold, Dulverton*.

- Tobruk to Alexandria (5–7 Feb.): Empty store ships. Escort: DDE *Heythrop, Hurworth*. Attacked by S.79s 5th.
- Tobruk to Alexandria (9–11 Feb.): Empty store ships. Escort: DDE *Avon Vale*, DC *Hyacinth*, AMT *Southern Sea*.
- Tobruk to Alexandria (13–15 Feb.): Empty store ships plus A Lighters. Escort: ABV *Antwerp*, DC *Gloxinia, Hyacinth*, plus 2xAMT. Attacked by submarine off Tobruk. Attacked by S.79s off Mersa Matruh.
- Tobruk to Alexandria (19–21 Feb.): Empty store ships. Escort: DDE *Southwold, Hurworth*, DC *Hyacinth*.
- TA.22 (23–26 Feb.): Empty stores ships. Escort: DDE *Beaufort, Eridge*, DC *Gloxinia*.
- TA.23 (25–26 Feb.): *Empire Patrol, Robert Maersk*. Escort: DDE *Dulverton, Hurworth*.
- TA.24 (28 Feb.–2 Mar.): Empty store ships. Escort: DD *Zulu, Lively, Jervis*, AMT *Southern Sea*.
- TA.25 (4–6 Mar.): Empty stores ships. Escort: DD *Hasty, Havock*, DDE *Dulverton, Hurworth*, DC *Gloxinia*. Attacked by S.79s 5th.
- TA.26. (7–9 Mar.): *Harboe Jensen* in tow of *St. Monace, Harrow*. Escort: DDE *Southwold, Beaufort*, AMT *Southern Maid*.
- TA.27 (12–14 Mar.): *Destro, Slavol*. Escort: DDE *Dulverton*, DC *Hyacinth*. Attacked by S.79s 13th.
- TA.29 (18–20 Mar.): *Toneline*. Escort: DDE *Avon Vale, Beaufort*, DC *Gloxinia, Peony*. Attacked by submarine 1700/18th.
- TA.30 (27–29 Mar.): *Cerion, Destro*. Escort: DDE *Eridge, Dulverton*, DC *Delphinium, Snapdragon*.

Table A2.1. **Summary of Malta Convoys**

Name	Dates	MM	Escort	Results
Astrologer I	11 Nov. 41 (sailed)	1	none	1xMM(sunk air)
Astrologer II	12 Nov. (sailed)	1	none	1xMM(sunk air)
MF1	16–18 Dec.	1	4xCL, 1xCLA, 14xDD	1xDD(D1 SURF), 1xDD(D1 air)
ME8	26–29 Dec.	4	2xCL, 1xCLA, 8xDD	1xDD(D2 air)
MF2W	5–8 Jan. 42	1	3xCL, 6xDD	Not spotted
MF2E	6–9 Jan. 43	1	4xDD	Not spotted
MF3– MW8	16–19 Jan.	4	4xCL, 1xCLA, 18xDD	1xCL(D1 air), 1 MM(sunk air), 1xDD (sunk sub)
MF4W	24–27 Jan.	1	3xCL, 1xCLA, 8xDD	Bombed no damage
ME9	25–28 Jan.	2	1xCL, 5xDD	Bombed no damage
MF5–MW9	12 Feb. (sailed)	3	3xCL, 1xCLA, 9xDD, 7xDDE	2xMM(sunk air), 1xMM (D2 air), 1xDD(D1 air)
ME10	13–15 Feb.	4	1xCL, 6xDD	1xCLA(D1 air), 1xDDE(D2 air)
MG1–MW10	20–23 Mar.	4	4xCL, 1xCLA, 11xDD, 7xDDE	1xMM (sunk air), 3xMM (damaged air), 2xCL(D2 SURF), 3xDD(D3 2xSURF, air), 1xDD(D2 SURF), 2xDD(D1 SURF), 2xDDE (sunk sub, mines)

D1 = superficial to light damage
D2 = light to moderate damage
D3 = moderate to heavy damage
D4 = heavy damage to disabled
SURF = surface forces
Only enemy inflicted damage is indicated.

ABBREVIATIONS

A/S	antisubmarine
ASV	air surface vessel (radar)
AU	Australian
B-Dienst	Beobachtungsdienst
BR	British
CS	cruiser squadron
DF	destroyer flotilla
DS	destroyer squadron
GC&CS	Government Code and Cypher School
GE	German
GK	Greek
GRT	gross registered tons
HA	high angle
IFF	Identification Friend or Foe
IT	Italian
kts	knots
Mk	mark
nm	nautical mile
NO	Norwegian
NZ	New Zealand
OBS	Oberbefehlshaber Süd
pdr	pounder
PO	Polish
QF	Quick-firer
RAF	Royal Air Force
SCU	Special Communications Unit

SIS	Servizio Informazioni Segrete
SLU	Special Liaison Unit
SU	Soviet Union
t	tons
TT	Torpedo tubes
XMAS	Tenth Light Flotilla or Decima Flottiglia MAS

Ship Types

ABV	armed boarding vessel
AMC	armed merchant cruiser
AMT	antisubmarine or minesweeping trawler
AO	tanker
BB	battleship
BM	monitor
CA	heavy cruiser
CL	light cruiser
CLA	antiair light cruiser
CV	aircraft carrier
DC	corvette
DD	destroyer
DDE	*Hunt*-type small destroyer
DS	sloop
GB	gunboat
MAS	*motoscafi armati siluranti* or *motoscafi anti sommergibili*
MFP	*marinefährprahm*
ML	minelayer or motor launch
MM	merchant vessel
MMS	motor minesweeper
MS	minesweeper
MTB	motor torpedo boat
S-boat	*schnellboote*
SC	submarine chaser
SS	submarine
TB	torpedo boat

NOTES

Abbreviations Used in the Notes

ACSR	Archivio Centrale dello Stato Roma
ADM	Admiralty Records
AIR	Air Ministry Records
AMWR	Air Mediterranean Weekly Reports
AUSMM	Archivio dell'Ufficio Storico della Marina Militare
AWD	Admiralty War Diary
AWM	Australian War Memorial
CAB	War Cabinet and Cabinet Memoranda
CCFN	Comando in Capo Forze Navali
CED	Corrispondenza e Direttive
CS	cruiser squadron
DEFE	Signals intelligence files series reference header
DSCS	*Diario Storico del Comando Supremo*
FRUS	Foreign Relations of the United States
GC&CS	Government Code & Cypher School
GWD	German Naval Staff War Diary
HW	Reference header for UK Communication records
Loc	location (on a Kindle)
Militär. Forsch	Militärgeschichtliches Forschungsamt
MK	Ultra files series reference header
MWD	Mediterranean War Diary
NARA	National Archives and Records Administration
NSH	Naval Staff History
OL	Ultra files series reference header
ONI	Office of Naval Intelligence (United States)

PT	*Partecipazione tedesca.* See Alberto Santoni and Francesco Mattesini. *La partecipazione aeronavale tedesca alla Guerra nel Mediterraneo.* Rome: Ateneo e Bizzarri, 1980.
ROP	Report of Proceedings
SIS	Servizio Informazione Segreto
USMM	Uffico Storia Marina Militare
VAMWD	Vice Admiral Malta War Diary
XMAS	Tenth Light Flotilla or Decima Flottiglia MAS
Z	Zone (Greenwich time)
ZTPI	Ultra files series reference header

Introduction

1. Woodman, *Malta Convoys*, 310.
2. Fioravanzo, *Nostri criteri*, 26. He was one of the admirals in charge of the Supermarina (naval high command) situation room and later commanded a cruiser division.
3. Thus, Ultra message MK 3411 regarding the departure of a convoy from Tripoli was stamped 1435/16/3/42 GMT (2:35 p.m., 16 March 1942). In Alexandria that would be 1735 (5:35 p.m., Z+3) and in Malta it would be 1635 (4:35 p.m. Z+2). The convoy in question departed at 2000 (Z+2), so, while at first glance it might appear that Ultra gave the British five and a half hours' warning, the advance notice actually was three and a half hours.

Chapter 1. Sea Power and the Mediterranean, 1940–41

1. Playfair, *Mediterranean and the Middle East* (hereafter, Playfair), I:116.
2. Quotations: Gooch, *Mussolini's Generals*, 338–39. Mattesini, ed., *Corrispondenza e Direttive* (CED), "Concetti Generali di azione in Mediterraneo," I/1:319.
3. Quotations: Roskill, *War at Sea*, I:10; Simpson, ed., *Cunningham Papers*, I:50, 49.
4. See Archivio Centrale dello Stato Roma (ACSR), "Direttive e Norme," for Italy's naval doctrine. For a critical summary of technical and doctrinal issues see Knox, *Italian Allies*, 132–35. Also, Sadkovich, *Italian Navy*, 39–43; Greene and Massignani, *Naval War*, 38–48; Bragadin, *Italian Navy*, 4–5.
5. Biagini and Frattolillo, ed., *Diario Storico del Comando Supremo* (DSCS), Daily summaries of traffic. This only counts ships displacing more than 1,000 GRT.
6. Quotations: War Cabinet and Cabinet Memoranda (CAB) 66/11/42, "Future Strategy," 5, 2, 5.
7. See the discussion in Boyd, *Eastern Waters*, 160–61.
8. CED, "Piano di Guerra," I/1:264–65. "The problem is therefore not to know if Italy enters or does not enter the war because Italy must go to war; it is only a matter of knowing how and when: it is a question of delaying as long as possible, consistent with honor and dignity, our entry into war."
9. CED, "Investimento di Malta," I/1:394.
10. Quotations: Naval Staff History (NSH) *Mediterranean*, I:12–13. Simpson, ed., *Cunningham Papers*, I:75. Hattendorf, ed., *Naval Strategy*, 61.

11. CAB 66/11/42, 5.

12. NSH, *Mediterranean*, I:xiv.

13. Uffico Storico Marina Militare (USMM), *Dati Statistici*, I:151–52; USMM, *Difesa del traffico*, IX:172–82.

14. NSH, *Mediterranean*, II:xiii, xiv-xv.

15. Playfair, I:362 says 130,000.

16. *London Gazette*, "Evacuation from Greece," 3041; Peter Cannon, Correspondence Lustre Convoys; USMM, *Difesa del traffico*, IX:12; USMM, *Sommergibili*, XIII:136–40; Santoni and Mattesini, *Partecipazione tedesca*, 48 (hereafter *PT*).

17. See Rocca, *Fucilate gli ammiragli*, 101 for the claim that the Germans forced the operation on Italy. For a relatively balanced account of Matapan see Seth, *Two Fleets Surprised*.

18. See Table 1.3 for sources.

19. NSH, *Mediterranean* II:xvii, 243, 245. Losses include Greek and Yugoslav vessels.

20. http://uboat.net/allies/technical/uk_radars.htm.

21. Simpson, ed., *Cunningham Papers*, I:406.

22. Playfair, II:269 and 280. Available aircraft included 20 Blenheims, 12 Wellingtons, 20 Swordfish, 10 Marylands, 75 Hurricanes, and 8 Beaufighters.

23. See sources in Appendix 2.

24. Weichold, *Naval Policy*, 58.

25. CAB 80/35/185, "Appointment of Supreme Commander," 22 March 1942. The navy favored the committee system because as Pound argued: "Should the enemy fleet put to sea . . . then it is the Naval Commander in Chief and not the Military Commander in Chief who must decide to what extent the Fleet can continue to assist the Army." The remarks that Stafford Cripps made to Churchill on 22 March 1942 while on a fact-finding mission to the Middle East are telling. He had just learned that Cunningham was being relieved. "It is, I think, most desirable that the new Commander-in-Chief, Mediterranean, should be stationed at Cairo and not at Alexandria, and should not be a seagoing admiral. Otherwise, co-operation on combined operations excessively difficult [sic] as has been proved on more than one occasion in the past." He asserted that Auchinleck and Tedder both felt the same way. CAB, 69/4/32, "Middle East."

26. Quotation: Kennedy, *Business of War*, 171–72. Percentage of sinkings: USMM, *Dati Statistici*, I:117.

27. CAB 80/60, "Possible Action in Middle East and Mediterranean," 4; and "Operation Whipcord Report."

28. USMM, *Dati Statistici*, I:32–33.

29. Gwyer and Butler, *Grand Strategy*, III/1:232. Militär. Forschungsamt, *Second World War*, III:707.

30. *Fuehrer Conferences*, 235.

Chapter 2. Communications, Intelligence, Logistics

1. Quotations: Deutsch, "The Ultra Secret," 20. Hinsley et al., *British Intelligence*, II:319.

2. Ferris, "The British 'Enigma,'" 168.

3. See Appendix 2 for a list of British convoys. Italian convoys are listed in USMM, *Difesa del traffico*, VII:373–409.

4. Kelly, *Big Machines*, 161. He estimates 10^{80} as the number of atoms in the universe.

5. Ferris, "The British 'Enigma,'" 165. Mulligan, "The German Navy Evaluates," 76. Standard works regarding Enigma and Ultra cited in the bibliography include those by Hinsley, Lewin, Kelly, Bennett, and Ratcliff.

6. Traffic volumes are based on a count of messages from *Signals Intelligence Files Series* (DEFE) reference header 3/690. The C 35 was a first-generation mechanical encoding machine seized by the Germans from the French and sold to the Italian air force.

7. Quotations: *Admiralty Records* (ADM) 223/88, *Special Intelligence*, 321. Dear, ed., *Oxford Companion*, 838.

8. Paterson, *Code Breakers*, 181.

9. Bennett, *Ultra*, 25.

10. ADM 223/88, *Special Intelligence*, 321. Quotation: Hinsley et al., *British Intelligence*, II:319.

11. Government Code and Cyber School (GC&CS), *Naval History*, XX:133.

12. UK Communication records (HW) reference header 50/15/5, 8G Naval Section, 6.

13. Simpson, ed., *Cunningham Papers*, I:535. Cunningham violated security by referring to Ultra in a radio communication.

14. See Ferris, "The British 'Enigma,'" 165.

15. National Archives and Records Administration (NARA), "Italian Communications Intelligence," 7.

16. For Fellows see, for example, Kahn, *Codebreakers*, 473. For the naval attaché in Istanbul see, for example, ACSR, Intercettazioni estere, 0890861, 11 October 1941.

17. Quotations: ADM 1/27186, "Review of Security," 65, 67, 71, 91.

18. Alvarez, "Left in the Dust," 402.

19. Mancini, "Porti," Part II; USMM, *Difesa del traffico*, VII:5.

20. CED, "Traffico Marittimo con la Libia," II/2:1220–21.

21. Between February 1941 and May 1942 of the 325 ships that sailed for Benghazi, including cargo ships and auxiliaries but not warships, 238 or 73 percent came from Tripoli. USMM, *Difesa del traffico,* VI and VII.

22. USMM, *Difesa del traffico*, VII:5. Cocchia, *Hunters and Hunted*, 96.

23. See CED, "Traffico Marittimo con la Libia," II/2:1220.

24. USMM, *Difesa del traffico*, VII:475–86.

25. USMM, *Dati Statistici*, I:277 for new supplies and 245 for consumption.

26. Supermarina, "Situazione Nafta per Caldaie," 21 February 1942 and 1 April 1942.

27. CED, "Consumo mensile di nafta," II/2:1060.

28. CED, "Problema del rifornimento di nafta." III/2, Doc. 228.

Chapter 3. Force K Arrives, October 1941

1. Quotation: Simpson, ed., *Cunningham Paper*, I:506 and 514.

2. ADM 199/415, "Mediterranean Command War Diary," 25.10.42. (hereafter MWD for Mediterranean War Diary). Quotations: *DSCS*, V:367, 387.

3. Quotations:: CED, II/2:1157–58. *DSCS*, V:423. For oil see USMM, *Dati Statistici*, I:245 and 277.

4. See DEFE 3/690, OL 1664, 1671.

5. Quotation: DEFE 3/690, OL 1731; also 1720, 1756. NARA, Admiralty War Diary, 1.11.41, "M/V damaged" (hereafter AWD for Admiralty War Diary). MWD, 1.11.41; USMM, *Difesa del traffico*, VII:40.

6. DEFE 3/690, OL 1738. MWD, 2.11.41.

7. AWD, 5–6.11.41. USMM, *Difesa del traffico*, VII:373. MWD, 5.11.41. *DSCS*, V:469.

8. DEFE 3/690, OL 1798, 1727, DEFE 3/834, ZTPI, 1800, 1803. Quotation: DEFE 3/690, OL 1831. AWD, 7.11.1941, "Enemy Convoy."

9. Quotations: AWD, 8.11.41, "Enemy Convoy Attacked"; USMM, *Difesa del traffico*, VII:41; CAB 80/31/680, "Weekly resume," 8–9. Also, MWD, 8.11.41.

10. USMM, *Difesa del traffico*, VII:44, 48–49. *Settembrini* tried to intercept Force K on its return to base and reached a position within five miles before the British force crossed her bow at high speed. USMM, *Sommergibili*, XIII:208.

11. USMM, *Difesa del traffico*, VII:150.

12. USMM, 45.

13. See AWD, 8.11.41 "Enemy Units"; ADM 199/897, *Aurora*, "Report of Proceedings" (ROP); USMM, *Difesa del traffico*, VII:51.

14. Hinsley et al., *British Intelligence*, II:319–20. DEFE 3/690 for the OL messages and DEFE 3/834 for the ZTPI intercepts. The British intercepted a message that gave the Beta Convoy's itinerary and schedule, but it was not translated until 19 November. See ZTPI 2234.

15. Quotation: Winton, ed., *War at Sea*, 145. ACDSR, SIS, *Intercettazioni estere*, 12672.

16. ADM 199/897, *Aurora*, "ROP," 8.

17. See Iachino, *Due Sirti*, 48 and the discussion of the *Conte Rosso* experience cited above. At the night action of Matapan the Italian cruisers did not use their main batteries.

18. Quotation: USMM, *Difesa del traffico*, VII:508, 64. ADM 199/897, *Aurora*, "ROP, Enclosure," 2.

19. Quotation: USMM, *Difesa del traffico*, VII:506. *Aurora* had three turrets, two forward and one aft called A, B, and Y respectively.

20. Times are within a minute or two of each other. See ADM 199/879, *Penelope*, "Gunnery Report," 2, 5. Quotation: ADM, *Penelope* "ROP."

21. Quotation: NSH, *Mediterranean*, II:192.

22. USMM, *Difesa del traffico*, VII:507.

23. CED, "Relazione azione," II/2:1165.

24. ADM 199/897, *Penelope*, "ROP," 2.

25. USMM, *Difesa del traffico*, VII:507.

26. Winton, ed., *War at Sea*, 146.

27. ADM 189/897, *Aurora*, "ROP."

28. ADM, *Aurora, Penelope, Lively*, "ROPs."

29. Allaway, *Hero of the* Upholder, 132.

30. Ciano, *Diaries*, 404. Quotations: Weichold, *Naval Policy*, 57; CED, "Conversazione Telefonica," II/2:1171; CED, "Relazione azione," II/2:1166.

31. Iachino, *Due Sirti*, 49–50. USMM, *Difesa del traffico*, VII:515.

32. DEFE 3/690, OL 1942, 1955, 1978.

33. Cavallero, *Diario*, 252. DSCS, V:528–30.

34. Fioravanzo, "Motovelieri," 37. Woodman, *Malta Convoys*, 251.

35. Quotation: Winton, ed., *War at Sea*, 154.

36. See MWD, 2.11.41. The destroyers were *Jaguar, Hasty, Jervis, Kandahar, Kimberley, Kingston, Napier, Nizam, Kipling, Jackal.*

37. MWD, 11.11.41.

38. MWD, 13.11.41.

Chapter 4. The Crusader Offensive, November–December 1941

1. This narrative relies mainly upon the accounts in Playfair III:33–102 and Miltär. Forschungsamt, III:725–54 for its overview of Operation Crusader's land aspects. Quotation: *DSCS*, V:563.

2. NSH, *Mediterranean*, II:199; MWD, 17.11.41 and 18.11.41.

3. Cavallero, *Diario*, 254.

4. DEFE 3/690, OL 1964 and 1965. AWD, 17.11.41, "Enemy Units Attacked." Quotation: AWD, 18.11.41, "M/V attacked." Also, USMM, *Difesa del traffico*, VII:80–81. Rohwer, *Allied Attacks*, 147 also says *Sokol* hit *Aviere* but the destroyer was escorting convoys a week later.

5. DEFE 3/745, MK 46, 48, 60.

6. DEFE 3/690, OL 2038.

7. USMM, *Difesa del traffico*, VII:99. Tedder is quoted in Austin, *Malta Strategic Policy*, 181.

8. Quotation: AWD, 20.11.41, "Enemy M/Vs attacked." USMM, *Difesa del traffico*, VII:376. DEFE 3/690, OL 2034.

9. DEFE 3/690, OL 2033, 2044; DEFE 3/834. ZTPI 2235. USMM, *Difesa del traffico*, VII:88.

10. DEFE 3/690, OL 1963, 2022, 2024, 2059, 2094; DEFE 3/745, MK 36, 58.

11. USMM, *Difesa del traffico*, VII:92. AWD, 22.11.41, "Enemy convoy attacked."

12. ACSR, Intercettazioni estere, 13125. The British aircraft transmitted the convoy's position, course, and speed at 0005/22nd. The SIS intercepted and decoded this report and generated a top priority alert six minutes later. See also 13131 regarding a British signal made at 0045 and passed along at 0049.

13. AWD, 22.11.41, "Enemy convoy attacked." Shores et al., *Hurricane Years*, 334. MWD, 22.11.41.

14. USMM, *Difesa del traffico*, VII:475–77.

15. AWM, *Yarra* "ROP, November."

16. Quotation: MWD, 21.11.41. M. T. means motor transport.

17. Playfair, III:39.

18. CAB 80/60 261, "Future Moves."

19. NSH, *Mediterranean*, II:205. Mattioli, *S.79*, Loc 651. Quotation: ADM 239/138, "Naval Gunnery," 16.

20. DEFE 3/834, ZTPI 2383. DEFE 3/745, MK 75. For *Procida* and *Maritza*, see DEFE 3/690, OL 1795, 1797, 1811, 1814.

21. DEFE 3/745, MK 116 for importance; MK 67 and 81 for departure; MK 91 and 105 for escort and route (incorrect); and MK 115 for route (correct). The last message to arrive before Force K sailed was MK 124 (1930Z/23rd), which gave the scheduled arrival. Regarding Churchill, see Hinsley et al., *British Intelligence*, II:320. Churchill's query was timed 1431Z/23rd, before GC&CS sent the message to the Middle East SCU.

22. USMM, *Difesa del traffico*, VII:112.

23. AWD, 24.11.41, "Enemy Units." ADM 199/897, *Penelope, Aurora*, "ROPs 24 November."

24. ADM 199/897, *Penelope, Aurora*, "ROPs 24 November"; USMM, *Difesa del traffico*, VII:113.

25. USMM, 526, USMM, 115.

26. ADM 199/897, *Penelope*, "ROP, 24 November."

27. USMM, *Difesa del traffico*, VII:527.

28. ADM 199/897 *Penelope*, "Gunnery Narrative." Quotation: AWD, 24.11.41, "M/Vs sunk by Force K." AWD, 26.11.41, "Fleet Operations."

29. ADM 199/897, *Penelope*, "ROP."

30. DEFE 3/745, MK 200; MWD, 27.11.41; USMM, *Difesa del traffico*, VII:380. AWD, 27.11.41, "Liner and Destroyer bombed." *DSCS*, V:638.

31. Quotations: ADM 1/11948, "Loss of HMS Barham," 13; ADM, "Witness Statements," 3.

32. ADM, "Message 2109/28 April."
33. Morgan and Taylor, *Attack Logs*, 163. Cavallero, *Diario*, 265. *DSCS*, V:629. ONI, German Naval Staff War Diary (hereafter GWD for German War Diary), 30.12.41, "Central and Eastern Mediterranean."
34. Morgan and Taylor, *Attack Logs*, 167–68.
35. Paterson, *U-Boats*, 51. Losses from Hughes and Costello, *Battle of the Atlantic*, 305; O'Hara et al., *On Sea Contested*, 74–75.
36. AWD, 28.11.41, "Air Operations." USMM, *Difesa del traffico*, VII:158. DEFE 3/745, MK 237.
37. AWD, 11.29.41, "Enemy Warships hit by P.31."
38. Quotation: ADM 199/897, "Passage of Force B to Malta," 1. See DEFE 3/745, MK 263 for the torpedo boat. See DEFE, MK 319 2245Z/28/11 for convoy. Position from AWD, 29.11.41. ADM 199/897, "Letter of Proceedings 30 November," 1.
39. AWD, 30.11.41, "Enemy units." Quotation: Cavallero, *Diario*, 267.
40. USMM, *Difesa del traffico*, VII:123–24.
41. ADM 199/897, *Aurora*, "ROP," 5 December 1941. ADM, 7th C.S., "ROP," 13 December 1941.
42. *DSCS*, V, Daily shipping summaries.
43. These losses are enumerated in Appendix 1.
44. Hezlet, *Submarine Operations*, Chapter 11. Rohwer, *Allied Attacks*, 146–48.
45. USMM, *Sommergibili*, XIII:213, 227.
46. AWD, 24.11.41, "Gov. Malta." ADM 199/413, *Vice Admiral Malta War Diary* (VAMWD), "Summary of Air Raid Alarms," 61. *DSCS*, V:433–638.

Chapter 5. Italy's Misery Mounts

1. CAB 80/60, "Combined Strategy with Russia," 5 December 1941.
2. GWD, 4.12.41, "Special Items." GWD, 7.12.41, "Items of Political Importance."
3. Quotation: CAB 80/60, "Future British Naval Strategy," 14.12.41, 1. This shift east assumed American forces would join the Home Fleet.
4. ADM 199/897, *Aurora*, "ROP," 5.
5. USMM, *Difesa del traffico*, VII:129; ADM 199/897, *Aurora*, "ROP."
6. DEFE 3/745, MK 326, 391.
7. ADM 199/897, "Letter of Proceedings," 30 November, 3–4.
8. They were designed as single-purpose guns and lacked the elevation and fire control to be effective anti-aircraft weapons.
9. USMM, *Difesa del traffico*, VII:133.
10. ADM 199/837, *Aurora*, "ROP," 4.
11. Quotations: USMM, *Difesa del traffico*, VII:136; USMM.
12. Quotation: ADM 199/837, *Aurora*, "ROP," 5. *DSCS*, V:682.
13. ADM 234/444, *Ships Damaged or Sunk*, 182. Mattioli, *S.79*, Loc. 610. MWD, 1.12.41. Langtree, *Kellys*, 128.
14. MWD, 2.12.41. DEFE 3/745, MK 406. Italian deliveries from USMM, *Difesa del traffico*, VII:487–95. In addition, Derna received two warship cargos, Benghazi seven, and Tripoli four.
15. See Appendix 2, Alexandria Convoys. MWD, 30.11–12.41. Quotation: AWM, *Yarra*, "ROP," 12.2.41.
16. Murphy, *Artillery*, 290. *DSCS*, V:706.
17. ADM 199/1178, *Flamingo*; AWM, *Yarra*, "Report of Attack 7.12.41." AWM, "ROP," 7.12.41. *PT*, 149.

18. MWD, 8.12.41, 10.12.41, 14.12.41. *DSCS*, V:742.
19. GWD, 2.12.41, "Transport of Supplies to North Africa."
20. CED, "Riunione," II/2:1217–19. Cavallero, *Diario*, 270–71.
21. Militär. Forschungsamt, *Second World War*, III:744–46.
22. DEFE 3/746, MK 526, 540, 601, 634, 678, 735.
23. Hezlet, *Submarine Operations*, Chapter 11. USMM, *Difesa del traffico*, VII:335. Supermarina, *Centauro*, "Rapporto," 13.12.41.
24. See Cavallero, *Diario*, 272, 274.
25. USMM, *Difesa del traffico*, VII:164. VAMWD, 9.12.41.
26. DEFE 3/745, MK 485, 493; DEFE 3/746, 660, 707.
27. Ghisotti, "Capo Bon," 16. USMM, *Difesa del traffico*, VII:481. Sources vary as to the exact amount of cargo carried. See also Mattesini, "Capo Bon," 63.
28. NSH, *Mediterranean*, II:216–17. AWD, 12.12.41, "Malta force."
29. Archivio dell'Ufficio Storico della Marina Militare (AUSMM), "Affondamento *Da Barbiano* e *Di Giussano*, 2–3.
30. See the discussion in Ghisotti, "Capo Bon," 30–31.
31. AUSMM, "Affondamento *Da Barbiano* e *Di Giussano*, 21.
32. AUSMM, 22.
33. AUSMM, 6.
34. NSH, *Mediterranean*, II:219.
35. DEFE 3/745, MK 522, 554, 564, 574, 583, 599, 617, 662, 664, 676, 698, 700, 759, 764, 777, 779, 801, 803, 811, 821, 976.
36. Quotations: MWD, 13.12.41; AWD, 12.12.41 "S/Ms."
37. Hezlet, *Submarine Operations*, Chapter 11 says three torpedoes hit *Del Greco*. The account in USMM, *Difesa del traffico*, VII:191–92 is followed here. See Cavallero, *Diario*, 309 for the German comments.
38. Bagnasco and De Toro, *Littorio*, 210. USMM, *Difesa del traffico*, VII:188.
39. USMM, VII:193.
40. Bagnasco and De Toro, *Littorio*, 336–37.
41. AWD, 14.12.41, "Malta Force." DEFE 3/746, MK 811.
42. Cavallero, *Diario*, 278.
43. CED, "Riunione," II/2:1236–38.
44. CED, "Traffico con la Libia," II/2:1242. Also De Toro, "La crisi," 63.
45. Cavallero, *Diario*, 282.

Chapter 6. Sudden Victories

1. Cavallero, *Diario*, 287. *DSCS*, V:806–13.
2. Santoro, *Aeronautica italiana*, 130. DEFE 3/746, MK 874, 878. See MK 881 for air strengths. Also MK 894 for crisis.
3. Quotations: MWD, 15.12.41; DEFE 3/746, MK 879; GC&CS, *Naval History*, XX:133.
4. GC&CS.
5. Quotation: ADM 199/897, 15th CS, "ROP," 2. *DSCS*, V:792. DEFE 3/835, ZTPI 3375, 3409.
6. Quotation: DEFE 3/746, MK 910, 917.
7. MWD, 16.12.41; AWD, 17.12.41, "Enemy Fleet," "Enemy Units. *Unbeaten*."
8. Quotations: GWD, 17.12.41, "Aerial Warfare, Mediterranean"; ADM 199/897, CS15, "ROP," 3. Connell, *Maelstrom*, 142. Also, AWD 17.12.41, "Enemy Attack"; *PT*, 150–51. *DSCS*, V:816.
9. ADM 199/897, CS15, "ROP," 4.
10. Marcon, *Ro.43/44*, 19.

11. CED, "Relazione," II/2:1243.
12. AUSMM, Prima Sirte, "Relazione di volo."
13. CED, "Relazione," II/2:1243. Iachino, *Due Sirti*, 98–101.
14. Quotations: Prideaux, "With A.B.C.," 49. GC&CS, *Naval History*, XX:133.
15. CED, "Relazione," II/2:1246.
16. Quotations: ADM 199/897, CS15, "ROP," 4. AUSMM, Prima Sirte, *Trento*, "Munizioni sparate."
17. The times are from *Littorio*'s report which says *Doria* was first to open fire. *Doria*'s report gives the time as 1757. See AUSMM, *Doria*, "Rapporto," and *Littorio*, "Rapporto di missione."
18. ADM 199/897, CS15, "ROP," 4.
19. Quotations: Lind, *N Class*, 89. Pack, *Sirte*, 20. Also, ADM 234/444, *Ships Sunk or Damaged*, 183. CED, "Relazione," II/2:1246.
20. Quotation: ADM 199/897, CS15, "ROP," 4. Also, AWM, *Nizam*, "ROP," 88. CED, "Relazione," II/2:1246.
21. Quotation: Iachino, *Due Sirti*, 117. AUSMM, *Doria*, "Rapporto," 3. Bagnasco and De Toro, *Littorio*, 212.
22. Quotations: ADM 199/897, CS15, "ROP," 5. *Aurora*, "ROP," 1–2.
23. "ROP," CS15, "ROP," 6.
24. Quotations: Roskill, *War at Sea*, I:535. Bragadin, *Italian Navy*, 151. GWD, 19.12.41, "Situation Italy. GC&CS *Naval History*, XX, 133.
25. CED, "Relazione," II/2:1247.
26. CED, II/2:1248.
27. AWD, 18.12.41, "Enemy Fleet." Rear Admiral Rawlings' flagship, *Ajax*, was in dock repairing a defect, and he did not sail with *Neptune* when she went to sea on the 17th for reasons that are not entirely clear.
28. AWD, "Situation Proposals for Forces B, K and T/Bs."
29. Quotation: Iachino, *Due Sirti*, 135. Also, AWD, 19.12.41, "M/Vs attacked." USMM, *Difesa del traffico*, VII:209–10. DEFE 3/835, ZTPI 3611 for damage to *Zeno*.
30. AWD, 19.12.41, "Malta Air Report."
31. Quotations: ADM 199/897, *Aurora*, "ROP, 18–19 December," 1. ADM 1/11947, *Penelope*, "ROP," 2.
32. The timing of this event is uncertain. *Penelope* has 0116, Aurora between 0112 and 0115 and *Lively* as 0125. See their respective reports in ADM 1/11947.
33. Quotations: ADM, *Lively*, "ROP," 2; *Kandahar*, "ROP," 2.
34. ADM, *Aurora*, "ROP," 1.
35. ADM, "Losses of *Neptune* and *Kandahar*," 94.
36. Quotations: http://www.hmsneptune.com/armstrong-account.htm. ADM 1/11947, *Kandahar*, "ROP," 3.
37. Quotation: GWD, 30.12.41, "Situation Italy." Also, USMM, *La Guerra di Mine*, XVIII:222–23; Cavallero, *Diario*, 301.
38. ADM 1/11947, *Jaguar*, "ROP," 2.
39. ADM, "Minutes of Evidence," 17.
40. Cavallero, *Diario*, 296.
41. Borghese, *Sea Devils*, summarizes the genesis of this unit.
42. Berrafato and Berrafato, *La Decima Mas*, 64.
43. Spertini and Bagnasco, *I mezzi d'assalto*, 37–49.
44. Quotation: ADM 223/583, "Torpedo Attacks," 5. AUSMM, Raccolta "QBC."
45. Quotation: DEFE 3/835, ZTPI 3371; also, 3409, 3424. Quotation: DEFE 3/746, MK 956.

46. Superaereo, Roma 1157 x 17/12 0800. Courtesy of Claudio Rizza, 9 March 2018.
47. HW 50/15/5, 6.
48. Quotations: NSH, *Mediterranean,* II:228–29. Wade, *Midshipman's War,* 119.
49. USMM, *Azioni navali,* IV:114. The reports of the SLC pilots are reprinted here: De la Penne, 112–120; Marceglia, 121–127; Martellotta, 127–133.
50. *Marceglia,* 122.
51. *De la Penne,* 115–16.
52. *De la Penne,* 118. NSH, *Mediterranean,* II:225. This history attributes the 0332 order to Cunningham.
53. Cunningham, *Odyssey,* 433. Wade, *Midshipman's War,* 119, 122.
54. USMM, *Azioni navali,* VI:119. Quotation: ADM 223/583, "Human Torpedo Attacks," 5. Knowingly exposing a prisoner of war to danger to extract information is a war crime according to the 1929 Geneva Conventions.
55. Quotations: Borghese, *Sea Devils,* 150, 151. Wade, *Midshipman's War,* 122. Cunningham, *Odyssey,* 433.
56. Quotations: ADM 234/444, *Ships Damaged or Sunk,* 16–17; Connell, *Maelstrom,* 145–46. Also, Burt, *British Battleships,* 121–22; Langtree, *Kellys,* 129.
57. DEFE 3/835, ZTPI 363 for damage. Quotation: GWD, 9.1.42, "Situation Italy"; 27.1.42, "Enemy Situation."
58. Corbett, *Principles,* 90.
59. Quotation: Simpson, ed., *Cunningham Papers,* I:557. For convoy statistics see, USMM, *Dati statistici.* I:122–25. For Malta convoys see Hague, *Allied Convoy System.*
60. De Belot, *Struggle for the Mediterranean,* 150.
61. Italian sources credit the submarine *Umbra* for these sinkings. (USMM, Navi Perdute, III:47 and *Difesa del traffico,* VII:390). British sources take no such credit. Rowher, *Allied Submarines,* 150 attributes Italian mines. Also see DEFE 3/835, ZTPI, 3752.
62. These departures are listed in USMM, *Difesa del traffico,* VII:390–91.
63. DEFE 3/747, MK 1002, 1249, 1388.
64. Quotation: MWD, 25.12.41. A year later Admiral Henry Harwood lost his job as commander of the Mediterranean Fleet in part because he did not reopen the Libyan ports quickly enough, at least in the eyes of General Bernard Montgomery. Although forces under Admiral Cunningham's command had at least equal problems in this regard, he was not criticized as Harwood was.
65. MWD, 17.12.41 and 18.12.41. Also, DSCS, V:815 and USMM, Difesa del traffico, VII:389. DEFE 3/747, MK 920, 1065 gave correct information on Probitas' departure and route. Lina was mentioned in MK 876 (departed Pantelleria at 0700Z/15th) and 891 (departed Pantelleria at 0540Z/15th). She actually departed 1600/16th.
66. See Appendix 2, Alexandria Convoys.
67. MWD, 21.12.41.
68. See MWD, 22–23.12.41. Rohwer, *Axis Successes,* 229. Niestlé, *U-Boat Losses,* 44.
69. ACSR, Intercettazioni estere, 14683. MWD, 24.12.41.
70. See MWD, 26–28.12.41. Rohwer, *Axis Successes,* 229. Niestlé, *U-Boat Losses,* 40.
71. Playfair, III:91.
72. AWD, 29.12.41 "Air Report," and "Situation Report." NSH, *Mediterranean,* II:232–33. DSCS, V:885. ADM 234/444, *Ships Damaged or Sunk,* 184.
73. DEFE 3/747, MK 1312 for *Monginevro* and 1343 for *Pisani.* VAMWD, 25.12 and 27.12.41.
74. DEFE 3/747, MK 1460 for *Sturla;* 1455 for *Ankara.*

75. Quotation: VAMWD, "December Summary." *DSCS*, V: December, 1941.
76. Hezlet, *Submarine Operations*, Chapter 11.
77. USMM, *Sommergibili*, XIII:220. Rohwer, *Axis Successes*, 228–29. ONI, U-Boats Diary, December 1941.

Intermezzo

1. USMM, *Dati statistici*, I:32–33. Roskill, *War at Sea*, 1:537–38 incorrectly claimed that in 1941 the Axis merchant marine experienced a "decline of nearly thirty per cent," dropping to 1.626 million GRT. He arrived at that figure using accurate Italian figures for inventory. He does not identify his source for Axis losses, which he overstates.
2. USMM, *Dati Statistici*, I:277 for new supplies and 245 for consumption. *DSCS*, V:912–13.
3. See CAB 80/60, 251, 263, and 283 for examples.
4. See CAB 80/60, 233, 235, 248, 250, 255, and 256, for examples.
5. CAB 80/61, "Reinforcement of the Far East," 1.
6. CAB 80/61, 3–4.
7. *Foreign Relations of the United States* (FRUS), First Washington Conference, 23–28.
8. Danchev and Todman, *Diaries*, 216.

Chapter 7. January 1942

1. Playfair, III:135.
2. See the MWD for a day-by-day description of these activities.
3. See Appendix 1. ADM 234/444, *Ships Damaged or Sunk*, 185.
4. AWD, 2.1.42, "Need for A/S Craft."
5. DEFE 3/78 and 3/79 cover January 1942. Also see Table 7.1.
6. Quotation: Weichold, *Naval Policy*, 71.
7. AUSMM, Promedia 1942, "*Relazione M 43.*" Cavallero, *Diario*, 309–10.
8. Quotation: DEFE 3/78, MK 1556. See also 1551. Quotation: AWD, 5.1.42, "Situation Report."
9. AUSMM, Promedia, "*Relazione M 43.*"
10. AWD, 4–6.1.42, "Enemy Fleet"; Iachino, *Due Sirti*, 156.
11. USMM, *Difesa del traffico*, VII:216. Quotations: AUSMM, Promedia, *Relazione M 43.*" MWD, 5.1.42.
12. GWD, 7.1.42, "Enemy Situation Mediterranean." Cernuschi and Tirondola, *Mediterraneo*, 260–61. Quotations: Iachino, *Due Sirti*, 156; Cavallero, *Diario*, 311, 12.
13. AWD, 8.1.42, "Malta Movements." GWD, 6.1.42, "Enemy Situation Mediterranean."
14. Playfair, III:156. CAB 79/17/4.
15. AWD, 1.16.42, "Movements Summary"; 1.17.42, "Operation M.F.3"; 1.25.42, "Operation M.F.3." MWD, 171.42; ADM 199/940, CS15, "ROP," 2.
16. "ROP," 2; "Enc. 4," 1.
17. Quotations: Morgan and Taylor, *Attack Logs*, 182. ADM 234/444, *Ships Damaged or Sunk*, 186. AWD, 1.17.42, "Tobruk." ONI, *Diary Captain U-Boats*, 1.17.42, 55; GWD, 1.17.42, "Aerial Warfare, Mediterranean." ADM 190/940, *Isaac Sweers*, "ROP."
18. ADM 199/940, CS15, "ROP," 3.
19. "ROP," 3, *Carlisle*, "ROP," 1. *PT*, 154.
20. *PT*, 154, 153; GWD 1.18.42, "Aerial Warfare, Mediterranean"; ADM 199/940; CS15, "ROP, Appendix III." Crusader Project, "Luftwaffe Air Report."
21. Naval History.net "Malta Supply"; Crusader Project, "Luftwaffe Air Report." Warsailors.com, "*Thermopylae.*" Quotations: ADM 199/940, *Havock*, "ROP."

22. ADM 199/940, Force K, "ROP."
23. Quotations: AWD, 1.25.42, "Operation M.F.3." ADM 199/940, CS15, "ROP, Enc. 5," 6. Also Austin, *Churchill and Malta's War*, 148.
24. See MWD, 10.1.42. "Bad weather again held up all work at Benghazi," 11.1.42: "At Benghazi, little progress was made due to the weather."
25. MWD, 14.1.42, 17.1.42.
26. *DSCS*, VI:190. MWD, 22.1.42. See Appendix 2, Alexandria Convoys.
27. USMM, *Difesa del traffico*, VII:394.
28. MWD, 7.1.42; USMM, *Difesa del traffico*, VII:394. For *Bosforo* see DEFE 3/748, MK 1757, 1759, 1845, 1852, 1915. For *Battista* see MK 1752, 1759, 1770, 1841, 1887.
29. For *Labor* see DEFE 3/748, MK 1561; *Bolsena*, MK 1615; *Perla*, MK 1616; *Probitas*, MK 1646, 1686. Also, MWD, 7.1.42. USMM, *Difesa del traffico*, VII:223; *DSCS*, VI:76.
30. DEFE 3/748, MK 1720 and 1742 gave a date range for the convoy's departure; 1768 date and course; 1786 destination changed; 1791 sailing delayed, 1809, destination changed again, 1826 already sailed.
31. DEFE 3/748, MK 1822. MWD, 14.1.42; AWD, 14.1.42. "Malta Report," *DSCS*, VI:131.
32. See DEFE 3/748, MK 1891, 1917. USMM, *Difesa del traffico*, VII:395. MWD, 18.1.42. *DSCS*, VI:170.
33. DEFE 3/748, MK 1926 for *Bixio* and 1940 for the *Allegri* convoy. VAMWD, 22.1.42.
34. ACSR, Intercettazioni estere, 15368. The prisoner count is from Playfair, III:97.
35. Playfair, III:142. Italy cracked the U.S. Diplomatic Code (Black Code) after army intelligence stole a copy from the U.S. embassy in Rome. Italy was also reading U.S. diplomatic traffic out of Kuibyshev, the temporary Soviet capital, and sharing the intelligence (but not the source) with the Germans. See *DSCS*, VI:239 for an example.
36. USMM, *Difesa del traffico*, VII:227–28.
37. DEFE 3/748, MK 1938, 1956, 1979, 1990, 1995, 2002, 2020.
38. AWD, 22.1.42, "Torbay." USMM, *Difesa del traffico*, VII:230. Quotation: MWD, 23.2.42.
39. AWD, 23.1.1942, "Movements of Enemy Fleet." VAMWD, 23.1.42."
40. AWD, 24.1.42, "M.E. Air Report." Air 22/165 "AMWR Analysis 14/7."
41. AWD, 24.1.42 "M.E. Air Report." MWD, 24.1.42, USMM, *Difesa del traffico*, VII:234–37.
42. USMM, VII:234–37, 235.
43. MWD, 24.1.42.
44. AWD, 23.1.42, "Situation Report." Also AWD, 24.1.42, "C.S.R. Malta."
45. Quotation: AWD, 24.1.42, "C.S.R. Malta." USMM, *Difesa del traffico*, VII:238. Air 22/165, "AMWR Analysis 14/7." *DSCS*, VI:228.
46. Hezlet, *Submarine Operations*, Chapter 14; Rohwer, *Axis Successes*, 151. Quotation: GWD, 25.1.42, "Transport of Supplies."
47. *DSCS*, VI:255. AWD, 26.1.42, "Heythrop bombed." AWD, 29.12.41, "Benghazi"; AWD, 19.1.42, "Benghazi"; AWD, 20.1.42, "Benghazi weather casualties"; AWD, 23.1.42, "Benghazi." MWD, 25–27.1.42.
48. ADM 199/940, CS15, "ROP"; AWD, 25.1.42 "C.S. 15 bombed." *PT*, 154. ADM 199/940, MF4, "Analysis of Air attacks." Quotation: Supermarina, *Diario*, 26.1.42.
49. *PT*, 155. ADM 199/940, CS15, "ROP."
50. Quotations: "ROP"; Force K, "ROP." Also ROP MTF4, "Analysis of Air attacks." AWD, 26.1.42 "Convoy M.E. 9 bombed"; *PT*, 155. *DSCS*, VI:255.
51. Cavallero, *Diario*, 325.

52. For *Tembien* see DEFE 3/749, MK 2135. For *Ariosto*, MK 2038. For *Bengasi*, MK 2109, 2121. For attacks on *Bengasi* see AIR 22/165, "AMWR, Analysis 15/7."

53. For *Sant'Antonio* see DEFE 3/749, MK 2168; for *Monginevro*, MK 2183; for *Napoli*, MK 2146; for route, MK 2154; for *San Giovanni Battista*, MK 2146, 2154.

54. USMM, *Difesa del traffico*, VII:397. AIR 22/165, 15/7.

55. USMM, *Difesa del traffico*, IX:392–98, VII:392–96. *DSCS*, VI:January 1942.

56. Quotation: Santoro, *Aeronautica italiana*, 265. VAMWD, 1.1942, 4. Also, AIR 22/165, "AMWR Analysis 11/7." *DSCS*, VI:January 1942.

57. Hezlet, *Submarine Operations*, Chapter 14. ONI, *Diary Captain U-Boats*. USMM, *Sommergibili*, XIII/2, 8.

Chapter 8. February 1942

1. Cavallero, *Diario*, 334. *DSCS*, VI:346–47.

2. Supermarina, "Appunto sulla situazione nafta."

3. CAB 79/18, 115.

4. AWD, 2.2.42, "Situation Report." AWD, 2.1.42, "Derna."

5. *DSCS*, VI:364; 404; AWD, VI:444. MWD, 5.2.42; 9.2.42. Shores and Massimello, *Air War*, 2:184. AWD, 9.2.42, "Farndale bombed." AWD, 10.2.42, "Hurworth bombed." AWD, 14.2.42, "Air attack on Convoy Chitty."

6. Quotation: Gregory-Smith, *Red Tobruk*, Loc 1544; AWD, 23.2.42, "Air Report." See Appendix 1.

7. DEFE 3/749, MK 2406, 2311, 2354. Quotation: *DSCS*, VI:358.

8. Mancini, "Porti," 43; DEFE 3/750, MK 2712.

9. DEFE 3/749, MK 2146, 2176, 2213, 2316, 2352, 2361. Hezlet, *Submarine Operations*, Chapter 14. USMM, *Difesa del traffico*, VII:398. AWD, 7.2.42, "Malta C.S.R." MWD, 7.2.41. *DSCS*, VI:376.

10. USMM, *Difesa del traffico*, VII: 243; AWD, 8.2.42 "Malta C.S.R." Supermarina, *Diario*, 8.2.42 "Perdita e danneggiamenti." Quotation: *DSCS*, VI:389.

11. AIR, 22/165, "Summary Attacks 7–15 February"; AWD, 14.2.42, "Malta C.S.R." Quotation: USMM, *Difesa del traffico*, VII:244. For the *Eritrea* convoy see DEFE 3/750, MK 2518 (wrong departure date); for *Argentea* see 2592 (escort information only). DEFE 3/750, MK 2579, which reported the sailing of the *Atlas* convoy, was generated at 0030/14th local, two hours after the convoy had been sighted. It mentioned the prisoners on board.

12. MWD, 30.3.42.

13. ADM 199/940, CS15, "ROP Appendix 1"; Carlisle, "Letter of 17 Feb.," 2–3. Quotation: USMM, *Azioni navali*, V:162.

14. AWD, 13.2.42, "*Carlisle* bombed." *PT*, 156. Quotation: ADM 199/940, "*Carlisle* Letter of 17 Feb." Also, MWD, 13.2.42. *DSCS*, VI:437. Supermarina, Promemoria, "Operazione nemica."

15. ADM 199/940, CS15, "Log of air attacks."

16. ADM 199/940, VA, Malta, "ROP 17.2.42." ADM 234/444, *Ships Damaged and Sunk*, 72, 188.

17. ADM 199/940, *Southwold*, "ROP 17.2.42."

18. Quotations: ADM 199/940, CinC, "ROP"; Force K, "ROP"; Gregory Smith, *Red Tobruk*, Loc 1707.

19. ADM 199/940, CS15, "Analysis of Air Attacks"; CS15, Force K, "Enclosure Signals." Quotation: Woodman, *Malta Convoys*, 285.

20. Supermarina, "Operazione nemica."

21. USMM, *Azioni navali*, V:164–65. Iachino, *Due Sirti*, 181.
22. Quotation: ADM 199/940, CS15, "Narrative," 16. CS15, "Enclosure," 4; *Southwold,* "ROP," 2.
23. Quotation: Santoro, *L'Aeronautica italiana*, 361. ADM 199/940, Force K, "ROP."
24. Quotation: Gregory-Smith, *Red Tobruk*, loc 1712. ADM 199/940, "Record of Air Attacks"; ADM CS15 "Enclosure," 3; ADM, *Carlisle*, "ROP," 2.
25. ADM 199/940, CS15, "Log of Air Attacks."
26. *PT,* 158.
27. Quotations: ADM 199/940, Force K, "Enclosure signals." Also, USMM, *Sommergibili,* XIII/2:13.
28. USMM, *Azioni Navali,* V:165.
29. Quotation: AIR 22/165, "Summary Attacks, 15.2.41–22.2.42." VAMWD, 15.2.42. USMM, *Azioni navali,* V:165.
30. Quotation: *DSCS,* VI: 470. MDW, 16.2.42.
31. AWD, 14.2.42, "Operation M.F. 5." GWD, 13.2.1942, "Situation Italy," GWD, 14.2.42, "Aerial Warfare, Mediterranean." Supermarina, "Operazione nemica." Quotation: GWD, 15.2.42, "Aerial Warfare."
32. ADM 199/940, "M.05639/42," 1–2.
33. DEFE 3/750, MK 2727, 2688.
34. See USMM, *Difesa del traffico,* VII:245–49.
35. Supermarina, *Diario,* 2.42, "Operazione K.7."
36. See DEFE 3/750, MK 2573, 2686, 2730, 2752, 2755, 2772, 2811 for Convoy 2. For Convoy 1 see 2573, 2601, 2606, 2771, 2813. For the heavy escort see 2772, and for the light escort, 2646, 2650. Quotation: MK 2601.
37. Quotation DEFE 3/750, MK 2772. Also, 2828, 2842.
38. AWD, 22.2.42, "Malta Air Report." Supermarina, *Diario,* 2.42, "Operazione K.7."
39. Quotation: USMM, *Difesa del traffico,* VII:247.
40. Supermarina, *Diario,* 2.42, "Operazione K.7."
41. AWD, 22.2.42, "*Penelope Legion.*"
42. AWD, "Mediterranean." Supermarina, *Diario,* 2.42, "Operazione K.7."
43. Hezlet, *Submarine Operations,* Chapter 14. Quotation: Supermarina, *Diario,* 23.3.42. "Operazione K7."
44. Quotation: USMM, *Difesa del traffico,* VII:247–48.
45. CAB 80/61, (49) "Reinforcements for Malta," 23.2.42.
46. CAB 79/18, 251, 303.
47. AWD, 27.2.42, "Defence of Malta." CAB 79/18, 339–41. Quotation: 341.
48. Supermarina, Direttive, "Attivitá della flotta."
49. DEFE 3/750, MK 2675, 2752, 2775, 2805, 2815, 2841.
50. DEFE MK 2769, 2811, 2802, 2810 gave accurate departure and route information for *Beppe, Vettor Pisani, Bengasi,* and *Argentea* respectively; 2908 gave *Tembien*'s details, except the ship departed a day later. USMM, *Difesa del traffico* VII:402–3. VAMWD, 24.2.42.
51. Hezlet, *Submarine Operations,* Chapter 14. USMM, *Difesa del traffico,* VII:250.
52. *DSCS,* VI:February 1942.
53. AIR 22/165, "Weekly Summaries," 15/3, 17/3. VAMWD, 2.42, Part III. *DSCS,* VI:February.
54. Hezlet, *Submarine Operations,* Chapter 14.
55. USMM, *Sommergibili* XIII/2:14. Rohwer, *Axis Successes,* 230. ONI, *Diary Captain U-Boats,* 2.42.

56. CAB 80/34/130, "Supplies to Malta," 22.2.42. Also, CAB, 79/18/62, 24.2.42.
57. CAB 79/18, "Malta Supply Situation 26.2.42," 329.

Chapter 9. Sirte Preliminaries

1. See CAB 80/61, "Shipping Situation," 13.2.42.
2. AWD, 1.3.42, "Troop Transports for Far East." AWD, 3.3.42, "Troop Transport."
3. CAB 80/61, "Situation in Libya," 1–4.
4. CAB Annex III.
5. Liddell Hart, ed., *Rommel Papers*, 191. Cavallero, *Diario* 357–64; AUSMM, "Esigenza C3."
6. GWD, 4.3.42, and 11.3.42, "Special Items." Also, Militär. Forschungsamt, *Second World War*, VI:338. Boyd and Yoshida, *Japanese Submarines*, 75.
7. Quotation: CAB 79/18. "Malta Supply Situation 26.2.42," MWD, 4.3.42. GWD, 9.3.42, "Mediterranean, Enemy Situation."
8. CAB 80/61, "Situation in Libya," 2.
9. AWD, 7.3.42. "*Cerion* Bombed." *DSCS*, VI:714. See Appendix 2, Alexandria Convoys.
10. Morgan and Taylor, *Attack Logs*, 221–24. Langtree, *Kellys*, 141. They also give *U652* credit for sinking *Slavol*. Rohwer, *Axis Successes*, 231 is followed here.
11. DEFE 3/751, ML 3012.
12. DEFE 3/750, MK 2680. Hezlet, *Submarine Operations*, Chapter 14 gives the date of the action as 6 March. See also AWD, 5.3.42, "P.31" and AWD, 13.3.42. For *Giordani* see DEFE 3/751, MK 3012, 3022, 3027.
13. GWD, 7.3.42, "Supplies to North Africa."
14. Cavallero, *Diario*, 351.
15. Quotation: DEFE 3/751, MK 3112. Also, 3148; 3171 for the north convoy. For *Manara* see DEFE 3/751, MK 3187. For *Monviso*, 3177 for incorrect departure and 3222 for departure after the fact.
16. Da Zara, *Pelle d'ammiraglio*, 318.
17. Supermarina, "Apprezzamento della Situazione," 10.3.42.
18. Quotations: USMM, *Difesa del traffico*, VII:254; AWD, 9.3.42, "Malta Air Report."
19. AWD, 11.3.42, "Air Report." AWD, 9.3.42, "Situation Report."
20. MWD, 9.3.42.
21. AWD, 10.3.42, "Attack on Enemy Convoy," "Malta Air Report." 11.3.42, "Malta Air Report." Hezlet, *Submarine Operations*, Chapter 14. Shores et al., *Malta: Spitfire Year*, 114.
22. AWD, 9.3.42, "Situation Report."
23. AWD, 11.3.42. "*Naiad* torpedoed and sunk"; "Situation report." Quotation: Vian, *Action this Day*, 84. GWD, 12.3.42, "Aerial Warfare." *DSCS*, VI:704–5.
24. USMM, *Difesa del traffico*, VII:254–55.
25. USMM, VII:405. DEFE 3/751; MK 3198, 3199. Also 3126 (pending), 3137 (escort), 3202 (escort changes), 3218 (departed).
26. DEFE MK 3308 and 3325.
27. Quotations: Simpson, ed., *Cunningham Papers*, I:582; *DSCS*, VI:730; AWD, 16.3.42, "attack on Rhodes." Also, Cernuschi, "La nave più brutta," 18.
28. USMM, *Difesa del traffico*, VII:256, 407. *Sirtori* returned to Messina.
29. USMM, VII:258–59.
30. DEFE 3/751; MK 3408 (1240Z/16) "German air operations suggest a convoy will arrive in Tripoli on the 18th"; 3427 (2220Z/16) "northbound convoy to meet southbound convoy, maybe 0500/18th"; 3465 (2035Z/17) assumed sailing

arrangements; 3466 (2115Z/17) time and place of rendezvous; 3497 (arrived). Also, VAMWD, 3.42, 2.
31. Quotation: USMM, *Difesa del traffico*, VII:259. Hezlet, *Submarine Operations*, Chapter 14; AWD, 17.3.42, "S/Ms."
32. Shores and Massimello, *Air War*, 2:194.
33. AWD, 18.3.43, "Una, P.34."
34. DEFE 3/751; MK 3463, 3465, 3411.
35. AWD, 18.3.42, "Air Operations." AIR 22/165, "15–22 March Attacks on Shipping."
36. Contrast Ireland, *Mediterranean*, 103, "to hide from the Italians the fact that their codes were compromised, a visible reconnaissance sighting always preceded an attack."
37. AWD, 18.3.42, "Malta Air Report." DEFE 3/751; MK 3427 (expected to leave with route), 3463 (route changed), 3464 (hurry departure), 3474 (departed and route). This was generated just hours before the actual attack.
38. DEFE 3/751; MK 3354.
39. USMM, *Guerra di mine*, XVIII:125, 157, 243, 269, 277–93; Frank, *S-Boats*, 78.
40. Cull and Galea, *Spitfires*, 10. The destroyers were *Active, Anthony, Blankney, Croome, Duncan, Laforey Lightning, Whitehall,* and *Wishart.*
41. Cull and Galea, *Spitfires*, 25.
42. ADM 223/548, "Convoy MG1," 195.
43. *DSCS*, VI:March 1942.
44. VAMWD, 3.42, 6.
45. See Jordan, *Merchant Fleets*, 447. Rohwer and Hummelchen, *Chronology*, 150 states that *Cuma* displaced 8,260 tons. The amount of collateral damage inflicted varies by source.
46. AIR 22/165, "Summary 15.3.42 to 22.3.42."
47. Hezlet, *Submarine Operations*, Chapter 14; Rohwer, *Allied Attacks*, 153–54.
48. Kemp, *Admiralty Regrets*, 173–74.
49. USMM, *Sommergibili*, XIII/2:20. Rohwer, *Axis Successes*; ONI, *Diary Captain U-Boats*, 3.42.
50. AWD, 9.3.42, "M.W.11. 14-knot ships."

Chapter 10. Second Battle of Sirte, 22 March 1942

1. The other two were *U559* and *U568*. Quotations: Gregory-Smith, *Red Tobruk*, Loc 1793; ADM 116/4631, Commander Cruiser Squadron 15, "Operation MG 1," 69. Morgan and Taylor, *Attack Logs*, 217–18.
2. Quotation: Morgan and Taylor, 218; ADM 116/4631, 69.
3. Quotation: Gregory-Smith, *Red Tobruk*, Loc 1824. *DSCS*, VI:786.
4. ADM 116/4631, 70.
5. ADM 115. For sighting, see AUSMM, "SIS Notiziario Speciale." Apparently, Kesselring's promise to improve Italo-German communications after the *Aosta* incident in February was still unrealized.
6. GWD, 20.03.42, "Mediterranean, Enemy situation." AUSMM, Supermarina, "Invio di un convoglio inglese." AUSMM, "SIS, Notiziario Speciale."
7. AUSMM, "Sansonetti, 1830/21."
8. AUSMM, "Sansonetti, 1945/21."
9. AUSMM.
10. AUSMM, Supermarina, "Invio di un convoglio inglese."
11. Santoro, *Aeronautica Italiana*, 364–65.

12. NSH, *Mediterranean Convoys*, 36.
13. ADM 223/548. "Convoy MG1 to Malta," 18; 14, 16, 20. Quotation: ADM 116/4631, 47.
14. Ultra messages include: DEFE 3/752, MK 3597, 3600, 3603, 3604, 3607, 3608, 3613, 3619, 3623; DEFE 3/839; ZTPI 7669, 7673, 7677, 7680, 7685, 7697, 7704.
15. AUSMM, Supermarina, SIS Notiziario Speciale, 10–16.
16. AUSMM, CCFN, "Intercettazioni estere"; ACSR, "Intercettazioni estere," 18564.
17. ACSR, SIS Notiziario Speciale. ACSR, "Intercettazioni estere," 18574, 18582, 18583.
18. ADM 116/4631, 28, 36, 42, 47.
19. Quotation: Simpson, ed., *Cunningham Papers*, I:558.
20. Quotation: Mattioli, *S.79*, Loc. 272. ADM 223/548, "Italian communique," 282–88. Also, Santoro, *Aeronautica Italiana*, 366. DSCS, VI:807.
21. AUSMM, "Missione 22 e 23 Marzo," 1.
22. AUSMM, 2. Quotation: ADM 223/548, "Message 1052B/22nd March," 20.
23. AUSMM, "Missione 22 e 23 Marzo," 5. USMM, *Azioni navali*, V:195.
24. ADM 116/4631, 47.
25. USMM, *Azioni navali*, V:199. Quotation: AUSMM, "Relazione del 22 e 23 Marzo." Iachino, *Due Sirti*, 229 for torpedo counts.
26. Quotations: ADM 116/4631, 43; ADM 223/548, "Message 1432B/21st," 70.
27. ADM 116/4631, 35. Quotation: ADM, 48. Also see, ADM, 100.
28. ADM, 79, 86. AUSMM, *Gorizia*, "Rapporto telegrafico." *Trento*, "Rapporto di tiro"; USMM, *Azione navali*, V:204.
29. Quotations: ADM 223/548, "Message 1445A/22nd," 69. AUSMM, "Relazione di volo 22 Marzo 1942."
30. Quotations: ADM 116/4631, 86, 60. Also, 67, 82; ADM 223/548, "Message 1506B/22nd," 67; AUSMM, *Trento*, "Rapporto di tiro."
31. First and third quotations: ADM 116/4631, 66, 65. Second quotation: ADM 223/548, "Message 2310B/23rd," 145.
32. Quotation: USMM, *Azioni navali*, V:202. ADM 116/4631, 82, 86.
33. AUSMM, "Relazione 22 e 23 Marzo," 2. "*Littorio*, Rapporto," 3. Postwar Iachino asserted that he never ordered Parona to lead the British to him and that such orders would have been unrealistic in any event. See Iachino, *Due Sirti*, 225.
34. Quotations: ADM 116/4631, 71; ADM 235/324, *Malta Convoys 1942*, 6. Also, *PT*, 168. Santoro, *Aeronautica Italiana*, 366.
35. Quotations: ADM 116/4631, 48, 49.
36. Iachino, *Due Sirti*, 229. AUSMM, "Missione 22 e 23 Marzo," 6.
37. Quotation: AUSMM, "Missione 22–23 Marzo," 7. Also, *Aviere*, "Rapporto," 2.
38. AUSMM, "Missione 22–23 Marzo," 7.
39. Iachino, *Due Sirti*, 234–35. Supermarina, "RO.43 No. 2, Relazione," 2.
40. ADM 116/4631, 58. Quotation: ADM, 49.
41. Quotations: Iachino, *Due Sirti*, 235. ADM 116/4631, 86.
42. Quotations: ADM 116/4631, 50, 56. Also, ADM, 105–6; Iachino, *Due Sirti*, 241.
43. ADM 116/4631, 60–61. AUSMM, *Aviere*, "Rapporto," 3.
44. Quotations: ADM 116/4631, 50. USMM, *Azioni navali*, V:211.
45. ADM 116/4631, 51. Quotation: Supermarina, *Trento* "Rapporto di Tiro."
46. Quotations: ADM 116/4631, 91. AUSMM, "Missione 22–23 Marzo," 8.
47. AUSMM, *Aviere*, "Rapporto," 4.
48. ADM 116/4631, 60. Quotation: 91.
49. Quotations: AUSMM, "Missione 22–23 Marzo," 9. Rapporto XI Sq, 5.
50. Gregory-Smith, *Red Tobruk*, Loc 1952.

51. AUSMM, "Relazione Ro.43. No.2," 2. ADM 116/4631, 97, 71.
52. ADM 116/4631, 82.
53. Quotations: *London Gazette*, "Battle of Sirte," 4375. Vian, *Action This Day*, 90. Roskill, *War at Sea*, II:53.
54. NSH, *Mediterranean Convoys*, 47 says 1735 but this is clearly too early.
55. Quotations: ADM 116/4631, 82; ADM, 67.
56. AUSMM, "Missione 22–23 Marzo," 11.
57. Quotations: ADM 116/4631, 61. Iachino, *Due Sirti*, 254.
58. Quotations: AUSMM, "Missione, 22–23 Marzo," 11 (first two). ADM 223/548, "Message 1733/22nd," 48. The actual distance was closer to twelve miles.
59. Quotations: ADM 116/4631, 52 (first and second), 87. Also, ADM, 102.
60. Quotation: ADM, 52–53. Some authors, like Bagnasco and De Toro, *Littorio*, 219, regard Vian's fixation on an enemy force to windward as proof that Iachino's tactics were defective. "Iachino's mistake was highlighted by Vian, whose repeated forays east reflected his incredulity at not seeing Italian forces appearing from the most dangerous direction." This analysis does not mention that Vian was acting on an exaggerated notion of Italian strength; he took all his cruisers each time he left; the Italians did not have enough time to work to windward; and finally, Vian himself later acknowledged that his forays were ill considered.
61. ADM 116/4631, 58.
62. AUSMM, "Missione del 22 e 23 Marzo."
63. Quotations: Thompson, *War at Sea,* 184; ADM 116/4631, 58.
64. ADM, 107.
65. ADM, 122; ADM 234/444, *Ships Damaged or Sunk*, 192. *Trento*, "Rapporto di Tiro."
66. ADM 116/4631, 122.
67. ADM, 108.
68. Quotations: ADM, 59, 61. ADM 223/548, "Message 1428C/14 April," 11.
69. Quotations: ADM 116/4631, 53, 83. Also, AUSMM, "Missione del 22 e 23 Marzo," 12.
70. Quotation: Winton, ed., *War at Sea*, 224. Also, ADM 116/4631," 87.
71. Quotations: ADM, 77, 61. Also, ADM 234/444, *Ships Damaged or Sunk*, 192.
72. AUSMM, "Missione del 22 e 23 Marzo, 11."
73. ADM 116/4631, 67.
74. Quotations: ADM 116/4631, 37. ADM, 97–98.
75. *PT,* 169. ADM 116/4631," 54. Santoro, *Aeronautica Italiana*, 366.
76. Quotation: Pollastri and Brown, "Loss of *Lanciere*," 196–97.
77. AUSMM, "Corrispondenza Iachino a Riccardi," 30 Marzo 1942.
78. First quotation: ADM 116/4631, 77. ADM 234/353, *Malta Convoys 1942*, 118. Thereafter *Pack*, *Sirte*, 81. Last Simpson, ed., *Cunningham Papers*, I:588.
79. MWD, 24.3.42.
80. Shores et al., *Desert Air War,* 2:196.

Chapter 11. After the Battle

1. Cull and Galea, *Spitfires*, 26–27.
2. Cull and Galea, *PT*, 170–71; Santoro, *Aeronautica Italiana*, 366.
3. Woodman, *Malta Convoys*, 309.
4. ADM 116/4631, 93.
5. Gregory-Smith, *Red Tobruk*, Loc 2107.
6. ADM 234/444, *Ships Damaged or Sunk*, 193. Quotation: ADM 223/548, "Message 1133/23rd," 95; "Message 1040B/23rd," 109.

7. Quotation: Cameron, *Red Duster,* 126. ADM 116/4559, Vice Admiral Malta, "Operation M.G. One," 46.
8. Quotation: ADM 116/4631, 100, 46.
9. Cull and Galea, *Spitfires,* 28. *PT,* 172.
10. ADM 116/4559, 36.
11. Quotations: ADM, 36–37. VAMWD, 03.42, Part II (1). After the fiasco with *Talabot* and *Pampas* the June convoys had a detailed unloading plan. This included centralized control and supervision, teams of stevedores provided with facilities, food, and transportation, a 24-hour work schedule, security measures to prevent pilfering, and dispersed storage yards.
12. *PT,* 172. ADM 116/4559, 37–38.
13. ADM 116/4631, 73.
14. Quotations: Cameron, *Red Duster,* 131; Gregory-Smith, *Red Tobruk,* Loc 2283; ADM 116/4559, 47.
15. Quotation: Gregory-Smith, *Red Tobruk,* Loc 2335. Also, *PT,* 173.
16. *PT,* 173. GWD, 26.3.42, "Aerial Warfare" and "Warfare in the Mediterranean."
17. ADM 116/4559, 25, 48.
18. Quotations: ADM, 2–3; 39–40.
19. Quotation: Playfair, III:171; ADM 116/4559, 40.
20. ADM, 41.
21. All quotations: ADM, 3–4.
22. ADM, 41, 45. The literature regarding the loss of MW.10's cargo is brief. In official accounts it is written off as an unfortunate, but inevitable occurrence. Among the few who tackle the subject critically, one author wrote, "The truth is that a priceless cargo . . . was largely lost because of a deadly combination of cowardice and lack of proper planning" (Jellison, *Besieged,* 162). This author faults the stevedores for cowardice and Governor Dobbie for lack of planning. Blaming civilian workers seems unfair. Indeed, they labored under fire and eight perished on board *Pampas* on 26 March. The assessment by another author is that the island's administrative council, consisting of the senior army, RAF, and navy officers along with the governor and lieutenant governor "should have discussed the unloading process at great length. All would have known the dangers, and plans for all circumstances— weather patterns included—should have been put in place long before the convoy ever reached Grand Harbour. A large number of troops as well as RAF ground crew should have been brought in for the operation. That none of them seemed to have thought of any of this was, frankly, astonishing" (Holland, *Fortress Malta,* 250). In fact, surprised by the sustained ferocity of the German attacks, Leatham bore the greatest responsibility for the failure.
23. ADM, 41.
24. Quotations: ADM, 5. Also, ADM 234/444, *Ships Damaged or Sunk,* 195–96.
25. Stead, *Leaf upon the Sea,* 61, 69.
26. All quotations: ADM 116/4559, 6–8.
27. ADM, 44.
28. Cunningham, *Odyssey,* 454.
29. Simpson, ed., *Cunningham Papers,* I:583: "I should feel happier if someone more experienced and better known to the personnel was to relieve me." This referred to Rear Admiral Henry Harwood, who assumed the command in mid-April.
30. ADM 223/548, "Naval Cypher 1948/24th," 194.
31. ADM, "Naval Cypher 1126A/25th," 241.

32. ADM 116/4631, 137.
33. Roskill, *War at Sea*, II:54; Playfair, III:17; Ireland, *Mediterranean*, 120. Barnett, *Engage the Enemy*, 500.
34. AUSMM, "Missione del 22 e 23 Marzo," 5.

Chapter 12. Conclusion: Six Victories

1. AWD, 9.11.41, "Report of Action."

BIBLIOGRAPHY

Primary Sources and Official Histories

Archivio Centrale dello Stato Roma (ACSR). Fondo Ministero della Marina, Gabinetto. "Condotta del tiro navale." January 1942.
———. "Direttive e Norme per l'impiego della Squadra nel conflitto attuale." January 1942.
———. "Norme di massima per l'impiego in guerra." January 1942.
———. Servizio Informazione Segreto (SIS). "Intercettazioni estere e informazioni." March 1942.
Archivio dell'Ufficio Storico della Marina Militare (AUSMM). Cartella Notizie sulle Azioni Navali, No. 53. "Affondamento degli incrociatori *Da Barbiano* e *Di Giussano.*" 12 January 1942.
———. *Centauro*, "Rapporto sul siluramento della M/N *Venier.* 13 December 1941.
———. "Esigenza C 3. Verbale della riunione tenuta il giorno 22 Febbraio 1942."
———. Raccolta di messaggi inglesi "QBC."
———. Relazione Prima Sirte: Comando in Capo della Squadra Navale. "Operazione M.42." 19 February 1942:
   Cesare: "Rapporto 16–19 Dicembre 1941"; "Navigazion."
   Doria: "Rapporto 16–19 Dicembre 1941."
   Littorio: "Relazion di missione"; "Relazion di volo"; "Statino consumi navigazione."
   Trento: "Rapporto azione;" "Munizioni sparate."
———. Relazione Segunda Sirte: 170 Sq: "Relazione sul volo effettuato il 22 Marzo 1942.Z.506 No. 3." No Date.
———. Comando in Capo Forze Navali (CCFN): "Relazione Riassuntiva sulla Missione del 22 e 23 Marzo 1942.XX, Allegato n. 1–6. 9 April 1942;
   CCFN: "Intercettazioni estere, 22 Marzo al 23 Marzo 1942." No date.
   CCFN: "Messaggi in arrivo, 22 Marzo al 23 Marzo 1942." No date.
   CCFN: "Missione 22–23 Marzo." 4 April 1942.
   Gorizia: "Rapporto telegrafico." No date.
   Littorio RO 43 No. 2: "Relazione di volo del giorno 22 Marzo 1942." 26 March 1942.
   Trento: "Rapporto di tiro."
   XI Sq.: "Rapporto di missione." 25 March 1942.
———. SIS Notiziario Speciale. "Operazione 20–24 Marzo 1942. No Date.
———. Superaereo: "Roma 1157 x 17/12 0800."
———. Supermarina: "Apprezzamento di Situazione, 10 March 1942."

———. Supermarina: Appunto sulla situazione nafta," 7 February 1942.

———. Supermarina: "Azione del 22 Marzo 1942 Primo apprezzamento." No date.

———. Supermarina: "Corrispondenza Iachino a Riccardi 30 Marzo 1942.

———. Supermarina: *Diario*, various dates.

———. Supermarina: Direttive 14 February 1942, "Attivitá della flotta."

———. Supermarina: Direttive 16 February 1942, "Situazione el attivitâ della flotta."

———. Supermarina: "fra Amm. Sansonetti e Amm. Barone." 1830/21; Amm. Iachino." 1945/21.

———. Supermarina: "Invio di un convoglio inglese a Malta operazioni navali nel Mediterraneo centrale per contrastarne il passaggio (20–23 Marzo 1942).

———. Supermarina: Promemoria. "Operazione nemica di protezione al traffico navale nel Mediterraneo Centrale dal 13 al 15 1942." 27 February 1942.

———. Supermarina: Promemoria. "Problema del rifornimento della nafta." 10 January 1942.

———. Supermarina: Promemoria. *"Relazione sintetica sull'operazione M 43."*

———. Supermarina: Promemoria. "Situazione Nafta per Caldaie," 21 February 1942.

———. Supermarina: Promemoria. "Situazione Nafta per Caldaie, al 1 Aprile 1942."

Australian War Memorial (AWM) 78. Reports of Proceedings HMA Ships and Establishments. HMAS *Hobart* 141/2 June 1941–September 1942; HMAS *Yarra*, HMAS *Nizam*, HMAS *Parrammara*.

Biagini, Antonello and Fernando Frattolillo, eds. *Diario Storico del Comando Supremo*. Vol. V (1.9.1941–31.12.1941) and VI (1.1.1942–30.4.1942). Rome: Ufficio Storico dello Stato Maggiore dell'Esercito, 1995 and 1996.

Coakley, Robert W. *Global Logistics and Strategy, 1940–1943*. Washington, DC: Office of the Chief of Military History, 1955.

Fuehrer Conferences on Naval Affairs, 1939–1945. London: Chatham, 2005.

Gwyer, J. M. A. and J. R. M. Butler. *Grand Strategy*. Volume III, *June 1941–August 1942*. London: HMSO, 1964.

Hinsley, F. H., et al. *British Intelligence in the Second World War*. 4 Volumes New York: Cambridge University Press, 1979–1984.

The London Gazette. "The Battle of Sirte of 22nd March 1942." Supplement, 18 September 1947.

———. "Evacuation of the Army from Greece." Supplement, 19 May 1948.

———. "Mediterranean Convoy Operations." Supplement, 11 August 1948.

Mattesini, Francesco, ed. *Corrispondenza e Direttive Tecnico–Operative di Supermarina*: *Volume Secondo II Tomo Giugno 1941–Dicembre 1941*. Rome: USMM, 2001.

Militärgeschichtliches Forschungsamt. *Germany and the Second World War*: Volume III. *The Mediterranean, South-east Europe, and North Africa 1939–1941*. Gerhard Schreiber, Bernd Stegemann, and Detlef Vogel. Oxford: Clarendon Press, 1995.

———. Volume VI. *The Global War*. Horst Boog, Werner Rahn and Reinhard Stumpf. Oxford: Clarendon Press, 2001.

Murphy, W. E. *2nd New Zealand Divisional Artillery*. Wellington: Historical Publications Branch, 1966.

Naval Staff History (NSH). *The Royal Navy and the Mediterranean Convoys*. Milton Park, England: Routledge, 2007. Reprint of Battle Summaries Nos. 18 and 32, *Selected Convoys (Mediterranean), 1941–1942*. Historical Section, Admiralty.

———. *The Royal Navy and the Mediterranean*. Two Volumes. London: Frank Cass, 2002. Reprint of *Mediterranean September 1939–October 1940* and *Mediterranean November 1940–December 1941*. Historical Section, Admiralty.

The National Archives, Kew, England. ADM 1/11941. "Loss of H.M. Ships *Neptune* and *Kandahar*." March 3, 1942.

———. ADM 1/11948. "Loss of H.M.S. Barham." March 20, 1942.

———. ADM 1/27186. "Review of Security of Naval Codes and Cyphers, 1939–1945."

———. ADM 53/115621. Ship's Logs, HMS *Cleopatra*; *Dido*, *Penelope*, *Euryalus*.

———. ADM 116/4559. Vice Admiral Malta: "Operation MG 1: Enemy air attacks on ships in Grand Harbour, Malta, and subsequent recommendations." 23 May, 1942.

———. ADM 116/4631. Commander Cruiser Squadron 15, "Operation MG 1: reports and recommendations for awards." March 31, 1942.

———. ADM 187/17. "Pink List." Mediterranean Fleet, 31 December 1941.

———. ADM 199/413. "War Diary, Vice Admiral Malta, October–December 1941."

———. ADM 199/415. "Mediterranean Command War Diary, 1941."

———. ADM 199/424. "War Diary, Vice Admiral Malta, January–March 1942."

———. ADM 199/650. "Mediterranean Command War Diary, 1942."

———. ADM 199/897. "HMS *Aurora*: Reports of Proceedings with Force K."

———. ADM 199/940. "Naval Operations in the Mediterranean, Reports."

———. ADM 199/1178. "Reports of Attack by Enemy Aircraft." Various ships and dates.

———. ADM 223/88. *Admiralty Use of Special Intelligence in Naval Operations.*

———. ADM 223/528. "Force K Convoy." 11 November 1941.

———. ADM 223/548. "Convoy MG 1 to Malta: Italian Fleet at Sea."

———. ADM 223/583. "Human Torpedo Attacks."

———. ADM 234/353. *Battle Summaries. No. 32, Malta Convoys 1942.*

———. ADM 234/444. *H.M. Ships Damaged or Sunk by Enemy Action 3 Sept. 1939 to 2 Sept. 1945.*

———. ADM 239/138. "Progress in Naval Gunnery 1942."

———. ADM 267/84. *Damage Reports and Files.* HMS *Cleopatra, Havock, Kingston, Legion, Penelope.*

———. ADM 267/106. Shell and bomb reports of *Kingston* and *Lively.*

———. AIR 22/165. A.M.W.R. Weekly Statistical Analysis: Mediterranean Area.

———. CAB 66/11/42. Future Strategy.

———. CAB 69/2–4. Defence Committee Memoranda. 26.7.41–7.8.42.

———. CAB 79/17–19. Chiefs of Staff Committee, Minutes of Meetings. 31.1.42–3.30.42.

———. CAB 79/56. Chiefs of Staff Committee, Minutes of Meetings. 9.1.42–13.8.42.

———. CAB 80/59–61. Chiefs of Staff Committee Memoranda. 24.7.41–25.3.42.

———. DEFE 3/690. "Intelligence from Intercepted German, Italian and Japanese Radio Communications, WWII." Cairo Series. OL 1501–2060. 11.10.41–19.11.41.

———. DEFE 3/745–3/752. "Intelligence from Intercepted German, Italian and Japanese Radio Communications, WWII." Cairo Series. MK 1–4000. 20.11.41–6.4.42.

———. DEFE 3/833–3/840. "Intelligence from Intercepted German, Italian and Japanese Radio Communications, WWII." ZTPI 1000–8265, 3.10.41–7.4.42.

———. HW 50/15/5. 8G and Naval Section WIT Watch.

National Archives and Records Administration (NARA), Washington D.C. Admiralty War Diaries, October 1941–April 1942.

———. G.C.&C.S. *Naval History Vol XX, The Mediterranean 1940–1943.* Record Group 38, Box 99.

———. "Italian Communications Intelligence." Record Group 457, Box 115.

———. "Interrogation Reports, Italian." Record Group 457, Box 167.

Playfair, I. S. O. *The Mediterranean and Middle East.* Four Volumes. Uckfield, England: Naval and Military Press, 2004.

Richards, Dennis and Hilary St. George Saunders. *The Royal Air Force 1939–1945.* Volume 2, *The Fight Avails.* London: HMSO, 1954.

Roskill, S. W. *The War at Sea 1939–1945.* Three Volumes. London: HMSO, 1954–1960.

Royal Air Force, Headquarters Middle East. *RAF Review No. 1.* Printing and Stationery Services MEF, 1943.

Santoro, Giuseppe. *L'Aeronautica italiana nella Seconda Guerra Mondiale.* Rome: Danesi, 1957.

Simpson, Michael, ed. *The Cunningham Papers.* Two Volumes. Aldershot, England: Ashgate, 1999–2006.

———. *The Somerville Papers.* Aldershot, England: Scolar, 1996.

Ufficio Storico della Marina Militare (USMM). *La Marina Italiana nella Seconda Guerra Mondiale.* Volume I. *Dati Statistici.* Rome, 1972.

———. Volume II. *Navi militari perdute.* Rome, 1965.

———. Volume III. *Navi perdute—Navi mercantili.* Rome, 1952.

———. Volume IV. *Le azioni navali in Mediterraneo dal 10 Giugno 1940 al 31 Marzo 1941.* Rome, 1976.

———. Volume V. *Le azioni navali in Mediterraneo dal 1 aprile 1941 al'8 Settembre 1943.* Rome, 1970.

———. Volume VI. *La difesa del traffico coll'Africa settentrionale dal 10 Giugno 1940 al 30 Settembre 1941.* Rome, 1958.

———. Volume VII. *La difesa del traffico con L'Africa settentrionale: dal 1 Ottobre 1941 al 30 Settembre 1942.* Rome, 1962.

———. Volume VIII. *La difesa del traffico con L'Africa settentrionale: dal 1 Ottobre 1942 alla caduta della Tunisia.* Rome, 1964.

———. Volume IX. *La difesa del traffico con L'Albania, la Grecia e l'Egeo.* Rome, 1965.

———. Volume XIII. Books 1 and 2. *I'sommergibili in Mediterraneo.* Dal 10 Giugno 1940 al 31 Dicembre 1941, and *Dal 1 Dennaio 1942 all'8 Settembre 1943,* Rome, 1972 and 1968.

———. Volume XVIII. *La guerra di mine.* Rome, 1988.

———. Volume XXI. *L'Organizzazione della Marina durante il Conflitto* Two volumes. Rome, 1972.

United States Department of State. Foreign Relations of the United States (FRUS) I. *The First Washington Conference (December 22, 1941–January 14, 1942),* 1942. University of Wisconsin Digital Collection.

United States War Department. *The Libyan Campaign: November 1941 to January 1942.* Washington, DC: Military Intelligence Service, 1942.

United States Navy, Office of Naval Intelligence (ONI). *War Diary, German Naval Staff Operations Division* (GWD). December 1941–March 1942.

———. *War Diary of Captain U-Boats Italy.* 8 December 1941–30 June 1942.

Weichold, Eberhard. *Axis Naval Policy and Operations in the Mediterranean 1939 to May 1943.* Washington DC: U.S. Navy, 1951.

Whelan, J. A. *Malta Airman.* Wellington: Historical Publications Branch, 1950.

Books

Allaway, Jim. *Hero of the Upholders: The Story of Lieutenant Commander M. D. Wanklyn VC, DSO** The Royal Navy's Top Submarine Ace.* Shrewsbury, England: Airlife, 1991.

Austin, Douglas. *Churchill and Malta: A Special Relationship.* The Mill, England: Spellmount, 2006.

———. *Churchill and Malta's War 1939–1945.* Stroud, England: Amberley, 2010.

——. *The Place of Malta in British Strategic Policy 1925–1943*. Thesis: University of London, 2001.

Bagnasco, Erminio. *Le armi delle navi italiane nella seconda guerra mondiale*. Parma: Ermanno Albertelli, 2007.

——. *In Guerra sul mare: navi e marinai italiani nel secondo conflitto mondiale*. Parma: Ermanno Albertelli, 2005.

——. *Submarines of World War Two*. London: Cassel & Co., 2000.

Bagnasco, Erminio, and Maurizio Brescia. *Cacciatorpediniere classi "Freccia/Folgore" "Maestrale" "Oriani."* Rome: Ermanno Albertelli, 1997.

Bagnasco, Erminio, and Enrico Censuschi. *Le navi da guerra italiane 1940–1945*. Parma: Ermanno Albertelli, 2003.

Bagnasco, Erminio, and Augusto de Toro. *The Littorio Class*. Annapolis, MD: Naval Institute Press, 2011.

Bagnasco, Erminio, and Mark Grossman. *Regia Marina: Italian Battleships of World War Two*. Missoula, MT: Pictorial Histories, 1986.

Bagnasco, Erminio, and Achille Rastelli. *Sommergibili in guerra*. Parma: Ermanno Albertelli, 2007.

Barnett, Correlli. *Engage the Enemy More Closely: The Royal Navy in the Second World War*. New York: W. W. Norton, 1991.

Bartimeus, *East of Malta, West of Suez*. Boston: Little, Brown and Company, 1944.

Bauer, Eddy. *The History of World War II*. New York: Galahad Books, 1979.

Bell, Christopher. *British Ideas of Sea Power, 1919–1941*. Calgary, Alberta: University of Calgary, Thesis, 1998.

Bennett, G. H. and R. Bennett. *Hitler's Admirals*. Annapolis, MD: Naval Institute Press, 2004.

Bennett, Ralph. *Ultra and Mediterranean Strategy*. New York: William Morrow, 1989.

Berrafato, Enzo and Laurent Berrafato. *La Decima Mas: les naguers de combat italiens de la Grande Guerre a Mussolini*. Paris: Histoire & Collections, 2001.

Bertke, Donald A., Don Kindell, and Gordon Smith. *World War II Sea War*. Volume IV and Volume V. Dayton, Ohio: Bertke Publications, 2012 and 2013.

Borghese, Valerio J. *Sea Devils: Italian Navy Commandos in World War II*. Annapolis, MD: Naval Institute Press, 1995.

Boyd, Andrew W. *The Royal Navy in Eastern Waters*. Barnsley, England: Seaforth, 2017.

Boyd, Carl and Akihiko Yoshida. *Japanese Submarine Force and World War II*. Annapolis, MD: Naval Institute Press, 1995.

Bragadin, Marc' Antonio. *The Italian Navy in World War II*. Annapolis, MD: Naval Institute Press, 1957.

Brown, David. *Warship Losses of WWII*. Annapolis, MD: Naval Institute Press, 1995.

Burt, R. A. *British Battleships 1919–1945*. Annapolis, MD: Naval Institute Press, 2012.

Cameron, Ian. *Red Duster, White Ensign: The Story of Malta and the Malta Convoys*. New York: Bantam Books, 1983.

Campbell, John. *Naval Weapons of World War II*. Annapolis, MD: Naval Institute Press, 2002.

Caruana, Joseph. *Malta*. Unpublished manuscript.

Cernuschi, Enrico. *Fecero tutti il loro dovere*. Rome: Rivista Marittima, 2006.

——. *Malta 1940–1943: La storia inconfessabile*. Vicenza, Italy: in edibus, 2015.

——. *"Ultra" la fine di un mito*. Milan: Mursia, 2014.

Cernuschi, Enrico, and Allesandro Gazzi. *Sea Power The Italian Way*. Rome: Ufficio Storico della Marina Militare, 2017.

Cernuschi, Enrico, and Andrea Tirondola. *Mediterraneo e oltre*. Rome, Ufficio Storico della Marina Militare, 2014.

Churchill, Winston S. *The Second World War*. Volume 3, *The Grand Alliance*. Boston: Houghton Mifflin, 1950.

Ciano, Galeazzo. *The Ciano Diaries 1939–1943*. Safety Harbor, FL: Simon Publications, 2001.

Cocchia, Aldo. *The Hunters and the Hunted*. New York: Arno, 1980.

Connell, G. G. *Mediterranean Maelstrom: HMS Jervis and the 14th Flotilla*. London: William Kimber, 1987.

Corbett, Julian S. *Principles of Maritime Strategy*. New York: Dover, 2004.

Cull, Brian, and Frederick Galea. *Spitfires over Malta: The Epic Air Battles of 1942*. London: Grub Street, 2005.

Cunningham, Andrew Browne. *A Sailor's Odyssey*. London: Hutchinson, 1951.

Da Zara, Alberto. *Pelle d'ammiraglio*. Rome: USMM, 2014.

De Belot, Raymond. *The Struggle for the Mediterranean 1939–1945*. Princeton, NJ: Princeton University Press, 1951.

Deakin, F. W. *The Brutal Friendship: Mussolini, Hitler and the Fall of Italian Fascism*. New York: Harper and Row, 1962.

Dear, I. C. B., ed. *The Oxford Companion to World War II*. New York: Oxford University Press, 1995.

Dunning, Chris. *Courage Alone: The Italian Air Force 1940–1943*. Manchester, England: Hikoki Publications, 2009.

Edwards, Kenneth. *Seven Sailors*. London: Collins, 1945.

Ellis, John. *World War II: A Statistical Survey*. New York: Facts on File, 1995.

Felmy, Hellmuth. *The German Air Force in the Mediterranean Theater of War*. U.S. Air Force Historical Study 161. Washington, DC: U.S. Air Force, 1955.

Fioravanzo, Giuseppe. *Nostri criteri strategici e tattici durante il conflitto 1940–1943*. Livorno: Istituto di Guerra Marittima, 1955.

Frank, Hans. *S-Boats in Action in the Second World War*. Annapolis, MD: Naval Institute Press, 2007.

Friedman, Norman. *Naval Anti-Aircraft Guns and Gunnery*. Annapolis, MD: Naval Institute Press, 2013.

———. *Naval Firepower: Battleship Guns and Gunnery in the Dreadnought Era*. Annapolis, MD: Naval Institute Press, 2008.

Gardiner, Robert, ed. *Conway's All the World's Fighting Ships 1906–1921*. Annapolis, MD: Naval Institute Press, 1986.

———. *Conway's All the World's Fighting Ships 1922–1946*. New York: Mayflower, 1980.

Gooch, John. *Mussolini and His Generals: The Armed Forces and Fascist Foreign Policy 1922–1940*. New York: Cambridge University Press, 2007.

Greene, Jack. *Mare Nostrum: The War in the Mediterranean*. Watsonville, CA: Typesetting, Etc., 1990.

Greene, Jack, and Alessandro Massignani. *The Naval War in the Mediterranean 1940–1943*. London: Chatham, 1998.

———. *Rommel's North African Campaign: September 1940–November 1942*. Cambridge, MA: Da Capo, 1994.

Gregory-Smith, Frank. *Red Tobruk: Memoirs of a World War II Destroyer Commander*. Barnsley, England: Pen and Sword, 2009.

Gröner, Erich. *German Warships 1815–1945*. Volumes 1 and 2. London: Conway Maritime, 1990–1991.

Hague, Arnold. *The Allied Convoy System 1939–1945.* Annapolis, MD: Naval Institute Press, 2000.

Hammond, Richard. *The British Anti-Shipping Campaign in the Mediterranean 1940–1944: Comparing Methods of Attack.* Exeter, England: University of Exeter, Thesis, 2011.

Harrison, Mark, ed. *The Economics of World War II: Six Great Powers in International Competition.* Cambridge: Cambridge University Press, 2000.

Hattendorf, John B., ed. *Naval Strategy and Policy in the Mediterranean, Past, Present and Future.* New York: Frank Cass, 2000.

Hezlet, Arthur. *British and Allied Submarine Operations in World War II.* Portsmouth, UK: The Royal Navy Submarine Museum. No date.

Howard, Michael. *The Mediterranean Strategy in the Second World War.* London: Greenhill, 1993.

Howarth, Stephen, and Derek Law, eds. *The Battle of the Atlantic 1939–1945.* London: Greenhill, 1994.

Hughes, Terry, and John Costello. *The Battle of the Atlantic.* Dial Press: New York, 1977.

Iachino, Angelo. *Le Due Sirti.* Verona: Arnoldo Mondadori, 1953.

———. *Operazione mezzo giugno.* Verona: Arnoldo Mondadori, 1955.

———. *Tramonto di una grande marina.* Verona: Arnoldo Mondadori, 1966.

Ireland, Bernard. *The War in the Mediterranean 1940–1943.* London, Arms and Armour, 1993.

Jellison, Charles A. *Besieged: The World War II Ordeal of Malta, 1940–1942.* Hanover, NH: University Press of New England, 1984.

Jordan, Roger. *The World's Merchant Fleets 1939.* Annapolis, MD: Naval Institute Press, 1999.

Kahn, David. *The Codebreakers: The Story of Secret Writing.* New York: Macmillan, 1967.

Kelly, Stephen J. *Big Machines: Cipher Machines of World War II.* Walnut Creek, CA: Aegean Park Press, 2001.

Kemp, Paul. *The Admiralty Regrets: British Warship Losses of the 20th Century.* Phoenix Mill, England: Sutton, 1999.

Kennedy, John. *The Business of War: The War Narrative of Major-General Sir John Kennedy.* New York, William Morrow, 1958.

Kesselring, Albert. *Kesselring: A Soldier's Record.* New York: William Morrow, 1954.

Knox, MacGregor. *Hitler's Italian Allies.* London: Cambridge University Press, 2000.

Krug, Hans-Joachim, et al., *Reluctant Allies: German-Japanese Naval Relations in World War II.* Annapolis, MD: Naval Institute Press, 2001.

Langtree, Christopher. *The Kellys: British J, K and N Class Destroyers of World War II.* Annapolis, MD: Naval Institute Press, 2002.

Levine, Alan J. *The War against Rommel's Supply Lines 1942–43.* Mechanicsburg, PA: Stackpool, 1999.

Lewin, Ronald. *Ultra Goes to War.* New York: McGraw-Hill, 1978.

Liddell Hart, Basil H. *The German Generals Talk.* New York: Quill, 1979.

———. *The Rommel Papers.* New York: Harcourt, Brace, 1953.

Lind, Lew. *N Class: The Story of HMA Ships Nizam, Nestor, Napier, Norman, and Nepal.* Sydney: Naval Historical Society of Australia, 1993.

Macintyre, Donald. *The Battle for the Mediterranean.* New York: W. W. Norton, 1965.

Marcon, Tullio. *C.R.D.A. Cant Z.501.* Torino, Italy: La Bancarella Aeronautica, 2001.

———. *Imam RO 43/44.* Torino, Italy: La Bancarella Aeronautica, 1999.

Mars, Alastair. *British Submarines at War 1939–1945.* Annapolis, MD: Naval Institute Press, 1971.

Mattioli, Marco. *Savoia-Marchetti S.79 Sparviero Torpedo Bomber Units.* Botley, UK: Osprey, 2014.

Maugeri, Franco. *From the Ashes of Disgrace.* New York: Reynal and Hitchcock, 1948.

Messenger, Charles, et al. *The Middle East Commandos.* Wellingborough, England: William Kimber, 1988.

Morgan, Daniel, and Bruce Taylor. *U-Boat Attack Logs.* Barnsley, England: Seaforth, 2011.

Niestlé, Axel. *German U-Boat Losses during World War II.* Annapolis, MD: Naval Institute Press, 1998.

O'Hara, Vincent P. *The German Fleet at War 1939–1945.* Annapolis, MD: Naval Institute Press, 2004.

———. *In Passage Perilous: Malta and the Convoy Battles of June 1942.* Bloomington, IN: Indiana University Press, 2013.

———. *Struggle for the Middle Sea.* Annapolis, MD: Naval Institute Press, 2009.

———. *Torch: North Africa and the Allied Path to Victory.* Annapolis, MD: Naval Institute Press, 2015.

O'Hara, Vincent P., W. David Dickson, and Richard Worth, eds. *On Seas Contested: The Seven Great Navies of the Second World War.* Annapolis, MD: Naval Institute Press, 2010.

Pack, S. W. C. *The Battle of Sirte.* London: Ian Allan, 1975.

Padfield, Peter. *War beneath the Sea: Submarine Conflict during World War II.* New York: John Wiley and Sons, 1995.

Parrish, Thomas, ed. *The Simon and Schuster Encyclopedia of World War II.* New York: Simon and Schuster, 1978.

Paterson, Lawrence. *U-Boats in the Mediterranean 1941–1945.* Annapolis, MD: Naval Institute Press, 2007.

Paterson, Michael. *Voices of the Code Breakers: Personal Accounts of the Secret Heroes of World War II.* Cincinnati, OH: D&C, 2007.

Pugsley, A. F. *Destroyer Man.* London: Weidenfeld and Nicolson, 1957.

Ratcliff, R. A. *Delusions of Intelligence: Enigma, Ultra, and the End of Secure Ciphers.* New York: Cambridge University Press, 2006.

Rocca, Gianni. *I disperati: la tragedia dell'Aeronautica italiana nella seconda guerra mondiale.* Milan: Arnoldo Mondadori, 1991.

———. *Fucilate gli ammiragli La tragedia della Marina italiana nella seconda guerra mondiale.* Milan: Arnoldo Mondadori, 1987.

Rohwer, Jürgen. *Allied Submarine Attacks of World War II.* Annapolis, MD: Naval Institute Press, 1997.

———. *Axis Submarine Successes of World War II.* Annapolis, MD: Naval Institute Press, 1999.

Rohwer, Jürgen, and Gerhard Hummelchen. *Chronology of the War at Sea 1939–1945.* Annapolis, MD: Naval Institute Press, 2006.

Roskill, S. W. *Churchill and the Admirals.* New York: William Morrow, 1978.

Ruge, Friedrich. *Der Seekrieg: The German Navy's Story 1939–1945.* Annapolis, MD: Naval Institute Press, 1957.

Sadkovich, James J. *The Italian Navy in World War II.* Westport, CT: Greenwood, 1994.

Santoni, Alberto, and Francesco Mattesini. *La partecipazione aeronavale tedesca alla Guerra nel Mediterraneo.* Rome: Ateneo e Bizzarri, 1980.

Seth, Ronald. *Two Fleets Surprised: The Story of the Battle of Cape Matapan.* London: Geoffrey Bles, 1960.

Shores, Christopher, Brian Cull, and Nicola Malizia. *Malta: The Hurricane Years.* London: Grub Street, 1987.

———. *Malta: The Spitfire Year 1942.* London: Grub Street, 1991.

Shores, Christopher, and Giovanni Massimello with Russell Guest. *A History of the Mediterranean Air War 1940-1945, Volume One: North Africa June 1940-January 1942.* London: Grubb Street, 2012.

Shores, Christopher, and Giovanni Massimello with Russell Guest, Frank Olynyk, and Winifred Bock. *A History of the Mediterranean Air War 1940-1945, Volume Two: North African Desert February 1942-March 1943.* London: Grubb Street, 2012.

Spertini, Marco and Erminio Bagnasco. *I mezzi d'assalto della X^a Flottiglia MAS.* Parma: Ermanno Albertelli, 2005.

Stead, Gordon W. *A Leaf upon the Sea: A Small Ship in the Mediterranean, 1941-1943.* Vancouver, Canada: University of British Columbia Press, 1988.

Stephen, Martin. *The Fighting Admirals: British Admirals of the Second World War.* Annapolis, MD: Naval Institute Press, 1991.

Stitt, George. *Under Cunningham's Command 1940-43.* London: George Allen & Unwin, 1944.

Symonds, Craig L. *World War II at Sea: A Global History.* New York: Oxford, 2018.

Thompson, Julian. *The War at Sea: The Royal Navy in the Second World War.* Osceola, WI: Motorbooks International, 1996.

Van Creveld, Martin. *Supplying War: Logistics from Wallenstein to Patton.* Cambridge: Cambridge University Press, 1977.

Vian, Philip. *Action This Day.* London: Frederick Muller, 1960.

Von der Porten, Edward P. *The German Navy in World War II.* New York: Thomas Y. Crowell, 1968.

Wade, Frank. *A Midshipman's War: A Young Man in the Mediterranean Naval War 1941-1943.* Victoria, Canada: Trafford, 2005.

Weal, John. *Junkers Ju 88* Kampfgeschwader *in North Africa and the Mediterranean.* Botley, UK: Osprey Press, 2009.

Whitley, M. J. *Battleships of World War Two.* Annapolis, MD: Naval Institute Press, 1998.

———. *Cruisers of World War Two.* Annapolis, MD: Naval Institute Press, 1995.

———. *Destroyers of World War Two.* Annapolis, MD: Naval Institute Press, 1998.

Willmott, H. P. *The Last Century of Sea Power, Volume 2: From Washington to Tokyo, 1922-1945.* Bloomington, IN: Indiana University Press, 2010.

Winton, John, ed. *The War at Sea: The British Navy in World War II.* New York: William Morrow, 1968.

Woodman, Richard. *Malta Convoys 1940-1943.* London: John Murray, 2000.

Worth, Richard. *Fleets of World War II.* Cambridge, MA: Da Capo, 2001.

Wynn, Kenneth. *U-Boat Operations of the Second World War.* Annapolis, MD: Naval Institute Press, 1997.

Zorini, Decio. *C.R.D.A. Cant Z 506.* Torino, Italy: La Bancarella Aeronautica, 1997.

Magazines and Chapters

Alvarez, David. "Axis Sigint Collaboration: A Limited Partnership." *Intelligence and National Security.* 14(1) (Spring 1999): 1-17.

———. "Left in the Dust: Italian Signals Intelligence 1915-1943. *International Journal of Intelligence and Counter Intelligence.* 14(3) (Fall 2001): 388-408.

Aylwin, Ken. "Malta's Years of Siege." *Naval Review* 82 (October 1994): 397–403.

Bernotti, Romeo. "Italian Naval Policy under Fascism." U.S. Naval Institute *Proceedings* 82 (July 1956): 722–31.

Burtt, John D., et al. "Operation Herkules." *Military Chronicles* 1(2) (Spring 2006): 30–41.

Caruana, Joseph. "I convogli britannici per Malta." *Storia Militare* 43 (April 1997): 15–24.

———. "Fighters to Malta." *Warship International* 43(4) (2006): 383–93.

Cernuschi, Enrico. "La nave più brutta della flotta." *Lega Navale Italiana* (July–August 2015): 15–21.

De Toro, Augusto. "La crisi del traffico con la Libia nell'autunno 1941 e il carteggio Weichold-Sansonetti." *Bollettino d'archivio dell'Ufficio Storico della Marina Militare* 23(1) (March 2009): 11–65.

Deutsch, Harold C. "The Historical Impact of Revealing the Ultra Secret." *Parameters* (7)3 (1977): 17–29.

Donolo, Luigi, and James J. Tritten. "The History of Italian Naval Doctrine." *Naval Doctrine Command* (June 1995).

Ferris, John. "The British 'Enigma': Britain, Signals Security and Cipher Machines, 1906–1953." In John Robert Ferris. *Intelligence and Strategy, Selected Essays*. New York: Routledge, 2005.

———. "The 'Usual Source': Signals Intelligence and Planning for the Eighth Army 'Crusader Offensive,' 1941." In David Alvarez, ed. *Allied and Axis Signals Intelligence in World War II*. London: Frank Cass, 1999.

Fioravanzo, Giuseppe. "Italian Strategy in the Mediterranean, 1940–43." U.S. Naval Institute *Proceedings* 84 (September 1958): 65–72.

———. "I motovelieri per missioni speciali (anni 1941–1943)." *Rivista Marittima* (February 1967): 29–48.

Ghisotti, Andrea. "La notte di Capo Bon." *Bollettino d'Archivio dell'Ufficio Storico della Marina Militare.* 23(4) (December 2009): 11–34.

Hammond, Richard. "An Enduring Influence on Imperial Defence and Grand Strategy: British Perceptions of the Italian Navy, 1935–1943. *The International History Review.* DOI: 10.1080/07075332.2017.1280520 (9 February 2017).

Kahn, David. "Codebreaking in World Wars I and II: The Major Successes and Failures, Their Causes and Their Effects." *The Historical Journal* (23)3 (September 1980): 617–39.

Lynn, Henry. "Malta: Effort and Sacrifice, 1940–42." *Naval Review* 86 (July 1998): 240–249.

Mancini, Renato. "I porti della Libia." *Storia Militare* 53 (February 1998): 20–27; 54 (March 1998): 40–47.

Marcon, Tullio. "Malta difesa a oltranza sinonimo di vittoria." *Storia Militare* 46 (July 1997): 4–16; 47 (August 1997): 35–45.

Mattesini, Francesco. "Lo scontro di Capo Bon (13 Dicembre 1941)." *Bollettino d'archivio dell'ufficio storico della Marina Militare* (September 1991): 54–63.

———. "La Seconda Battaglia della Sirte 22 Marzo 1942." *Naval History Quaderno 2014.* Rome: Società Italiana di Storia Militare, 2014, 591–658.

Mulligan, Timothy. "The German Navy Evaluates Its Cryptographic Security, October 1941." *Military Affairs,* 49(2) (April 1985): 75–79.

Nailer, Roger. "Aircraft to Malta." *Warship 1990.* Annapolis, MD: Naval Institute Press, 1990, 151–65.

Pollastri, G., and David K. Brown. "The Loss of the Destroyer *Lanciere.*" *Warship 1994.* London: Conway Maritime Press, 1994.

Poynder, C. F. T. "Midshipman 1942." *Naval Review* 84 (July 1996): 256–61.

Prideaux, A. G. "With 'A.B.C.' in the Med." *Naval Review* 65 (April 1977): 133–40; (July 1977): 270–77; (October 1977): 351–60; 66 (January 1978): 46–54.

Rodwell, E. "The Destruction of Force K." *Naval Historical Review* (June 1979): 1–5.

Roucek, Joseph S. "The Geopolitics of the Mediterranean." *American Journal of Economics and Sociology.* 12(4) (July 1953): 347–54; 13(1) (October 1953): 71–76.

Sullivan, Brian R. "Downfall of the Regia Aeronautica, 1933–1945." In *Why Air Forces Fail: The Anatomy of Defeat,* edited by Robin Higham and Stephen J. Harris. Lexington, KY: The University Press of Kentucky, 2006.

——. "A Fleet in Being: The Rise and Fall of Italian Sea Power, 1861–1943." *International History Review* 10 (February 1988): 106–24.

——. "Prisoner in the Mediterranean: The Evolution and Execution of Italian Naval Strategy, 1919–42." In *Naval History: The Seventh Symposium of the U.S. Naval Academy,* edited by William B. Cogar. Wilmington, DE: Scholarly Resources, 1988.

Tamkin, Nicholas. "Britain, the Middle East, and the 'Northern Front,' 1941–1942." *War in History* 15(3) (2008): 314–336.

Internet

Convoy Web. http://www.convoyweb.org.uk/ (19 March 2018).

Crusader Project, Luftwaffe Report—Air Attacks on Convoy Operation MF 3. http://rommelsriposte.com/2012/02/26/luftwaffe-report-air-attacks-on-convoy-operation-mf-3-16-to-19-jan-42/ (19 March 2018).

Hammerton, John. *The War Illustrated.* Various Volumes. http://www.ibiblio.org/pha/TWI/ (19 March 2018).

HMS Neptune. http://www.hmsneptune.com. (23 April 2018).

Hyperwar: A Hypertext History of World War II. http://www.ibiblio.org/hyperwar (19 March 2018).

Naval History.net. http://www.naval-history.net (19 March 2018).

Naval Weapons, Naval Technology and Naval Reunions. http://www.navweaps.com (19 March 2018).

People's War. http://www.bbc.co.uk/ww2peopleswar (19 March 2018).

Uboat.net. http://uboat.net/index.html (March 19 March 2018).

Warsailors.com. Thermopylae http://www.warsailors.com/singleships/thermopylae.html (20 March 2018).

INDEX

Note: *t* indicates a table.

About the Author

Vincent P. O'Hara is an independent scholar and the author of eleven works, most recently *Torch: North Africa and the Allied Path to Victory* (Naval Institute Press, 2015) and *Clash of Fleets: Naval Battles of the Great War, 1914–1918* (Naval Institute Press, 2017). He holds a history degree from the University of California, Berkeley, and lives in Chula Vista, California.

The **Naval Institute Press** is the book-publishing arm of the U.S. Naval Institute, a private, nonprofit, membership society for sea service professionals and others who share an interest in naval and maritime affairs. Established in 1873 at the U.S. Naval Academy in Annapolis, Maryland, where its offices remain today, the Naval Institute has members worldwide.

Members of the Naval Institute support the education programs of the society and receive the influential monthly magazine *Proceedings* or the colorful bimonthly magazine *Naval History* and discounts on fine nautical prints and on ship and aircraft photos. They also have access to the transcripts of the Institute's Oral History Program and get discounted admission to any of the Institute-sponsored seminars offered around the country.

The Naval Institute's book-publishing program, begun in 1898 with basic guides to naval practices, has broadened its scope to include books of more general interest. Now the Naval Institute Press publishes about seventy titles each year, ranging from how-to books on boating and navigation to battle histories, biographies, ship and aircraft guides, and novels. Institute members receive significant discounts on the Press' more than eight hundred books in print.

Full-time students are eligible for special half-price membership rates. Life memberships are also available.

For a free catalog describing Naval Institute Press books currently available, and for further information about joining the U.S. Naval Institute, please write to:

Member Services
U.S. Naval Institute
291 Wood Road
Annapolis, MD 21402-5034
Telephone: (800) 233-8764
Fax: (410) 571-1703
Web address: www.usni.org